About Island Press

Island Press is the only nonprofit organization in the United States whose principal purpose is the publication of books on environmental issues and natural resource management. We provide solutions-oriented information to professionals, public officials, business and community leaders, and concerned citizens who are shaping responses to environmental problems.

In 1994, Island Press celebrated its tenth anniversary as the leading provider of timely and practical books that take a multidisciplinary approach to critical environmental concerns. Our growing list of titles reflects our commitment to bringing the best of an expanding body of literature to the environmental community throughout North America and the world.

Support for Island Press is provided by Apple Computer, Inc., The Bullitt Foundation, The Geraldine R. Dodge Foundation, The Energy Foundation, The Ford Foundation, The W. Alton Jones Foundation, The Lyndhurst Foundation, The John D. and Catherine T. MacArthur Foundation, The Andrew W. Mellon Foundation, The Joyce Mertz-Gilmore Foundation, The National Fish and Wildlife Foundation, The Pew Charitable Trusts, The Pew Global Stewardship Initiative, The Rockefeller Philanthropic Collaborative, Inc., and individual donors.

About the Rainforest Alliance

The Rainforest Alliance is an international nonprofit organization dedicated to the conservation of tropical forests for the benefit of the global community. Our mission is to develop and promote economically viable and socially desirable alternatives to the destruction of this endangered, biologically diverse natural resource. We pursue this mission through education, research in the social and natural sciences, and the establishment of cooperative partnerships with business, governments, and local peoples.

Founded in 1987, the Rainforest Alliance has headquarters in New York City and conservation operations worldwide. Our major efforts include certifying sustainable sources of timber and agricultural products, improving global communications about tropical ecology, and promoting the equitable management of tropical biodiversity, including forests, fisheries, and wildlife. The Alliance also provides financial and technical support to grassroots conservation groups in the tropics and grants research fellowships appropriate to our mission.

GREENING
THE
COLLEGE
CURRICULUM

GREENING THE COLLEGE CURRICULUM

A GUIDE TO
ENVIRONMENTAL TEACHING
IN THE LIBERAL ARTS

EDITED BY JONATHAN COLLETT AND STEPHEN KARAKASHIAN

A Project of the Rainforest Alliance

ISLAND PRESS
Washington, D.C. ● Covelo, California

Library of Congress Cataloging-in-Publication Data

Greening the college curriculum: a guide to environmental teaching in
    the liberal arts: a project of the Rainforest Alliance / edited by
    Jonathan Collett and Stephen Karakashian.
        p.   cm.
    Includes bibliographical references and index.
    ISBN 1-55963-421-9 (cloth.) — ISBN 1-55963-422-7 (pbk.)
    1. Education, Humanistic—United States—Curricula.
    2. Environmental education—United States—Curricula. 3. Education,
    Higher—United States—Curricula. I. Collett, Jonathan.
    II. Karakashian, Stephen. III. Rainforest Alliance.
    LC1023.G74   1996
    370.112'071'1—dc20   95-39225
                                                                    CIP

Contents

Foreword

One of the prominent casualties of the last quarter century of upheaval in higher education was the idea that there are certain fundamental, universally recognized bodies of knowledge to which all students should be exposed. In the liberal arts, the notion of the ideal curriculum of great books and great thoughts disintegrated after the academic discovery—late, as usual—that there are other directions besides west, other sexual identities besides male, other colors besides white. It is possible that the revolution went too far, as revolutions often do, in stigmatizing as politically incorrect much of our previously accepted and long-accumulated wisdom, but this is a question that others can debate elsewhere. Here, a related but different problem wants our attention. For not long after the political awakening of academia has come the environmental awakening, still in its early stages, and the timing of the two awakenings is rather unfortunate.

No sooner did we begin to get used to the new liberal arts curriculum—with its freedom from the insistence that one *must* know this and one *must* have read that—than along comes the environmental crisis, forcing us to proclaim that ecological ignorance is dangerous, that gaining environmental understanding *must* be an essential goal of every student's education. As David Orr notes in the first chapter, "We are still educating the young as if there were no planetary emergency." This is clearly wrong. But emergencies call for mobilization, concerted planning, and if not a unified response, at least not a haphazard one. So it looks as if we are back to the idea of the necessary curriculum, with its prescribed subject matter and carefully defined set of objectives.

The howls will surely go up, because the introduction of a single organizing principle—people and the environment—into every discipline from architecture to zoology will appear to some to be the end of pluralism, the end of democracy, the end of freedom in education. Such fears will be unfounded, as discussed below; meanwhile, we cannot ignore the urgent call for environmental literacy. This is not merely a clash of rival cultures that we are about to witness, important as that may be; no "Western Civilization 101" versus "Native American Cultures 111." This time, survival is the issue: survival of our institutions, survival of our society, survival of nature, survival of ourselves. The environment is one subject about which there is a clear and overriding need for all students to be informed. There is no right that grants students and teachers the freedom to be ignorant of the central concern that affects human civilization in this, its greatest struggle for life.

Greening the College Curriculum has arrived at a timely moment. Assembling a large, complex body of information, sources, and curricular insights, which up to now has been hopelessly scattered, the book takes the concept of environment-as-interdisciplinary-focal-point beyond the talking stage. Equally important, it should help calm the fears of those who see the environmental viewpoint as narrow and authoritarian. The working bibliographies that are the critical part of nearly every chapter contain a refreshing diversity of opinion, a wide range of assumptions and viewpoints. The only guiding premises are: (1) our environment is in serious trouble; (2) the modern relationship between people and nature is fraught with problems, some of them unique to our time; and (3) if students learn about the environment and our interactions with it, they will be in a position to make positive changes in the relationship. Here are premises that transcend the politics of race, culture, and gender— premises inspired by both a noble altruism and the highest form of enlightened self-interest.

Greening the College Curriculum is indeed, as the editors state, a gold mine of accessible environmental thought and information, beautifully arranged for use in teaching. Organized by discipline for the benefit of real teachers in real departments of real colleges and universities, it nevertheless has the potential of providing a rare, integrated view of the world, as the theme of environment is explored in complementary ways while students move from one subject area to the next.

Those who use this book—I hope there will be many—should understand that it is a beginning, not the final word. First, a few environmentally rich disciplines have not been included: chemistry, psychology, fine arts, and one or two others. This provides a challenge to the readers to help fill in the gaps, and an opportunity for the editors when they prepare the second edition. More important, when teaching about the environment, bibliographies are not enough. *Greening the College Curriculum* is only a teacher's guide for a text; the text itself is outdoors. Go and look. Then, take your students.

I know that for most of us the idea of reading the environmental text is a daunting prospect, but *Greening the College Curriculum* is not the only gold mine around. Every college and university has a cadre of emeritus professors and current faculty who are familiar with the flora, fauna, landscapes, soils, or geology of your region. Find them and ask them to lead field trips for you and other faculty—many will be delighted, especially if you make the arrangements. Afterward, you will come back to *Greening the College Curriculum* with the practical insights and sustained enthusiasm that environmentally inclusive education requires and deserves.

David Ehrenfeld
Rutgers University
New Brunswick, New Jersey

Acknowledgments

This book breaks new ground in that its purpose is to "mainstream" teaching about the environment in higher education. It is not conservation activism, it is not merely environmental scholarship, nor is it traditional environmental studies.

Two people recognized the project's importance immediately, even though in neither case was the project central to their organization's mission. Mary Pearl, executive director of Wildlife Preservation Trust International, and Daniel Katz, executive director of the Rainforest Alliance, were helpful in providing encouragement and contacts throughout. The Rainforest Alliance has sponsored the project and given us material support.

Our contributors, too, have stretched beyond their customary scholarly stance to combine teaching with disciplinary content as they address environmental issues. We appreciate their creativity and cooperativeness.

In the early stages, we formed an advisory committee. We want to acknowledge the helpful criticism they offered, particularly Margaret O'Brien, president of Hollins College; William Burch, Hixon Professor of Natural Resource Management at Yale University; and Louis Iozzi, professor of natural resources at Rutgers University.

Barbara Dean, executive editor at Island Press, also recognized immediately the importance of moving into this new instructional territory and has been a consistent and much appreciated advocate. Finally, Barbara Youngblood, developmental editor at Island Press, has been patient and encouraging. She has somehow maintained a sense of humor through all our tribulations.

Introduction

Jonathan Collett
State University of New York, College at Old Westbury
and
Stephen Karakashian
The Rainforest Alliance

Helping Harried Professors Teach Their Convictions

From the start, as we prepared this book, we have had in mind the assistant professor at Heartland State University who is concerned about the environment but has not yet seen a way to incorporate this concern into her teaching. She has the big "Intro" course each semester and a required course for majors, leaving her room only for the course in her specialty, for which, after all, she was hired. How could she include anything on the environment? And, isn't that the province of the new Environmental Studies Program anyway?

For those who remember teaching in the 1970s this may all sound like the predicament we were in then with African-American Studies and Women's Studies. It has taken until the 1990s for the curriculum, textbooks, and individual faculty to catch up and begin to represent issues of race and gender in a wide range of liberal arts courses, although still not without controversy. We believe strongly that we cannot wait 20 years to make it possible for the majority of students in the liberal arts to confront the challenges of an environmentally sustainable future. Their lives and the life of our planet are already deeply affected by environmental change. Because of the particular role of the United States in the

1

world's economy and politics, we have a special responsibility to see that students of American higher education are environmentally literate.

So, we offer Professor Green at Heartland State a guide that will help her in several ways:

(1) It will provide her with a rationale for including material on the environment in the teaching of the basic concepts of her discipline.

(2) It will show her how to construct a unit or a full course at the introductory level that is a basic course in the discipline yet makes use of environmental subjects. She may be ready to propose an upper-division course in her department, perhaps cross-listed in Environmental Studies, and *Greening the College Curriculum* gives her sample course plans, with a wealth of ideas about bringing the subject matter to life.

(3) It serves as a compendium of annotated resources, both print and nonprint, for materials in her own and related disciplines.

As she becomes aware of the possibilities, Professor Green will discover that she has some allies. No doubt there is a student environmental action group on campus. Its leaders may well have attended the "Campus Earth Summit" at Yale, where they signed a "Blueprint for a Green Campus," recommending among other things a goal of integrating "environmental knowledge into all relevant disciplines." Regional organizers from national organizations like the Student Environmental Action Coalition or the Campus Ecology Program may be available to help students enact the "Blueprint's" recommendations. And her students, quite at home in the electronic information age, will be quick to use the plentiful resources provided on EcoNet, Envirolink (started by a student at Carnegie Mellon), and other on-line facilities expanding exponentially on the Internet.

Perhaps stretching the environmental awareness surrounding her a bit, let's suppose that in town Professor Green discovers an organization of environmentally concerned citizens that is affiliated with the Citizens Network for Sustainable Development, an umbrella structure of individuals and groups across the country following up on issues raised at the 1992 Rio "Earth Summit." The editor of the local paper has been running a series of articles on water pollution and the city council members are feeling pressure from both sides as they prepare to vote on a redistricting measure that would allow a huge shopping mall to be built on ecologically valuable marshland. The student government has just called for an environmental audit of the campus, to include evaluations of waste disposal, hazardous substances, purchasing policies, energy consumption, and other matters of concern. A student in Professor Green's class says he is part of a team that will study the environmental soundness of the academic building in which the class is held, an idea developed and practiced on several campuses by David Orr, something of a guru to students in the environmental movement (and author of a chapter in this book).

So, Professor Green can begin planning to include environmental material in her courses with the confidence that she is responding to a need felt with urgency by increasing numbers of citizens, especially the young (if not yet by her departmental colleagues!). It is our conviction that within the next decade a graduation requirement in environmental literacy, championed by student activists, will be common in higher education, along with full majors in environmental studies. Professor Green, and many others like her who share her concern for an environmentally sustainable future, can begin now to incorporate their convictions into their teaching. Based on the experience of the authors represented in this book, she will find that this exploration will involve her and her students in rethinking the basic structure and terminology of her discipline. As she tries out the ideas presented here, she is likely to find herself reaching across the traditional boundaries of her discipline: what is central content for one discipline can easily become part of the background for a course in another. And just as this material should heighten her understanding of the discipline, both its strengths and its limitations, so should it bring a new light to her teaching as she tries out new strategies and finds students responding to a subject that is closely related to their own concerns.

The Audience for *Greening the College Curriculum*

It should be clear, then, that the Professor Greens of academia are this book's primary audience, a wide spectrum of college and university faculty who, after seeing the stimulating coursework offered here, might be motivated to start infusing this material into courses in their own disciplines. A secondary audience is the committed faculty who are already teaching in environmental studies programs who, nonetheless, are always eager to find additional ideas and resources, especially in disciplines that are not their own. A further audience would be citizen groups of all kinds for whom the instructional materials presented here, although written for college teachers, might serve as a useful guide in pursuing self-study of environmental questions.

A vast array of published materials on the environment is already available, but these publications have, for the most part, not been written with faculty in mind. An exception is the American Sociological Association's collection of course syllabi for environmental sociology, which we feel makes a chapter on sociology here unnecessary. (See Chapter 12,

"Revinventing the Classroom," for details.) For teachers in other disciplines to do the background reading necessary from all the available material and then design course units, find appropriate texts to assign students, and come up with stimulating classroom activities is asking a lot from today's overworked faculty. We hope that this book makes the task much easier, even inviting.

A Disciplinary Picture with an Interdisciplinary Frame

Despite the holistic nature of the content, we have chosen to structure the book, with two exceptions, around disciplinary chapters. We have done this for two reasons, one practical and the other itself pedagogical. First, in most institutions courses still have to be offered within a departmental context. We want to encourage the book's use at the very many institutions whose curricula are organized in traditional ways, but where individual faculty members may be open to a more innovative approach. Second, there are some advantages to the structure we have adopted. While it is true that the world is not neatly compartmentalized, and this is especially true for the balance of nature, the fact is that the disciplines do have a somewhat unique methodology and content. These diverse viewpoints, when juxtaposed as they are in this book, can provide a rich and multidimensional view of the subject. The conflicting demands of a holistic subject matter and the diverse perspectives of the disciplines produce an inevitable tension that we hope animates the book with a creative force. The opening chapter, "Reinventing Higher Education," and the final chapter, "Reinventing the Classroom: Connected Teaching," provide an interdisciplinary frame for the book. We hope that because of this frame and the many cross-references within chapters the reader is more prepared to view the disciplinary foreground in each chapter against the background of other disciplines.

There is no lack of relevant, substantive topics that are at the core of liberal arts concerns. Each of the chapter authors considers what areas of his or her discipline have been most receptive to inclusion of environmental issues and where there is the most resistance. In anthropology, for example, Balée uses the teaching of environmental materials as a powerful instrument to probe the most fundamental assumptions of the discipline, going to the very heart of the reciprocal relationship between the human species and its nonhuman environment. In their chapter on biology, Campbell and Durkee warn of the current unprecedented extinction of species due to the destruction of the earth's wild places, but they wisely note that "for students to mourn the loss of Earth's diversity (and hence to become motivated to do something about it), they first must celebrate it." In economics, Smith would have students look critically at the presuppositions of conventional economists who prescribe price adjustment and technological development for any temporary resource insufficiencies in an ecosphere seen as having unlimited natural resources. In their chapter on history, Opie and Black counsel against environmental history as merely a "revisionist critique" of environmental practices through time, and they suggest a broader role in providing historic background for a better understanding of our constantly shifting perceptions of the natural world.

Chapter authors find that viewing the discipline through the environmental lens gives students a powerful new perspective, although some in the field would argue that the picture is distorted. Grossman and Filemyr argue for a broad definition of environmental journalism that includes issues like poverty, racism, and overpopulation, and they question the traditional standard of "objective" reporting. In philosophy, Rolston points out that "what we wish to conserve depends on what we value," and takes us down a value-laden path, transparent in its clarity, pointing out contradictions and assumptions each step of the way. Kraft points to the considerable interest in environmental policy and politics in various professional associations and in college courses in political science, but he warns that behaviorism with its emphasis on quantitative analysis is still dominant in the field and that movements toward interdisciplinary connections are often viewed suspiciously. In religion, Rockefeller explores how the environmental crisis has stimulated interest in existing religions of the East and in Native American spirituality, while stimulating new developments in Christian and Jewish theology.

There would seem to be less controversy about the inclusion of environmental topics in geography and literature, perhaps because each quite naturally cuts across disciplinary boundaries and moves with ease from a perspective of individual actions to the broadest global scope (literally, in geography, the view from a space satellite). Naughton-Treves and Young demonstrate how geography encompasses the biological, social, and physical sciences, and they offer intriguing suggestions for linking classroom projects with global issues. Many in literature would support Grumbling's position that the tradition of nature writing has "heroically attempted to subvert the dominant western industrial paradigm of human domination over the biosphere."

Teaching Environmental Courses in the Liberal Arts

From a purely pedagogical standpoint, this subject matter provides a nearly ideal educational tool, since it encourages students to think critically and to look for unexpected connections between their discipline and the real world in which they live. With a challenging subject matter and students primed to learn about issues that are important to them, all that remains is for teachers to do their part to bring students and subject matter together in effective ways. Although it required them to think and write in a very different manner than they are accustomed to, the teacher/scholars who authored the chapters in this book take obvious satisfaction in describing the course objectives, the readings, class projects, and other teaching strategies that they have used successfully. College teachers seldom talk about the art of teaching, but we do spend much of our careers doing it and we know from our own experience that inspired teaching can make a difference in the lives of students. In addition to the wealth of ideas about teaching offered in individual chapters, we provide a separate, final chapter on "connected teaching" that contains resources both for teaching in general and for teaching environmental subjects in particular.

How to Use This Book

Begin, if you like, with your own discipline. Despite its familiarity, you may find the author's treatment stimulating. Then, move on to related disciplines. You will note that there is considerable overlap between chapters. We consider this desirable, illustrating as it does how the same material is viewed from surprisingly different perspectives. Curiosity will lead you, we trust, to sample even those disciplines that may seem far removed from yours. You will be encouraged to find how informative the chapter introductions and course plans are. (We know—editing has been an adventure!) Remember that teaching methods may well be transferred, even if the content lies far afield.

The book is a gold mine, we think, for the creative browser, and we have employed a number of devices to facilitate browsing. For example, we have inserted cross-references in the text in places where the same topic is treated from a different perspective in another chapter. We also asked chapter authors to work within a uniform organizational format:

(1) Each chapter begins with an introduction that asks, "What can the content and methodology of this discipline bring to the study of the environment?" and conversely, "What challenges and opportunities does this material create for teaching basic concepts in this discipline?"

(2) Next, sample plans are presented, either for course units or for full courses. Generally, material for introductory or lower division courses precedes that for advanced or upper division courses.

(3) The chapters each conclude with a resource section that includes teaching materials, print and nonprint, and background material for the instructor.

Within this general uniformity of format there is, of course, some variation according to the particular approach of individual authors.

We anticipate that prospective teachers will find the resource sections valuable and may not necessarily want to take the time to read through detailed course plans, especially in subjects somewhat remote from their own. Accordingly, we have tried to make the resource sections browsable by encouraging authors to annotate liberally. In addition, page references in brackets at the end of certain resource listings direct the reader to the location in the course plans where the resource is used.

A Final Word

We believe strongly that the most important element of learning and of citizenship is the ability of the individual to gather and assess all available information, make decisions, and act on them. This requires intellectual honesty and an openness to new ideas. A careful reading of this book will show that it is in no sense a polemic. As Theodore Roszak has recently pointed out, battering at people's denial and playing on their guilt is counterproductive. It is also educationally antithetical. Our chapter authors are a diverse group with many different perspectives, although it is safe to say that they share a common view, hardly controversial, that there is an environmental crisis upon us. Most important, they all share a conviction that education involves teaching students to think, not force-feeding a predigested point of view.

Chapter 1

Reinventing Higher Education

David W. Orr
Oberlin College

Toward the conclusion of his book *Preparing for the Twenty-First Century,* Yale historian, Paul Kennedy, calls for "nothing less than the re-education of humankind" (Kennedy 1993, p. 339). Implicit in Kennedy's proposal is the idea that formal education has failed to prepare us for the rigors of the next century, which he describes in great detail. But what does it mean to re-educate humanity, and how will it be done, and by whom?

Most of the present debate about reforming education has to do with preparing the young to compete more effectively in global markets. There are, however, better reasons to rethink education that have to do with the rapid decline in the habitability of the earth. The kind of education that enabled us to industrialize the earth will not necessarily help us heal the damages caused by industrialization. Kennedy is right, I think, in believing that our capacity to respond effectively to the great crises of the 21st century will require a fundamentally different education, one that prepares the young to live harmoniously on a planet with a biosphere. Those now being educated will have to do what we, the present generation, have been unable or unwilling to do: stabilize world population, now growing at the rate of a quarter of a million each day; reduce the emission of greenhouse gases that threaten to change the climate—perhaps disastrously; protect biological diversity, now declining at an estimated 100–200 species per day; reverse the destruction of rainforests (both tropical and temperate), now being lost at the rate of 116 square miles or more each day; and conserve soils, being eroded at the rate of 65 million tons per day. They must learn how to use energy and materials efficiently. They must learn how to run civilization on sunlight. They must rebuild the economy in order to eliminate waste and pollution. They must learn how to conserve resources for the long term. They must begin the great work of repairing, as much as possible, the damage done to the earth in the past 200 years of industrialization. And they must do all of this while reducing poverty and egregious social inequities. No generation has ever faced a more daunting agenda.

For the most part, however, we are still educating the young as if there were no planetary emergency. It is widely assumed that environmental problems will be solved by technology of one sort or another. Better technology can certainly help, but the crisis is not primarily one of technology. Rather, it is one of mind and hence within the minds that develop and use technology. The disordering of ecological systems and of the great biogeochemical cycles of the earth reflects a prior disorder in the thought, perception, imagination, intellectual priorities, and loyalties inherent in the industrial mind. Ultimately, the ecological crisis is a crisis of education that purports to shape and refine the capacity of minds to think clearly, to imagine what could be and is not, and to act faithfully. Resolution of the great challenges of the next century, then, will require us to reconsider the substance, process, and purposes of education at all levels.

Another Yale University historian, Yaroslav Pelikan, has recently questioned "whether the university has the capacity to meet a crisis that is not only ecological and technological, but ultimately educational and moral." He goes on to question "the readiness of the university community to address the underlying intellectual issues and moral imperatives of having responsibility for the earth, and to do so with *an intensity and ingenuity matching that shown by previous generations in obeying the command to have dominion over the planet*" (emphasis added) (Pelikan 1992, pp. 20–21). Why have colleges and universities, the very institutions that purport to induct young people into responsible adulthood, failed to respond with "intensity and ingenuity" to environmental deterioration that is undermining the world the young will inherit?

Higher Education in Ecological Perspective

First, institutions of higher education are products of the Enlightenment era and were shaped by its explicit optimism about progress. To the

Enlightenment mind, ignorance was a solvable problem. Every victory for knowledge meant a corresponding defeat for ignorance, superstition, and darkness. In the language of game theory, this was thought to be a "zero sum" game. We now know that the relationship between knowledge and ignorance is not that simple. Knowledge advances, but ignorance does not necessarily retreat as once assumed; sometimes it advances as well. The discovery of chlorofluorocarbons, for example, represented a significant gain in knowledge, but no one thought to ask what such a substance might do to the atmosphere until it was too late to prevent significant damage to the biosphere and to human health. In this case, as in so many others, we were ignorant of the larger effects of our actions that were based on increased knowledge. As the scale and complexity of science and technology have grown, so too have the possibilities for disasters that we could not foresee.

The Enlightenment also bequeathed to the modern university its distinctive mission of conquering nature. The idea came from Francis Bacon, but it is now the operating creed of the modern research university. Simply put, Bacon proposed that power and knowledge should join forces to render nature everywhere subservient to human purposes. When humanity was small relative to the biosphere and our technology crude, a little domination was tolerable. No longer. (For more on this subject, see the discussion of full earth versus empty earth scenarios in Chapter 4, Economics.) Humanity is causing major disruption of the biosphere, but the idea of domination has no stopping point. Bacon didn't tell us when to quit. The university, likewise, has no notion of enough applicable, say, to technology or to the extent of the human domain on earth. If it did, it would be a significantly different kind of institution.

Second, we've organized higher education like a system of mailbox pigeonholes, by disciplines which are abstractions organized for intellectual convenience. Hardly one scholar in ten could say why or when this came to be, but most would state with great conviction that it is quite irrevocable. The "information explosion" has further added to the impulse to divide knowledge by smaller and smaller categories, and the end is not in sight.

There is, nonetheless, a good bit of grumping about academic specialization, intellectual narrowness, and pigeonhole thinking. But despite decades of talk about "interdisciplinary courses" or "transdisciplinary learning," there is a strong belief that such talk is just talk. Those thought to be sober, or at least judiciously dull, mostly presume that real scholarship means getting on with the advance of knowledge organized exclusively by disciplines and subdisciplines. It doesn't seem to matter that some knowledge may not contribute to an intelligible whole, or that some of it is utterly trivial, or that parts of it are contradictory, or that there are significant and life-enhancing things omitted.

If this were all that happened as a consequence of the way we organize knowledge, the results would be merely unfortunate, but the truth is that they are, in a deeper sense, tragic. The great ecological issues of our time have to do in one way or another with our failure to see things in their entirety. That failure occurs when minds are taught to think in boxes and not taught to transcend those boxes or to question overly much how they fit with other boxes. We educate lots of in-the-box thinkers who perform within their various specialties rather like a dog kept in the yard by an electronic barrier. And there is a connection between knowledge organized in boxes, minds that stay in those boxes, and degraded ecologies. Many suspect where all of this is going but believe themselves powerless to alter it.

Our situation is tragic in another way. Often those who do comprehend our plight intellectually cannot feel it, and hence they are not moved to do much about it. This is not merely an intellectual failure to recognize our dependence on natural systems, which is fairly easy to come by. It is, rather, a deeper failure to join intellect with affection and foster loyalty to particular places, which is to say a failure to bond minds and nature. It is no accident that this bonding happens far less often than we might hope. Professionalized and specialized knowledge isn't about loyalty to places or to the earth, or even to our senses, but rather about loyalty to the abstractions of a discipline. The same can be said of the larger knowledge "industry" that was intended to make us rich and powerful by industrializing the world. This may help to explain why increasingly sophisticated analyses of our plight coincide with a paralysis of will and imagination to get at its roots.

Third, colleges and universities are expensive institutions that can only work expensively. As a result, fund raising is now the chief occupation of college and university administrations virtually everywhere. Financial need has made administrators increasingly subservient to corporations and government and all the less likely to think deeply about "having responsibility for the earth." This is not a new condition. Henry Adams, writing in 1912, complained that "capital has long owned the leading universities by right of purchase . . . and has used the universities, in a general way, to develop capitalistic ideas" (quoted in Smith 1984, p. 115). It is worse now than Adams could have imagined. It is not uncommon for whole university departments to hang out "for sale or rent" signs. The result is a growing trend toward corporate–university research in areas such as computer science, nanotechnologies, and genetic engineering, which creates constant pressures to define knowledge in ways that can turn a profit. Commercialization, in turn, creates its own kind of pressure to conform, which undermines any intense or ingenious effort to get at the roots of technologically induced ecological disorder. And I think that Adams was both right and prescient in saying that: "Capital has preferred the specialized mind and that not of the highest quality, since it has found it profitable to set quantity before quality to the limit the market will endure" (Smith 1984, p. 115).

Fourth, higher education has not responded with intensity and ingenuity to the ecological crisis because of a failure of leadership. College presidents and trustees have, on balance, provided little vision about the place of higher education in relation to the large issues looming ahead. The result has been an erosion of a sense of the larger purposes of learning beyond the creation and certification of specialists to carry out the further industrialization of the earth. In ecologist Stan Rowe's words:

> Years ago the university shaped itself to an industrial ideal—the knowledge factory. Now it is overloaded and top-heavy with expertness and information. It has become a know-how institution when it ought to be a know-why institution. Its goal should be deliverance from the crushing weight of unevaluated facts, from bare bones cognition or ignorant knowledge: knowing in fragments, knowing without direction, knowing without commitment (Rowe 1990, p. 129).

Institutions of higher education became "know-how" institutions with hardly a whimper of protest from administrators. Most, in fact, welcomed the change and did not stop to question the reasons for it or the likely results. Caught between financial duress on one side and a sense of intellectual complacency on the other, college and university presidents have rarely asked how the work of their institution adds up, and whether it adds up ecologically over the long haul. In fact, I doubt that the environment is taken seriously by more than a few college and university presidents or their trustees for that matter. I have a further hunch that the majority of them know little more about the global emergency looming ahead than what appears on the financial and business pages of the paper or *Forbes Magazine*, unlikely sources of ecological enlightenment. Finally, I doubt that one college president in 20 has pondered what his or her institution costs the earth each year through routine operations.

In sum, colleges and universities have not been entirely hospitable places for uncomfortable ecological truths and the kind of ideas that will be necessary to build what is now called a "sustainable society." In the words of former Harvard President, Derek Bok:

> Our universities excel in pursuing the easier opportunities where established academic and social priorities coincide. On the other hand, when social needs are not clearly recognized and backed by adequate financial support, higher education has often failed to respond as effectively as it might, even to some of the most important challenges facing America (Bok 1990, p. 105).

Rather like the U.S. auto industry in the 1970s and 1980s, colleges and universities have been complacent in the face of mounting evidence of serious challenges. When moved to innovate, they have mostly done so by tinkering at the edge of the status quo. They continue to graduate a high percentage of students who are ecologically illiterate, by which I mean ignorant of how the earth works as a physical system and why that knowledge is important to them. By and large, colleges and universities are overmanaged and underled. And most important, they are increasingly infused with a kind of fundamentalism that prevents them from the institutional self-analysis necessary to re-examine the basic foundational assumptions of modern education. What can be done?

The Greening of Higher Education

What would it mean for higher education to respond with intensity and ingenuity to the planetary emergency now upon us? No satisfactory answer to that question can be given until we know more than we now know. I am certain, however, that the same institutions that enabled us to industrialize the earth will require radical overhaul if we are to consolidate our tenure on the earth in any kind of humane and ecologically sustainable manner. To this end I would like to propose three broad changes in education having to do with: (1) the standards by which we judge colleges and universities; (2) the architecture of places where learning occurs; and most important, (3) changes in curriculum and pedagogy.

Educational Standards

Like that done by *U.S. News and World Report*, most ranking systems are based on such things as peer reputation, SAT scores of incoming freshmen, GRE scores of graduating seniors, the size of endowments, number of books in the library, percentage of PhD's on the faculty, publications by faculty, tuition, faculty/student ratios, and so forth. These purport to describe, in one way or another, the capacity of educational institutions to educate.

Judging the capacity of a college to cultivate the higher qualities of life and mind, however, is considerably more subtle and complex than most indicators of educational quality would lead us to believe. In fact, in an ecological perspective, many of the indicators now used to rank educational institutions are highly misleading or wrong altogether. Peer reputation may measure only the excellence with which some institutions do what should not be done. It can also be an index of snobbery and intellectual inbreeding. Faculty publications may even be a tolerable indicator of student dissatisfaction and the decline of forests. Large endowments might be a reasonable index of the strength of institutional attachment to the status quo. The volume of research grants may, on occasion, reflect ties to corporate and military activities, the effect of which is ecological ruin.

And there is that unavoidably embarrassing fact that colleges and universities have played a major role in the industrial devastation wrought on the world roughly in proportion to their national rankings. Current budgets, dependent on endowment earnings from stock held in major corporations, will cause even more of it. We have, as a result, several centuries of hard work ahead of us to clean up the mess: sequestering toxic and radioactive wastes; restoring depleted and mined land; cleaning up lakes, seas, and rivers; stabilizing climate; replanting forests; protecting whatever biological diversity we can; rebuilding decayed urban areas; and bringing the vital signs of earth back to health.

For this reason I propose a different ranking system for colleges based on whether the institution and its graduates move the world in more sustainable directions or not. Do four years at a particular institution instill knowledge, love, and competence toward the natural world or indifference, ignorance, and incompetence? Are its graduates equipped for a responsible life on a planet with a biosphere? What kinds of indicators would suggest such possibilities?

The first basis for ranking has to do with how much of various things the institution consumes or discards per student. Arguably the best indicator of institutional impacts on the sustainability of the earth is how much carbon dioxide it releases per student per year from electrical generation, heating, and direct fuel purchases. Other ratios of interest would include amounts of paper, water, materials, and electricity consumed per student. These can only be determined by careful audits of how much of what enters and leaves the campus (Smith 1992; Eagan and Orr 1992).

A second criterion has to do with the institution's management policies for materials, waste, recycling, purchasing, landscaping, energy use, and building. What percentage of institutional purchases is made from recycled materials? What percentage of its material flows is recycled? Does it limit the use of toxic chemicals on the grounds and in buildings? Does it emphasize energy efficiency and solar energy in renovations and new buildings? Does it use nontoxic materials?

Third, does the curriculum provide the essential tools for ecological literacy? Do graduates know the basic principles of ecology and thermodynamics and why these are important to their prospects? Do they understand that no good economy can be built on the ruins of natural systems? Are they encouraged to become ecologically competent? Is there opportunity and encouragement to help restore some part of the nearby rivers, prairies, worn out farmland, or strip-mined land? Do they have a coherent ecological ethic? Do they understand the difference between:

optimum and maximum
stocks and flows
design and planning
renewable and nonrenewable
dwelling and residing
sufficiency and efficiency
can do and should do
health and disease
development and growth
intelligence and cleverness?

And are they equipped with the essential tools necessary for the transition to a sustainable society, such as least-cost end-use analysis, full-cost accounting, ecological and solar design, and ecological engineering? Do they understand the basic principles of environmental ethics, sustainable agriculture and forestry, and restoration ecology? These, in turn, presume that the faculty itself is ecologically literate and comprehends the relation between the environment and their particular disciplines. In this regard, the recent Tufts University effort to weave ecological literacy throughout its curriculum stands out as a model for other institutions.

My fourth criterion has to do with institutional finances. Does the institution use its buying power to help build sustainable regional economies? What percentage of its food purchases come from nearby farmers? In studies of food buying at Hendrix College, Oberlin College, St. Olaf College, and Carleton College, for example, students discovered significant opportunities to increase food quality, decrease costs, and help the local economy. The same approach could be applied throughout all institutional purchases, giving priority to local craftspersons, merchants, and suppliers. Use of institutional buying power to help rebuild local and regional economies is also a prudent hedge against future price shocks associated with higher energy costs coming from supply interruptions, future scarcity, and the eventual imposition of carbon taxes to reduce emission of greenhouse gases.

Colleges and universities also have investment power. To what extent are their funds invested in enterprises that move the world toward sustainability? Admittedly, this involves complex calculations for which there is as yet no good investment screen. Nevertheless, all institutions should aim to harmonize their investments with the goal of sustainability, seeking out companies and investment opportunities related to things that need to be done to move the world in sustainable directions.

Fifth, institutions might be ranked on the basis of what their graduates do in the world. On average, what price does the planet and future

generations pay for the manner in which graduates of particular institutions live? How much do they consume over a lifetime? How much CO_2
do they contribute to the atmosphere? How many trees do they plant?
How do they earn their keep? How many work through business, law,
social work, education, agriculture, communications, research, or whatever to create the basis for a sustainable society? Are they part of the
larger ecological enlightenment that must precede the transition to a
sustainable society, or part of the rear guard of a vandal economy? Most
colleges make serious efforts to discover who among their alumni have
attained unto wealth. I know of none that has surveyed its graduates to
determine their cumulative environmental impacts.

Architecture and Pedagogy

My second suggestion has to do with rethinking the design of the places
where learning occurs. It is paradoxical that buildings on college and
university campuses, places where the stock-in-trade is good thinking,
characteristically show so little thought, imagination, sense of place, ecological awareness, and relation to any larger pedagogical intent. The typical academic building would seem to have the architectural elegance
and performance standards common to shopping malls, motels, and
drive-through funeral parlors; places where considerations of "through-
put" are uppermost in the minds of designers.

The problem is not just that many academic buildings are unsightly,
do not work very well, or that they do not fit their place or region. The
deeper problem is that we have assumed, wrongly I think, that learning
takes place in buildings but that none occurs as a result of how they are
designed or by whom, how they are constructed and from what materials, how they fit their location, and how and how well they operate. My
point is that academic architecture is a kind of crystallized pedagogy and
that buildings have their own hidden curriculum that teaches as effectively as any course taught in them.

We have not thought of academic buildings as pedagogical, but they
are. We have not exercised much imagination about the design of academic buildings, and it shows in a manifest decline in our capacity to envi-
sion alternatives to the urban and suburban excrescence oozing all
around us. We have assumed that people who know little about learning
and pedagogy were competent to design places where learning is supposed to occur. They aren't, not alone anyway. What do I propose?

Let's begin by asking what might be learned from the design, construction, and operation of the places where formal education takes
place? First, the process of design and construction is an opportunity for
a community to deliberate over the ideas and ideals it wishes to express
and how these are rendered into architectural form. What do we want

our buildings to say about us? What will they say about our ecological prospects? To what large issues and causes do they direct our attention? What problems do they resolve? What kind of human relationships do they encourage? These are not technical details, but first and foremost issues of common concern that should be decided by the entire campus community. When they are so decided, the design of buildings fosters civic competence and extends the idea of citizenship.

Second, the architectural process is an opportunity to learn something about the relationship between ecology and economics. For example, how much energy will a building consume over its lifetime? How much of what kinds of materials will be required for its upkeep? What unpriced costs do construction materials impose on the environment? Are such materials toxic to manufacture, install, or, later, to discard? How are these costs paid? What is the total energy embodied in materials used in the structure? Is it possible to design buildings that repay those costs by being net energy exporters? If not, are there other ways to balance ecological accounts? Can buildings and the surrounding landscape be designed to generate a positive cash flow?

These questions cannot be answered without engaging issues of ethics. How are building materials extracted, processed, manufactured, and transported? What ecological and human costs do various materials impose where and on whom? What in our ethical theories justifies the use of materials that degrade ecosystems, jeopardize other species, or risk human lives and health? Where those costs are deemed unavoidable to accomplish a larger good, how can we balance ethical accounts?

Third, within the design, construction, and operation of buildings is a curriculum in applied ecology. Buildings can be designed to recycle organic wastes through miniature ecosystems that can be studied and maintained by the users. Buildings can be designed to heat and cool themselves using solar energy and natural air flows. They can be designed to inform occupants of energy and resource use. They can be landscaped to provide shade, break winter winds, propagate rare plants, provide habitat for animals, and restore bits of vanished ecosystems. Buildings and landscapes, in other words, can extend our ecological imagination.

Fourth, they can also extend our ecological competence. The design and operation of buildings is an opportunity to teach students the basics of architecture, landscape architecture, ecological engineering for cleaning waste water, aquaculture, gardening, and solar engineering. Buildings that invite participation can help students acquire knowledge, discipline, and useful skills that cannot be acquired other than by doing.

Finally, good design can extend our imagination about the psychology of learning. The typical classroom empties quickly when not required to be used. Why? The answer is unavoidable: it is most often an uninteresting and unpleasant place, designed to be functional and nothing more. And the same features that make it unpleasant make it an inadequate place in which to learn. What makes a place a good educational environment? How might the typical "classroom" be altered to encourage ecological awareness? creativity? responsiveness? civility? How might materials, light, sounds, water, spatial configuration, openness, scenery, colors, textures, plants, and animals be combined to enhance the range and depth of learning? My hunch is that good learning places are places that feel good to us—human scaled places that combine nature, interesting architecture, materials, natural lighting, and "white" sounds (e.g., running water) in interesting ways that resonate with our innate affinity for life.

My point is that the design, construction, and operation of academic buildings can be a liberal education in a microcosm that includes virtually every discipline in the catalog. The act of building is an opportunity to stretch the educational experience across disciplinary boundaries and across those dividing the realm of thought from that of application. It is an opportunity to work together on projects with practical import and to teach the art of "good work." It is also an opportunity to lower life-cycle costs of buildings and to reduce a large amount of unnecessary damage to the natural world incurred by careless design.

As a test of these ideas I worked with 25 students in 1992–1993 to determine the feasibility of designing a building of approximately 5,000 square feet that would:

(1) heat and cool itself with natural energy flows,

(2) be constructed from nontoxic and recycled materials,

(3) recycle all organic wastes on site,

(4) produce more energy over its lifetime than it consumes in construction and operations through application of photovoltaic technology,

(5) generate a positive cash flow, and

(6) meet the highest aesthetic standards.

At the end of two semesters of investigation, which included presentations by a dozen of the best architects and designers in the United States, we concluded that it is not only possible to build structures that meet such criteria but that it is advantageous on strictly economic grounds as well. Further, we came to realize that the common effort to design buildings that conform to our highest ethical, technical, ecological, and pedagogical standards represents a worthy part of a liberal arts education.

Curriculum and Pedagogy

My third suggestion calls for extending this idea by rethinking old and worn out assumptions about the purposes and structure of liberal education. John Henry Newman, in his classic *The Idea of A University*, drew a distinction between practical and liberal learning that has influenced education from his time to our own. Liberal knowledge, according to Newman, "refuses to be informed by any end, or absorbed into any art" (Newman [1852] 1982, p. 81). Knowledge is liberal if "nothing accrues of consequence beyond the using." "Liberal education and liberal pursuits," he wrote, "are exercises of mind, of reason, of reflection." All else, which he regarded as practical learning, had no place in the liberal arts. To this day, Newman's distinction between practical and liberal knowledge is de rigueur in liberal arts institutions.

Harvard philosopher and mathematician, Alfred North Whitehead, had a different view of the liberal arts. "The mediocrity of the learned world," he wrote in 1929, could be traced to its "exclusive association of learning with book-learning" (Whitehead [1929] 1967, p. 51). Real education required "first-hand knowledge," by which he meant an intimate connection between the mind and "material creative activity." Others, like John Dewey and J. Glenn Gray, reached similar conclusions. "Liberal education," Gray once wrote, "is least dependent on formal instruction. It can be pursued in the kitchen, the workshop, on the ranch or farm . . . where we learn wholeness in response to others" (Gray 1984, p. 81). A liberally educated person, in Gray's words, "is one who has fully grasped the simple fact that his[/her] self is fully implicated in those beings around him[/her], human and non-human, and who has learned to care deeply about them" (Gray, p. 34). The inclusion of practical experience in the curriculum, then, is essential to the development of mind, character, and the art of good thinking. It is, moreover, the basis for the ecological competence the young will need to rebuild households, farms, institutions, communities, corporations, and economies that: (1) do not emit heat trapping gases; (2) operate on renewable energy; (3) conserve biological diversity; (4) use materials and water efficiently; and (5) recycle materials and organic wastes.

The old liberal arts curriculum was shaped around the goal of extending human dominion over the earth to its fullest extent. The new liberal arts curriculum must be organized around the need to develop the analytic abilities, ecological wisdom, and practical wherewithal essential to making things that fit in a world of microbes, plants, animals, and entropy: what can be called the "ecological design arts." Ecological design requires the ability to comprehend patterns that connect, which means getting beyond the boxes we call disciplines to see things in their larger context. Ecological design is the careful meshing of human purposes with the larger patterns and flows of the natural world, and the careful study of those patterns and flows to inform human purposes.

Competence in ecological design means incorporating intelligence about how nature works into the way we think, build, and live. Design applies to the making of nearly everything that directly or indirectly requires energy and materials or that governs their use. When houses, farms, neighborhoods, communities, cities, transportation systems, technologies, energy policies, and entire economies are well designed, they are in harmony with the ecological patterns in which they are embedded. When poorly designed, they undermine those larger patterns, creating pollution, higher costs, social stress, and ecological havoc. Bad design is not simply an engineering problem, although better engineering would often help. Its roots go deeper.

Good designs everywhere have certain common characteristics, including the right scale, simplicity, efficient use of resources, a close fit between means and ends, durability, redundance, and resilience. They are often place-specific or in John Todd's words they are: "elegant solutions predicated on the uniqueness of place." Good design also solves more than one problem at a time and promotes human competence (instead of addiction and dependence), efficient and frugal use of resources, sound regional economies, and social resilience. Where good design becomes part of the social fabric at all levels, unanticipated positive side-effects multiply. When people fail to design with ecological competence, unwanted side-effects and disasters multiply.

What are the possibilities for integrating ecological design into a liberal arts education? Is it possible to engage young people and faculty together in the effort to design ecologically smart solutions to real problems? We face what Winston Churchill once described as "insurmountable opportunities." Beginning with campus buildings and institutional resource flows, opportunities for learning and demonstrating ecological design are everywhere.

COURSE PLANS

How do we move from ideas to institutional change, and most important, to students equipped to make a positive difference in the world? In addition to the architectural design project mentioned above, let me offer three other examples from my own experience.

(1) Institutional resource flows. In 1986–1987 I helped to organize studies of the food systems on four college campuses that aimed both to establish the true costs of food systems and to identify better and more sustainable alternatives within the region. In each case the studies showed that college dining systems were part of larger food and agricultural patterns that were neither sustainable nor just. They also established the fact that the possibility of supplying some part of food needs from local farms had been systematically overlooked, often for no

good reason. The students who conducted the studies discovered their complicity in unraveling the world as well as the possibilities to do better.

At Oberlin we have extended the idea by offering a course in which students analyze campus food, energy, water, materials, and waste flows. Data from that course has been instrumental in changing the college's energy and water use, resulting in savings and avoided costs of $400,000 in the first two years on an initial investment of $300,000. Student research from that class also revealed the potential to save one-third to one-half of the electricity used in the town of Oberlin with attractive pay back times. Results from that effort helped to convince the local school district to invest $500,000 to improve energy efficiency.

(2) For the past four years Oberlin students have been involved in developing a data base on the local watershed: the Black River. Their work has been helpful in the creation of a county-wide organization, the Friends of the Black River, and in developing the necessary scientific data for a "Remedial Action Plan" to restore the river to a semblance of its former health. The college now offers a course on the Black River in which students continue to expand the base of scientific knowledge about the river and in the process learn biology, local history, law, and how to put their education to good use.

(3) A third example is taken from a month-long project in January of 1993 in which 35 graduate and undergraduate students and faculty representing a dozen disciplines and as many institutions worked for three weeks as a team of ecological design consultants to the owners of a financially troubled resort hotel in Virginia. The project was organized around problems of purifying waste water, nonpoint pollution in a nearby lake, landscape design, energy efficiency, and ways to better integrate the facility with its locality. In the process, students came up with several dozen good ideas to increase efficiencies, save money, reduce environmental damages, and redefine the mission of the facility around themes of place, ecological design, and environmental restoration.

There is great potential to extend this idea. Virtually all schools and institutions of higher education are located in places that are losing biological diversity and the means for right livelihood—rural and urban places alike that are polluted, overexploited, and increasingly derelict. What do we faculty and students alike know that might restore such places? How might the effort to solve real problems be made a part of the conventional curriculum? How might the discipline of designing and helping to implement ecological solutions change how we think about education and the organization and purposes of knowledge?

Suggestions for class projects with a journalistic bent can be found in Chapter 8, Media and Journalism. The instructor looking for additional ideas and some tips on how to proceed can profitably peruse the case studies offered in Smith (1992), *Campus Ecology;* Eagan and Orr (1992), *The Campus and Environmental Responsibility*; and Keniry (1995), *Ecodemia*. In addition, the Campus Earth Summit at Yale University on February 18–20, 1994 produced a document entitled, *Blueprint for a Green Campus*, a project of the Heinz Family Foundation. It is available through Campus Green Vote, 1400 16th Street NW, Box 24, Washington, DC 20036. Phone: (202) 939-3338; fax: (202) 797-6646; E-mail: shadow@ igc.apc.org. The *Blueprint* contains a wealth of suggestions about activist curriculum initiatives, student organizations, and others working at the local level on campuses.

The educational advantages of studies such as these and similar projects being carried out on many other campuses are numerous and substantial. First, for students they reduce large and unsolvable global problems to a manageable scale. Students cannot solve the problem of global warming for example, but they can comprehend and help to solve the problem of energy efficiency on their own campus. In the process they learn that many things that appear to be hopeless are, in fact, amenable to reason, effort, and an ecologically disciplined intelligence. Second, students learn how to analyze problems in order to render them solvable. The analysis of resource flows requires mastery of full-cost accounting, careful science, and skill in analyzing how systems work and why they sometimes do not work. Third, by having to help identify solutions, students arrive at a more reasonable and sometimes sympathetic view of power. The result is less polarization, accusation, and finger-pointing. Fourth, results of these studies that lead to positive change are the best antidote I know to despair in the face of seemingly overwhelming problems.

Education that builds on solving real problems requires broadening what we take to be our constituency to include communities in which educational institutions are located. It requires institutional flexibility and creativity which in turn presuppose a commitment to make knowledge count for the long-term health of local communities and people. It requires that we overcome the outmoded idea that learning occurs exclusively in classrooms, laboratories, and libraries. It requires acknowledgment of the possibility that learning sometimes occurs most thoroughly and vividly when diverse people possessing different kinds of knowledge pool what they know and join in a common effort to accomplish something that needs to be done. When they do, they discover ways to communicate that disciplinary education alone cannot produce. They quickly learn to distinguish what's important from what's not. And students and faculty alike discover that they are able to change things that otherwise appear to be unchangeable.

Conclusions

Institutions of higher education have been remarkably blasé about the declining prospects for human survival. Not everywhere and always to be sure, but all too often. They've become "know-how" places content to churn out armies of specialists of one sort or another and mountains of research that seldom advances the human prospect in any clear way, whatever it does for particular prospects. If that's all that could be said, the situation would still cry out for change. There is, however, more to be said. The human prospect now depends a great deal on the ability of educational institutions to respond with intensity and ingenuity to the larger ecological disorders of our time. Paul Kennedy's view quoted at the beginning of this essay calling for "nothing less than the re-education of humankind" is, I think, entirely correct. It raises, however, a prior question: Who will re-educate the re-educators?

References

Bok, D. 1990. *Universities and the Future of Higher Education*. Durham, NC: Duke University Press.

Eagan, D. and D. Orr. 1992. *The Campus and Environmental Responsibility*. San Francisco: Jossey-Bass.

Gray, J. G. 1984. *Re-Thinking American Education*. Middletown, CT: Wesleyan University Press.

Keniry, J. 1995. *Ecodemia*. Washington, DC: National Wildlife Federation.

Kennedy, P. 1993. *Preparing for the Twenty-First Century*. New York: Random House.

Newman, J. H. [1852] 1982. *The Idea of A University*. Notre Dame, IN: Notre Dame University Press.

Pelikan, Y. 1992. *The Idea of The University*. New Haven: Yale University Press.

Rowe, S. 1990. *Home Place*. Edmonton: NeWest.

Smith, A. 1992. *Campus Ecology: A Guide to Assessing Environmental Quality and Creating Strategies for Change*. Los Angeles: Living Planet Press.

Smith, P. 1984. *Dissenting Opinions*. San Francisco: North Point Press.

Whitehead, A. N. [1929] 1967. *The Aims of Education*. New York: The Free Press.

Chapter 2

Anthropology

William Balée
Tulane University

The discipline of anthropology offers unique opportunities for teaching college students about biodiversity and environmental conservation. As the most holistic discipline that studies humankind, anthropology encompasses a vast subject matter on relationships between past and present sociocultural systems and the biotic and physical environments associated with them (Anderson 1973). Partly because of its temporal and spatial scope, anthropology is highly appropriate for decoding and explaining what anthropologist Carole Crumley (1993, p. 1) has termed "complex chains of mutual causation in human-environment relations." Of the four subdisciplines of anthropology—sociocultural anthropology, archaeology, physical anthropology, and linguistics—the first, sociocultural anthropology, is arguably most immediately pertinent to contemporary biocultural and environmental crises, such as mass species extinctions, ecological extinctions, conversion of tropical forests to pastureland, destruction of coral reefs, global warming and air pollution, eutrophication of lakes and rivers, and the loss of indigenous knowledge concerning local habitats and biotic resources. This is because sociocultural anthropology encompasses the scientific study of contemporary human cultures and societies. The role of sociocultural anthropology in greening the curriculum, therefore, is the proper focus of this chapter, even if the other three subdisciplines of anthropology also investigate human–environmental relations.

Specifically, in the United States, issues of biodiversity and environmental conservation most often surface in sociocultural anthropology under course rubrics such as Ecological Anthropology and Human Ecology, which I treat here as synonyms. These courses tend to be taught by specialists in sociocultural anthropology, although in principle ecological anthropology is intersubdisciplinary. That is because it examines relations between humans and the environment in the present and recent past (by research in sociocultural anthropology) and in prehistory (by research in archaeology) as well as in terms of how people classify and name local biota and habitats (by research in linguistics). Ecological anthropology as a course is often organized around one or more theoretical perspectives that despite some shared terminology and concepts are sufficiently different from one another as to be distinguished by specific labels. These include cultural ecology, sociobiology, ethnoecology, and, more recently, historical ecology.

Cultural ecology holds that given environmental conditions, such as limits on soil fertility and availability of water, affect social life and work patterns; sociobiology posits that certain subsistence behaviors in given settings may contribute to increased reproductive fitness of those who practice them; ethnoecology prioritizes the classification, nomenclature, and knowledge of surrounding habitats, landscapes, and bioecological processes by local peoples; and historical ecology holds that the interpenetration of human societies, local landscapes, and the biosphere over time represents a dialectical relationship itself amenable to scientific study. Each of these theoretical perspectives together with the research carried out within them has contributed to ecological anthropology, the study of the complex relationships that obtain among human communities, their learned behaviors, and their infrahuman biotic and physical environs.

Contrary to what so many nonanthropologists have assumed (e.g., Pianka 1983, p. 2), most of the early literature in ecological anthropology was not concerned with human effects on other organisms and the environment, but rather with the presumed effects of local environments on small-scale sociocultural systems over time. This literature is associated with the paradigm of cultural ecology, originally espoused by Julian Steward (1938) [see commentary in Balée 1993 and Roosevelt 1991]. By contrast, I, along with others, contend that ecological anthropology ought to include analysis of the mutual relationships between human beings and the environment. In the past, different authors have linked any sort of ecological anthropology to environmental determinism, economic determinism, and even vulgar materialism (e.g., Friedman 1974; Sahlins 1976). In other words, ecological anthropology often has been seen as adhering to the axioms of microeconomics and mini-max theories, such that human cultural behavior is believed to be overdetermined by forces and conditions external to it. This view, as such, conflates the field of ecological anthropology with one of its theoretical perspectives, namely, cultural ecology. From the foregoing, one can see that ecological anthropology, as a field, is experiencing something of an identity crisis.

Ultimately it will probably have to deliberately encompass a diversity of theoretical perspectives, which includes both those that emphasize a determining effect of the environment and a historical ecology focusing on human influences on natural surroundings and the formation of distinctively human landscapes (Crumley 1994). Teachers of ecological anthropology can make their courses exciting by encouraging their students to grapple with these rival paradigms. (See sample unit "The Emergence of Historical Ecology" from an upper division unit for Ecological Anthropology and the sample course on Ecological Anthropology below.)

Courses with decidedly regional foci are now appearing, such as "The Amazon in Crisis: Ecology and Development," taught by Professor Emilio Moran at Indiana University, and "Human Ecology of the Amazon," jointly taught by Professors William H. Durham and Dominique Irvine at Stanford University. Both of these courses evaluate the impact of development, as conventionally understood, on indigenous and folk peoples in the Amazon basin. Both courses also discuss the reciprocal impact of aboriginal and modern sociocultural systems and species-rich Amazonian environments. In the introduction to his course's syllabus, for example, Moran states:

> This course provides an introduction to the ecology of the Amazon Basin of South America, by focusing on its habitats, the use and conservation of the environment by its native inhabitants, and by examining the forces of development that threaten its very existence. The course will survey the historical context of current developments, the differences found in native cultures and the diverse ways in which they deal with environmental differences.

Moran (1993) has recently published a comprehensive and timely introductory text on Amazonian human ecology appropriate for such a course, called *Through Amazonian Eyes*. Durham's and Irvine's team-taught course stresses themes similar to those found in Moran's course:

> The Amazon Basin contains the largest expanse of tropical rainforest in the world today. In the last 20 years the forest and its peoples have been subject to tremendous pressures as national governments with Amazonian territory have multiplied their efforts to develop

the resources of the region . . . This course will explore the human ecology of the Amazon in the context of these development pressures. How does an understanding of the rainforest environment and the ways that its indigenous inhabitants have adapted to and used it in the past help to formulate solutions to the dilemmas posed by Amazonian development today? (from the syllabus by W. Durham and D. Irvine)

Because they are somewhat specialized, regional courses are usually offered at the upper division or graduate levels.

A more general course on ecological anthropology could also be oriented by major world regions, as is Bernard Campbell's (1983) textbook, *Human Ecology*. This course could survey the relationships among sociocultural systems and diverse world environments and life-zones (including tropical forests, savannas, semi-arid steppes, deserts, mountains, and circumpolar zones). Alternatively, the course could examine how different systems of human subsistence both affect and are affected by local bioecological conditions and resources, comparing and contrasting, for example: pastoral nomadic societies in the Old World; foraging societies of deserts, savannas, tropical forests, and the circumpolar zones; horticultural societies that depend on the hoe and rainfall only, as in West Africa; horticultural societies that rely on slash-and-burn as well as rainfall; early state societies and modern peasant societies that utilize intensive agriculture; and modern industrial states that require mechanized agriculture and the burning of fossil fuels. Netting's (1986) text called *Cultural Ecology* utilizes such an organizational plan and would be well assigned. This course would be listed in the upper division of the undergraduate curriculum.

At the lower division, issues of biodiversity and environmental conservation can appropriately be incorporated into the introductory course in cultural and/or social anthropology. However, biodiversity and environmental conservation can also be treated in more narrowly specialized, lower division courses. For example, with creative planning a regional course, such as one focusing on the Amazon, might well be taught so as to emphasize basic principles, and thus be suitable as a lower division course. In the spring of 1993 I taught a freshman seminar at Tulane entitled "Tropical Forests." See the sample unit below, "Human Cultures and Tropical Forests Through Time." Although this multidisciplinary course had a narrow focus, it was appropriate for the general curriculum, partly because it capitalized on the students' keen interest in and curiosity about tropical forests. In addition, through support from my department and the university administration, it was possible to cover important topics beyond my own specialty by bringing in distinguished speakers who also carry out research on tropical forests within different disciplines or subdisciplines, such as botany (Dr. Michael J. Balick of the New York Botanical Garden), ecology (Dr. Julie Denslow, then of Tulane University, now of Louisiana State University; and Dr. David G. Campbell of Grinnell College), archaeology (Dr. Anna C. Roosevelt of the Field Museum of Natural History and the University of Illinois at Chicago), and sociology (Dr. J. Timmons Roberts of Tulane University). The course was aimed at the relatively few students who would be most likely to specialize later in anthropology, biology, ecology, tropical forestry, or an allied field. But it could be adapted easily as a course for nonmajors who wish to learn a multidisciplinary approach to conservation thinking.

By contrast to these more specialized lower division courses, broader introductory courses on cultural anthropology attract enrollments of between 300,000 and 350,000 students every year on U.S. campuses (G. Michael Queen, pers. comm., 1994), and they thus present a real opportunity to reach a great many students with an enlightened environmental approach. In my teaching of Cultural Anthropology, I tend to emphasize the clash of relativist and rationalist doctrines. (See sample unit below, "Human Nature and the Environment" for a lecture course in Cultural Anthropology [lower division] or Ecological Anthropology [upper division].) Extreme relativists hold that human behavior is entirely plastic and very much a product of the social and natural environment. Extreme rationalists contend, in contrast, that human behavior is to a large extent biologically determined. Relativists emphasize the differences among human sociocultural systems, suggesting that the similarities are borrowed, coincidental, or the result of underlying psychic uniformity (and therefore not in need of explanation). Rationalists stress the similarities among sociocultural systems, finding the differences to be on the order of surface noise.

While students should comprehend that there is a core of human nature that is essentially biological and unitary across our species, they should also be trained to question supposed sociocultural universals that would supply evidence for and define the boundaries of that nature. Such questioning reflects the empiricist hallmark of general anthropology that has sought to falsify biologically and psychologically reductionist explanations of human behavior. Much human behavior is plastic and at least partially learned rather than fixed and simply biological. This approach can lead to an enlightening tension in the classroom, even in lecture courses, and students can be encouraged to debate the matter in recitations or in term papers.

With regard to biodiversity, it may be argued that two doctrines concerning human nature seem to be in competition within sociocultural anthropology: the Noble Savage, on the one hand, and *Homo devastandus*, its opposite, on the other. The Noble Savage implies that indigenous (especially foraging) peoples are either unable because of cultural norms to diminish biodiversity (e.g., Hughes 1983; Martin 1992; Reichel-Dolmatoff 1976) or culturally programmed to increase it. Only industrialized societies, from this position, are associated with environmental ills and reductions in biodiversity. Those who subscribe (if only implicitly) to *Homo devastandus* argue that indigenous peoples, as with human beings everywhere, contribute to lowered biodiversity and are naturally destructive of local environments (Diamond 1992; Rambo 1985; Redford 1991). The Noble Savage doctrine holds that it is human nature to be custodial of the environment, the relationship becoming corrupted only after the rise of civilization. The doctrine of *Homo devastandus*, in contrast, holds humankind itself accountable for the destruction of natural habitats and other species, as in commonly heard statements about the inborn, environmental destructiveness and greed of "man." These radically opposed viewpoints have been applied to nonstate societies, where, for better or worse, anthropologists have most sought to bolster or falsify specific theories about human nature (see Sponsel 1992).

Indeed, some anthropologists have raised doubt as to whether any of the paradigms thus far developed in ecological anthropology can apply to research carried out in state-level societies. In their surprise over the lack of congruence between cultural ecology and their empirical findings in a complex society of the Italian Alps, anthropologists John Cole and Eric Wolf (1974, pp. 284–285) noted that:

> Because the study of homeostatic systems has been emphasized in ecological anthropology, the only kind of change that this discipline has considered is systemic divergence through movement into different microenvironments. . . . This kind of analysis is most applicable to the process of fission in isolated primitive societies; it is least applicable to the process of fusion and synthesis that governs the rise of complex societies. Complex societies are ecologically grounded, but the rise of the state introduces into the ecological set a specifically political element that transforms problems of ecological limitations into decisions of a political economy.

They were arguing that ecological anthropology offers explanations of complex (state-level) society that perforce are weaker and more irrelevant than those deriving from the field of political economy.

This interpretation of the limits of ecological anthropology indicates a crisis in the applicability of anthropological theory more generally. In other words, if ecological anthropology can only satisfy itself with explanations of "primitive" or egalitarian societies (where the paramount distinctions among individuals' power tend to be connected to age and gender only), then it is obviously not fulfilling the holistic, panhuman commitments of anthropology as a discipline. On the other hand, one might argue that it is more likely that ecological anthropology is not inherently restricted to the study of egalitarian societies. Rather, the problem may be that its chief paradigm until recently, cultural ecology, has merited such a description (Balée 1993; Roosevelt 1991; cf. Moran 1990 and cf. Murphy 1970). In other words, Cole and Wolf (1974) seem to have fused ecological anthropology to environmental determinism and cultural ecology exclusively, as did Sahlins and Friedman at about the same time and as have many students since. Even the late Robert M. Netting, who was perhaps more a historical ecologist (although he did not so label himself) than a cultural ecologist, used the term *ecological anthropology* interchangeably with cultural ecology in his important textbook, *Cultural Ecology* (1986). In a course on ecological anthropology, it is important to stress the differences between the field of inquiry itself and its component, rival paradigms. (See sample course below on Ecological Anthropology, week 1.)

Cultural ecology excludes historical process in the determination of the sociopolitical structure of small-scale, egalitarian societies. Cultural ecology tended to confine its explanations to such societies, including the hunting-and-gathering Shoshone of the Great Basin Plateau (e.g., Steward 1938), the !Kung San of the Kalahari Desert (e.g., Lee and DeVore 1976), and numerous South American Indian peoples (e.g., Gross 1975; Meggers 1971). These native peoples lived in environments that earlier researchers considered harsh and constraining with respect to culture, such as deserts and tropical forests. From the point of view of cultural ecology, the more rudimentary the culture, the more rigorous the environment (and vice versa), in terms of stringent, quantifiable limits on rainfall, soil quality, temperature, dietary protein availability, and the like. In contrast, recent research in historical ecology (e.g., Balée 1989; Bailey and Headland 1991; Cronon 1983; Denevan 1992; Vansina 1990) demonstrates that indigenous peoples, in both temperate and tropical regions of the world, profoundly altered supposedly pristine environments as the effects of their daily economic activities unfolded over time. In anthropologist Jan Vansina's words, "Jungle is as much a myth as Tarzan is" (1990, p. 39). Likewise, the authors of a recent textbook on general ecology pointed out that "The ecologist who tries to study undisturbed communities (such as virgin forest) is likely to spend his whole life trying to find one!" (Begon, Harper, and Townsend 1990, p. 740). (For more on the human concept of a forest, see Chapter 6, History.)

If certain cultures are adapted to given physical environments, or if they are somehow limited by isolated geophysical factors in those environments, as the paradigm of cultural ecology has held, it should also be admitted that some of those environments are, paradoxically, also culturally (and historically) determined. In other words, some of those environments are, in reality, landscapes that exhibit characteristic human signatures. As such, the current collision between environmental and cultural (or historical) determinisms in sociocultural anthropology can be fruitfully explored and evaluated in class discussion during courses on ecological anthropology and in units of cultural anthropology that assess relationships between humans and the infrahuman environment.

In the sections outlining sample units and courses that follow, in addition to including material on lower division courses on tropical forests and cultural anthropology, I include one sample unit from an upper division course on ecological anthropology and a set of topics for another full course on ecological anthropology that would be appropriate both for graduate students and advanced undergraduate students.

References for the Introduction

Anderson, J. N. 1973. "Ecological Anthropology and Anthropological Ecology." In *Handbook of Social and Cultural Anthropology*. J.J. Honigmann, ed. Chicago: Rand McNally.

Bailey, R. C. and T. N. Headland. 1991. "The Tropical Rainforest." *Human Ecology* 19(2):261–285.

Balée, W. 1989. "The Culture of Amazonian Forests." *Advances in Economic Botany* 7:1–21.

Balée, W. 1993. "Indigenous Transformation of Amazonian Forests: An Example from Maranhão, Brazil." *L'Homme* 126–128, XXXIII(2–4): 231–254.

Begon, M., J. L. Harper, and C. R. Townsend. 1990. *Ecology: Individuals, Populations and Communities*. Boston: Blackwell Scientific Publications.

Campbell, B. 1983. *Human Ecology*. New York: Aldine de Gruyter.

Cole, J. W. and E. R. Wolf. 1974. *The Hidden Frontier*. New York: Academic Press.

Cronon, W. 1983. *Changes in the Land*. New York: Hill and Wang.

Crumley, C. L. 1993. "Analyzing Historic Ecotonal Shifts." *Ecological Applications* 3(3):377–384.

Crumley, C. L. 1994. "Introduction." In *Historical Ecology*. C. L. Crumley, ed. Santa Fe: School of American Research Press.

Denevan, W. M. 1992. "The Pristine Myth: The Landscape of the Americas in 1492." *Annals of the Association of American Geographers* 82(3):369–385.

Diamond, J. M. 1992. "The Golden Age That Never Was." In *The Third Chimpanzee: The Evolution and Future of the Human Animal*. J. M. Diamond, ed. New York: HarperCollins Publishers.

Friedman, J. 1974. "Marxism, Structuralism, and Vulgar Materialism."
Man, n.s., 9:444–469.

Gross, D. R. 1975. "Protein Capture and Cultural Development in the
Amazon Basin." *American Anthropologist* 77:526–549.

Hughes, J. D. 1983. *American Indian Ecology*. El Paso: Texas Western
Press.

Lee, R. B. and I. DeVore, eds. 1976. *Kalahari Hunter-Gatherers: Studies
of the !Kung San and Their Neighbors*. Cambridge: Harvard University Press.

Martin, C. L. 1992. *In the Spirit of the Earth: Rethinking History and
Time*. Baltimore: The Johns Hopkins University Press.

Meggers, B. J. 1971. *Amazonia: Man and Culture in a Counterfeit Paradise*. Chicago: Aldine.

Moran, E. F. 1990. "Ecosystem Ecology in Biology and Anthropology: A
Critical Assessment." In *The Ecosystem Approach in Anthropology:
From Concept to Practice*. E. F. Moran, ed. Ann Arbor: The Univer-
sity of Michigan Press.

Moran, E. F. 1993. *Through Amazonian Eyes*. Iowa City: University of
Iowa Press.

Murphy, R. F. 1970. "Basin Ethnography and Ethnological Theory." In
Languages and Cultures of Western North America. E. H. Swanson,
Jr., ed. Pocatello: Idaho State University Press.

Netting, R. M. 1986. *Cultural Ecology*, 2nd ed. Prospect Heights, IL:
Waveland Press.

Pianka, E. R. 1983. *Evolutionary Ecology*, 3rd ed. New York: Harper and
Row.

Rambo, A. T. 1985. *Primitive Polluters*. Ann Arbor, MI: Museum of
Anthropology.

Redford, K. H. 1991. "The Ecologically Noble Savage." *Cultural Survival
Quarterly* 15(1):46–48.

Reichel-Dolmatoff, G. 1976. "Cosmology as Ecological Analysis: A View
from the Rain Forest." *Man* 11:307–318.

Roosevelt, A. C. 1991. *Moundbuilders of the Amazon: Geophysical
Archaeology on Marajo Island, Brazil*. San Diego: Academic Press.

Sahlins, M. 1976. *Culture and Practical Reason*. Chicago: University of
Chicago Press.

Sponsel, L. E. 1992. "Myths of Ecology and Ecology of Myths: Were Indi-
genes Noble Conservationists or Savage Destroyers of Nature?" In
*The Second Annual Conference on Issues of Culture and Communi-
cation in the Asia/Pacific Region*. Honolulu, HI: East–West Center.

Steward, J. H. 1938. *Basin-Plateau Aboriginal Sociopolitical Groups*.

Bureau of American Ethnology, Bulletin 120, pp. 1–346. Washington, DC: United States Government Printing Office.

Vansina, J. 1990. *Paths in the Rainforests*. Madison: University of Wisconsin Press.

COURSE PLANS

Lower Division Course Units

Human Cultures and Tropical Forests Through Time (Portion of a freshman seminar on tropical forests)

Course Objectives. The seminar focuses on the past and present state of knowledge about tropical forests together with the peoples and sociocultural systems that have inhabited them. The historical, ecological, and cultural forces that have molded the biological and geophysical conditions of many tropical forests are discussed. The long-term effects of prehistoric and historic human occupations of tropical forests worldwide are critically reviewed. The current prospects for survival of tropical forests and associated peoples and cultures are assessed.

UNIT 1. PRIMARY VERSUS SECONDARY FORESTS; HUMAN EFFECTS ON TROPICAL FORESTS

The focus in this session is the distinction between forests that have and have not been disturbed by human beings. The instructor may compare several types of human disturbance (by hunter-gatherers, by horticulturalists, by modern state-level societies). Discussion by students could profitably focus on what constitutes disturbance and whether any nondisturbed forests and other "natural" areas truly exist today.

Readings
- Vansina 1990, *Paths in the Rainforest*, chapters 1 and 2
- Denevan 1992, "The Pristine Myth"
- Balée 1989, "The Culture of Amazonian Forests"

UNIT 2. PREHISTORY OF TROPICAL FORESTS (GUEST SPEAKER: DR. ANNA C. ROOSEVELT, FIELD MUSEUM OF NATURAL HISTORY, CHICAGO)

Part of the student interest in this session is the guest speaker herself. They have read her work before the class meeting. This session deals with the archaeological aspects of tropical forest environments and the richness of their flora and fauna. This topic follows logically from Unit 1 above because it suggests that human occupation, and hence disturbance of tropical forests and their rich biological diversity, is quite ancient.

Readings
- Vansina 1990, *Paths in the Rainforest,* chapters 3 and 4
- Roosevelt et al. 1991, "Eighth Millennium Pottery. . . "

UNIT 3. ABORIGINAL SOCIOPOLITICAL STRUCTURES OF TROPICAL FORESTS

This session analyzes the various types of sociopolitical structures known from tropical forests, including hunting-and-gathering, horticultural, and intensively agricultural societies. The objective is to get students to think about whether different types of sociopolitical organization involve differential impacts on biodiversity and local environments.

Readings
- Vansina 1990, *Paths in the Rainforest,* chapter 5
- Bailey and Headland 1991, "The Tropical Rainforest"

UNIT 4. INDIGENOUS KNOWLEDGE OF TROPICAL FOREST HABITATS AND RESOURCES

The point of this session is to evaluate whether indigenous peoples of tropical forests consciously considered the effects their economic activities had on biodiversity and local environments. Of particular relevance is the debate between Posey and Parker concerning the apêtê forest islands of the Kayapó Indians of central Brazil, wherein Posey affirms that these are anthropogenic and Parker claims that they are not.

Readings
- Vansina 1990, *Paths in the Rainforest,* chapters 7, 8, 9
- Posey 1984, "Indigenous Ecological Knowledge and Development of the Amazon," pp. 135–144
- Parker 1992, "Forest Islands and Kayapó Resource Management in Amazonia"
- Posey 1992, "Reply to Parker"

Human Nature and the Environment *(unit for a lower division course in Cultural Anthropology or upper division course in Ecological Anthropology)*

Unit Objectives. This unit is devoted to the definition of human nature, based on the concept of sociocultural universals. It can appropriately include discussion of relationships among humankind, biodiversity, and the environment.

LECTURE 1. THE CONCEPT OF CULTURE

The biologically determined capacity of the human species to learn language and be enculturated into given social contexts is presented. Cultures and cultural behaviors are based on learning, not instinct. (Readings are discretionary.)

LECTURE 2. SOCIOCULTURAL UNIVERSALS AND HUMAN NATURE

Sociocultural universals are used in defining human nature. The more specific the behavioral characteristic in question, the less likely it is to be universal. G. P. Murdock (1945) listed 73 sociocultural universals or "common denominators of cultures," most of which are quite general, such as cooking, games, magic, music, and visiting. (Readings are discretionary.)

LECTURE 3. HUMAN BEINGS AND INFRAHUMAN NATURE

Here we consider the relationship between human beings and the environment in different sociocultural and historical contexts. Basic types of human subsistence strategies known from the ethnographic record are examined, such as hunting and gathering, horticulture, intensive agriculture, and industrial agriculture. Specific sociopolitical types are related to each subsistence type; for example, nation-states are not anywhere associated with a hunting-and-gathering subsistence strategy but are found only with either intensive or industrial agriculture. (Readings are discretionary.)

LECTURE 4. *HOMO DEVASTANDUS* OR THE NOBLE SAVAGE?

This lecture builds and depends upon the three previous ones. It contrasts the view that human nature is essentially benign toward nature with the opposite view, that human nature is incompatible with maintaining the given biological and ecological diversity of the globe. The juxtaposition of these views can be highly instructive for beginning students. The exercise encourages them to evaluate for themselves whether either does justice to the complexity that underlies human nature and culture, or whether a more critical perspective offers a better window onto the intricate relationships between any human society and its immediate surroundings.

Readings

• Posey 1984, "Indigenous Ecological Knowledge and Development of the Amazon," pp. 135–144

- Rambo 1985, *Primitive Polluters,* chapters 1 and 2
- Redford 1991, "The Ecologically Noble Savage"

Upper Division Courses

The Emergence of Historical Ecology (unit for a course in Ecological Anthropology)

WEEK 1. ENVIRONMENTAL DETERMINISM OF EGALITARIAN SOCIETIES

In this section we evaluate the research axioms associated with cultural ecology, especially the view that egalitarian societies (nonstate-level societies with status distinctions based principally on age and gender only) are mostly at the mercy of their local environments.

Readings
- Gross 1975, "Protein Capture and Cultural Development in the Amazon Basin"
- Steward 1972, chapter 2, "The Concept and Method of Cultural Ecology"
- Meggers 1954, "Environmental Limitation on the Development of Culture"

WEEK 2. PROBLEMS IN THE IDENTIFICATION OF ENVIRONMENTALLY LIMITING FACTORS

Here we directly question the assumptions raised in the immediately preceding section that protein, soils, or some other supposed environmentally limiting factor of egalitarian society is actually operational, at least at the level of magnitude suggested by its proponents. Each of the readings in this section challenges the findings discussed in one of the readings in the preceding section.

Readings
- Beckerman 1979, "The Abundance of Protein in Amazonia: A Reply to Gross"
- Carneiro 1961, "Slash-and-Burn Cultivation Among the Kuikuru. . ."
- Bettinger 1991, "Aboriginal Occupation at High Altitude. . ."

WEEK 3. HISTORICALLY DETERMINED ENVIRONMENTS

The hypothesis that egalitarian societies are limited (or determined) by their environments is evaluated in the light of evidence that egalitarian peoples over time have actually transformed their environments, including those that in the past have been customarily seen as pristine.

Readings
- Denevan 1992, "The Pristine Myth"
- Balée 1989, "The Culture of Amazonian Forests"
- Gómez-Pompa, Flores, and Sosa 1987, "The 'Pet-Kot': A Man-Made Tropical Forest of the Maya"

WEEK 4. HISTORICAL ECOLOGY

A new paradigm, historical ecology, is emerging. This new paradigm holds that historical not evolutionary events are responsible for the principal changes in relationships between human societies and their immediate environments. Historical ecology seeks to synthesize human–environmental interactions within specific societal, biological, and regional contexts. Its focus is a relationship, not an organism, species, or society. This relationship, itself an empirical object of inquiry, is between human groups and their immediate physical surroundings (i.e., landscapes).

Readings
- Bailey and Headland 1991, "The Tropical Rainforest"
- Cronon 1983, *Changes in the Land*, chapters 1 and 2
- Vansina 1990, *Paths in the Rainforest*, chapter 2

Ecological Anthropology (*a complete course for upper division undergraduates or graduate students*)

Course Objectives. Ecological theories concerning human behavior will be evaluated in light of several case studies in diverse ethnographic milieus. The global environmental crisis of our time will be addressed from perspectives that are unique to ecological anthropology.

WEEK 1. ECOLOGICAL ANTHROPOLOGY AS A FIELD OF INQUIRY RATHER THAN AS A SET OF AXIOMS

In other words, this section presents ecological anthropology (or human ecology) as a domain of research that includes more than one paradigm or theoretical perspective, such as cultural ecology and historical ecology. It discusses definitions of ecological anthropology and human ecology from a historical perspective.

Readings
- Steward 1972, *Theory of Culture Change,* pp. 1–77
- Anderson 1973, "Ecological Anthropology and Anthropological Ecology"
- Bates 1953, "Human Ecology" (graduate students)

WEEK 2. THE INFLUENCE OF ENVIRONMENTAL DETERMINISM AND 19TH CENTURY EVOLUTIONISM ON ECOLOGICAL ANTHROPOLOGY

This section presents the historical background to ecological anthropology beginning with Enlightenment theories of climatic determinism and proceeding through the unilinear models of Morgan, Tylor, and other 19th century theoreticians of cultural evolution.

Readings
- Steward 1972, *Theory of Culture Change,* pp. 78–172
- Helm 1962, "The Ecological Approach in Anthropology" (graduate students)
- White 1959, "Energy and Tools" (graduate students)

WEEK 3. MULTILINEAR AND GENERAL SCHEMES OF EVOLUTION; ENVIRONMENTAL DETERMINISM AND THE BEGINNINGS OF CULTURAL ECOLOGY

Here we evaluate the return of evolutionist thinking in 20th century anthropology, which coincides with the emergence of cultural ecology. The distinction between general evolution of the human species and culture as a whole and specific evolution of given sociocultural systems and its implications for ecological anthropology are discussed.

Readings
- Steward 1972, *Theory of Culture Change,* pp. 173–222
- Meggers 1954, "Environmental Limitation on the Development of Culture" (graduate students)

WEEK 4. MANIFEST VERSUS LATENT FUNCTIONS

We examine human behaviors, distinguishing those explicitly recognized by subjects themselves and those known consciously only to outside observers.

Readings
- Harris 1979, *Cultural Materialism,* pp. 1–76

- Merton 1968, "Manifest and Latent Functions," pp. 73–138 (graduate students)
- Moore 1982, "Divination: A New Perspective," pp. 120–128 (graduate students)

WEEK 5. EARLY POST-WAR TRENDS: SYNCHRONIC RESEARCH IN ECOLOGICAL ANTHROPOLOGY

Applications of cultural ecological and functionalist theories to specific ethnographic milieus are considered here.

Readings
- Harris 1979, *Cultural Materialism,* pp. 77–140
- Piddocke 1982, "The Potlatch System of the Southern Kwakiutl. . . ," pp. 130–156 (graduate students)

WEEK 6. CULTURAL MATERIALISM AND MODERN CULTURAL ECOLOGY

These two subdisciplines are compared in order to determine whether they are essentially the same paradigm or whether differences significant enough to warrant their separation exist. Marvin Harris argued in his earlier work, *The Rise of Anthropological Theory,* that Steward was anthropology's first cultural materialist. This section examines whether cultural ecology, as practiced by Steward, reached the holistic level of explanation of cultural similarities and differences that Harris has claimed for cultural materialism as a research strategy.

Readings
- Harris 1979. *Cultural Materialism,* pp. 141–341
- Vayda and Rappaport 1967. "Ecology, Cultural and Noncultural," pp. 477–497 (graduate students)

WEEKS 7 AND 8. LIEBIG'S LAW OF THE MINIMUM; LIMITING FACTORS; MODERN VERSIONS OF ENVIRONMENTAL DETERMINISM

This section discusses the use of the concept of limiting factors, such as soils and protein in parts of the tropics, by some researchers working in modern ecological anthropology.

Readings
- Rappaport 1979, pp. 1–259 (all)
- Ross 1978 (graduate students)
- Gross 1975, "Protein Capture and Cultural Development in the Amazon Basin" (graduate students)

- Beckerman 1979, "The Abundance of Protein in Amazonia: A Reply to Gross" (graduate students)

WEEK 9. THE ECOSYSTEM AS AN ANALYTICAL UNIT IN HUMAN ECOLOGY; CULTURALLY CREATED VERSUS NATURAL ECOSYSTEMS; ENERGETICS AND THE DEVELOPMENT OF CULTURE

We ask here, can human ecology be understood in terms of bounded, self-enclosed units such as ecosystems? We also discuss exchanges of energy between specific human societies and surrounding environments in light of technological and cultural aspects of those societies.

Readings
- Moran 1990, *The Ecosystem Approach in Anthropology,* pp. 1–187
- Alland 1975, "Adaptation" (graduate students)
- Orlove 1980, "Ecological Anthropology" (graduate students)

WEEK 10. ECOLOGICAL AND MATERIALIST THEORIES IN ARCHAEOLOGY; STUDYING THE ECOLOGY OF COMPLEX SOCIETIES

Here we consider the impact of theories from ecological anthropology (which is usually concerned with modern societies) on archaeology. Likewise, the impact of ecological theory on the study of the development of complex (state-level) societies is examined.

Readings
- Moran 1990, *The Ecosystem Approach in Anthropology,* pp. 188–319
- Kent 1992, "The Current Forager Controversy. . ." (graduate students)

WEEK 11. MODERN EVOLUTIONISM IN BIOLOGY; EVOLUTIONARY ECOLOGY; OPTIMAL FORAGING THEORY; BEHAVIORAL ECOLOGY

This section deals with the influence of evolutionary theories in biology on new approaches in ecological anthropology.

Readings
- Moran 1990, *The Ecosystem Approach in Anthropology,* pp. 323–457
- Charnov 1976, "Optimal Foraging, the Marginal Value Theorem" (graduate students)
- Hames and Vickers 1983, "Introduction" (graduate students)
- Pierce and Ollason 1987, "Eight Reasons why Optimal Foraging Theory is a Complete Waste of Time" (graduate students)

WEEK 12. ETHNOECOLOGY
This section deals with perspectives of native peoples on their own environments

Readings
- Smith 1991, *Inujjuamiut Foraging Strategies,* pp. 1–141
- Posey 1984, "Indigenous Ecological Knowledge and Development of the Amazon," pp. 135–144 (graduate students)

WEEKS 13 AND 14. HISTORICAL ECOLOGY
Treatment as in preceding course, lecture 4 (above).

Readings.
- Smith 1991, *Inujjuamiut Foraging Strategies,* pp. 143–409
- Headland 1987, "The Wild Yam Question. . ." (graduate students)
- Hardin 1968, "The Tragedy of the Commons" (graduate students)
- Redford 1991, "The Ecologically Noble Savage" (graduate students)
- Feeney et al. 1990, "The Tragedy of the Commons: Twenty-two Years Later." (graduate students)

RESOURCES

Page numbers appearing in brackets at the end of some entries indicate where the reference is cited in a course plan.

Alland, A., Jr. 1975. "Adaptation." *Annual Review of Anthropology* 4:59–73. [p. 40]
Criticizes the use of the biological concept of adaptation in ecological anthropology.

Anderson, J. N. 1973. "Ecological Anthropology and Anthropological Ecology." In *Handbook of Social and Cultural Anthropology.* J. J. Honigmann, ed. Chicago: Rand McNally. [p. 38]
This is one of the most lucid (and unfortunately most underread) statements of the holistic goals of ecological anthropology and of the possibility of an anthropological ecology.

Bailey, R. C. and T. N. Headland. 1991. "The Tropical Rainforest." *Human Ecology* 19(2):261–285. [pp. 34, 37]

Argues against the view that the tropical rainforest, understood as a pristine entity, is a habitat rich enough in natural food sources to support exclusively hunting-and-gathering lifestyles. Points out that traditional hunters and gatherers depend on cultivated and other resources in zones of agriculture within tropical forests, not within the forests themselves.

Balée, W. 1989. "The Culture of Amazonian Forests." *Advances in Economic Botany* 7:1–21. [pp. 33, 37]

This paper holds that 12% of the Brazilian Amazon consists of old, anthropogenic forests established through the economic activities of past indigenous peoples.

Bates, M. 1953. "Human Ecology." In *Anthropology Today*. A. L. Kroeber, ed. Chicago: University of Chicago Press. [p. 38]

One of the earliest attempts to survey and delimit the field of "human ecology."

Beckerman, S. 1979. "The Abundance of Protein in Amazonia: A Reply to Gross." *American Anthropologist* 81:533–560. [pp. 36, 40]

Directly questions Gross's theory that environmental protein exercised a limiting effect on native Amazonian populations by arguing, somewhat anecdotally, that there is in fact a wealth of protein in Amazonia, especially if one considers plant, insect, and fish sources of dietary protein in addition to the mammalian, terrestrial fauna.

Bettinger, R. L. 1991. "Aboriginal Occupation at High Altitude: Alpine Villages in the White Mountains of Eastern California." *American Anthropologist* 93:656–679. [p. 36]

This paper directly contradicts Steward's (1938) hypothesis that because of environmental limitations, human habitation was impossible in the alpine range of the indigenous Shoshone (Numic-speaking) habitat.

Carneiro, R. 1961. "Slash-and-Burn Cultivation Among the Kuikuru and its Implications for Cultural Development in the Amazon Basin." In *The Evolution of Horticultural Systems in Native South America, Causes and Consequences: A Symposium*. J. Wilbert, ed. *Antropológica, Supplement Publication no. 2*, Caracas. Reprinted in P. J. Lyon, ed. 1985. *Native South Americans*. Prospect Heights, IL: Waveland Press. [p. 36]

This paper challenges Meggers' theory (and environmental determinism in general without calling it by that name) that poor soils effected limitations on the development of complex society in lowland South America by showing that slash-and-burn agriculture does not necessarily result in soil exhaustion and that the widely noted mobility of peoples in lowland South America cannot be ascribed to environmental limitations.

Charnov, E. L. 1976. "Optimal Foraging, the Marginal Value Theorem." *Theoretical Population Biology* 9:129–136. [p. 40]
Original formulation of one of the principal axioms of optimal foraging theory, namely, that predators will abandon patches or expand their choice of food types as productivity from given types of prey becomes limiting.

Cronon, W. 1983. *Changes in the Land.* New York: Hill and Wang. [p. 37]
A pioneering account of interrelationships between indigenous peoples and local environments in New England, both before and after contact with Europeans. Although he is a historian, Cronon specifically utilizes theory and data from ecological anthropology, especially the work of Roy Rappaport.

Denevan, W. M. 1992. "The Pristine Myth: The Landscape of the Americas in 1492." *Annals of the Association of American Geographers* 82(3):369–385. [pp. 33, 37]
Argues that much of the Americas shows the lasting effects of past perturbations by indigenous peoples: undermines the view that the Americas constituted simply a vast wilderness at the time of the Conquest.

Feeny, D., F. Berkes, B. J. McCay, and J. M. Acheso. 1990. "The Tragedy of the Commons: Twenty-two Years Later." *Human Ecology* 18(1):1–19. [p. 41]
Based on recent research, takes issue with Hardin's hypothesis of the "tragedy of the commons."

Gómez-Pompa, A., J. S. Flores, and V. Sosa. 1987. "The 'Pet-Kot': A Man-Made Tropical Forest of the Maya." *Interciencia* 12(1):10–15.
This interesting article proposes that certain tropical forests of the Maya region are in fact the living artifacts of prehistoric Mayan forest management.

Gross, D. R. 1975. "Protein Capture and Cultural Development in the Amazon Basin." *American Anthropologist* 77:526–549. [pp. 36, 39]
The classic statement of the famous "protein hypothesis," in which it is argued that Amazonian forest dwellers have not been able to achieve sedentary, densely populated, politically complex sociocultural systems because of the low density of environmental protein in Amazonia.

Hames, R. B. and W. T. Vickers. 1983. "Introduction." In *Adaptive Responses of Native Amazonians.* R. B. Hames and W. T. Vickers, eds. New York: Academic Press. [p. 40]

Reviews ecological approaches to Amazonian indigenous peoples, arguing for more empiricism in research and less speculation as to the principal causes of settlement patterns, population densities, warfare, and so on.

Hardin, G. 1968. "The Tragedy of the Commons." *Science* 162:1243–1248. [p. 41]

Classic article which propounds the notion that common lands will inevitably be degraded because no one senses individual responsibility for them, assuming individuals are always trying to maximize their own benefits and minimize their own costs in economic and subsistence activity.

Harris, M. 1968. *The Rise of Anthropological Theory*. New York: T. Y. Crowell.

This book is one of the most comprehensive studies of the history of anthropological theory from the Enlightenment to the time of publication. It is highly focused on showing how diverse theories of past anthropological scholars led away from or converged toward cultural materialism, which is the theoretical orientation of the author. The book is sometimes criticized for its polemical tone, but that is paradoxically often seen as one of its strengths. The author is quite deliberate and explicit about the theoretical axe he has to grind.

Harris, M. 1979. *Cultural Materialism*. New York: Random House. [pp. 38, 39]

Major treatise on cultural materialism by its principal apologist; compares it, as a paradigm, to other theoretical orientations in anthropology, especially to those without an ecological focus.

Headland, T. N. 1987. "The Wild Yam Question: How Well Could Independent Hunter-Gatherers Live in a Tropical Rain Forest Ecosystem?" *Human Ecology* 15(4):463–491. [p. 41]

One of the first papers to question the concept that foraging populations can survive independently of agricultural interventions in tropical forests.

Helm, J. 1962. "The Ecological Approach in Anthropology." *The American Journal of Sociology* 57:630–639. [p. 38]

Useful summary by an anthropologist of the competing trends and major findings of ecological anthropology from the 1930s to the date of publication.

Kent, S. 1992. "The Current Forager Controversy: Real versus Ideal Views of Hunter-Gatherers." *Man* 27:45–70. [p. 40]

Reviews some of the principal controversies surrounding the ecological portrayal of hunters and gatherers, with specific focus on San peoples of southern Africa.

Meggers, B. 1954. "Environmental Limitation on the Development of Culture." *American Anthropologist* 56:801–824. [pp. 36, 38]

This is one of the most cogent arguments in the history of anthropology for environmental determinism, phrased in terms of environmentally limiting factors on egalitarian sociocultural systems which prevented these systems from evolving into full-fledged states and civilizations.

Merton, R. 1968. "Manifest and Latent Functions." In *Social Theory and Social Structure*. R. Merton, ed. New York: The Free Press. [p. 39]

Although written by a sociologist and not concerned with ecology per se, this reading is extremely relevant to the history of ecological anthropology. The distinction between manifest function (of which people are consciously aware) and latent function (of which people are not consciously aware) is one of the most important implicit concepts in many of the synchronic studies in cultural ecology carried out during the 1960s.

Moore, O. K. 1982 [1965]. "Divination: A New Perspective." In *Environment and Cultural Behavior*. A. P. Vayda, ed. Austin: University of Texas Press. [p. 39]

An important illustration of the ecological implications of a distinction between manifest and latent functions. Argues that scapulimancy (ostensibly a divinatory practice without practical connotations) randomizes hunting focus and therefore contributes to ecological stability among the Montagnais-Naskapi indigenous people of Labrador.

Moran, E. F., ed. 1990. *The Ecosystem Approach in Anthropology*. Ann Arbor: The University of Michigan Press. [p. 40]

Collection of important papers on applications of the ecosystem concept to modern and prehistoric societies. This is the major statement concerning the relevance of the concept of ecosystem to ecological anthropology, although the orientation of the book is not primarily theoretical.

Murdock, G. P. 1945. "The Common Denominator of Cultures." In *The Science of Man and the World Crisis*. N. R. Linton, ed. New York: Columbia University Press. [p. 35]

This famous paper draws on the earlier concept formulated by Clark Wissler of a universal pattern in human cultures; that is, a concatenation of traits all cultures presumably share as part of our human, biological heritage. Murdock suggests that while a universal pattern exists, the more specifically cultural traits are defined, the less general their occurrence can be. As an example, eating is universal; eating with chopsticks is not. Culture traits can be defined even more specifically than this, such that, according to Murdock, "It is highly doubtful . . . whether any specific element of behavior has ever attained genuinely universal distribution" (p. 125).

Orlove, B. S. 1980. "Ecological Anthropology." *Annual Review of Anthropology* 9:235–273. [p. 40]

Reviews history of ecological anthropology. Argues that ecological anthropology should focus on individuals and constraints on individual choices and actions in given environments rather than on cultures and populations per se. Seeks to develop "actor-based models" in the context of a "processual ecological anthropology." This article is often understood as a precursor to sociobiological models in ecological anthropology, insofar as it reifies the costs and benefits of subsistence practices to individuals rather than groups. In sociobiology, such costs and benefits are in principle measured in terms of reproductive fitness.

Parker, E. 1992. "Forest Islands and Kayapó Resource Management in Amazonia: A Reappraisal of the Apête." *American Anthropologist* 94:406–440. [p. 34]

Argues that Posey's findings on forest management by the Kayapó are mostly unsubstantiated in Parker's own research. Takes the relatively extreme position that the Kayapó do not manage trees and other forest resources and that there is no evidence that forest islands on the savanna are man-made or even influenced by human subsistence activities.

Piddocke, S. 1982 [1965]. "The Potlatch System of the Southern Kwakiutl: A New Perspective." In *Environment and Cultural Behavior.* A. P. Vayda, ed. Austin: University of Texas Press. [p. 39]

This paper argues that the Kwakiutl potlatch, which had often been seen as irrational economic behavior because of the giving away and even destruction of wealth that it entailed, in fact had the useful latent ecological function of spreading the risk of food shortages in the region of Vancouver Island and therefore lessening the chance of deprivation in any particular locale.

Pierce, G. J. and J. G. Ollason. 1987. "Eight Reasons why Optimal Foraging Theory is a Complete Waste of Time." *Oikos* 49(1):111–117.

As the title implies, this article attempts to show that optimal foraging theory is unprovable and lacks a rigorous empirical basis. [p. 40]

Posey, D. A. 1984. "Indigenous Ecological Knowledge and Development of the Amazon." In *The Dilemma of Amazonian Development.* E. Moran, ed. Boulder, CO: Westview Press. [pp. 34, 35, 41]

Argues that indigenous knowledge of natural resources and processes, as demonstrated by the Kayapó Indians of central Brazil, can be used by Western planners for the elaboration of more ecologically rational, less destructive development projects in the Amazon region.

Posey, D. A. 1992. "Reply to Parker." *American Anthropologist* 94:441–443. [p. 34]

Holds that Parker's (1992) critique of his work with the Kayapó is itself flawed, in part because Parker did not spend enough time in the field, did not use a rigorous methodology, and did not master the Kayapó language which would be requisite to falsifying Posey's hypotheses with regard to Kayapó forest management.

Rambo, A. T. 1985. *Primitive Polluters.* Ann Arbor, MI: Museum of Anthropology. [p. 36]

Represents the *Homo devastandus* doctrine in arguing that "all human societies, primitive as well as civilized, cause environmental change, often the sort of degradation popularly referred to as 'pollution'. . . "

Rappaport, R. A. 1979. *Ecology, Meaning, and Religion.* Berkeley, CA: North Atlantic Books. [p. 39]

Further development of many of the ideas originally expressed in the 1968 edition of *Pigs for the Ancestors.* Some but not all of these ideas are reprinted in the 1984 edition of *Pigs for the Ancestors.*

Rappaport, R. A. 1984 [1968]. *Pigs for the Ancestors: Ritual in the Ecology of a New Guinea People.* New Haven: Yale University Press.

This is the best known work in the field of ecological anthropology. It presents the view that the Tsembaga Maring live within a closed ecosystem in the New Guinea Highlands that sustains itself through time without environmental degradations via the ritual activities of the people themselves. My students in Ecological Anthropology have tended to consistently rank this monograph as one of their favorites.

Redford, K. H. 1991. "The Ecologically Noble Savage." *Cultural Survival Quarterly* 15(1):46–48. [pp. 36, 41]

Argues that indigenous peoples of the New World tropics may not be any more custodial of nature than Western societies.

Roosevelt, A. C., R. A. Housley, M. Imagio da Silveira, S. Maranca, and R. Johnson. 1991. "Eighth Millennium Pottery from Prehistoric Shell Midden in the Brazilian Amazon." *Science* 254:1621–1624. [p. 34]

This paper argues that the Amazon harbors the earliest pottery yet known in the Western Hemisphere and suggests that resource poverty did not limit cultural evolution in the tropics.

Ross, E. B. 1978. "Food Taboos, Diet, and Hunting Strategy: The Adaptation to Animals in Amazon Cultural Ecology." *Current Anthropology* 19(1):1–36. [p. 39]

Well-known article which sought to prove that taboos on game animals in South American indigenous cultures were actually ecologically adaptive to the people who possessed such taboos. As with Rappaport's and Moore's works, this paper seeks to show the ecological rationality of religious behavior and belief.

Smith, E. A. 1991. *Inujjuamiut Foraging Strategies*. New York: Aldine de Gruyter. [p. 41]

This is a difficult book, but it can be manageable for upper division and graduate level students in ecological anthropology. The book solidly evaluates diverse ecological theories in anthropology. Ultimately, in the excellent quantitative analysis of Inujjuamiut (Eskimo) foraging strategies, the book adopts a modified version of optimal foraging theory.

Steward, J. H. 1972 [1955]. *Theory of Culture Change*. Urbana and Chicago: University of Illinois Press. [pp. 36, 38]

Although the second chapter of Steward's main theoretical work argues that cultural ecology is not merely environmental determinism, it also states categorically that "The simpler cultures are more directly conditioned by the environment than advanced ones" (p. 40). Despite or perhaps because of his originality, Steward was often self-contradictory in his theoretical writings. In any case, this is the principal theoretical work Steward completed during his lifetime. (An alternative and equally useful book of Steward's writings, treating some of the same subjects, was published posthumously as *Evolution and Ecology: Essays on Social Transformation* [1977, University of Illinois Press] under the editorship of J. C. Steward and R. F. Murphy.) It is important to include a major work such as this one in the course, however dated the research may seem, because Steward was the founder of cultural ecology.

Vansina, J. 1990. *Paths in the Rainforest: Toward a History of Political Tradition in Equatorial Africa*. Madison, WI: University of Wisconsin Press. [pp. 33, 34, 37]

This volume undermines the illusion that equatorial Africa lacks history and traditions. By using historical linguistics, the author reconstructs many long-standing lifeways in equatorial Africa, including ways of using and managing land and biological resources. The book also attacks the belief that the African "jungle" is pristine, having been subject, rather, to millennia of human occupation and utilization.

Vayda, A. P. and R. A. Rappaport. 1967. "Ecology, Cultural and Noncultural." In *Introduction to Cultural Anthropology*. J. A. Clifton, ed. Boston: Houghton Mifflin. [p. 39]

A classic paper that attempted to revise Steward's cultural ecology so as to substitute "human population" for "culture." This made ecological anthropology more like the general ecology of the time in terms of its principal units of analysis (populations of organisms, not behaviors or cultures).

White, L. A. 1959. "Energy and Tools." In *The Evolution of Culture: The Development of Civilization to the Fall of Rome*. L. A. White, ed. New York: McGraw-Hill. [p. 38]
Excerpt from one of the major statements on 20th century cultural evolutionism by one of its principal founders. Theorizes a relationship between energy capture per capita and cultural complexity.

Acknowledgments

Professors William Durham, Dominique Irvine, and Emilio Moran generously shared with me their syllabi relevant to this chapter. The editors, Jonathan Collett and Stephen Karakashian, offered quite helpful editorial suggestions on the original manuscript. Thanks are due Dan M. Healan and James F. Kilroy of Tulane University for encouraging development of the Freshman Seminar on Tropical Forests that I taught in 1993.

Chapter 3

Biology

David G. Campbell
and
Vern Durkee
Grinnell College

The virtue of Earth that separates it from the rest of the universe (as far as we know) is its thin mantle of life. Earth would better be named "Vita." The evolution, diversification, and extinction of life over the past 3.5 billion years is Earth's greatest saga.

It comes as no surprise, therefore, that "biodiversity" has become one of the catch words of our time. Its analysis, evaluation, preservation, and teaching are now cottage industries for scientists, educators, politicians, conservationists, agriculturalists, philosophers, and even religious leaders. In recent years this word has been used in every sector of global society and in the dialogue of north versus south and rich versus poor, and it has been repeatedly interpreted—and misinterpreted—by the press. Few subjects touch so many. An ecologist regards biodiversity in a very different manner than an agronomist. A traditional conservationist argues for inviolate reserves; a pragmatist regards humans as a component of the biosphere. Conservative politicians consider the preservation of biodiversity to be a threat to economic development; liberal ones consider it necessary for human survival. A Judeo-Christian religious scholar, steeped in the concept of human dominion over the planet, may well be at philosophical odds with a Hindu.

Regardless of these differences, it is clear that Earth is losing its skin of life and is entering a pulse of extinction, due to human activities, that is equal in magnitude to most others in geological time—probably not as great as the extinction of marine invertebrate species at the end of the Permian period, 250 million years ago, but at least of the magnitude of the extinction of the ammonites, dinosaurs, and other fauna at the Cretaceous/Tertiary boundary, 65 million years ago (Raup 1991; Wilson 1992). This places a staggering responsibility on our generation. The decisions that we will make regarding biodiversity during the next several decades will leave their imprimatur on the planet for tens of millions of years. Scholars (assuming that any survive into the distant future) will debate the environmental and moral implications of the primacy of *Homo sapiens* on this Earth long after the damage is done.

As educators, we strive to define the issues that pertain to biodiversity, and to bring them into a manageable context. But the task is daunting, the literature vast and confusing. This chapter presents several successful methods of teaching biodiversity in the undergraduate curriculum. But first, a few definitions and motifs—some quite unexpected—are in order.

What Is Biodiversity?

Biodiversity literally means "biological diversity." The concept embraces the full hierarchy of nature's echelons—DNA, genes, proteins, varieties, subspecies, species, genera, families, orders, classes, etc.—and also the full spectrum of communities of plants and animals, of ecosystems and biomes. It is meaningless to consider a species outside of its ecological context, that is, its association with the biotic and abiotic components of its environment. Therefore biodiversity, in its elemental sense, incorporates all of Earth's environments and their living components.

Most biologists would argue that the fundamental units of the community—and therefore of diversity—are species. (But species are not necessarily the fundamental units of evolution; many argue that individuals, or even the frequencies of genes, which are sub-organismal, are the units of evolution.) Yet evolutionary biologists are still quibbling over the definition of "species," which has evolved in this century from the exemplar of a type specimen to embrace molecular and population biology. The technologies of taxonomy are also changing, from morphological, to cladistic, to biochemical (for a modern review, see Ereshefsky 1992). Are species real natural entities or convenient—and largely arbitrary—impositions of order on the natural world by humans? Most biologists would argue the former, embracing the *biological-species concept,* which states that "a species is a population whose members are able to interbreed freely under natural conditions" (Sokal and Crovello 1992; Wilson 1992). But the limits of an inbreeding population are not always obvious to the taxonomist, whose job it is to define and describe species. Consider, for example, that a slight difference in behavior—say, for example, the timing of mating—can differentiate species which are outwardly identical and occupy the same territory.

Likewise, it is meaningless to study a species without a consideration of its evolutionary context. The conservation of a last survivor of a lineage, such as the black rhinoceros, is very different from that of a suite of closely related species, all descended from one, or several, common ancestors that have undergone explosive adaptive radiation in a new environment (such as the cichlids in East African lakes). The implication here is fundamental, and often overlooked by teachers of biodiversity: an understanding of biodiversity must embrace the biological-species concept and necessarily, therefore, evolution. Without an exact definition for species, it is impossible to describe, let alone preserve, biological diversity (Rojas 1992).

What Is Ecological Diversity?

Ecologists differentiate between two principal kinds of diversity: (1) *alpha diversity* is a measure of the diversity in a circumscribed area (be it a small island or a continent); (2) *beta diversity* is a measure of the rate of change in species composition over distance, in other words, the heterogeneity of species in space. Further, ecologists define alpha diversity as a statistic that encompasses both the species richness (the number of species per unit area) and the evenness of distribution of those species. Most non-biologists are unaware of these distinctions, and thus use "diversity" in a simple sense, as an ecologist would use "alpha species richness." It is important, therefore, to understand the scholarly vantage point of the writer when considering discussions of biological diversity. The two types of diversity are often confused in the popular literature. For example, by virtue of their isolation, island or mountaintop environments often have low alpha diversities, yet because their biotas are close to 100% endemic they have high beta diversities relative to neighboring peaks or islands.

How Many Species Are There on Earth?

More than 230 years after the death of Carolus Linneaus, the founder of modern taxonomy, biologists do not know, even to the nearest order of magnitude, how many species exist on Earth. Estimates range from 5 million to 30 million. Yet, as of now, only about 1,400,000 species of protists, fungi, plants, and animals have been described by taxonomists (May 1990). (Even more elusive than estimates of how many species there *are* on Earth are models to estimate how many species there *could be* [May 1992b].) Tropical Central America, South America, and the West Indies provide an example. It is estimated that there are approximately 90,000 species of flowering plants in these regions. As of 1988, only 4,254 species—only 4.7% of the estimated total—had been formally described in *Flora Neotropica,* the series of floristic monographs that is considered definitive for the region. Since 1988 an average of 236 species per year have been added to *Flora Neotropica.* At this rate, it will take 381 years to complete the inventory of flowering plants. The situation is more grave for fungi, of which about 50,000 species are believed to occur in the tropical Americas. As of 1988, only 949 species—1.8% of the total—had been described in *Flora Neotropica,* and it is estimated that it will take 948 years to finish the inventory of fungi. The neotropical fungi and flowering plants are not exceptions in the tropics. It is obvious that most life on Earth has yet to be described (May 1992a).

Just as obviously, the pace of biological inventory is not keeping up with extinction, and many species are becoming extinct anonymously, before their existence is ever formally noted by taxonomists (Campbell 1989a & 1989b). Decisions relating to conservation and development are therefore being made, particularly in tropical areas, without an adequate understanding of biodiversity, and tropical communities are essentially "black boxes" presumed to have a high, but undefined, species richness. Regardless, conservation cannot wait for inventory, and it is necessary to assign priorities for conservation in the tropics, the so-called "hot spots," without using reliable quantitative criteria.

The Celebration of Diversity

There are abundant esthetic and moral reasons for conserving diversity. However, it is hard to teach these reasons to a hungry citizen of a developing country who must resort to short-term destruction of a tropical forest in order to get through the next few months, or even to an urban American student, who has little appreciation, or understanding, of a tropical forest. Much of the recent literature has therefore focused on utilitarian reasons for preserving diversity, ranging from the questionable relationship between diversity and environmental stability, to the extraction of medicines from tropical forest plants (Farnsworth et al. 1985; Myers 1984; see The Socioeconomic Paradigm, Unit 4C, below). Thus, for crass reasons, biological diversity is perceived as necessary for human welfare. (For a discussion of intrinsic versus utilitarian regard for nature, see Chapter 9, Philosophy.)

Teaching students to value biological diversity for more than the utilitarian reasons presented above is perhaps the greatest challenge to the educator. For students to *mourn* the loss of Earth's diversity (and hence to become motivated to do something about it), they first must *celebrate* diversity. Our experience has been that no course can be a dirge and still be effective. Therefore a course in biodiversity should first devote itself to exploring, at least broadly, the splendid panoply of living things, and the adventure of exploring it, before coming to grips with the reasons for its loss.

COURSE PLANS

Our search of syllabi has produced three general paradigms for teaching biodiversity: (1) the museum approach, (2) the ecosystems/conservation biology approach, and (3) the global socioeconomic approach. It is important to note that none of the syllabi we consulted conformed exactly to any one of the paradigms and that most derived components from all three paradigms. Regardless, in the section that follows we present excerpts from representative syllabi (the first and third are direct excerpts; the second is a chimaera of two syllabi), accompanied by text references and other resources, that generally conformed to each of the paradigms.

A Nonmajor, Introductory Course

The Museum Approach: The Classical Presentation of Plant Taxonomy, Animal Taxonomy, and Comparative Anatomy

Traditionally, zoology and botany have been taught in this manner, accompanied by dissection of specimens and visits to herbaria and museums. Most modern biology texts devote many pages (usually relegated to the back of the book) to the iteration of taxonomies. A generation ago, biologists were trained in this manner, which can be a splendid and engrossing experience (Darwin, after all, began by collecting beetles). But a new generation of biologists has emerged since the 1960s, raised in the exciting era of cellular-molecular biology. Constrained for time and grappling with an exponentially increasing amount of information that demands some sort of restraint, the planners of biology curricula have often neglected a formal consideration of diversity. This *triage* has resulted in a poverty of taxonomic biologists, just at the time when the inventory of Earth's life forms is most critical (Wilson 1985). Succumbing to the fad, entire departments have "gone molecular." Courses in invertebrate zoology (including entomology), plant taxonomy, mammalogy, and so on are disappearing from the undergraduate curriculum (and most depressing, from the *nonmajor* curriculum) and are now available only in the more specialized graduate universities.

Fortunately, there are exceptions to this trend. One exemplar is Professor Monte Lloyd's nonmajor, undergraduate course, entitled "Biodiversity," at the University of Chicago. The text is *Understanding Biology* (Raven and Johnson 1988), one of the basic, unspecialized, undergraduate biology primers that devotes a large section to the description of taxonomic hierarchies, but almost any text (such as Campbell 1993) would serve this function. What distinguishes Lloyd's course is the use of the collections of the Field Museum of Natural History, the Shedd Aquarium, and the Lincoln Park Zoo. Students do not visit these institutions with the professor in formal classes but instead go individually at their convenience. (The 254-page laboratory manual, which is a trove of observations and ideas, even shows bus routes to the museum.)

Lloyd's course (which defies outlining) begins in the great hall of the dinosaurs at the Field Museum. The laboratory manual is so detailed that it even points out on which sides of the display the labels (which are often challenged) are placed. It invites the students to interpret for themselves, for example, the nuances of dentition and bone structure of a dinosaur skeleton, and then to predict the method of locomotion, physiology, social behavior, and habitat—in other words, to think like a scientist. "Go to the end of the case and look *Dimetrodon* straight in the face," writes Lloyd. "It had partially binocular vision, made possible by its very thin snout." What student would ever forget being eyeball-to-socket with a dinosaur? The supplementary reading for the section is Bakker (1988), an iconoclastic and well-illustrated popular book that promulgates the theory that dinosaurs were warm-blooded. Inevitably, the section ends with a discussion of extinction and Walter and Louis Alvarez's extraterrestrial collision hypothesis (for a review, see Raup 1991) which, in turn, introduces the concept of the transience of species. Having spent an afternoon in the Cretaceous, the students now have a perspective from which to compare the modern day pulse of extinction.

After dinosaurs, the excursions are as follow: birds, plants, fish, mammals, insects, and marine invertebrates, each in its own particular museum hall, aquarium, or zoo. The course ends with discussions of ecological succession, global climate, human demography, and tropical deforestation. Lloyd's course has a liberal use of documentary films: Adrian Colwell's "The Decade of Destruction," and episodes from the popular television series, "Nature." Leaving nothing to chance, Lloyd presents transcripts of the films in his manual. The course is ideal for the undergraduate nonmajor: it is experiential, tactile, designed to be interesting, and diversionary from the humdrum of university life. The stu-

dent is seduced by curiosity, and learns, perhaps for the first time, that
there is value in biodiversity.

An Upper Division Course

The Ecosystems Approach, Including Theories and Modeling of Biodiversity

Course Description and Objectives. This approach often begins with a
"taxonomy" of ecosystems: their characteristics, principal components,
and importance to humans. Requisite to this approach is an introduction
to the measures of the biological complexity of communities, species
richness, diversity, equitability, alpha and beta diversity, as well fundamentals of evolution, extinction, and the geographical distribution of life
on the planet. In many ways, this material fills the role (as does Lloyd's
course) of "celebrating" diversity. Next comes the pragmatic section on
teaching the conservation of biodiversity (including human crop diversity), embracing the design of parks and reserves, the principles of island
biogeography, population size and genetic viability, and the restitution of
damaged ecosystems.

John Terborgh (Duke University) has been an innovator in the application of theoretical, empirical, and applied ecology to the tropics, working with both animals and plants. His course, entitled "Tropical Ecology,"
is an excellent example of the ecosystems approach to teaching biodiversity at an upper level. M. A. Davis (Macalester College) teaches "Global
Biodiversity and the Biology of Conservation," a nonmajor, undergraduate course that "explores the reasons behind the alarming loss of biodiversity throughout the world today." Davis's course overlaps much of Terborgh's but has a greater emphasis on restoration ecology. We present a
hybrid syllabus of Terborgh's and Davis's courses (with references) below.
We have also added some references of our own.

UNIT 1. PLANTS

  A. Causes of climate. Fundamental, but often overlooked, questions: Why
      are the tropics warm? What are the global weather patterns that define
      the tropics? Have the tropics always been warm? (Pianka 1978, chap-
      ter 3).

  B. Global patterns of vegetation. How have organisms adapted to patterns
      of climate? What are the latitudinal patterns of diversity? (Walter
      1985).

  C. Evolution of species diversity I: historical biogeography. Is the extrava-
      gant diversity of the tropics due to long-term stability, a constancy and
      predictability of physical conditions? The maintenance of tropical
      diversity. Equilibrium and disequilibrium models (Ashton 1989; Burger
      1985; Gentry 1989).

D. Evolution of species diversity II: the Pleistocene and Holocene. Or is the diversity of the tropics due to short-term disruption during the Ice Ages, when the tropical-forested parts of South America and Africa may have been broken up into island refugia (Gentry 1989; Haffer 1969; Haffer 1982; Prance 1982).

E. Ecology of deserts, savannas, and forests. What are the adaptations of organisms to these disparate climatic regimes? What are the patterns of diversity within these regimes? (Walter 1985).

F. Tropical plant diversity: the horizontal component. How are organisms distributed on the surface of the Earth, over large and small scales? In tropical forests, how much of distribution is explained by the "source and sink" model of tropical forest trees? (Hubbell 1979). How do patterns of diversity relate to soil quality, light, successional stage, altitude, rainfall? (Clark and Clark 1984; Gentry 1988a; Gentry 1988b; Huston 1979; Janzen 1970).

G. Tropical plant diversity: the vertical component. The majority of species in tropics occur in the forest canopy (Erwin 1988; Terborgh 1985a).

H. Tropical plant succession. The dynamic mosaic of tropical forest vegetation. The changes that occur after trees fall. The vegetation of light gaps as a function of gap size and age. The concept of the climax. Is there such a thing as climax in tropical forests? (Denslow 1987; Foster 1985; Uhl, Bushbacker & Serrão 1988; Uhl, Clark et al. 1988; Whitmore 1989).

I. Phenological cycles. How do patterns of flowering and fruiting in tropical forests correspond with annual climatic changes? How do propagules and pollinators adapt to these changes? (Baker et al. 1983; Foster 1985; Wright and Cornejo 1990).

J. Frugivory in tropical forests. What, in terms of taste, nutrients, and phenology, constitutes the ideal fruit? Does seed predation explain the scattered distribution of many tropical forest plant species? (Clark and Clark 1984; Janzen 1970; Terborgh 1986; Wheelwright 1988).

K. Herbivory in tropical forests. The evolutionary race between herbivores and plants. The evolution of secondary plant substances. Ant–plant interactions (Benson 1985; Coley, Bryant, and Chapin 1985; Janzen 1983; Leigh and Smythe 1978).

UNIT 2. ANIMALS

A. Ecology of distributions I: the role of interspecific competition. How do animal species differentiate their niches? The concept of niche packing (Terborgh 1971).

B. Ecology of distributions II: the role of ecotones and physical factors. Physical barriers often circumscribe the distribution of organisms, communities, and biomes. Certain organisms specialize in ecotones, which are zones where communities meet (Terborgh 1985b).

C. Tropical animal diversity I: the temperate tropical gradient (Owen 1983). See Unit 1 D above.

D. Tropical animal diversity II: horizontal and vertical components of diversity. See Unit 1 F & G above (Bourliére 1983; Erwin 1988).

E. Convergence and nonconvergence in animal communities. Animal communities in tropical Africa and South America appear to be strikingly similar in terms of the niches they contain, yet the species, even families, of animals in these guilds are often only distantly related (Terborgh and van Schaik 1987).

F. Predator/prey relations in savanna and forest. Under what conditions does predation foster diversity? diminish diversity? (Emmons 1987).

UNIT 3. CONSERVATION BIOLOGY IN THE TROPICS

A. Applications of island biogeography to the design of reserves. The number of species on an island is a function of area, the distance from a source of colonists, whether the island is oceanic or continental, and the antiquity of colonization (Williamson 1981). These same factors apply to parks and reserves, which are virtual islands (Shafer 1990). Parks and reserves can be designed incorporating the theory of island biogeography (Spears 1988). Reserves can also be designed taking into account Pleistocene refugia (Prance 1977).

B. Habitat fragmentation and its implications. When habitats are fragmented, they lose diversity as a function of fragment size and the amount of edge relative to fragment area (Terborgh 1988; Alverson et al. 1988). The Amazon minimum critical size experiment is designed to test the relationship between refugia (island) size and the maintenance of species diversity (Lovejoy et al. 1983).

C. The role of zoos, botanical gardens, and gene banks (Ashton 1988; Cade 1988; Conway 1988; Dresser 1988; Seal 1988).

D. Managing tropical forests I: nontimber products including fruits, nuts, rubber, and traditional medicines (Johns 1988; Peters et al. 1989). See also Unit 4 in the course, "Nations and the Global Environment," below.

E. Managing tropical forests II: timber. Is the removal of timber from tropical forests inevitably damaging to biodiversity? (Laarman 1988; Uhl and Vieira 1989).

F. The ecology of invading species. Tropical biotas, especially island biotas, are susceptible to introduced species. Examples are mongooses on the Hawaiian Islands, the brown snake on Guam, the marine toad in tropical Queensland, and Eurasian weeds on the American prairie (Crosby 1986).

G. Restoration ecology. Can damaged tropical ecosystems ever recover? Do "restored" ecosystems ever have their original diversity? (Cairns 1988; Jordan 1988; Todd 1988; Uhl 1988; Zedler 1988).

H. Sustainable development in the tropics: Is it possible? There may not be such a thing as sustainable development (Sanchez and Benites 1987).

General Course for Lower or Upper Division Students from a Variety of Majors

The Socioeconomic Paradigm: Nations and the Global Environment

Course Description and Objectives. This is a multidisciplinary undergraduate course in the Environmental Studies Concentration at Grinnell College. It is taught by the senior author, although it would be highly conducive to being team-taught, by a natural scientist and a social scientist, for example. The course has general appeal, attracting upper and lower level students, including those in the sciences, social sciences, and the humanities, as well as environmental studies. Just about everybody finds something novel in the course, which embraces subjects as disparate as the evolution of Earth's atmosphere, atmospheric warming, ozone depletion, human demography, and biodiversity. The section on biodiversity begins with elements of both the ecosystem and conservation biological approaches, described above. The focus is on neotropical forests.

A fundamental theme of the course, especially as it relates to the conservation of biodiversity, is economic development in both rich and poor countries and the revelation that, although most of Earth's biodiversity resides in the poorer, tropical nations, the fundamental reasons for its destruction lie in the developed North.

Basic to this approach is the "demographic transition," the three stages of population growth that accompany economic growth: (1) the first stage is when the population is in equilibrium because both the birth and death rates are high, (2) the second stage is when the death rate declines but, for cultural reasons, the birth rate remains high and the population soars, and (3) the third stage is when the population is once again at equilibrium, with low birth and death rates (Keyfitz 1991; Livi-Bacci 1989; Piel 1992). Stated another way, the third stage of the transition is the economic threshold after which it is adaptive for a father and mother to invest their resources in educating a few children, rather than producing as many children as possible. Most of Europe crossed the third stage of the demographic transition during the last century, and population growth dropped concomitantly—so much so that some countries, especially in the former Soviet bloc, have declining populations. (There is, of course, a flip side to the third stage demographic transition: per capita consumption—and therefore the per capita burden placed on the environment—also increases dramatically.) However, many countries in Africa, South America, and Asia are stuck in the second stage of the transition, and they are kept from shifting to the third stage for the reasons stated above. The subjects in the syllabus below are all presented in the context of the demographic transition.

UNIT 1. THE PACE OF BIOLOGICAL EXPLORATION

Unit Objectives. What is the pace of biological exploration; how long will it take to complete the inventory of Earth's biodiversity? Can this process ever be completed in areas that are stuck in the second stage of the transition? (Campbell 1989a and 1989b; Janzen 1988; Kubitzki 1977; Myers 1988).

UNIT 2. PUBLIC HEALTH ASPECTS OF DEFORESTATION

Unit Objectives. How does deforestation foster epidemic disease? Do these epidemics, by increasing infant mortality, delay the third stage of the transition? (Garrett 1994; Yuill 1983).

UNIT 3. ECONOMIC DISINCENTIVES TO PRESERVE BIODIVERSITY

Unit Objectives. Many economies, national and global, provide short-term incentives for the destruction of biological diversity (McNeely 1988; Rich 1994; Schmink and Wood 1984).

A. The status of women and the environment. Throughout the developing world, the isolation of women from the decision-making processes of their nations and their families, in the contexts of politics, the economy, and contraception, is perhaps the most important barrier to the rational use of natural resources, including biological diversity. This is particularly important in the context of family planning and therefore the pace at which a nation crosses the demographic transition. Key references are Boserup (1970) and Jacobson (1992). The Chikpo ("tree hugging") movement in India, in which women actually placed themselves in the path of bulldozers and chainsaws, is described in Rudda (1992) and Shiva (1989). See also Sontheimer (1991).

B. International debt. The huge debts that developing nations owe to wealthy nations often drive their economies toward policies that generate rapid revenue, yet are inimical to biological diversity. The Serra das Carajás iron-mining enterprise, in eastern Brazilian Amazonia, is the classic example (Rich 1994). Debt-for-nature swaps are an alternative (Brown and Jacobson 1987).

UNIT 4. ALTERNATIVES TO TROPICAL DEFORESTATION

A. Agroforestry. The basic principles of nutrient cycling in tropical forests (Herrera 1985; Jordan 1983). Examples of agricultural strategies that preserve the nutrient cycling; the Lacandon Maya (Nations and Nigh 1980). For examples in Amazonia, refer to Peck (1990) and Taylor (1988).

B. Extractivism and extractive reserves. The extractivism of valuable tropical forest products is being explored as an alternative to deforestation. The Brazilian rubber boom and peonage extractivism (Hecht and Cockburn 1989). Extractive reserves; the alliance of native people and extractors (Allegretti 1990; Anderson 1990; Peters 1990; Stone 1985). Utilization of flooded forest (Goulding 1985). The farming of native animals: river turtles, agoutis, and East African antelopes (to name a few) produce as much, or more, meat per hectare as environmentally destructive introduced domesticates, such as cattle (Ocana et al. 1988; Robinson and Redford 1991).

C. The pharmacopeia of the forest. For their war on insects, and on each other, plants have evolved chemical defenses that provide a largely untapped botanical pharmacy. Key references are Farnsworth et al. (1985), Janzen (1978, 1985), and Plotkin (1988). Do secondary plant substances of tropical forest plants have potential as pharmaceuticals? (Myers 1984). The intellectual property rights of indigenous people: how should native informants be compensated for the information that they provide to drug researchers? (Boom 1990).

D. Economic valuation of forest. Positive effects: is the long-term extraction of forest products worth more than the short-term gain from deforestation? (Peters et al. 1989; Prance et al. 1987). Negative effects: what if the economy changes and the forest products are no longer valuable? What if they are grown on plantations elsewhere, or are synthesized? Is it wise to attach a monetary value to tropical forests? (Ehrenfeld 1988; Norton 1988).

Resources

Page numbers appearing in brackets at the end of some entries indicate where the reference is cited in a course plan.

The texts and monographs described immediately below are suitable for those who are new to the field, or who have neither the time nor resources to enter the primary literature. The videotapes would enrich either lower or upper division courses. Next, several journals are described which contain many of the most important articles on the conservation of biodiversity. The instructor of an upper division course would be wise to follow these with some regularity. Finally, references cited in the course plans are given. These are ideal for upper level courses, for which exposure to the primary literature is desirable, or as supplemental material for advanced students. Because the titles are quite descriptive, we have not annotated these references.

General Texts and Monographs

Huston, M. 1994. *Biological Diversity: The Coexistence of Species on Changing Ecosystems*. Cambridge: Cambridge University Press.

A magnificent compendium of knowledge, with 98 pages of references, that covers all aspects of biological diversity.

Ricklefs, R. E. and D. Schulter, eds. 1993. *Species Diversity in Ecological Communities*. Chicago: University of Chicago Press.

A replete and competent review of current issues in the historical and geographical perspectives of biological diversity, with a look toward trends of future inquiry. The edited volume is divided into four parts, each with at least five chapters: (1) local patterns and processes, (2) coexistence at the mesoscale, (3) regional perspectives, and (4) historical and phylogenetic perspectives. Although a thorough review of these issues, it is not quantitative, and therefore is suitable for undergraduates who are not science majors.

Terborgh, J. 1992. *Diversity and the Tropical Rain Forest*. New York: Scientific American Library.

In many ways this book is structured in the same manner as Terborgh's course, described above. Its nine chapters are a succinct review of tropical forest biology. Among others, headings are: the paradox of tropical luxuriance, the global diversity gradient, sunlight and stratification, the evolution of diversity, conserving biodiversity, and managing tropical forests. Illustrated with beautiful color photographs.

Wilson, E. O. 1992. *The Diversity of Life*. Cambridge, MA: Belknap.

This book is a treasure, a personal inquiry into biodiversity by a man of science and of conscience. It is both a celebration of life's bouquet and a lament for its diminution. But the book is also an excellent nuts-and-bolts primer for the nonmajor on species, evolution, the pace of biological exploration, and conservation.

Wilson, E. O. and F. M. Peter, eds. 1988. *Biodiversity*. Washington, DC: National Academy Press.

An edited volume with 57 chapters by experts in their fields, it has become the benchmark of the literature on biodiversity. It deals with subjects as wide-ranging as "Ecological Diversity in Coastal Zones and Oceans" (G. C. Ray), "Screening Plants for New Medicines" (N. Farnsworth), "Using Science and Technology to Reestablish Species Lost in Nature" (T. J. Cade), and "Mind in the Biosphere; Mind of the Biosphere" (M. E. Soulé). It is simply indispensable.

Videotapes

"The Decade of Destruction." [p. 55]

Six hours long, this film documents the destruction of the tropical forests and native peoples of the Brazilian state of Rondônia by disillusioned colonists along the Trans Amazon Highway. Written and filmed by Adrian Colwell, it is as much a work of art as a didactic tool. When the film was broadcast in Brazil it galvanized the conservation movement and spawned several nongovernmental organizations dedicated to preserving Amazonia. A production of PBS's "Frontline." To purchase copies, contact WNET: 800-345-9638.

"Nature." [p. 55]

A series of splendidly photographed wildlife films, narrated by George Page, that is a production of WNET in New York. This is a good way to imbue an esthetic sense of biological diversity. Take your pick from the extensive catalogue of tapes. To purchase copies, contact WNET: 800-345-9638.

"NOVA."

A series of films devoted to all aspects of science, including biology and biodiversity, produced by WGBH in Boston. To order tapes, contact WGBH: 800-828-9424.

Journals

Ambio, the Journal of the Human Environment.

Published by the Royal Swedish Academy of Sciences, it is a source of papers on the interface of humans and biodiversity.

Conservation Biology.

The benchmark journal for issues of biodiversity, applied and theoretical. Published for the Society for Conservation Biology.

Biotropica.

The voice of the Association for Tropical Biology, it is a source of short, technical articles, ideal for upper level courses.

Trends in Ecology and Evolution.
Elsevier Science Publications. A timely source of short, succinct articles that
are ideal for nonmajors.

Additional References

We are aware that many of the papers listed below, although useful as
first-hand resources for the classroom, may be out of the reach of some
small institutions. Interlibrary loan (ILL) is one way of acquiring these
papers. The information highway provides yet a quicker method.
Uncover is a commercial computer service that can fax current papers to
any phone as quickly as a few hours. The cost per paper averages about
$12.00 (depending on copyright fee), which is comparable to the cost of
most ILL retrievals. For further information, contact the Uncover Company, 3801 E. Florida, Suite 200, Denver, CO 80210. Phone: 800-787-
7979; fax: 303-758-5946; E-mail: uncover@carl.org.

Allegretti, M. H. 1990. "Extractive Reserves: An Alternative for Recon-
    ciling Development and Environmental Conservation in Amazonia."
    In *Alternatives to Deforestation: Steps Toward Sustainable Use of the
    Amazon Rain Forest.* A. B. Anderson, ed. New York: Columbia Uni-
    versity Press. [p. 61]

Alverson, W. S., D. M. Waller, and S. L. Solheim. 1988. "Forests Too Deer:
    Edge Effects in Northern Wisconsin." *Conservation Biology*
    2(4):348–358. [p. 58]

Anderson, A. B. 1990. "Extraction and Forest Management by Rural
    Inhabitants in the Amazon Estuary." In *Alternatives to Deforestation:
    Steps Toward Sustainable Use of the Amazon Rain Forest.* A. B.
    Anderson, ed. New York: Columbia University Press. [p. 61]

Ashton, P. S. 1988. "Conservation of Biological Diversity in Botanical
    Gardens." In Wilson and Peter (1988). [p. 58]

Ashton, P. S. 1989. "Species Richness in Tropical Forests." In *Tropical
    Forests: Botanical Dynamics, Speciation and Diversity.* L. B. Holm-
    Nielson, I. C. Nielson, and H. Balslev, eds. London: Academic Press.
    [p. 56]

Baker, H. G., K. S. Bawa, G. W. Frankie, and P. A. Opler. 1983. "Repro-
    ductive Biology of Plants in Tropical Forests." In *Tropical Rain For-
    est Ecosystems.* F. B. Golley, ed. Vol. 1, *Structure and Function.*
    Amsterdam: Elsevier. [p. 57]

Bakker, R. 1988. *The Dinosaur Heresies.* New York: Morrow. [p. 55]

Benson, W. 1985. "Amazon Ant-Plants." In *Amazonia*. G. T. Prance and T. E. Lovejoy, eds. Oxford: Pergamon Press. [p. 57]

Boom, B. 1990. "Giving Native People a Share of the Profits." *Garden*. 14(6):28–31. [p. 61]

Boserup, E. 1970. "Male and Female Farming Systems." In *Woman's Role in Economic Development*. E. Boserup, ed. Reading: Earthscan Library. [p. 60]

Bourliére, F. 1983. "Animal Species Diversity in Tropical Forests." In *Tropical Rain Forest Ecosystems*. F. B. Golley, ed. Vol. 1, *Structure and Function*. Amsterdam: Elsevier. [p. 58]

Brown, L. and J. L. Jacobson. 1987. *Our Demographically Divided World*. Washington, DC: Worldwatch. [p. 60]

Burger, W. C. 1985. "Why Are There So Many Kinds of Flowering Plants in Costa Rica?" In *The Botany and Natural History of Panama*. W. G. D'Arcy and M. D. Correa A., eds. St. Louis: Missouri Botanical Garden. [p. 56]

Cade, T. J. 1988. "Using Science and Technology to Reestablish Species Lost in Nature." In Wilson and Peter (1988). [p. 58]

Cairns, J. 1988. "Increasing Diversity by Restoring Damaged Ecosystems." In Wilson and Peter (1988). [p. 58]

Campbell, D. G. 1989a. "The Importance of Floristic Inventory." In *Floristic Inventory of Tropical Countries*. Campbell, D. G. and D. H. Hammond, eds. New York: The New York Botanical Garden. [p. 60]

Campbell, D. G. 1989b. "Rates of Botanical Exploration in Asia and Latin America; Similarities and Dissimilarities with Africa." *Mitt. Inst. Allg. Bot. Hamburg*. 23a:155–167. [p. 60]

Campbell, N. 1993. *Biology*, 3rd ed. Redwood City, CA: The Benjamin Cummings Publishing Company. [p. 55]

Clark, D. A. and D. B. Clark. 1984. "Spacing of a Tropical Rain Forest Tree: Evaluation of the Janzen-Connell Model." *American Naturalist* 124:769–788. [p. 57]

Coley, P. D., J. P. Bryant, and F. S. Chapin III. 1985. "Resource Availability and Plant Antiherbivore Defense." *Science* 230:895–899. [p. 57]

Conway, W. 1988. "Can Technology Aid Species Preservation?" In Wilson and Peter (1988). [p. 58]

Crosby, A. W. 1986. *Ecological Imperialism: The Biological Expansion of Europe, 900-1900*. New York: Cambridge University Press. [p. 58]

Denslow, J. S. 1987. "Tropical Rain Forest Gaps and Tree Species Diversity." *Annual Review of Ecology and Systematics* 18:431–451. [p. 57]

Dresser, B. L. 1988. "Cryobiology, Embryo Transfer, and Artificial Insemination in Ex Situ Animal Conservation Programs." In Wilson and Peter (1988). [p. 58]

Ehrenfeld, D. 1988. "Why Put a Value on Biodiversity?" In Wilson and Peter (1988).[p. 61]

Emmons, L. H. 1987. "Comparative Feeding Ecology of Felids in a Neo-Tropical Forest." *Behavior Ecology and Sociobiology* 20:271–283. [p. 58]

Ereshefsky, M., ed. 1992. *The Units of Evolution.* Cambridge: Massachusetts Institute of Technology Press.

Erwin, T. L. 1988. "The Tropical Forest Canopy: The Heart of Biotic Diversity." In Wilson and Peter (1988). [pp. 57, 58]

Farnsworth, N. R., O. Akerele, A. Bingel, D. Soejarto, and Z. Guo. 1985. "Medicinal Plants in Therapy." *Bulletin of the World Health Organization* 63(6):965–981. [p. 61]

Foster, R. 1985. "Plant Seasonality in the Forests of Panama." In *The Botany and Natural History of Panama.* W. G. D'Arcy and M. D. Correa A., eds. St. Louis: Missouri Botanical Garden. [p. 57]

Garrett, L. 1994. *The Coming Plague: Newly Emerging Diseases in a World Out of Balance.* New York: Farrar, Straus and Giroux. [p. 60]

Gentry, A. 1988a. "Tree Species Richness of Upper Amazonian Forests." *Proceedings of the National Academy of Sciences* 85:156–159. [p. 57]

Gentry, A. 1988b. "Changes in Plant Community Diversity and Floristic Composition on Geographical and Environmental Gradients." *Annals of the Missouri Botanical Garden* 75:1–34. [p. 57]

Gentry, A. H. 1989." Speciation in Tropical Forests." In *Tropical Forests: Botanical Dynamics, Speciation and Diversity.* L. B. Holm-Nielson, I. C. Nielsen, and H. Balslev, eds. London: Academic Press. [pp. 56, 57]

Goulding, M. 1985. "Forest Fishes of the Amazon." In *Amazonia.* G. T. Prance and T. E. Lovejoy, eds. Oxford: Pergamon Press. [p. 61]

Haffer, J. 1969. "Speciation in Amazonian Forest Birds." *Science* 165:131–137.

Haffer, J. 1982. "General Aspects of the Refuge Theory." In *Biological Diversification in the Tropics.* G. T. Prance, ed. New York: Columbia University Press. [p. 57]

Hecht, S. and A. Cockburn. 1989. *The Fate of the Forest: Developers, Destroyers, and Defenders of the Amazon.* New York: Verso. [p. 61]

Herrera, R. 1985. "Nutrient Cycling in Amazonian Forests." In *Amazonia.* G. T. Prance and T. E. Lovejoy, eds. Oxford: Pergamon Press. [p. 61]

Hubbell, S. P. 1979. "Tree Dispersion, Abundance, and Diversity in a Tropical Dry Forest." *Science* 203:1299–1309. [p. 57]

Huston, M. 1979. "A General Hypothesis of Species Diversity." *American Naturalist* 113:81–101. [p. 57]

Jacobson, J. L. 1992. *Gender Bias: Roadblock to Sustainable Development.* Washington, DC: Worldwatch. [p. 60]

Janzen, D. H. 1970. "Herbivores and the Number of Tree Species in Tropical Forests." *American Naturalist* 104:501–528. [p. 57]

Janzen, D. H. 1978. "Complications in Interpreting the Chemical Defenses of Trees Against Tropical Arboreal Plant-Eating Vertebrates." In *The Ecology of Arboreal Folivores.* G. G. Montgomery, ed. Washington, DC: Smithsonian Institution Press. [p. 61]

Janzen, D. H. 1983. "Food Webs: Who Eats What, Why, How and With What Effects in a Tropical Forest?" In *Tropical Rain Forest Ecosystems.* F. B. Golley, ed. Vol. 1, *Structure and Function.* Amsterdam: Elsevier. [p. 57]

Janzen. D. H. 1985. "Plant Defenses Against Animals in the Amazonian Rainforest." In *Amazonia.* G. T. Prance and T. E. Lovejoy, eds. Oxford: Pergamon Press. [p. 61]

Janzen, D. H. 1988. "Tropical Dry Forests: The Most Endangered Tropical Ecosystem." In Wilson and Peter (1988). [p. 60]

Johns. A. D. 1988. "Effects of 'Selective' Timber Extraction on Rain Forest Structure and Composition and Some Consequences for Frugivores and Folivores." *Biotropica* 20(1):31–37. [p. 58]

Jordan, C. F. 1983. "Productivity of Tropical Rain Forest Ecosystems and the Implications for Their Use as Future Wood and Energy Sources." In *Tropical Rain Forest Ecosystems.* F. B. Golley, ed. Vol. 1, *Structure and Function.* Amsterdam: Elsevier. [p. 61]

Jordan, W. R. 1988. "Ecological Restoration: Reflections on a Half-Century of Experience at the University of Wisconsin-Madison Arboretum." In Wilson and Peter (1988). [p. 58]

Keyfitz, N. 1991. "Population Growth Can Prevent the Development That Would Slow Population Growth." In *Preserving the Global Environment.* J. T. Mathews, ed. New York: W. W. Norton & Company. [p. 59]

Kubitzki, K. 1977. "The Problem of Rare and of Frequent Species: The Monographer's View." In *Extinction is Forever.* G. T. Prance and T. S. Elias, eds. New York: New York Botanical Garden. [p. 60]

Laarman, J. G. 1988. "Export of Tropical Hardwoods in the Twentieth Century." In *World Deforestation in the Twentieth Century.* J. F.

Richards and R. P. Tucker, eds. Durham, NC: Duke University Press. [p. 58]

Leigh, E. G., Jr. and N. Smythe. 1978. "Leaf Production, Leaf Consumption, and the Regulation of Folivory on Barro Colorado Island." In *The Ecology of a Tropical Forest: Seasonal Rhythms and Long-term Changes.* G. G. Montgomery, ed. Washington, DC: Smithsonian Institution Press. [p. 57]

Livi-Bacci, M. 1989. *A Concise History of World Population.* Cambridge: Blackwell. [p. 59]

Lovejoy, T. E., R. O. Bierregaard, J. Rankin, and H. O. R. Schubart. 1983. "Ecological Dynamics of Tropical Forest Fragments." In *Tropical Rain Forest: Ecology and Management.* S. L. Sutton, T. C. Whitmore, and A. C. Chadwick, eds. Oxford: Blackwell Scientific Publications. [p. 58]

May, R. M. 1990. "How Many Species?" *Philosophical Transactions of the Royal Society of London* 330 (series B):293–304.

May, R. M. 1992a. "Taxonomy of Taxonomists." *Nature* 356:281–282.

May, R. M. 1992b. "How Many Species Inhabit the Earth?" *Scientific American* 267(4):42–48.

McNeely, J. A. 1988. *Economics and Biological Diversity.* Gland: International Union for the Conservation of Nature and Natural Resources. [p. 60]

Myers, N. 1984. "Pharmaceutical Factories." In *The Primary Source: Tropical Forests and Our Future.* N. Myers, ed. New York: Norton. [p. 61]

Myers, N. 1988. "Tropical Forests and Their Species: Going, Going . . . " In Wilson and Peter (1988). [p. 60]

Nations, J. D. and R. B. Nigh. 1980. "The Evolutionary Potential of Lacandon Maya Sustained-Yield Tropical Forest Agriculture." *Journal of Anthropological Research* 36(1):1–30. [p. 61]

Norton, B. 1988. "Commodity, Amenity, and Morality: The Limits of Quantification in Valuing Biodiversity." In Wilson and Peter (1988). [p. 61]

Ocana, G., I. Rubinoff, N. Smythe, and D. Werner. 1988. "Alternatives to Destruction: Research in Panama." In Wilson and Peter (1988). [p. 61]

Owen, D. F. 1983. "The Abundance and Biomass of Forest Animals." In *Tropical Rain Forest Ecosystems.* F. B. Golley, ed. Vol. 1, *Structure and Function.* Amsterdam: Elsevier. [p. 58]

Peck, R. B. 1990. "Promoting Agroforestry Practices Among Small Producers: the Case of the Coca Agroforestry Project in Amazonian

Ecuador." In *Alternatives to Deforestation: Steps Toward Sustainable Use of the Amazon Rain Forest.* A. B. Anderson, ed. New York: Columbia University Press. [p. 61]

Peters, C. M. 1990. "Population Ecology and Management of Forest Fruit Trees in Peruvian Amazonia." In *Alternatives to Deforestation: Steps Toward Sustainable Use of the Amazon Rain Forest.* A. B. Anderson, ed. New York: Columbia University Press. [p. 61]

Peters, C. M., A. H. Gentry and R. O. Mendelsohn. 1989. "Valuation of an Amazonian Rainforest." *Nature* 339:91–93. [pp. 58, 61]

Pianka, E. R. 1978. *Evolutionary Ecology.* New York: Harper and Row. [p. 56]

Piel, Gerard. 1992. *Only One World, Our Own to Make and to Keep.* New York: W. H. Freeman & Co. [p. 59]

Plotkin, M. J. 1988. "The Outlook for New Agricultural and Industrial Products From the Tropics." In Wilson and Peter (1988). [p. 61]

Prance, G. T. 1977. "The Phytogeographic Subdivisions of Amazonia and Their Influence on the Selection of Biological Reserves." In *Extinction is Forever.* G. T. Prance and T. S. Elias, eds. New York: New York Botanical Garden. [p. 58]

Prance, G. T., ed. 1982. *Biological Diversification in the Tropics.* New York: Columbia University Press. [p. 57]

Prance, G. T., W. Balée, B. Boom, and R. Carneiro. 1987. "Quantitative Ethnobotany and the Case For Conservation in Amazonia." *Conservation Biology* 1(4):296–310. [p. 61]

Raup, D. 1991. *Extinction: Bad Genes or Bad Luck?* New York: W. W. Norton & Co. [p. 55]

Raven, P. and G. B. Johnson. 1988. *Understanding Biology.* St. Louis: Times Mirror/Moseby College Publishers. [p. 55]

Rich, B. 1994. *Mortgaging the Earth: The World Bank, Environmental Impoverishment, and the Crisis of Development.* Boston: Beacon Press. [p. 60]

Robinson, J. G. and K. H. Redford, eds. 1991. *Neotropical Wildlife Use and Conservation.* Chicago: University of Chicago Press. [p. 61]

Rojas, M. 1992. "The Species Problem and Conservation: What Are We Protecting?" *Conservation Biology* 6(2):170–178.

Rudda, A. 1992. *Women and the Environment.* Atlantic Highlands, NJ: Zed Books. [p. 60]

Sanchez, P. A. and J. R. Benites. 1987. "Low-Input Cropping For Acid Soils of the Humid Tropics." *Science* 238:1521–1527. [p. 58]

Schmink, M. and C. H. Wood., eds. 1984. *Frontier Expansion in Amazonia.* Gainesville: University of Florida Press. [p. 60]

Seal, U. S. 1988. "Intensive Technology in the Care of Ex Situ Populations of Vanishing Species." In Wilson and Peter (1988). [p. 58]

Shafer, C. 1990. *Nature Reserves: Island Theory and Conservation Practice*. Washington, DC: Smithsonian Institution Press. [p. 58]

Shiva, V. 1989. *Staying Alive*. Atlantic Highlands, NJ: Zed Books. [p. 60]

Sokal, R. and T. Crovello 1992. "The Biological Species Concept: A Critical Evaluation." In *The Units of Evolution*. M. Ereshefsky, ed. Cambridge: Massachusetts Institute of Technology Press.

Sontheimer, S. 1991. *Women and the Environment*. New York: Monthly Review Press. [p. 60]

Spears, J. 1988. "Preserving Biodiversity in The Tropical Forests of the Asian Region." In Wilson and Peter (1988). [p. 58]

Stone, R. D. 1985. *Dreams of Amazonia*. New York: Viking. [p. 61]

Taylor, K. I. 1988. "Deforestation and Indians in Brazilian Amazonia." In Wilson and Peter (1988). [p. 61]

Terborgh, J. 1971. "Distribution on Environmental Gradients: Theory and a Preliminary Interpretation of Distributional Patterns in the Avifauna of the Cordillera Vilcabama, Peru." *Ecology* 52(1):23–40. [p. 57]

Terborgh, J. 1985a. "The Vertical Component of Plant Species Diversity in Temperate and Tropical Forests." *American Naturalist* 126:760–776. [p. 57]

Terborgh, J. 1985b. "The Role of Ecotones in the Distribution of Andean Birds." *Ecology* 66(4):1237–1246. [p. 58]

Terborgh, J. 1986. "Community Aspects of Frugivory in Tropical Forests." In *Frugivores and Seed Dispersal*. A. Estrada and T. H. Fleming, eds. Dordrecht, The Netherlands: W. Junk. [p. 57]

Terborgh, J. 1988. "The Big Things That Run the World—A Sequel to E. O. Wilson." *Conservation Biology* 2:402–403. [p. 58]

Terborgh, J. and C. P. van Schaik. 1987. "Convergence vs. Nonconvergence in Primate Communities." In *Organisation of Communities Past and Present*. J. H. R. Ghee and P. S. Giller, eds. Oxford: Blackwell. [p. 58]

Todd, J. 1988. "Restoring Diversity: the Search For a Social and Economic Context." In Wilson and Peter (1988). [p. 58]

Uhl, C. 1988. "Restoration of Degraded Lands in the Amazon Basin." In Wilson and Peter (1988). [p. 58]

Uhl, C., R. Bushbacher, and E. A. S. Serrão. 1988. "Abandoned Pastures in Eastern Amazonia. I. Patterns of Plant Succession." *Journal of Ecology* 76:663–681. [p. 57]

Uhl, C., K. Clark, N. Desseo, and P. Maquirino. 1988. "Vegetation Dynamics in Amazonian Treefall Gaps." *Ecology* 69(3):751–763. [p. 57]

Uhl, C. and I. C. G. Vieira. 1989. "Ecological Impacts of Selective Logging in the Brazilian Amazon: A Case Study From the Paragominas Region of the State of Pará." *Biotropica* 21(2):98–106. [p. 58]

Walter, H. 1985. *Vegetation of the Earth and Ecological Systems of the Geobiosphere.* Berlin: Springer-Verlag. [pp. 56, 57]

Wheelwright, N. T. 1988. "Fruit-Eating Birds and Bird-Dispersed Plants in the Tropics and Temperate Zone." *Trends in Ecology and Evolution* 3(10):270–274. [p. 57]

Whitmore, T. C. 1989. "Canopy Gaps and the Two Major Groups of Forest Trees." *Ecology* 70:536–538. [p. 57]

Williamson, M. 1981. *Island Populations.* Oxford: Oxford University Press. [p. 58]

Wilson, E. O. 1985. "Time to Revise Systematics." *Science* 230:4731. [p. 54]

Wright, S. J. and F. H. Cornejo 1990. "Seasonal Drought and Leaf Fall in a Tropical Forest." *Ecology* 71(3):1165–1175. [p. 57]

Yuill, T. M. 1983. "Disease-Causing Organisms: Components of Tropical Forest Ecosystems." In *Tropical Rain Forest Ecosystems.* F. B. Golley, ed. Vol. 1, *Structure and Function.* Amsterdam: Elsevier. [p. 60]

Zedler, J. B. 1988. "Restoring Diversity in Salt Marshes: Can We Do It?" In Wilson and Peter (1988). [p. 58]

Acknowledgments

The authors thank Dr. Mary Ashley (Lake Forest College), Dr. Robin Chazdon (University of Connecticut), Dr. David W. Crumpacker (University of Colorado), Dr. M. A. Davis (Macalester College), Dr. Don Farrar (Iowa State University), Dr. Carolyn Jaslow (Rhodes College), Dr. Monte Lloyd (University of Chicago), Dr. Mark McKone (Carleton College), Dr. Sumner Richman (Lawrence University), Dr. John Terborgh (Duke University), and Dr. David Pimentel (Cornell University).

Chapter 4

Economics

Gerald Alonzo Smith
Mankato State University

Economics promotes understanding about how persons within communities make the necessary choices both to provision themselves and also to fashion a life of quality and fulfillment. As such, economics is a discipline that is bounded on one side by the material planet, the world of limited natural resources, the world of entropy and passing time, only partially offset by technology, and on the other side by the immaterial and timeless world, the world of values and ultimate concerns.

Consequently there are two fundamental questions that need to be addressed at the beginning of any course in economics: (1) What is the impact upon the planet earth of this economic system? and (2) Does this economic system promote high-quality and fulfilled human lives? Conventional economic thought, however, ignores these fundamental questions, believing that such questions are irrelevant to its self-defined goal: maximizing utility in a resource-abundant world by choosing efficiently from among acts of production and consumption that will satisfy as many desires as possible. Thus, for the first question, conventional economists presuppose that the planet's resources are virtually unlimited and that we do not have to worry about destroying our natural resource infrastructure. When pressed on this issue, they will turn to the ability of the marketplace to resolve particular "bottleneck" scarcities by raising prices of particular scarce commodities. Added to this is the belief that in the presence of such higher prices, technology will resolve such scarcities either by inventing a technically more efficient machine or by discovering some substitute that will fulfill the need or desire that first generated this particular scarcity. Thus, while recognizing the possibility of particular or relative scarcities, they cannot recognize the possibility of absolute or universal scarcity. As a result, conventional economics fails to give a full and explicit discussion of sustainability. It simply cannot be a problem, given its foundational premises and the definition of what the discipline of economics is all about.

As to as the second question: "Does the economic system lead to high-quality and fulfilled human lives?", the answer to this question, too, is presupposed without being explicitly asked. Economists assume that the self-professed goal expressed in the phrase "maximization of utility" explains it all. Though they have vastly refined it, economists really have never progressed philosophically beyond the positivism of early Utilitarian thought. As they themselves state in their textbooks, the human being is perceived as a "homo economicus" or, in less elegant but more clear words, as a "basket of desires." For some examples of this consider the following statements from two much-used economics texts: "According to the view of humans as homo economicus, individuals always want more, no matter how much they have" (Byrnes and Stone, 1989, *Microeconomics* [question #41 in testbank]); and "The principal task of the economy is to attain the maximum fulfillment of society's unlimited material wants" (McConnell 1984, *Economics*, p. 16).

Ideally, economics courses would have as prerequisites both a course on the environment, where questions about the plenitude and fragility of the natural resources required for the economic system would be examined, and a course in philosophy, where questions about the purpose of life and the nature of a "high-quality and fulfilled life" would be explored. Since this is not likely, economics instructors must at least raise these issues and start students thinking. To ignore these questions is to allow them to be answered by default, by the ideology of the market economy, and/or by the powerful and the persuasive, by the rich, and by the media, with its 30-second television commercials. A proposed answer to the question of what is a high-quality life in a Western culture, where individualism is prized, might be stated briefly: the quality of life for an individual is directly related to that person's ability to develop his or her potential to the fullest.

It is also essential to a high-quality and fulfilled life that the workings of the economy do not destroy our human communities and sense of identity: our families, our social groupings, and our heritage. If these social bonds are lacking, we tend to substitute material possessions that are destructive of the environment. As Donella Meadows has written:

> People don't need enormous cars; they need respect. They don't need closetsful of clothes; they need to feel attractive and they need excitement, variety, and beauty. People need identity, community, challenge, acknowledgment, love, joy. To try to fill these needs with material things is to set up an unquenchable appetite for false solutions to real and never-satisfied problems. The resulting psychological emptiness is one of the major forces behind the desire for material growth. A society that can admit and articulate its nonmaterial needs and find nonmaterial ways to satisfy them would require much lower material and energy throughputs and would provide much higher levels of human fulfillment (Meadows et al. 1992, "Executive Summary," p. 3).

In summary, an attitude about life that seeks fulfillment in terms only of material goods does not fit into the world, for this attitude toward life has no limiting principle and the environment is strictly limited.

Economists have to keep all of this in mind as they go about studies of how to achieve a desirable economic system. As Herman Daly has stated, we need an alternate economic theory that is both more materialistic and immaterialistic. The goals of this alternate economic system are to preserve the biophysical environment and to promote high-quality, fulfilled lives for as many as possible.

As we explore course units that might be helpful in leading the discipline of economics toward the goal of a more sustainable and fulfilling life, it is necessary to remember the importance of beginning at the beginning. The reason that conventional economic thought as it is commonly taught is destructive of the environment and unsuccessful in achieving human fulfillment is not a lack of intellectual ability and knowledge of factual information, nor a lack of good will, nor a lack of sophistication in economic models. Instead, it is a result of starting out with basic visions and definitions that are taken for granted and unquestioned. Any economics instructor who would correct this situation must begin classes with a thorough discussion of these fundamental assumptions.

COURSE PLANS

The Introductory Course in Economics

The teacher of economics who feels that the current approach of economic theory is becoming intolerably disabling to people and damaging to the earth is in somewhat of a quandary. Should this teacher teach conventional standard economic theory and attempt to critique it as he or she goes along, or should the teacher jettison all of it and attempt to teach some alternative, more ecologically sound and humane theory? My solution is to do more of the former in introductory courses and more of the latter in upper division courses. Thus in introductory microeconomics I attempt to teach the basic conventional theory with a vengeance. By this I mean that I spell out very clearly and precisely all the details of the fundamental premises of standard microeconomic thought as they relate to the environment and to the fulfillment of life. In this way I hope to accomplish two things: I hope to make students not only knowledgeable about these premises but also ready to question them. It is also my belief that it is necessary to teach them the generally accepted core material that is commonly taught in first-level economics texts. Otherwise these students would be ill-prepared for the next level.

What follows immediately are two examples of how I attempt to do this. The first unit is an exploration of the fundamental premises that underlie conventional economic theory. The second unit explores the meaning of some key innocent-looking words that carry a tremendous weight of hidden premises in them and that should be vigorously investigated whenever they are first met in any economics texts. I call them "red flag" words.

UNIT 1. BASIC PREMISES IN CONVENTIONAL ECONOMICS AS THEY RELATE TO THE ENVIRONMENT

It is absolutely essential for anyone concerned with the impact of the economy on the environment to begin a course in economics with a study of the premises of economic theory as they relate to the environment. This is so because these basic premises ultimately determine what conclusions will be reached. One way to begin a study of economics is to explore the location of the science of economics along the spectrum of academic disciplines. The place of economics in the realm of academic disciplines can be shown by the ends–means spectrum of knowledge as shown in Figure 4.1. Several lessons can be learned from this spectrum, including:

(1) The science of economics is constrained and indeed determined, on the one hand, by one's sense of the biophysical limits of the planet earth and its biosphere and, on the other hand, by one's view of what is the final goal of life.

(2) It is thus essential for the student of economics either to have some previous knowledge of both the limits of the material world and the immaterial ideas of what is a high-quality life or else to be given the opportunity at the beginning of the economics class to explore these fundamental questions.

For a thorough and well-reasoned discussion of this question, students can read Daly and Cobb (1989) *For the Common Good: Redirecting the Economy Toward Community, the Environment, and a Sustainable*

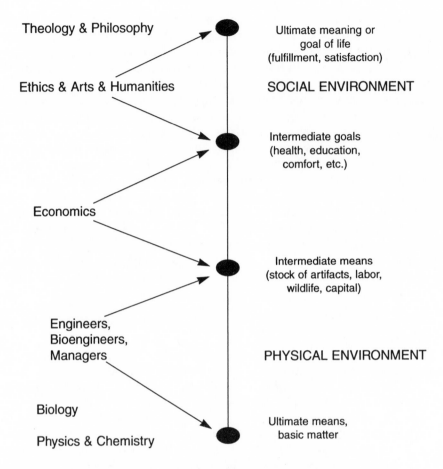

Figure 4.1. End–Means Spectrum (adapted from Herman E. Daly and K. Townsend, eds. [1993], *Valuing the Earth: Economics, Ecology, Ethics,* p. 20).

Future. (The first two parts should be read by all, with individual chapters of the third part according to interest.)

As I pointed out in the introduction, because of their uncritically accepted preanalytic view that the biosphere has virtually unlimited resources, most traditional economists immediately deduce that it is not necessary to be concerned about natural resource depletion or biospheric pollution on a global scale. Students can be shown that conventional economists turn their attention to the problem of scarcity and choice in another dimension. Instead of focusing on the question of how individuals within society make choices about how to provision themselves on a limited planet and how to make a more fulfilled life for themselves that is sustainable, their analysis focuses on the unlimited desires of individuals and the limited productive capacity of the manufacturing and service economy, taking the natural environment for granted. Natural resources are viewed essentially as free and unlimited. The only limits are human ingenuity in utilizing the resources of the earth. Thus all beginning economics texts spend most of their chapters investigating the market, consumer behavior, and the typical firm's behavior in order to see if their actions are efficient (i.e., fulfill the most desires possible).

The crucial premise to be explored at this point in the unit is the difference between the full-world scenario and the empty-world scenario. See Figures 4.2 and 4.3 for a graphical representation of these two opposing preanalytical views. In Figure 4.2 the economy is visualized as having grown to such an extent that it is now brushing up against the biophysical limits of the earth with the danger that it may exhaust or destroy the earth. In Figure 4.3, the empty-world scenario, the economy is visualized as affecting a relatively small portion of the biosphere and

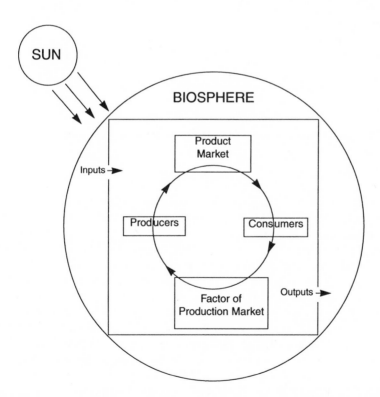

Figure 4.2.   Ecologically Englightened Economics View (Full-World Scenario).

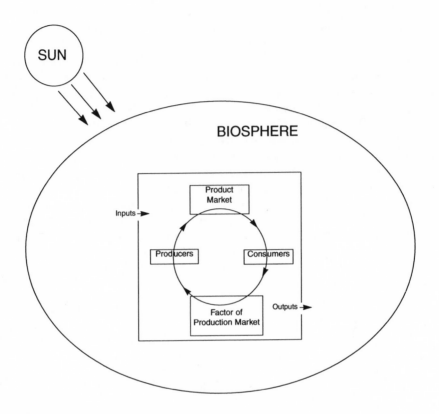

Figure 4.3. Conventional Economics View of Biosphere and Economy (Empty-World Scenario).

therefore has much room to grow. It is necessary to point out that if one begins with the empty-world scenario and with the conviction that there are unlimited wants and that such wants and desires are absolute ends in themselves (i. e., final goals of life), then more is always better and one necessarily has to conclude that economic growth as measured by the GNP is desirable. One's premises have forced such a conclusion. One can also reason backward at this point by showing that since the conventional introductory text does take fulfillment of any and every desire (all of which are treated as equal and final goals) by unceasing economic growth as the ultimate goal of the economy, then it is necessary to conclude that economists have rather uncritically accepted the empty-world scenario and the yuppie philosophy of life.

On the other hand, if one starts with the full-world scenario and the belief that enough is enough and that desires have to be subjected to one's reason and its definition of what is a high-quality life, then one has to conclude that sustainability is a main goal. Thus the important questions that have to be discussed are (1) whether the full-world scenario or the empty-world scenario is correct and (2) whether passing desires are the determinant of value or whether society should attempt to evaluate such desires depending upon how they fulfill the person's life.

Students might see some of these issues more clearly by being presented with the premises of the two scenarios and asked to arrive at differing conclusions. There is a large amount of literature that supports each of these two conflicting views. Much of this literature eventually revolves around the importance of the entropy law and the possibility of technology in cleverly bypassing the apparent limits of the entropy law. For contrasting views by biological and physical scientists on this issue of a full-world scenario versus an empty-world scenario, see the article by Vitousek et al. (1986) entitled "Human Appropriation of the Products of Photosynthesis," wherein the authors conclude that the human species and its economy appropriate about 40 percent of the products of photosynthesis for itself. They also argue that 40 percent is about the maximum that one species can appropriate. For the other empty-world scenario, see the influential article by Goellner and Weinberg (1976). In this article the authors have gone through the entire periodic system, examining all of the elements plus some important compounds, in order to determine whether there is reason for concern that society will be running out of any vital resource. On the basis of their scrutiny, they announce the principle of infinite substitutability: With the exception of phosphorus and some trace elements for agriculture, and finally the carbohydrates or fossil fuels (coal, oil, and gas), society can exist on near-inexhaustible resources for an indefinite period. One could have a class debate on these issues.

Related very closely to this discussion of a full-world/empty-world scenario is a discussion about the role of technology in the future. The conventional belief is that forthcoming technology will resolve all future environmental problems. As Herman Daly (1991) has noted, "Technology is the rock upon which the growthmen build their church" (*Steady-State Economics*, p. 105). Those concerned with the economy and its environmental damage take a much more cautious view. It is their perception that technology has been a two-edged sword. It has both resolved environmental problems and caused new and extremely dangerous pollutants, as well as the exhaustion of resources. As such, technology is perceived to have the potential to be as much a problem as a solution. For an insightful discussion of the dubious role of technology in preserving the environment and fulfilling human lives, see the article by Cobb (1992) "Reflections of a Neo-Luddite." For the opposite "optimistic" view that human ingenuity and technology will resolve all future environmental problems see Simon (1980), "Resources, Population, Environment: An Oversupply of False Bad News." (See Orr's discussion of the limitations of technology in Chapter 1.)

I would place this discussion of basic premises in the very beginning of an introductory class of either microeconomics or macroeconomics. As a matter of fact, I would use it for the first day's class as an introduction to the discipline of economics and its subject matter. It could take either one or two or more class periods, depending on how much reading is required.

UNIT 2. DEFINING KEY CONCEPTS IN ECONOMICS: EFFICIENCY, VALUE, MARKETS, EXTERNALITIES, AND THE ENVIRONMENT

Efficiency is a key concept in conventional economic theory that is met early in introductory economics texts. However, efficiency is an ambiguous word in the sense that its meaning always depends on some further goal. For example, when found in the phrase "economic efficiency" it means that society is allocating its resources so as to produce the most possible value where value is both defined and measured by the satisfaction that customers receive in consuming economic commodities. The final goal is the satisfaction of consumers' desires by maximizing consumption possibilities.

Before going on one needs to note this meaning of the concept "value." In conventional economic thought, a commodity is considered to be of "value" if it satisfies any consumer's desires. A less traditional view is a definition that states that a commodity is of "value" if it helps one to achieve his or her full potential as a human person. These are obviously different meanings of the word *value,* and they are definitions that will have a substantial impact on the substance and conclusions of economic teachings and on what is "efficient" in an economics system and what is not.

For more on this discussion of efficiency, see Goodwin (1991) *Social Economics: An Alternative Theory.* Goodwin correctly writes that "this fall-back upon efficiency is often not enough, for the question arises: Efficiency to what end? We shall see throughout this book instances of where this untenable situation is uneasily resolved by the injection of normative elements back into the foundations of the field from which they are supposed to be absent" (p. 84).

From these premises the conventional economist can easily show that the market efficiently resolves the important question of how much of any commodity to produce. The argument goes as follows: The market is a combination of consumers' demand and producers' supply. The demand curve is a graphical device that shows the various quantities of a commodity that people will purchase at different prices and thus is used as a measurement of people's desires for that product (see Figure 4.4). In

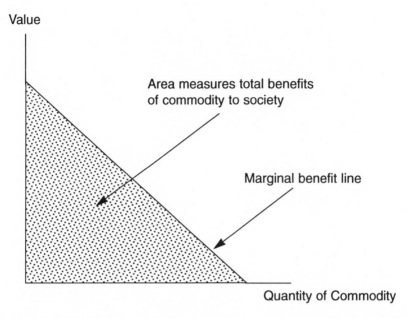

Figure 4.4.   Demand Curve as a Measurement of a Commodity's Benefit to Society.

other words, it is not only a demand curve but it is also an indicator of how much satisfaction (i.e., value) people obtain from a particular commodity. The supply curve is correspondingly a cost curve. In other words, it is an indicator of how much satisfaction people give up (i.e., disvalue) as they consume a particular commodity. Accordingly, the intersection point of the demand curve and the supply curve is the efficient quantity of production and consumption (see Figure 4.5). The easiest way to show this is to take any quantity either to the left or right of the equilibrium intersection point on a supply and demand market graph. One can then show that value as so defined is not maximized.

This would be all well and good if the demand curve did indeed measure authentic value and the supply curve measured all the costs. However such is not necessarily the case. Much of what we desire is not authentic in the sense that it brings contentment and fulfillment. For a discussion of this important point, see chapter 3, "The Dubious Rewards of Consumption," chapter 9, "The Cultivation of Needs," and chapter 10, "A Culture of Permanence," in Durning (1992), *How Much is Enough? The Consumer Society and the Future of the Earth*. Alternatively students may be referred to *The Poverty of Affluence* by the psychologist P. Wachtel (1983). In a country that has more malls than high schools and

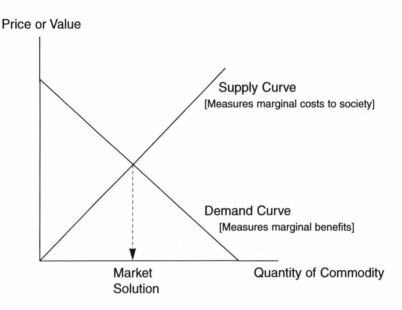

Price or Value

Supply Curve
[Measures marginal costs to society]

Demand Curve
[Measures marginal benefits]

Market   Quantity of Commodity
Solution

Figure 4.5.   Measurement of Maximum Value and Efficiency.

that spends $495 annually per person on advertising, perhaps it should not be surprising that all of our desires are not authentic, in this sense.

Also one can question the authenticity of the supply line as a cost line. Does it measure the ecological costs to the planet? Does it measure the costs to future generations? For example, does the supply of automobiles measure the following: (1) the cost of its carbon dioxide and other emissions? (2) the depletion of resources both to build it and to run it? (3) the costs of highways and paved areas? (4) the disruption of communities that such highways cost? For two books on the costs and benefits of the automobile, see Zuckermann (1992) *End of the Road: The World Car Crisis and How We Can Solve It* and Sachs (1991) *For Love of the Automobile: Looking Back into the History of Our Desires.*

Thus there are some real and serious questions about the authenticity of the demand line as an indicator of value and the supply line as cost. Economists recognize this and bring in the concept of externalities to resolve these anomalies. They argue that in the presence of such third-party costs or nonauthentic values the market will not bring about an efficient solution and that in such circumstances the government has the obligation to interfere with the market solution through appropriate fees, taxes, prohibitions, etc. But what if almost everything that we do in a crowded world has serious externalities attached to it? What if externalities are pervasive throughout the economic system? Just as the Ptolemaic theory of the universe viewed the earth as the center of the universe and used epicycles to resolve problems, so current conventional economic theory views unlimited consumer desires as its center and uses externalities to resolve anomalies. If such is the case, perhaps what is needed is a new and different economic theory, one that has sustainability and human fulfillment as its primary goals and thus efficient allocation would be that allocation which promotes such ideals. For books that advocate such a change in economic theory, the teacher might read either Daly and Cobb (1989), *For the Common Good: Redirecting the Economy toward Community, the Environment, and a Sustainable Future* or Elkins and Max-Neef, eds. (1992), *Real-Life Economics: Understanding Wealth Creation.* For students, the film *An Introduction to Ecological Economics* would be helpful. For a favorable view of externalities as a solution to the problem of the environment, see the article by Alper (1993), "Protecting the Environment with the Power of the Market."

Material in this section can be used as needed throughout the semester (i.e., whenever these concepts are first met). Generally speaking, the discussion on efficiency, values, and market is needed early on whenever the market is discussed. This will add about a class period to the discussion. The discussion on the pervasiveness and importance of externalities can be left to the chapter when your introductory microeconomics text deals with the environment, usually one of the last few chapters.

Upper Division Courses

Economics and the Environment: Theoretical Questions (sample units)

In an upper division course the instructor is not so constrained to covering the core teachings of the discipline as he or she is in an introductory level course. This indeed is the time to go beyond questioning such teachings and doctrines and present alternatives. The following are a few examples of how this might be done.

UNIT 1. THE PLACE OF ECONOMICS IN THE SPECTRUM OF KNOWLEDGE

The discussion of this topic is a logical and necessary introduction to any course on economics and the environment. If it is left out, as it usually is, then economics can and oftentimes does become an isolated, independent, and unbounded discipline. As such it can then self-define its own goals and the importance of environmental and natural resource limits to the economy. It will be guilty of living in a "splendid isolation" or, as has been noted by more than one critic, the science of economics can then be compared to the emperor who has no clothes.

In order to avoid such a state of affairs, economics as a discipline and the economy as a social institution must be related to the physical environment. Useful questions in this context are: What impact does the economy have on the environment? Is the economy operating in an empty world with abundant resources, as the conventional economists apparently believe? Is the economy operating in a full world and in danger of destroying the planet? As much as possible it is necessary to explore what actual impact the economy has had upon the earth and the biosphere. One way to do this is to conduct a debate between the "optimistic" or "cornucopian" position, which views resources and the environment as being so abundant and provident technology so forthcoming that the economist can safely ignore talk of limits, and the "pessimistic" or "neo-Malthusian" position, which holds that the economy is already in the process of destroying the planet earth. First, have all of the class read chapters 10 and 11 of Georgescu-Roegen's (1971) *The Entropy Law and the Economic Process.* Then have half of the class read Simon (1980), "Resources, Population, Environment: An Oversupply of False Bad News" and have the other half read Vitousek et al. (1986) "Human Appropriation of the Products of Photosynthesis." The students will then be properly prepared to debate the issue. After the debate, all of the class could read Orr's (1992) resolution to this debate in "Pascal's Wager and Economics in a Hotter Time."

UNIT 2. THE ROLE OF THE MARKET IN DETERMINING HOW MUCH AND WHAT TO PRODUCE

The beginning chapters of any basic economics textbook will contain a discussion of how the market works and its importance. This discussion is considered to be foundational in any basic economics text. Ever since Adam Smith wrote his famous theory of "the market's invisible hand," it is a fundamental belief of conventional economic thought that the market is the essential mechanism in an economy for determining the quantity of all items to be produced from primary raw materials to finished final products.

Some of this emphasis on the market is justified. The market is a wonderful mechanism for distributing goods and resources. Individual people do know better than anyone else their own needs. Individual producers do have better information about their capacities and options than anyone else. However, once again, it is important to realize the limitations of the market and the impact that this market mechanism for allocating goods and services has on the environment.

One issue that needs to be discussed as we explore the market's impact on the environment is whether the market mechanism adequately takes into account the current and future value of the natural environment. The market relies totally on the passing desires of current consumers and producers to determine directly the demand and indirectly the supply curves, the combination of which in turn determines the market quantity produced and consumed. In this process, there is much evidence to suggest that the market does not correctly value such natural resources. One new school of ecological economists has decided to explore the real value of the environment. For a summary view of this school of thought, see Costanza, ed. (1992) *Ecological Economics: The Science and Management of Sustainability.* For a particular example of how a natural resource should be valued, see the film *What Price Clean Air?*

It is one thing to state that the market is the most efficient distributor of commodities and that it works best without interference from any governmental regulations. But frequently in such discussions economists also imply that there are no objective criteria of better and worse or good and bad by which an individual can make his or her choice. Quantity and price would seem to be the only relevant factors. Why do economists draw this implication? Daly and Cobb (1989) have responded: "The answer is that their mechanical, mathematical models abstract from final causation. The policies consistently recommended are designed to increase the total quantity of goods available to those able to buy them. To introduce into this picture judgments about relative values or purposes not correlated with price would disrupt the entire discipline" (p. 93). Once again we see that economists prefer to work in "splendid isolation" rather than be relevant; or as Daly and Cobb concluded, "the temptation to deny the facts in favor of theory is great" (p. 93).

For a further discussion of the role of the market, see either the chapter "Misplaced Concreteness: The Market" in Daly and Cobb (1989), or for a more extended discussion, Schmookler (1993), *The Illusions of Choice: How the Market Economy Shapes Our Destiny.*

UNIT 3. CONCEPT OF "UTILITY" IN ECONOMIC THOUGHT

The concept of "utility" is not usually addressed directly in economic texts until the chapter on consumer behavior, where the "maximization of utility" is defined as both the ultimate goal of consumers and consequently as the ultimate goal of any economic system. Nonetheless, the concept of utility is behind the scenes in every page of every economics text and, as such, the concept has a great influence on how the economy impacts on the environment.

Conventional economic theory defines the maximization of utility as the ultimate goal of the human person. When one explores the picture of human nature presented in the pages of economics texts, one finds an amazing caricature. Basically, the human person is defined as an isolated human being who is a "basket of desires." And the fulfillment or enjoyment or contentment that comes from satisfying these passing desires is named "utility."

This view of human beings has a harmful impact on the environment because it promotes a consumeristic set of values that is utterly destructive to the planet. With its emphasis on material things and satisfying every passing desire, it has created an environmental nightmare. And the evidence is mounting that it is also a social and psychological disaster. Utility, as defined by the economists, must be subjected to a much more vigorous inquiry than it has routinely received in the past.

For a study of how the consumeristic set of values harms the planet, read chapter 4, "The Environmental Costs of Consumption," in Durning (1992) *How Much is Enough?: The Consumer Society and the Future of the Earth*. To see how this consumeristic set of values with its final goal of maximization of utility harms the human personality, see Wachtel (1983), *The Poverty of Affluence*, or Scitovsky (1976), *The Joyless Economy*.

UNIT 4. CONCEPT OF "EFFICIENCY" IN ECONOMIC THOUGHT

As noted above, efficiency is a key word in economic thought. Yet in a very real sense *efficiency* is one of the most slippery and ambiguous words in the English language. Whether one is efficient or not depends totally upon one's sense of what is valuable. To its credit, the science of economics has defined what it considers to be valuable and that is, as noted in the previous section, the satisfaction or "utility" that one gets from consuming economic goods and services.

From this definition it follows directly that for an economy to be efficient, it must satisfy as many desires as possible. The problem with this conclusion is that every passing desire for any and every economic good or service becomes an absolute end in itself. To paraphrase Descartes, such a philosophy is based upon the fundamental premise: I make and I buy, therefore I am. In such a philosophical perspective people's reason becomes subject to the desires of the acquisitive side of their nature rather than being the dominant partner in the orientation and direction of their activities. Thus it is necessary in the teaching of economics to raise further questions of value whenever some activity is promoted because it is "efficient."

If the human person is only a "basket of desires," then the planet is in serious trouble. We then would have what Alan Durning has defined as "the conundrum of consumption," namely, (1) the philosophy of consumerism is destroying the planet, and (2) a person's success and fulfillment is measured by the amount of possessions that he/she consumes. If both of these assumptions were indeed true, then there could be no satisfactory conclusion to this conundrum. Either we would end up destroying the planet or we would end up leading unfulfilled lives. Fortunately, as Durning also shows, such is not the situation. While it is true that the consumerist mentality would destroy the planet, it definitely is not the situation that a person's fulfillment can be measured by the amount of one's economic possessions. Yet many Americans and indeed much of the world's population tacitly accept this second premise (Durning 1992, p. 25).

It is clear, therefore, that the salvation of the planet depends upon a shift in values. This shift in values will in turn make what was formerly considered to be efficient to appear as inefficient and vice versa.

This would be a good place to attempt to get class members to think about the meaning and the importance of the word *efficiency* in the United States' culture. One way to start such a discussion is by asking the question: Is the U.S. farmer efficient? On average one U.S. farmer feeds 85 people, which is the highest ratio in the world. At the same time one U.S. farmer uses more herbicides, pesticides, and fossil fuel energy and other scarce natural resources than any other farmer. Is this efficient or not? The answer depends upon whether one values labor or natural resources more, which in turn depends upon how much one values the future.

Economics and the Environment: Applied Questions *(sample units)*

UNIT 1. USE OF COST–BENEFIT ANALYSIS TO RESOLVE ENVIRONMENTAL DECISIONS

At an earlier stage in the history of environmental economics, it was believed that social cost–benefit analysis could resolve decisions that would have a substantial and long-lasting impact on the environment. An example of such a situation was the question of whether to build a dam in Hell's Canyon on the Snake River, which separates Oregon from Idaho. It is now pretty clear that the claims for cost–benefit analysis were overblown and that the use of such analysis can be misleading. It is true that theoretically cost–benefit analysis could resolve environmental questions by simply measuring the costs of a project, on the one hand, and the benefits of the project on the other hand, and going forward whenever the benefits of a project outweighed the costs; nonetheless problems with cost–benefit analysis have quickly become apparent. First and primary, who is to decide what is a cost and what is a benefit? Who is to decide how great are the costs and how great are the benefits? When the costs and benefits are in the future, how can we compare costs and benefits across generations? What about uncertainties when we are unsure of the environmental risks? See the article by Kelman (1981),

"Cost-Benefit Analysis—An Ethical Critique," for further discussion of this area of thought. See chapter 8, "Benefit-Cost in Practice: Implementing the Efficiency Standard," in Goodstein (1995), *Economics and the Environment,* for several examples of benefit–cost analysis.

UNIT 2. HOW TO DEAL WITH FUTURE COSTS AND BENEFITS

The science of economics frequently boils this decision of the future down to a discussion of what is the appropriate discount rate. When dealing with decisions such as resource depletion and persistent pollutants whose impacts will last long into the future, economists will attempt to compare future costs and benefits to present costs and benefits by discounting the future at a certain percentage rate on an annual basis. This is called the present value criterion and the goal is to maximize net present value. It is clear that such an approach depends upon having and knowing a satisfactory discount rate. But this introduction of an appropriate discount rate to resolve the problem of comparing costs and benefits of different time periods may raise more questions than answers. Should we discount our children's and their children's generations? It would seem better to deal with these issues directly as ethical and ecological issues (as does most of the literature by conservationists) rather than obfuscate them by using future discounted benefits and costs.

For a thorough discussion of these two methods of resolving questions that compare intertemporal costs and benefits, see chapter 7, "The Present Value Criterion," and chapter 8, "The Conservation Criterion," in Page (1977), *Conservation and Economic Efficiency.* See the quotation on page 250 of that book for implications of use of the discount rate.

UNIT 3. IMPACT OF WORLD TRADE ON THE DEGRADING OF NATURAL ENVIRONMENTS

World trade as such is an extension of the market mechanism to the international arena. As such, all the arguments already made in the above section on the role of the market can also be made in this context. Yet there is an important further discussion that needs to be undertaken when the issue is trade between nations. In the current world political situation, for better or worse, it is nation-states with their boundaries that define an individual's identity and community more than any other political unit. More than any other criterion, people identify themselves as members of a particular nation. Thus if people want to protect their environment they naturally turn to their particular nation as the area in which to act. One danger of international trade is that it will lead to a reduction in such safeguards. There are several reasons why this will happen.

First, if one nation maintains and protects its environment by putting into place appropriate legislation that manufacturers in that nation must observe and a second nation does not pass such legislation, this will put the former nation's manufacturers at a disadvantage, at least in the short run, since they have to incur higher environmental protection costs than the second nation's manufacturers. This will lead to their demise in a free trade area. Rather than allow this to happen the government of the first nation will be under intense pressure to lower its environmental standards. Rather than weaken these standards because of free trade, it would be preferable to apply a tariff on the goods of a nation that does not enforce strict environmental standards. This would also have the desirable effect of putting into place an incentive for the second nation to draw up and enforce legislation to protect its environment.

Second, world trade leads to a disregard for problems pertaining to the environment and resource depletion. All nations now feel that they can import raw materials and export final produced goods and at the same time they can export their toxic wastes and other pollutants. Such a belief in world trade breaks down individual accountability and responsibility.

In order for the world to be sustainable, individuals and nations will have to take responsibility for their actions. Although one could make an argument that nation-states are, on the whole, too large to make an individual feel responsible for his or her actions that impinge upon the environment, nonetheless they are the only political community that does exist. If environmental safeguards are going to come from anywhere, they will have to come from nation-states. However, international trade in toxic wastes and pollutants removes the incentives for such nation-states to act responsibly. For a general treatment of this important issue, see chapter 11, "Free Trade versus Community," in Daly and Cobb (1989). For more on the effects of free trade on the environment, see the debate on this topic by Bhagwati and Daly (1993) in *Scientific American*.

UNIT 4. MARKET VERSUS CENTRALLY PLANNED ECONOMIES

Neither the market nor centrally planned economies tend to be concerned about issues of sustainability, justice, fairness, or authentic fulfillment in one's life. This leads one to the conclusion that has been advanced throughout this chapter: that it is not the particular economic models that are so much at fault as something more fundamental than these models. It is the view of both capitalism and communism that the earth is unlimited in its resources and that progress in human affairs can be measured by economic production and consumption. What is called for is not a discussion of whether central government, small groups, or individuals should make decisions. Obviously individuals should make decisions when individuals are affected, small groups when small groups are affected, and governments when society as a whole is affected, but what is needed is a more fundamental rethinking of issues of sustainability. As it now stands we do not know nor are we in any position to learn which of our economic activities affect the environment in a significant way and which do not, because we refuse to ask the right questions. There seems to be a need for a third economic theory that will ask these and other related questions. Perhaps better than any other scholars, Neva Goodwin and her colleagues at the Global Development And Environment Institute have explored the need for a third theory and what it would look like. See her *Social Economics: An Alternative Theory* (1991) for a full discussion of this issue.

UNIT 5. PARTICULAR TOPICS FOR PRESENTATIONS OR PAPERS

As time and interest dictate, study of particular issues such as global warming, ozone depletion, acid rain, energy and other resource supplies, water contamination, forests, and solid waste landfills can be undertaken. In an economics class the focus should be upon how the economy interacts with the environment in each of these particular areas. For example, in the question of ozone depletion, besides studying the chemistry and extent of ozone depletion, it is important to study the purposes for which CFCs are used in the economy. Are there any substitutes? How important are these products? A good example of the type of research needed in these specific projects is Shea (1989), "Protecting the Ozone Layer."

Resources

Page numbers appearing in brackets at the end of some entries indicate where the reference is cited in a course plan.

Alper, J. 1993. "Protecting the Environment with the Power of the Market." *Science* 260:1884–1885. [p. 83]

According to this article, if you add in all the hidden and external costs, you can give consumers a better idea of the consequences of their purchases and they then would make more environmentally sound decisions.

Bhagwati, J. 1993. "The Case for Free Trade." *Scientific American* 269(5):42–49. [p. 89]

This article argues for free trade because the benefits resulting from such free trade may be the best way to pay for the costs of protecting the environment. The other side is presented by Daly in the same issue.

Byrnes, R. T. and G. W. Stone. 1989. *Microeconomics Testbank*. New York: HarperCollins.

This is simply used to show values and premises of conventional economic thought.

Cobb, C. 1992. "Reflections of a Neo-Luddite." *The Human Economy Newsletter* 13(3):1–10. [p. 79]

In this article Cobb investigates the impact of technology on modern life. It is his conclusion that such technology has led to a myth of perpetual progress that blinds our society to the items of real value in our life.

Cobb, C. and J. Cobb, Jr. 1994. *The Green National Product: A Proposed Index of Sustainable Economic Welfare.* New York: University Press of America.

This book proposes to improve on the GNP as an indicator of national prosperity. It does this by including as costs the damage to and deterioration of the environment, as well as taking many other issues relating to sustainability and human well-being into account.

Costanza, R., ed. 1992. *Ecological Economics: The Science and Management of Sustainability.* New York: Columbia University Press. [p. 85]

This book brings together many of the leading scholars who are concerned that the present economy is not sustainable. They explore what is needed to make it so.

Daly, H. E. 1977, 1991. *Steady-State Economics.* Washington, DC: Island Press. [p. 79]

Still the most complete and thorough summary of what an economy could and should look like if it were concerned about being sustainable.

Daly, H. E. 1993. "The Perils of Free Trade." *Scientific American* 269(5):50–57.

This article argues against free trade because of the mobility of financial capital. One loses control over the environment if one has to compete economically with nations that do not practice sound environmental management of their natural resources. The other side is presented by Bhagwati in the same issue.

Daly, H. E. and J. Cobb, Jr. 1989. *For the Common Good: Redirecting the Economy Toward Community, the Environment, and a Sustainable Future.* Boston: Beacon Press. [pp. 75, 83, 85, 89]

In this book, Daly, an economist, and Cobb, a theologian, team up to roam over a wide range of topics, all of which need to be covered if society is to both be sustainable and have a high-quality life.

Daly, H. E. and K. Townsend, eds. 1993. *Valuing the Earth: Economics, Ecology, Ethics.* Cambridge, MA: MIT Press.

In this collection of essays, the editors bring together many of the leading thinkers in the field of ecological economics to make a forceful argument for the necessity of an alternative economic approach.

Durning, A. 1992. *How Much is Enough? The Consumer Society and the Future of the Earth*. New York. W. W. Norton & Company. [pp. 81, 86, 87]

In this important book Durning explores the question: How much is enough? What level of consumption can the planet sustain? When do more things cease to add appreciably to human fulfillment? This is the second book in the Worldwatch Institute's "Environmental Alert" series. [p. 83]

Elkins, P. and M. Max-Neef, eds. 1992. *Real-Life Economics: Understanding Wealth Creation*. London: Routledge. [p. 83]

This book explores the causes of such problems as environmental degradation, the erosion of culture and community, and the loss of social values. Perhaps the most important contribution of this book is its outline of a new school of economic thought.

Georgescu-Roegen, N. 1971. *The Entropy Law and the Economic Process*. Cambridge, MA: Harvard University Press. [p. 84]

For an encyclopedic overview of the basic theoretical problems involved in the relationship between the economic system and the environment, this book has not been surpassed. It is difficult reading in places.

Goellner, H. E. and A. M. Weinberg. 1976. "The Age of Substitutability." *Science* 191:683–689. [p. 79]

This is the seminal article for the empty world view or the optimistic approach to the world's resources. Basically this article concludes that because of the possibility of substituting resources such as iron and aluminum that are practically inexhaustible for more scarce resources, there is plenty of reason for optimism. On the basis of their scrutiny of geological and technological data, Goellner and Weinberg pronounce the principle of infinite substitutability: With the exception of phosphorus and some trace elements for agriculture, mainly cobalt, copper, and zinc, and finally the carbohydrates, society can exist on near-inexhaustible resources for an indefinite period.

Goodstein, E. 1995. *Economics and the Environment*. Englewood Cliffs, NJ: Prentice-Hall. [p. 88]

This environmental textbook incorporates some but not all of the premises that are necessary for a sustainable society.

Goodwin, N. 1991. *Social Economics: An Alternative Theory*. New York: St. Martin's Press. [pp. 80, 90]

Although a little dense in spots, for the most thorough and balanced approach to an alternative economic theory, this book is unsurpassed.

Kelman, S. 1981. "Cost-Benefit Analysis—An Ethical Critique." *Regulation* (Jan.-Feb.):33–40. [p. 87]

In this article the author concludes that attempts to expand the use of cost–benefit analysis probably are ill-advised. He points out clearly that cost–benefit analysis depends upon one's ethical premises.

Krishnan, R. , J. Harris, and N. Goodwin. 1995. *A Survey of Ecological Economics*. Washington, DC: Island Press.

This survey summarizes 95 seminal articles in the field of ecological economics. Each summary is two to three pages in length and is far more comprehensive than a typical abstract.

McConnell, C. 1984. *Economics*. New York: McGraw-Hill.

This is an example of a much-used text in economics. See chapter 1 for a statement of conventional economics premises.

Meadows, D., D. Meadows, and J. Randers. 1992. *Beyond the Limits: Confronting Global Collapse and Envisioning a Sustainable Future*. Published simultaneously in English by Chelsea Green (United States), McClelland & Stewart (Canada), and Earthscan (United Kingdom).

This is a sequel to the international bestseller *The Limits to Growth* and updates and expands the authors' original analysis and projections of world growth trends. In addition to the book there are a variety of teaching and research aids for classroom use: role playing simulations, technical illustrations, and software programs. Copies of the Executive Summary of this book or the book itself may be ordered through Chelsea Green Publishing Company, P.O. Box 130, Post Mills, VT 05058.

Orr, D. 1992. "Pascal's Wager and Economics in a Hotter Time." *Ecological Economics* 6(July):1–6. [p. 84]

In this essay David Orr explores what is the prudent response when society is faced with issues of potential disaster, such as global warming.

Page, T. 1977. *Conservation and Economic Efficiency*. Baltimore: Resources for the Future. [p. 88]

Though this is an older book, chapter 7, "The Present Value Criterion," chapter 8, "The Conservation Criterion," and chapter 9, "The Criteria Reconciled," are still very useful summaries of the basic two contrasting positions by an economist. The first six chapters of this book deal with the more specific problem of recycling and are useful if one is dealing with that issue.

Sachs, W. 1991. *For Love of the Automobile: Looking Back into the History of Our Desires*. Berkeley, CA: University of California Press. [p. 82]

Written in a lively style and illustrated by a wealth of cartoons, this book explores the nature of Germany's love affair with the automobile. In the conclusion Sachs appeals for the cultivation of new dreams born of the futility of the old ones.

Schmookler, A. B. 1993. *The Illusions of Choice: How the Market Economy Shapes Our Destiny*. Albany: State University of New York Press.

This book shows that the free market gives us certain freedoms but at the same time takes certain opportunities away. Several chapters deal with the impact of the market economy on the environment.

Schmookler, A. B. 1993. *Fool's Gold: The Fate of Values in a World of Goods*. San Francisco: Harper. [p. 85]

This book is a sequel to *The Illusions of Choice* and reveals how a system that regards nothing as sacred, everything as a mere commodity, creates illusions and devalues everything from art to the planet's resources.

Scitovsky, T. 1976. *The Joyless Economy: An Inquiry into Human Satisfaction and Consumer Dissatisfaction*. Oxford: Oxford University Press. [p. 86]

A book by an economist trying to figure out why, in the midst of such an abundance of economic goods, we have such a stressed and joyless society.

Shea, C. P. 1989. "Protecting the Ozone Layer." In *State of the World 1989*, L. Brown et al., eds., pp. 77–97. New York: W.W. Norton & Co. [p. 90]

This is a good example of how a particular environmental problem is caused by the economy. Not only does it investigate the chemical reactions that are the immediate cause of the hole in the ozone layer, it also shows the costs and benefits of constraining the production of CFCs, the culprits in causing the ozone thinning.

Simon, J. L. 1980. "Resources, Population, Environment: An Oversupply of False Bad News." *Science* 20:1431–1438. [pp. 80, 84]

In this essay Simon summarizes the conventional economic approach that there really is no environmental problem. It is all a product of flimsy evidence or no evidence at all and is published in the face of contradictory evidence. This article is included in Simon's (1981) book *The Ultimate Resource*. Princeton: Princeton University Press.

Solow, R. 1974. "The Economics of Resources or the Resources of Economics." *American Economic Review* 64 (May):1–14.

In this article Solow went as far as to proclaim not only the conditional possibility but the empirical likelihood that "the world can, in effect, get along without natural resources" (p. 11). What he means, however, is that the world can get along without exhaustible resources.

Vitousek, P., P. Ehrlich, A. Ehrlich, and P. Matson. 1986. "Human Appropriation of the Products of Photosynthesis." *Bioscience* 36 (June):368–373. [pp. 79, 84]

This article explores what percentage of potential terrestrial net primary productivity of photosynthetic activity is used directly, co-opted, or foregone because of the activity of the human species. The authors conclude that these biological realities make further economic growth highly unlikely.

Wachtel, P. 1983. *The Poverty of Affluence: A Psychological Portrait of the American Way of Life*. New York: Free Press. [pp. 82, 86]

In this insightful book the author, a psychologist, shows that the increased production and consumption of economic goods and services has not made most Americans more happy and/or fulfilled.

World Development Report 1992: Development and the Environment. 1992. Published for the World Bank by Oxford University Press.

This is the 15th in an annual series. Each year this series focuses on a specific problem and in 1992 it focused on economic development of the nonindustrialized world and the environment.

Zuckermann, W. 1992. *End of the Road: The World Car Crisis and How We Can Solve It*. Post Mills, VT: Chelsea Green Publishing Co. [p. 82]

The emphasis in this book is on sustainable transportation and planning our cities not around the automobile but around transportation systems that best meet people's needs for transportation.

Journals

Ecological Economics. This journal is published by The International Society for Ecological Economics, which is concerned with extending and integrating the study and management of "nature's household" (ecology) and "humanity's household" (economics). This integration is necessary because conceptual and professional isolation have led to economic and environmental policies that are mutually destructive rather than mutually reinforcing in the long run. For more information, write to International Society for Ecological Economics, P. O. Box 1589, Solomons, MD 20688.

The Human Economy Newsletter was started soon after the death of E. F. Schumacher to keep alive his research and thought. It can be ordered from *The Human Economy Newsletter*, Box 28, West Swanzey, NH 03469.

Journal of Environmental Economics and Management. This journal attempts to resolve environmental problems mainly using conventional economic premises and analysis. However, it does also deal with some of the issues mentioned in this chapter.

Films

An Introduction to Ecological Economics. 1991. 45 minutes. $19.95. In this film Gaylord Nelson, Herman Daly, and John Cobb, Jr. join others in a fascinating glimpse into new economic principles that would radically redefine the discipline of economics. This film can be obtained from Griesinger Films, 7300 Old Mill Road, Gates Mills, OH 44040. There is also a brief study guide that will be sent with this film. [p. 83]

What Price Clean Air? 1992. 57 minutes. $185.00 for purchase, $87.00 for rental. This film documents the price that society will eventually have to pay for health and environmental damages, if existing Clean Air standards continue to be relaxed. This film also gives global perspective to the issue of Clean Air, citing evidence from Sweden, Canada, and Japan to show that we do not need to relax our Clean Air standards. Order from Richter Productions, 330 West 42nd St., New York, NY 10036. [p. 85]

Chapter 5

Geography

Lisa Naughton-Treves
University of Florida
and
Emily Young
University of Arizona

Geography as an Environmental Science

Conservation ideology is in transition. The conventional model—preserving nature in parks and reserves entirely isolated from human activities—has proven inadequate. Biologists now recognize that most parks and reserves are too small to support populations of large vertebrates, or to sustain ecological processes that generate and maintain high levels of biodiversity. Numerous case studies of parks in the tropics also prove that prohibiting all human use of protected areas is often socially infeasible. Conservationists have thus turned to a more holistic approach, where ecosystems are managed beyond the scale of a single park, and human resource use is incorporated in management strategies. This broad-scale, integrated approach requires an understanding of how humans adapt to and transform their biophysical environs. But how do we thoroughly evaluate environmental change on a large spatial and temporal scale? How do we distinguish land degradation from sustainable land use? These questions lie at the core of geographic inquiry. Geographers are well suited to explore the interface between local actions and global concerns. Geography leads students to examine the physical and social consequences of human interaction with the biosphere. Geography students also explore the evolution of environmental conservation as an ideology across time and culture. The goal of an introductory geography course is to prepare students to evaluate how they shape their local—as well as global—environment.

Emphasis on Spatial Pattern and Focus on Human Agency in Shaping Landscapes

Geography is founded on an age-old intellectual tradition of observing human influence on the biophysical environment. During the past three centuries, as human capacity to alter the environment has escalated in scale, rate, and intensity, geographers have chronicled human degradation of physical habitats (Turner et al. 1992). At the turn of the 18th century, Alexander von Humboldt documented human influence on vegetation in his exploration of remote Andean regions. Sauer (1956, p. 49) later noted the ever-expanding role of humans as "ecologic dominants." This school of thought persists in geography, characterized by the view that pristine or "untouched" ecosystems are, by and large, nonexistent (Denevan 1992). (See Chapter 2, Anthropology, for further discussion of this perspective.)

The approach of geographers to the study of environmental change emphasizes spatial pattern, a large scale of inquiry (over space and time), and the integration of social and natural sciences. Geographers typically conduct research at the level of landscape or region; for example, considering land use patterns and their impact on vegetation in a drainage basin or watershed. Recently, geographers have begun working at much broader scales. Such a study is under way in Mexico, where Liverman (1990) is investigating the capacity of small-scale farmers to cope with climatic change over several decades. Research elsewhere documents local adaptation in land management upon elevated exposure to storms, oil spills, flooding, and other forms of environmental risk (Kates and Burton 1986).

While geography as a discipline encompasses a broad realm of inquiry, geographers as individuals tend to specialize in either human or physical studies, often borrowing methods of analysis from other disciplines. Geographers traditionally break the study of human transformation of the biosphere into four fields: (1) regional studies, (2) people–environment studies, (3) environmental processes and resources, and (4) spatial analysis.

Regional Studies

Geographers working in this tradition address conservation issues relevant to a particular place. A regional focus allows students to understand how the physical characteristics and social history of a place have led to a unique land use system. Students may draw on this insight to evaluate the sustainability of a land use system and to predict how changing external and internal factors may result in the transformation or degradation of a landscape (Leighly 1969). For example, many Latin Americanist geographers examine how deforestation in the Amazon is driven by distinctive regional characteristics such as land tenure patterns, demographic features, government policies, and agricultural and economic systems (Hecht and Cockburn 1989; Smith 1982).

People–Environment Studies

Within this broad focus, geographers explore the relationship between society and nature in terms of causes and consequences. The justification for environmental conservation is likely to vary dramatically according to a society's own view of its relationship with nature. Ancient writers such as Hippocrates, Ptolemy, and Strabo expressed a profound desire to define the human role in the natural world. Since then, many philosophies have developed, ranging from the Christian doctrine of defining man as master of nature (Glacken 1956) (see Chapter 11, Religion), to Romantic/Arcadian ideas of humanity in harmony with nature (O'Riordan 1981) (see Chapter 7, Literature), to deterministic theories akin to social Darwinism that individual and social characteristics are formed by the physical environment (Semple 1911), to notions that human choice is influenced primarily by cultural and historical factors (Lewthwaite 1966). (These latter viewpoints are discussed fully in Chapter 2, Anthropology.) Accordingly, the aim of conservation will vary in terms of what type of human intervention in ecosystems a given society considers desirable.

The concept of humanity as modifier of nature now dominates geographic theory (Turner et al. 1992). Today geographers further divide the realm of people–environment studies into three broad categories: environmental perception, cultural ecology, and political ecology.

Under the rubric of environmental perception, geographers address conservation, environmental ethics, and resource management by revealing cultural attitudes to wilderness and wilderness preservation. These perceptions are shaped by religious tradition and socioeconomic conditions (Doughty 1981; Graber 1976; Tuan 1971; Tuan 1974). Human awareness of and experience with natural hazards, for example, vary considerably among different groups of people at local, national, and global levels, hampering the degree to which people can effectively cope with such calamities (Palm 1990).

In the field of cultural ecology, geographers examine human interaction with their environment through the process of adaptation. Their studies of subsistence systems in rural areas of developing countries reveal that many aboriginal and peasant societies possess a wealth of information regarding their biophysical surroundings, which enables them to manage local resources in a manner favoring long-term ecological stability (e.g., Brower 1990; Grossman 1984; Nietschmann 1973). Findings from these studies have been used to promote new models of development and conservation that incorporate ecologically sound resource management practices from local groups (e.g., Clarke 1977; Denevan 1980).

The political ecology approach evolved out of earlier works in cultural ecology, broadening the focus to explore interactions between local land use and political and economic institutions at regional, state, and international levels (Blaikie and Brookfield 1987; Bryant 1992). For example, Watts (1983) combines environmental and political economy approaches to analyze peasant food production, famine, and desertification in Nigeria. Most of these studies emphasize agricultural systems. Less well studied are the dimensions of human use of terrestrial and marine fauna and whether human activities are compatible with the long-term survival of these biological resources.

Environmental Processes and Resources

Geographers who study biogeography, climatology, and geomorphology are distinguished from their colleagues in other natural sciences by their scale of inquiry and their attention to human agency in modifying or altering environmental processes. An introductory course in biogeography will help students understand the relationship between abiotic and biotic elements in the landscape as well as human impact on vegetation (Veblen 1989). Since biogeographers record and explain changing patterns of floral and faunal assemblages across space and time (Veblen 1989), their work is important to the selection of priority areas for protection. Biogeographers provide an alternative to the single species approach to biodiversity conservation, as they are likely to focus on higher taxa or communities at regional scales (Gunderson et al. 1995; Veblen et al. 1992). Biogeography research often explores patterns of vegetation disturbance and succession under varying degrees of human influence, while also documenting the consequences of human-introduced species (Parsons 1972).

Spatial Analysis

The rapid advance in technologies of remote sensing, Geographic Information Systems (GIS), and computer cartography provides geographers with powerful tools of analysis to monitor and evaluate human impact on landscape. GIS is a broad term used to refer to any computer system composed of software used to collect, store, and manipulate spatially referenced data. The land management utility of GIS is obvious—it allows an investigator to rapidly change, correct, and compare maps and thus carry out complex and comparative analysis of such phenomena as land use change or change in vegetation cover. While GIS has been employed for environmental impact assessment in forestry and agriculture for two decades, geographers are also beginning to expand the use of GIS as an analytical and predictive tool (Odland et al. 1989). Such work has the potential to aid conservation decisions, including the selection of an appropriate scale of management.

COURSE PLANS

Environmental conservation is an increasingly popular theme in geographic research. Most geography departments in the United States (and many abroad) currently offer undergraduate level courses addressing conservation issues. Introductory geography courses provide students with a broad framework for understanding the impact of humans on the biosphere, as well as the influence of the physical environment on human society. This synthesis of social and life sciences is valuable to nonmajors who may take only a single course in environmental studies, or who may later specialize in a different field related to conservation. Upper division geography courses initiate students in research methods and theory and offer detailed case studies related to specific environmental issues.

The following material is offered as a sample of the diverse approaches used within geography to teach about environmental conservation. Some course units are most suited for physical geography courses, others for human geography courses. Depending on the course emphasis and the level of students, professors most likely will want to expand on or delete specific subjects. We also present outlines of two upper level courses that focus on environmental conservation. The references cited are ones readily available on most U.S. campuses and written at a level accessible to the average undergraduate reader.

Within each unit we stress three teaching goals: (1) to cause students to recognize their role in shaping environments at many scales, (2) to encourage personal reflection on environmental responsibility, and (3) to introduce students to research tools and case studies enabling their participation in environmental management decisions. The material may additionally be of use to professors teaching introductory courses with environmental themes in disciplines of anthropology, area studies, conservation biology, sociology, or history. The reader is urged to compare the material in this chapter with that presented in chapters in this book on allied disciplines.

Lower or Upper Division Course Units

Land Degradation as a Social Problem

Unit Objectives. This unit can be integrated into a lower division, human geography course on peoples, places, and cultures or an upper division course in culture, environment, and development. The goal in either case is to allow students to explore land degradation as a social problem and to question common assumptions about the causes of environmental destruction and prospects for conservation in lesser developed countries. Both courses focus on people as increasingly dominant agents in shaping environmental processes at the global level.

(1) Land degradation and society (concepts: Blaikie and Brookfield 1987, pp. 1–26, plus case studies).

  (a) How do human activities influence natural processes of reproduction and degradation (e.g., agriculture and chemical pollution from pesticides)?

  (b) Link between economic–institutional settings and environmental problems (e.g., market-oriented monocropping and soil erosion).

  (c) Role of land management in checking and/or enhancing natural processes of damage and repair (e.g., polycropping versus cattle ranching in tropical rainforests).

  (d) Perspectives on "sustainability." The meaning of the term varies dramatically according to who uses it (Redclift 1987; Sanderson and Redford 1992). See also ecological systems theory cited in course unit, Tropical Deforestation and Subsistence Agriculture, below.

(2) Using the regional political ecology approach to understand land degradation.

  (a) Definition: regional political ecology, that is, how interactions between regional, state, and international political and economic institutions and local land management render particular environmental outcomes (Blaikie and Brookfield 1987, p. 17).

  (b) Case study #1: tropical deforestation in Borneo and the Malay Peninsula (Brookfield et al. 1992, pp. 495–512).

  (c) Case study #2: desertification in the Sahel, Northern Nigeria (Watts 1983).

Class Assignment (lower division): Choose an environmental issue in your home town (e.g., watershed deterioration, smog, landfill shortage, habitat fragmentation) and determine the nature of the problem using a regional political ecology approach. Discuss impediments to and possible strategies for resolution of environmental conflict.

Class Assignment (upper division): Form a team of students to carry out the assignment outlined above for the lower division course. The assignment will then be presented in front of the class in the form of a public hearing to discuss proposals for conflict resolution, with team members playing roles of politicians, bureaucrats, private interests, community activists, and so on who would be involved. The rest of the class provides "public input" from the community at large. Later invite local guest speaker(s) who are actually working on resolving the problem.

Tropical Deforestation and Subsistence Agriculture

Unit Objectives. This course unit can be integrated into a lower division human geography course on peoples, places, and cultures or upper division courses in either biogeography or culture, environment, and development. The purpose is to allow students to examine biophysical and sociocultural aspects of tropical deforestation, as well as to explore how local knowledge can contribute to conservation strategies in tropical forests, using Amazonia as a regional example. For the lower division human geography course, it fits within its larger aim to study the earth as home to human beings. For the upper division courses in biogeography and culture, environment, and development, it serves as a regional case study for applying more general principles, concepts, and ideas.

(1) Basic ecological characteristics of tropical forests.

   (a) Introduction: What are tropical forests? How are they unique? Describe location, climate, and soils, plus paleoecology (Forsyth and Miyata 1984, pp. 1–15; Longman and Jenik 1974).

   (b) Plant and animal communities. Describe structure and biomass. Introduce concept of niches and keystone species.

   (c) Biological diversity. Distinguish species richness from species diversity. Describe different scales of diversity beyond the species level. (See also Chapter 3, Biology.)

   (d) Patterns of disturbance and succession. Gap dynamics, natural succession; discuss resilience versus stability (Holling 1986, pp. 292–320).

   (e) Evidence of human management. Recent research reveals human impact on rainforest composition and distribution long before the colonial period (Balée 1989; see also Chapter 2, Anthropology).

(2) Swidden cultivation as an agricultural system.

   (a) Concepts/definitions: for example, indigenously developed agriculture, subsistence economy, extensive versus intensive agriculture, shifting cultivation (Denslow and Padoch 1988, pp. 111–140).

   (b) Swidden cultivation as an ecologically viable versus environmentally destructive agricultural system. Case studies from the Amazon.

(i) Shipibo Indians of eastern Peru—sustainability of a traditional agricultural system (Bergman 1980).

(ii) Destructive development of the Amazon: deforestation, cattle ranching, and soil degeneration (Hecht and Cockburn 1989).

(c) Subsistence hunting and impact on faunal resources. Describe how population growth, changes in hunting technology and market penetration cause over-exploitation of faunal resources (Redford 1992).

(d) Local knowledge, sustainable resource management, and biodiversity conservation in tropical rainforests: future prospects. Discuss strategies for conservation ranging from inviolate parks to extractive reserves. What consequences do they have for cultural survival and ecosystem conservation (Denevan and Padoch 1988; Posey and Balée 1989; Browder 1987)?

(e) What can you do? Discuss alternatives for activism. Provide examples of brochures from conservation groups working in tropical forests and discuss their various approaches.

Class Assignment (lower division): Develop a plan for marketing rainforest products from the Amazon to your home town, in a manner that is both ecologically sustainable and economically viable, making use of local knowledge of indigenous and folk societies who inhabit the region. Think about the kinds of products that could be marketed, how they would be produced, appropriate (if any) governmental measures, and marketing strategies.

Class Assignment (upper division); (for both Biogeography and Culture, Environment, and Development): Draw up a plan for a biosphere reserve in the old growth forests of the Pacific Northwest that addresses the concerns of both environmentalists and loggers.

Cartography, Geographic Information Systems (GIS), and Environmental Management

Unit Objectives. This course unit can be integrated into a lower division cartography course. The purpose is to use maps and aerial photos as a basis for exploring human–nature relationships and environmental problems. It fits within the larger aim of the course to introduce students to properties, uses, and interpretation of maps and remote sensing images to provide a useful tool for relating to our surroundings.

(1) Interpreting the physical environment (adapted from Muehrcke 1980).

(a) Four physical realms: lithosphere, atmosphere, hydrosphere, and biosphere.

(b) Integrating environmental realms using cartographic methods.

(c) Case study: cartographic analysis of mammalian biogeography in the Trans–Mexican neovolcanic belt (Fa 1989).

(2) Interpreting the human environment (adapted from Muehrcke 1980).

(a) Four component factors: governmental, technological, social, and economic.

(b) Integrating human factors using cartographic methods.

(c) Case study: Landsat images of tropical deforestation along the Mexico–Guatemala order (Stuart 1992).

(3) Interpreting people–environment interactions (adapted from Muehrcke 1980).

(a) Influence of human factors on the environment (e.g., wetland destruction in the United States).

(b) Influence of physical factors on people (e.g., agricultural land use).

(c) Feedback relations between people and environment (e.g., acid rain).

(d) Case study: map using geographical information systems to examine ecological responses to natural and human-induced influences in El Malpais Conservation Area and National Monument (Carroll 1991).

Course Assignment: Act as the local naturalist and map the distribution of flora and fauna on campus. Think about why some species of flora and fauna are more prevalent than others. Which species are endemic and which are introduced? Which are most tolerant of disturbed habitats? Where could "nature reserves" be established on campus?

Upper Division Courses

Human Impact on Vegetation *(adapted from a course given by Dr. Thomas Vale at University of Wisconsin–Madison)*

Course Objectives. This biogeography course first offers students an explanation of how environmental conditions influence wild vegetation structure and composition at the level of landscapes. Modification of vegetation by various human activities is then explored and compared to historical patterns of natural disturbance. The course thus offers insight and methods for evaluating what is "natural" vegetation—a core question for habitat conservation and restoration.

(1) Natural vegetation in the landscape.

    (a) Physical features.

    (b) Biotic factors.

    (c) Disturbance—concepts of stability and resilience (Hill 1987; Holling 1986, pp. 292–320).

    (d) Overview of vegetation as integrator of environmental conditions (Vale 1982).

(2) Studying vegetation change: historical and ecological sources (Miles 1979).

(3) Human activities as a cause of vegetation change. Abundant case studies exist. Examples that are relevant to local or regional habitats should be selected.

    (a) Introduction of exotic species (Crosby 1986, pp. 145–194; Parsons 1972).

    (b) Altered fire regimes (Wade and Lundsford 1990; Sanford et al. 1985).

    (c) Livestock grazing (Parsons 1972; Veblen and Lorenz 1988).

    (d) Logging (Franklin and Forman 1987).

    (e) Hunting elimination of wildlife (Redford 1992).

    (f) Other: use local examples, such as off-road vehicles, construction activities, air pollution, etc.

(4) Altered vegetation: impacts on wildlife; wildlife impacts on vegetations. See Schule 1992 for tropical examples.

(5) Altered vegetation: impacts on soils and hydrology (Miles 1979; Goudie 1982).

(6) Vegetation change and human purposes. Notions of "natural" vegetation debunked (Denevan 1992).

Field Trip and Class Assignment: Travel to a local park or reserve where students will individually describe what appears to be natural or human-created in the landscape. As a group, outline research projects for assessing vegetation change at various temporal and spatial scales. Each student then writes a "mock" short proposal to the appropriate conservation authority for support of research.

Wilderness Conservation: Ideas and Practices *(adapted from a course by Dr. J. T. Wood, "Conservation and Environmental Education," at Atkinson College of York University, Ontario)*

Course Objectives. This course provides an historical account of the development of North American conservation ideology based on societal

attitudes toward nature. It then explains the evolution of the conservation movement on a regional or statewide basis. Finally, students examine the history of a local park or reserve in terms of its conservation
goals, public constituency, and conflicts.

(1) History and principles of conservation.

    (a) Discuss philosophical foundation of the North American conserva-
tion movement. Present thoughts of key wilderness authors: Pinchot, Muir, Leopold, Carson, etc. Discuss radicalism in conservation
(see Lewis 1992). Focus on the tension between utilitarian and aesthetic goals. (On this latter point, see Chapter 9, Philosophy.)

    (b) How have recent shifts in our understanding of ecosystem function
(e.g., nonlinear processes and multistable states) influenced our
management of nature (Zimmerer 1994)?

    (c) Discuss the exportation of North American conservation ideology to
the neotropics (Olwig and Olwig 1979).

(2) Current conservation strategies at the regional and local level.

    (a) Does a unique conservation ethic exist at a local or regional level?
How did it evolve? How have conservation areas been selected in
your state? How much of your state's area is included in protected
areas?

(3) Integrating conservation theory and practice.

This portion of the course is ideally taught in the field at a protected
area. Through interviews and readings, students learn how and why the
area was declared protected. Representatives of various institutions
(City Council, Department of Natural Resources, university departments) explain to students the challenges and controversies involved in
managing the site.

Course Assignment 1: Maintain a personal journal as a record of what
you have learned in class. Share your response to main themes in class.
How has your attitude to nature been formed? How does it compare with
models of nature presented in North American conservation literature?
Or with those of modern ecosystem theory? What role does nature, as
you perceive it, play in your daily life? Entries should be weekly, at a
minimum, and be comprehensible to someone other than you or the professor. (Adapted from Yi-Fu Tuan's course on Environment and the Quality of Life offered at the University of Wisconsin–Madison.)

Course Assignment 2: In small groups, write up a management plan for
a local protected area. Establish policy on public access, research activities, and habitat management. Assuming limited budgets, what are priority management activities?

Resources

Page numbers appearing in brackets at the end of some entries indicate where the reference is cited in a course plan.

Culture, Environment, and Sustainable Development

Anderson, D. and R. Grove, eds. 1987. *Conservation in Africa: People, Policies and Practices.* New York: Cambridge University Press.

An interdisciplinary treatment of how conservation can and must be integrated with human development throughout Africa.

Bergman, R. W. 1980. *Amazon Economics: The Simplicity of Shipibo Indian Wealth.* Dellplain Latin American Studies, No. 6. Ann Arbor, MI: University Microfilms International. [p. 104]

Comprehensive study of the subsistence ecology of the Shipibo Indians in eastern Peru, examining different livelihood strategies, including swidden agriculture, fishing, and hunting.

Blaikie, P. and H. C. Brookfield. 1987. *Land Degradation and Society.* London: Methuen. [p. 102]

Provides a conceptual overview and case studies that explore social underpinnings of land degradation, with an emphasis on the relationship between local land use/management and regional institutions and political structures.

Brookfield, H. C., F. J. Lian, L. Kwai-Sim, and L. Potter. 1992. "Borneo and the Malay Peninsula." In *The Earth as Transformed by Human Action.* B. L. Turner II, W. C. Clark, R. W. Kates, J. F. Richards, J. T. Mathews, and W. B. Meyer, eds. Cambridge: Cambridge University Press. [p. 102]

A historical overview of how colonial and neocolonial structures have led to destructive transformation of tropical ecosystems.

Browder, J. O., ed. 1987. *Fragile Lands of Latin America: The Sustainable Basis for Alternative Agriculture.* Boulder, CO: Westview Press. [p. 104]

Provides case studies of land use in neotropical steep slopes and humid lowlands. Argues that in these zones, local management systems are more sustainable than intensive, high-tech systems.

Brower, B. 1990. "Range Conservation and Sherpa Livestock Management in Khumbu, Nepal." *Mountain Research and Development* 10(1):34–42.

Case study of traditional resource management among the Sherpa in the Himalayas of Nepal.

Bryant, R. L. 1992. "Political Ecology: an Emerging Research Agenda in Third World Studies." *Political Geography* 11(1):12–36.

Introduces the approach of political ecology; emphasizes how political structures influence land use systems toward sustainability or degradation.

Butzer, K. W. ed., 1992. "The Americas Before and After 1492: Current Geographical Research." *Annals of the Association of American Geographers* 82(3).

Contains articles describing the American landscape and land use systems before European contact, arguing against conceptions of a pristine wilderness prior to 1492.

Butzer, K. W. 1994. "Towards a Cultural Curriculum for the Future: A First Approximation." In *Re-Reading Cultural Geography*. K. E. Foote, ed. Austin: University of Texas Press.

Devises a cultural curriculum for future geographers, including a provocative discussion of environmental management and sustainability.

Clarke, W. C. 1977. "The Structure of Permanence: The Relevance of Self-Subsistence Communities for World Ecosystem Management." In *Subsistence and Survival*. T.P. Bayliss-Smith, ed. London: Academic Press.

Discusses why examples of sustainable subsistence land use systems are relevant to land management at a broader scale in industrial society.

Clarke, W. C. and R.E. Munn, eds. 1986. *Sustainable Development of the Biosphere*. Cambridge: Cambridge University Press.

Collection of papers by geographers, ecologists, and social scientists on processes of environmental transformation.

Dasmann, R. F. 1985. "Achieving the Sustainable Use of Species and Ecosystems." *Landscape Planning* 2:211–219.

Attempts to define sustainability from an ecological perspective.

Denevan, W. M. 1980. "Latin America." In *World Systems of Traditional Resource Management*. G. Klee, ed. New York: Halsted Press.

Reviews past and present traditional resource management techniques employed by Latin American farmers and emphasizes their practical value for present agricultural systems.

Denevan, W. M. 1992. "The Pristine Myth." *Annals of American Association of Geography* 82(3):369–385. [p. 106]

See Butzer 1992 above.

Denevan, W. M. and C. Padoch, eds. 1988. *Swidden-Fallow Agroforestry in the Peruvian Amazon. Advances in Economic Botany,* Vol. 5. Bronx, NY: New York Botanical Garden. [p. 104]

Ethnoecological study of swidden-fallow management among the Bora Indians of eastern Peru for the harvest of useful plants.

Denslow, J. S. and C. Padoch, eds. 1988. *People of the Tropical Rainforest.* Berkeley: University of California Press. [p. 103]

Provides interdisciplinary perspective on traditional peoples of rainforest environments from across the tropics. Documents various threats to their culture and to the rainforest. Breathtaking photos.

Glacken, C. J. 1956. *Traces on the Rhodian Shore: Nature and Culture in Western Thought from Ancient Times to the End of the Eighteenth Century.* Berkeley: University of California Press.

A massive work documenting the history of environmental thought in Western society. Most appropriate for upper level courses.

Grossman, L. S. 1984. *Peasants, Subsistence Ecology, and Development in the Highlands of Papua New Guinea.* Princeton, NJ: Princeton University Press.

Analysis of socially and ecologically destructive impacts of commodity production on traditional patterns of resource use and subsistence production in Papua New Guinea.

Hecht, S. B. and A. Cockburn. 1989. *The Fate of the Forest: Developers, Destroyers, and Defenders of the Amazon.* London: Verso. Also, New York: Harper, 1990. [p. 103]

Examines how markets and governmental policies have encouraged agricultural settlers to adopt destructive land management practices.

IUCN/UNEP/WWF. 1991. *Caring for the Earth. A Strategy for Sustainable Living.* Gland, Switzerland.

Provides a working definition of sustainability used among international development agencies and Washington-based environmental groups.

Kates, R. W. and I. Burton. 1986. "The Great Climacteric 1798–2048: Transition to a Just and Sustainable Human Environment." In *Essays on Themes from Works of G. F. White.* R. W. Kates and I. Burton, eds. Chicago: University of Chicago Press.

G. F. White is a major figure in human geography and is considered by many to be the founder of theory and research on environment as potential hazard. This volume provides an introduction to his work and is appropriate for an interdisciplinary audience.

Leighly, J., ed. 1969. *Land and Life: A Selection from the Writings of Carl O. Sauer*. Berkeley: University of California Press.

A seminal collection of essays that emphasize the possibility for humane use of the earth and the value of past human experience in resolving present problems of destructive resource use.

Liverman, D. M. 1990. "Drought Impacts in Mexico: Climate, Agriculture, Technology and Land Tenure." *Annals of the Association of American Geographers* 80(1):49–73.

Detailed study of how different forces acting at different scales shape the impact of climatic change on agricultural communities in Mexico.

Marsh, G. P. [1864] 1965. In *Man and Nature*. D. Lowenthal, ed. Cambridge, MA: Belknap.

Landmark study on the destructive environmental consequences of human activities.

Nietschmann, B. Q. 1973. *Between Land and Water: The Subsistence Ecology of the Miskito Indians, Eastern Nicaragua*. New York: Seminar Press.

Examines how global markets disrupted traditional patterns of resource use and fueled the overexploitation of sea turtles.

Oldfield, M. L. and J. B. Alcorn. 1991. *Biodiversity: Culture, Conservation and Ecodevelopment*. Boulder, CO: Westview Press.

Broad collection of papers offering an interdisciplinary approach to the conservation and sustainable use of biological resources in developing countries.

Palm, R. 1990. *Natural Hazards: An Integrative Framework for Research and Planning*. Baltimore: Johns Hopkins University Press.

Discussion of natural disasters in a U.S. context, moves beyond a behavioral approach to analyze how political, social, and economic forces shape a community's capacity to cope with environmental hazards.

Posey, D. A. and W. Balée, eds. 1989. *Resource Management in Amazonia: Indigenous and Folk Strategies. Advances in Economic Botany*, Vol. 7. Bronx, NY: New York Botanical Garden. [p. 104]

A series of studies in conservation and management of tropical rainforests, focusing on environmental perception and resource management strategies among native Amazonian groups.

Redclift, M. 1987. *Sustainable Development: Exploring the Contradictions*. London: Methuen. [p. 102]

A classic work exploring the concept of social sustainability in rural land use systems.

Sanderson, S. and K. Redford. 1992. "The Brief, Barren Marriage of Sustainability and Development." *Bulletin of the Ecological Society of America* 73:26–39. [p. 102]

Provides a short, critical perspective on the misuse of the term sustainability in reference to environmental issues within development assistance.

Sauer, C. O. 1956. "The Agency of Man on the Earth." In *Man's Role in Changing the Face of the Earth*. W. L. Thomas, Jr., ed. Chicago: University of Chicago Press.

A classic essay in geography about human influence on natural landscapes.

Semple, E. C. 1911. *Influences of Geographic Environment*. New York: Henry Holt and Co.

A seminal work on how the environment has influenced human societies.

Smith, N. J. H. 1982. *Rainforest Corridors: The Trans-Amazon Colonization Scheme*. Berkeley: University of California Press.

Critical assessment of the successes and failures of Trans-Amazon colonization scheme and problems of agricultural development in a frontier rainforest.

Turner, B. L. II, W. C. Clark, R. W. Kates, J. F. Richards, J. T. Mathews, and W. B. Meyer, eds. 1992. *The Earth as Transformed by Human Action: Global and Regional Changes in the Biosphere over the Past 300 Years*. Cambridge: Cambridge University Press.

A large volume covering 300 years of human influence on the biosphere from the perspective of geographers, historians, and environmental scientists. Provides regional case studies as well as overarching discussions concerning driving forces in human transformation of earth. Certain chapters are appropriate for beginning level courses, but by and large, this is an upper division resource book.

Watts, M. 1983. *Silent Violence: Food, Famine, and Peasantry in Northern Nigeria*. Berkeley: University of California Press. [p. 102]

A seminal work that integrates institutions and international structures into explanations of how food production and drought result in famine and desertification. Appropriate for upper level courses only.

World Commission on Environment and Development. 1987. *Our Common Future* ("The Brundtland Report"). New York: Oxford University Press.

Explores concepts of sustainability, seeks operational definition.

Zimmerer, K. S. 1994. "Human Geography and the New Ecology. The Prospect and Promise of Integration." *Annals of the American Association of Geographers* 84(1):108–125. [p. 107]

A timely discussion of the implications of the reorientation of ecological thought (i.e., challenging the notion of persistent stability in natural systems) for human geography.

RECOMMENDED JOURNALS: *Ambio*; *Cultural Survival Quarterly*; *Environment*; *Global Environmental Change: Human and Policy Dimensions*; *Research and Exploration* (National Geographic Society); and *Science*.

Biogeography, Ecosystem Theory, and Biodiversity Conservation

Anderson, J. M. 1981. *Ecology for Environmental Sciences: Biosphere, Ecosystems, and Man.* New York: John Wiley and Sons.

Textbook exploring ecological concepts at the ecosystem level, with an emphasis on people–environment interactions.

Balée, W. 1989. "The Culture of Amazonian Forests." *Advances in Economic Botany* 7:1–21. [p. 103]

Presents evidence of human influence on paleoecology of Amazonian forests.

Burton, I. and R. W. Kates, eds. 1985. *Readings in Resource Management and Conservation.* Chicago: University of Chicago Press.

A collection of readings that focus on applications of science to environmentally sound resource management.

Crosby, A. W. 1986. *Ecological Imperialism—The Biological Expansion of Europe, 900–1900.* New York: Cambridge University Press. [p. 106]

A history of the introduction and profound impact of European ecosystems, plants, and animals in the New World, Australia, and New Zealand.

Dasmann, R. 1984. *Environmental Conservation*, 5th ed. New York: John Wiley and Sons, Inc.

One of the best textbooks on issues of the environment and natural resource conservation.

Deshmukh, I. 1986. *Ecology and Tropical Biology*. Palo Alto, CA: Blackwell Scientific Publications.

Provides a clear introduction to principles of ecology with special emphasis on the tropics.

Fa, J. E. 1989. "Conservation-Motivated Analysis of Mammalian Biogeography in the Trans-Mexican Neovolcanic Belt." *National Geographic Research* 5(3):296–316. [p. 105]

Useful case study example of how spatial analysis through choropleth maps of biogeographic patterns can be employed to select areas for the conservation of mammals.

Forsyth, A. and K. Miyata. 1984. *Tropical Nature*. New York: Charles Scribner's Sons. [p. 103]

A captivating introduction to the ecology, beauty, and mystery of neotropical rain forests.

Franklin, J. F. and R. T. T. Forman. 1987. "Creating Landscape Patterns by Forest Cutting: Ecological Consequences and Principles." *Landscape Ecology* 1(1):5-18. [p. 106]

Adds a landscape perspective to studies on the ecological effect of logging. Discusses implications of creating edge environment in the landscape.

Goudie, A. S. 1982. *The Human Impact: Man's Role in Environmental Change*. Cambridge, MA: MIT Press. [p. 106]

Textbook exploring human influence on biological and physical environments. Includes graphics.

Gunderson, L., C. S. Holling, and S. Light, eds. 1995. *Barriers and Bridges for the Renewal of Regional Ecosystems*. New York: Columbia University Press.

An interdisciplinary, ground-breaking effort to manage ecosystems at the regional scale. Provides case studies from temperate and tropical systems, both marine and terrestrial.

Hill, A. R. 1987. "Ecosystem Stability: Some Recent Perspectives." *Progress in Physical Geography* 11:315–333. [p. 106]

Discusses and defines stability and argues for its importance in ecosystem research and conservation.

Holling, C. S. 1986. "The Resilience of Terrestrial Ecosystems: Local Surprise and Global Change." In *Sustainable Development of the Biosphere*. W. C. Clarke and R. E. Munn, eds. Cambridge: Cambridge
University Press. [pp. 103, 106]

Departs from linear models of ecosystem change to describe discontinuous
change; presents concepts of connectedness and the importance of scale in
understanding ecosystem process.

Longman, K. A. and J. Jenik. 1974. *Tropical Forest and its Environment*.
London: Longman. [p. 103]

Clearly describes ecological characteristics of tropical rainforests, particularly useful for providing examples from African and Asian forests.

Miles, J. 1979. *Vegetation Dynamics*. London: Chapman & Hall; New
York: Wiley. Distributed in the United States by Halsted Press.
[p. 106]

Explores dynamics of vegetation change, focusing on historical and ecological sources.

Parsons, J. J. 1972. "The Spread of African Pasture Grasses to the American Tropics." *Journal of Range Management* 25:12–17. [p. 106]

Redford, K. H. 1992. "The Empty Forest." *Bioscience* 42(6):412–422. [pp.
104, 106]

Describes the importance of faunal community to rainforest function and
how it is often decimated in what appears to be an intact forest.

Sanford, R. L., J. Saldarriaga, K. Clark, C. Uhl, and R. Herrera. 1985.
"Amazon Rain-Forest Fires." *Science* 227:53–55. [p. 106]

Offers empirical evidence of large fires in the Amazon and thus questions the
portrayal of the Amazon as an undisturbed, stable ecosystem.

Schule, W. 1992. "Vegetation, Megaherbivores, Man and Climate in the
Quaternary and the Genesis of Closed Forests." In *Tropical Forests
in Transition*. J. G. Goldammer, ed. Boston: Birkhauser Verlag. [p.
106]

Hypothesizes that through elimination of megaherbivores and increasing
burning, humans have created closed-canopy forests.

Simmons, I. G. 1979. *Biogeography: Natural and Cultural*. London:
Edward Arnold.

Examines human attitudes and activities that influence the biosphere.
Includes graphics.

Troll, C. 1968. *Geo-Ecology of the Mountainous Regions of the Tropical Americas.* Bonn: Ferdinand Duemmler.
A classic work on Andean biogeography.

Vale, T. R. 1982. *Plants and People: Vegetation Change in North America.* Washington, DC: Association of American Geographers. [p. 106]
A concise but comprehensive look at human impacts to North American vegetation (both deliberate and unintended) from a variety of ecological perspectives, including an extensive bibliography.

Veblen, T. T. 1989. "Biogeography." In *Geography in America.* G. L. Gaile and C. J. Willmott, eds. Columbus, OH: Merrill Publishing Company.
Presents the intellectual traditions of biogeography and the new directions in biogeographical research.

Veblen, T. T. and D. C. Lorenz. 1988. "Recent Vegetation Changes Along the Forest/Steppe Ecotone of Northern Patagonia." *Annals of the Association of American Geographers* 78(1):93-111. [p. 106]
Offers a clear depiction of various sources of disturbance and resulting change in vegetation structure in a dynamic environment.

Veblen, T. T., T. Kitzberger, and A. Lara. 1992. "Disturbance and Forest Dynamics Along a Transect From Andean Rain Forest to Patagonian Shrubland." *Journal of Vegetation Science* 3:506–520. [p. 106]

Wade, D. D. and J. Lundsford. 1990. "Fire As a Forest Management Tool: Prescribed Burning in the Southern United States." *Unasylva* 41(162):28-38. [p. 106]

RECOMMENDED JOURNALS: *Journal of Biogeography; Environmental Conservation; Biological Conservation; Conservation Biology;* and *Landscape Ecology.*

Environmental Perception and Conservation Ideology

Doughty, R. W. 1981. "Environmental Theology: Recent Trends in Christian Thought." *Progress in Human Geography* 5(2):234–238.

Graber, L. 1976. "Wilderness as a Sacred Space." *Annals of the Association of American Geographers* 78(1):93–111. [p. 107]

Lewis, M. W. 1992. *Green Delusions: An Environmental Critique of Radical Environmentalism.* London: Duke University Press.

An excellent and thought-provoking work that explores the problems and contradictions underlying radical environmentalist thought.

Lewthwaite, G. R. 1966. "Environmentalism and Determinism: A Search for Clarification." *Annals of the Association of American Geographers* 56(1):1–23.

McNeely, J., K. Miller, W. Reid, R. Mittermeier, and T. Werner. 1990. *Conserving the World's Biological Diversity.* Washington, DC: World Resources Institute.

Offers a global perspective toward conservation, integrating social concerns into a conservation agenda.

Nash, R. 1976/1982. *Wilderness and the American Mind,* 3rd ed. New Haven: Yale University Press.

A classic historical work on American attitudes toward nature.

Olwig, K. and K. Olwig. 1979. "Underdevelopment and the Development of 'Natural' Park Ideology." *Antipode* 11(2):17–25. [p. 107]

Structuralist analysis describing the suffering of local populations who have lost access to resources in a park in the Caribbean; it argues that parks serve urban elite of industrialized countries.

O'Riordan, T. 1981. *Environmentalism.* London: Pion.

A useful reference text which provides an overview and analysis of the history of the conservation movement as well as a number of contemporary environmental issues with a North American and British focus.

Tuan, Y.–F. 1971. *Man and Nature.* Washington, DC: Association of American Geographers.

Tuan, Y.–F. 1974. *Topophilia: A Study of Environmental Perception, Attitudes, and Values.* Englewood Cliffs, NJ: Prentice-Hall.

Explores society–nature relations, including how a sense of place (and love for a place) is developed in individuals.

Williams, M. 1989. *Americans and their Forests: A Historical Geography.* Cambridge: Cambridge University Press.

A massive work describing the meaning of the forest in American history and culture. Describes forest use from pre-European times to the present.

Worster, D. 1977. *Nature's Economy: A History of Ecological Ideas.* Cambridge: Cambridge University Press.

Provides a historical overview of the development of ecological thinking and perspectives on people–environment relations in various disciplines.

RECOMMENDED JOURNALS: *Progress in Human Geography* and *Antipode*

Spatial Analysis

Mason, R. J. and M. T. Mattson. 1990. *Atlas of United States Environmental Issues*. New York: Macmillan Publishing.

Presents a variety of local and regional environmental data on maps to visually illustrate the complexity of environmental issues.

Muehrcke, P. C. 1980. *Map Use: Reading, Analysis, and Interpretation*, rev. ed. Madison, WI: JP Publications. [pp. 104, 105]

A comprehensive introduction to map use that is easily accessible to the student and full of examples of concepts presented in text.

Odland, J., R. G. Golledge, and P. A. Rogerson. 1989. "Mathematical and Statistical Analysis in Human Geography." In *Geography in America*. G. L. Gaile and C. J. Willmott, eds. Columbus, OH: Merrill Publishing Company.

Stuart, G. E. 1992. "Maya Heartland Under Siege." *National Geographic* 182(5):94–107. [p. 105]

Demonstrates how satellite imagery can be employed to illustrate land use threats to Maya Biosphere Reserve and other protected areas in Guatemala.

RECOMMENDED JOURNALS: *GIS World*; *Cartography and Geographic Information Systems*; *International Journal of GIS*; *Photogrammetic Engineering and Remote Sensing (PE & RS)*; and *GEOCARTO International: A Multidisciplinary Journal of Remote Sensing*.

Maps

Burton, J. A. 1991. *The Atlas of Endangered Species*. New York: Macmillan Publishing Company.

Provides an overview of problems facing species at risk in different biogeographic regions and includes numerous photos and maps.

Carroll, C. S. 1991. *El Malpais Conservation Area and National Monument*. Albuquerque, NM: U.S. Bureau of Land Management. [p. 105]

Map models biophysical units with a geographical information system to illustrate ecological responses (i.e., in space and time) to biophysical and cultural influences.

Dahl, T. E. 1991. *Wetland Resources of the United States.* St Petersburg, FL: U.S. Fish and Wildlife Service.

Map illustrating the extent of wetlands in the United States.

De Souza, A., ed. 1992. "The Coexistence of Indigenous People and the Natural Environment in Central America." *National Geographic Research and Exploration* 8(2):232–240. (See also in same issue, M. Chapin, "Field Notes: Indigenous Peoples and the Environment in Central America," pp. 232–234.)

Order from Research and Exploration, National Geographic Society, P.O. Box 1111, Washington, DC 20013–9990.

Garver, J. B. 1990. "Africa Threatened." *National Geographic* 182(6):insert.

A colorfully illustrated map representing plant and animal species at risk on the African continent.

Lean, G. and D. Hinrichsen. 1994. *Atlas of the Environment.* Santa Barbara, CA: ABC-CLIO.

Offers basic information about natural and human environments, along with the impacts of people on the environment. Includes maps, charts, graphs, etc.

Acknowledgments

In preparing this chapter, we received valuable comments from several "conservation–minded" geographers, in particular B. Brower, O. Coomes, K. Dow, R. Doughty, K. Foote, P. Keating, B. Sterrenberg, B. L. Turner II, and T. Vale. W. M. Denevan and W. E. Doolittle offered particularly valuable suggestions for geographic references—including works both classic and exploratory. We also greatly appreciate Katherine Robbins' editorial skills.

Chapter 6

History

John Opie
New Jersey Institute of Technology
and

Michael Black
San Francisco–based policy analyst

The great environmental essayist, Loren Eiseley, tells of a stroll through some woods while his dog Beau raced around in excitement. "I looked on, interested and sympathetic, but aware that the big black animal lived in a smell prison as I, in my way, lived in a sight prison." Each generation has its own view about Nature's embrace. Considering the 25 generations since 1500, each lived in its own "prison" shaped by technological agility, language, and history. Hindsight can create its own sentimental blinders. Fifty years ago we believed that the Indians lived in an untouched primeval forest; today we know Native Americans did much to shape their environment for their benefit, like regular forest burning to create better deer habitats. We also know their touch was lighter than ours. Our environments, past and present, are always moving points on moving lines.

When European settlers arrived in the unexpected New World, they located their new geography in the frame of the classic three-storied universe of Heaven, Earth, and Hell. Colonial Puritans believed the demonic underworld erupted to the surface bearing frightening witches and their familiars. A more secular Enlightenment view imagined the world as a tidy mechanism that could become known by scientific laws and exploited by new technologies. Modern capitalism and industrialization imprisoned the environment as a mere commodity. Today, the view from space shows Earth as a small and vulnerable globe where humanity paradoxically still claims ownership.

There are at least three ways in which our views of the world's environment can affect how we see the human experience, past, present, and future. First, it can be treated as humanity's fixed physical base that undergirds our economics, politics, society, and culture. Most history textbooks will have one physiographic map as a frontispiece; they hardly refer to America's physical environment again except in simple maps of continental expansion. We must include lessons on how beliefs about a landscape also changed over time. The first European visitors only gradually experienced America's geography, which began for them as an unknown eastern edge of an unknown "barrier island" to the fabled Orient. Just as colonial Americans did not know that a revolution and independence were coming, they had no idea that the new nation might include a Midwest over the horizon or a West to the distant Pacific. Doubtless they could never have imagined a cornucopia of consumer goods nor an interstate highway system that would allow them to cross the nation in tens of millions of private vehicles, simultaneously clouding and poisoning the air.

Second, an environmental viewpoint can be a template by which to measure success or failure in civilizations, past and present. Most textbook approaches have generally discounted environmental problems like resource depletion or the real costs of pollution. Thus an environmental viewpoint is usually a revisionist critique arguing that these earlier approaches are excessively exploitative and wasteful of the nation's biological and physical heritage. Often environmentalists feel a deep current of melancholia. The philosopher John Tallmadge wrote of Aldo Leopold, "To love a place is to suffer doubly when it perishes. . . . The price of ecological wisdom is loneliness, isolation and an aching sense of loss. . . .Leopold finds truth in the wilderness and comes back to warn a society with little sense of its own spiritual danger. . . .He takes his place with Thoreau as an American Jeremiad, judging his culture against the standard of wild nature" (Tallmadge 1987, p. 122). There is a lot of truth to this revisionist approach, but it remains adversarial and divisive, and it lacks breadth.

A third approach can treat humanity and nature as integrated, not oppositional, by exploring the relationship in a holistic and inclusive way. From such a perspective the world's environment—global, regional, or local—is itself perpetually dynamic and infrequently predictable. This viewpoint offers a multidimensional plane that combines the environment (seen through the eyes of ecological science) with the political process, economic development, social institutions, cultural change, and intellectual life. Changing public perceptions—"climates of opinion"—

are powerful forces molding how humanity has interacted with its environment over time. Thus the human invasion of any wilderness, together with its settlement, domestication, and emergence into today's urban industrial landscape, goes through multifold changes of psychological attitude, technological power, and societal need involving the environment as humanity's "living tether." This viewpoint does not deny human technological dominance of the environment by seeking to return to some idyllic "golden age." More realistically, it informs contemporary environmental conflicts (and, with luck, future trends) by uncovering their historic foundations. This third approach simultaneously can offer an attractive reinterpretation of history.

COURSE PLANS

Lower Division Courses

Global Environmental History: The Legacy of Western European Conquest (full course)

Course Description and Objectives. The package of six units described below could also form the core of an entire course that can substitute for the traditional freshman–sophomore course in Western Civilization, 1500–present. Alternatively, the first three units can be taught in other basic survey courses as two-week units (six one-hour classes each). Units four through six can similarly be covered in two weeks each, or, they are particularly effective as major class projects.

A journalist once asked Mahatma Gandhi what he thought of Western civilization. "Yes," he replied, "I think it would be a good idea." Gandhi's remark playfully unmasked a Eurocentric belief system that, by the 15th century, comfortably rationalized a worldwide pattern of European imperial conquest. We can do no better than quote from William Woodruff (1966):

> All civilizations have transferred ideas about man, as well as ideas about art, science, and technology, but until the European Age no civilization had transferred them on a world-wide scale, with such speed, with such a degree of activity, or with such tremendous effect; in so many parts of the world Europe's intrusion shattered the traditional static order of things. No civilization prior to the European had occasion to believe in the systematic material progress of the whole human race. . . . It makes no difference to argue that much of the promised gold of progress has proved to be dust. Mankind is not drunk with this idea of progress because of what it has achieved in a material and physical sense, but because of what it promises. The idea that with western methods there might be removed from man

the eternal haunting skeleton of want is so powerful that it might well, for a period, capture the imagination of the whole human race. (pp. 16–17)

From an environmental perspective, today's global dominance by Western ideals and institutions has not been universally enlightening or beneficial.

UNIT 1. MODERNIZATION AND EUROPEANIZATION

Why did the world become dominated by European thinking and culture, rather than, say, Chinese or Moslem? A combination of forces—aggressive competing national states, Renaissance Humanism, and superior military technologies—did much to assure European domination. A Eurocentric perspective was also attractive because of its emphasis on material well-being—the higher standard of living apparently reachable through industrialization.

Readings

• McNeill 1964, *The Rise of the West*
• Headrick 1981, *The Tools of Empire: Technology and European Imperialism in the Nineteenth Century,* chapters 4, 5, and 7 on European weapons, chapters 9 and 13 on steamboats and railroads

UNIT 2. RATIONALISM, SCIENCE, TECHNOLOGY, AND SECULARIZATION

European values and institutions became worldwide between 1500 and today. Contrary to the usual textbook view, they created a distinctive point of view sometimes called European "hubris" (meaning overweening pride in being aggressive, zealous, bigoted, and perhaps self-destructive). It was a contradictory combination of Christian exclusiveness and missionary zeal, of the materialism of capitalism and consumerism, and of scientific rationalism. Non-European views, often based on ancient mythic traditions, tolerance, and the sacredness of nature, have been largely discarded. The result is the worldwide spread of an anti-environmentalism that sees nature as solely consisting of natural resources, of little intrinsic value—raw material to be mastered.

Readings

• Mumford 1970, *The Pentagon of Power*, chapters 3, 5, 6, and 10
• Berman 1981, *The Reenchantment of the World,* chapters 1, 3, and 4

UNIT 3. ECOLOGICAL IMPERIALISM

Recent research details the environmental impact of European global expansion. Europeans carried with them powerful nonhuman organisms, plants, animals, and virulent diseases that reshaped local and regional environments. European "nuisance" diseases such as measles, smallpox, and tuberculosis wiped out millions of native peoples in the Americas and thus allowed relatively easy European conquest of the New World. The exchanges of plants and animals between Old and New World transformed human and environmental history: large draft animals, such as the horse, ox, cow, and donkey were introduced into the New World and crops like the potato and corn into the Old World.

Reading
• Crosby 1972, *The Columbian Exchange,* chapters 1, 2, and 3

UNIT 4 (or major course project). AGRICULTURE, SCORCHED EARTH, AND THE COMMON WEED

This is based on a student survey of local indigenous plant and animal species. Seek out several local botanists or thoroughly knowledgeable members of a local native plant society. (1) Under the experts' tutelage have students inventory a small patch of accessible, relatively untouched land. Be sure that students exercise particular care in cataloging surviving native plant species. (2) Use historic materials to reconstruct what this landscape may have looked like prior to the arrival of European émigrés. (3) Identify which fauna coevolved with native flora and catalogue remnants of what remains. (4) Would undertaking a sustained effort at ecological restoration make sense in that particular landscape? (5) What managerial strategies would be required to sustain a serious restoration effort? Would community protests likely occur? Why?

Readings
• Crosby 1986, "Weeds." In *Ecological Imperialism*
• Jackson 1980, *New Roots for Agriculture.* Read the entire work.

UNIT 5 (or major course project). EUROPEANS LOST IN ALIEN ENVIRONMENTS: COMPARING CONRAD'S *HEART OF DARKNESS* WITH COPPOLLA'S "APOCALYPSE NOW."

The film about America's ill-fated Vietnam War was roughly based on Conrad's novella about European self-degradation in central Africa, with a common character in the mysterious Kurtz and a common theme of the journey up river into the great unknown as a mythic rite of passage. Going up the river, be it the Congo or the Mekong, was like a regression back in time to a terrifying primitiveness that Europeans say they have conquered, but that recaptures them (the primal opposite of Kubrick's 2001. Is HAL the equivalent of Kurtz?). The river charms them like a snake charms a chicken. A gunboat shells the African shore, and "nothing happened"; the heavily armed patrol boat blasts away into the Southeast Asian jungle pointlessly and just as ineffectually. In both novella and film a primary theme is the collapse of European civilization's veneer, including its vaunted technology and compelling hubris, as it encounters an entirely alien world that it only appears to master. In both cases Kurtz is feared because he has "gone native," done the unthinkable by denying European civilization, and therefore must be eliminated. Both novella and film end up damning white man's pretense. Conrad has the company say, "What saves us is efficiency," while Coppolla's Kurtz speaks of someone being "clear in his mind but his soul is blind" (also like Melville's Ahab: "All my methods are sane but my goal is insane"). The moral is that there are still natural and cultural environments beyond European understanding, like central Africa or Southeast Asia, which also show that Europeans do not know their own souls despite their technological agility. We in the West, like Icarus, are quite far removed from the gods.

Reading

• Kimbrough, ed. 1988. *Norton Critical Edition of Joseph Conrad, Heart of Darkness.* Contains an excellent analysis of both novella and film. Coppolla's film is readily available as a video.

UNIT 6 (or major course project). THE "LIMITS TO GROWTH" DEBATE

In 1972 the European think-tank, the Club of Rome, funded the controversial research project and book by Donella H. Meadows and an MIT simulation team, *The Limits to Growth.* It became the first computer-based analysis of global economic and environmental forces. The book was controversial because it argued, in opposition to the dynamic of Western materialism, capitalism, and economic growth incentives, that there are naturally impassable limits to population growth, industrialization, pollution, food production, and resource depletion. Herman Kahn and his Hudson Institute, among others, took exception, and the debate polarized within several themes:

• world as finite pie or unlimited pie

• technology and capital as largely illusory/counterproductive versus their capacity to "solve almost all problems"

• resources are steadily depleted versus continuous discovery of new resources

• current growth rates are cancerous versus growth is desirable and healthy

• new technologies produce more and new problems versus technology as essentially benign and good
• poverty and injustice are real and growing problems versus misformulated problems
• industrialization can be disastrous versus necessary for wealth and progress
• quality of life in decline versus the future will be better

The debate led to the current discussions concerning "sustainable development," meaning our right to our own well-being without penalizing the right of future generations to their own well-being. (See discussion of the same theme in Chapter 4, Economics.)

Readings
• World Commission 1987, selections from *Our Common Future*
• Meadows et al. 1992, *Beyond the Limits*

American Environmental History (units for an introductory course in United States History)

Unit Objectives. The two units described below will introduce students to spatial and environmental awareness. The first is particularly effective early in the course; it can lead to excellent class presentations by students as well as provocative discussion. At least two class periods are needed, and four are recommended. The second unit effectively involves students with their contemporary urban environment.

UNIT 1. COGNITIVE MAPPING: LEARNING TO READ YOUR PERSONAL HISTORY IN YOUR NEIGHBORHOOD ENVIRONMENT

As a teaching tool to encourage better understanding of the role of the immediate geographical setting in human history, students are asked to draw a map of their home neighborhood at age 11 (6th grade). At that age they are still curious, home-centered kids but have greater mobility, can ride bikes but not yet drive a car. Have students mark out the routes and landmarks on the way to school, friends' homes, parks and sports fields, school, church, relatives' homes, stores, and other common destinations. Be certain to color key friendly and hostile places (where the dog bit them or the bully beat them up). Give some indication of terrain. Most students will find a zone approximately one mile square, unless they live on a farm or are army brats or immigrants. This exercise teaches geographical awareness, a sense of place, and the importance of environmental memory.

Reading

- Meinig 1978, *The Interpretation of Ordinary Landscapes.* Read several provocative essays, especially "The Beholding Eye: Ten Versions of the Same Scene."

UNIT 2. LEARNING TO READ HISTORY IN THE URBAN LANDSCAPE

In our case we used the city of Newark, New Jersey, which students first saw as forbidding. Many of the nation's inner cities have "disappeared" or are forgotten places, seemingly erased from public consciousness. Or they give rise to stereotypes that include drugs, violence, destitution, AIDS, environmental pollution, all pointing to dystopia. But cities are our ultimate artifacts. The environmental simulation game, *SimCity,* is a particularly thought-provoking tool. Students can also learn the environmental infrastructure (the "living tether") of a place by studying the incomparable Sanford Fire Insurance maps (available in many large or research libraries) for most major U.S. cities, which show streets, buildings, water mains and lines, electrical systems, underground tunnels, etc. Visits to the local city engineer and to the property archives are also useful. Students need to compare this "library" work with on-the-street analysis of a manageable urban space like an intersection or a commercial block. The emphasis here is how technological actions create environmental problems that can only be understood in broad infrastructural terms.

Reading

- Watts 1975, *Reading the Landscape of America.* Entertaining and provocative. Will be hard to put down.

Environmental History of the United States *(topics for individual course units, not necessarily in sequence)*

UNIT 1. THE COLUMBIAN EXCHANGE

This topic is taken from Alfred Crosby's pathbreaking study of the impact of new plants, new animals, and especially disease upon the New World. Crosby adds to these environmental impacts the aggressiveness and insensitivity of white Europeans to the richness and diversity of the New World.

Readings

- Crosby 1972, *The Columbian Exchange*
- Crosby 1986, *Ecological Imperialism*

UNIT 2. NATIVE AMERICANS

The story is now familiar that the Indians, while vulnerable before European technology and hubris, enjoyed sophisticated cultures with features that could be called superior to their European invaders, including their "light" touch on the environment.

Reading
- Cronon 1983, *Changes in the Land,* a pathfinding comparison between native and Puritan uses of the wilderness

UNIT 3. PEOPLE OF THE LAND

Our urban industrial society tends to forget that most of human history was hunter-gatherer and thereafter agricultural. In 1800, nine out of ten Americans lived on the farm; in 1930, it was still 30 percent; today it is 2 percent. Farm life everywhere was closely connected with the land, seasons, and climate.

Readings
- Cronon 1983, *Changes in the Land*
- Merchant 1989, *Ecological Revolutions*
- Williams 1989, *Americans and Their Forests*

UNIT 4. THE CHANGING POLITICAL GEOGRAPHY OF THE UNITED STATES

American expansion across the continent was every bit as dramatic but much less influential than independence from England. Independence from the crown forced political experimentation with representative government. While eastern industrial cities adopted highly centralized, Hamiltonian solutions to governance, isolated frontier living invited absolute reliance upon neighbors. These highly atomized, Jeffersonian solutions to government among frontier communities nonetheless remained at odds with the ideology of liberty, with the requirement of state intervention to deliver and maintain essential services like water mobilization, and with intrusive monopolies such as the railroads. Make selections from the concepts, units, and bibliography below for an upper level course, The American West in Environmental Perspective.

UNIT 5. WILDERNESS ROMANTICISM

Americans began to idealize the "untouched wilderness" as a paradise instead of a dangerous place. This utopian "Original America" was the place of recovery, renewal, cleansing, and purification. A major pantheon of writers promoted the importance of wilderness: Henry David Thoreau, Ralph Waldo Emerson, John Wesley Powell, John Muir, Loren Eiseley, Joseph Wood Krutch, Edward Abbey, Annie Dillard, and others.

Readings
- R. Nash 1983, *Wilderness and the American Mind*
- Oelschlaeger 1991, *The Idea of Wilderness.* May be too challenging except for advanced classes.

UNIT 6. ENVIRONMENTAL COSTS OF INDUSTRIAL AMERICA

Industrial wastes, treated as economic "externalities," were dumped into the public "commons" for generations. Today's cleanup, to save the health of the nation, will cost hundreds of billions of dollars indefinitely into the future. It is a sad and terrible burden upon our children, grandchildren, and future generations. (See Chapter 4, Economics.)

Readings
- Barbour et al. 1982, *Energy and American Values*
- Petulla 1988, *American Environmental History,* especially chapter 9
- Opie, forthcoming, *United States Environmental History,* especially chapters on industrialization and pollution

If more traditional units are desired in a class, we recommend a close examination of historical resources in Merchant (1993), while major contemporary environmental issues are covered well in Goldfarb (1993).

Upper Division Courses

The American West in Environmental Perspective (two sample units)

Course Description and Objectives. The American West, particularly when it is treated as a frontier region, is commonly offered as an upper level undergraduate (or graduate) course. The two units below, each intended for two weeks (six one-hour classes), represent current environmental approaches. The first is useful because it puts the famous Turner "frontier thesis" of American history in environmental perspective. The second reflects the attempts of environmental historians to take a fresh look at geographical regions.

Because environmental changes have been so dramatically compressed in a relatively short time and accelerated by new technologies, the American West is a microcosm where the changing relationship between humanity and the nonhuman world is vividly displayed. All of humanity's technological and cultural shifts of the past 25,000 years are concentrated in a single rectangular region 1500 by 1000 miles that leaped from a subsistence economy to a consumer society, sometimes in less than 50 years, as was the case with California's hydraulic civilization. The West's settlement and modernization are more recent, more fluid, and more clearly dependent upon a local geography than in the East, such as the mix of climate, soil, and groundwater on the Kansas High Plains or in California's San Joaquin Valley. Patricia Limerick writes that western settlement provided, "a more focused and revealing case study of how the United States as a nation conducted conquest."

UNIT 1. ENVIRONMENTAL HISTORY AND THE TURNER THESIS

Here we compare the usual romantic and idealistic view of the frontier with a highly critical environmental perspective. Frederick Jackson Turner was honestly shocked when in 1890 he first learned that the nation's frontier had ended. To Turner, American expansion into its empty western regions provided the stimulus for a unique national character: "The wilderness masters the colonist." It was both a *place*, the zone of free land beyond the western edge of settlement, and a *process*, where old habits fell before the pragmatic needs of wilderness survival. While the Turner Thesis is perhaps the single most powerful and long-lasting interpretation ever put forth by an American historian, it soon began stirring up scathing criticism. Critics argued that single-cause explanations of American history failed to account, among other phenomena, for urbanization, immigration, and industrialization, much less British and Continental influences. Yet, even in the late 20th century, Americans are still drawn to Turner's frontier thesis.

Environmental historians have shed Turner's triumphal story for a tragic and cautionary tale about unrelenting European conquest. Participants in a "New Western History" observe that western landscapes were treated as wasted empty land until the white man's intervention. Europeans moved single-mindedly to guarantee the fastest possible capital growth regardless of the long-term consequences. Europeans wiped out existing Indian societies that enjoyed a close and vital relationship with nature. "Gut and get out" was the true European spirit, as Frank Norris once wrote about California. As a result, millions of tons of soil eroded away, extremely scarce water was wasted and polluted, limited supplies of gold, silver, copper, oil, and coal were extracted from the ground, and wilderness began to disappear forever. Donald Worster adds that, "Far from being a child of nature, the West was actually given birth by modern technology and bears all the scars of that fierce gestation, like a baby born of an addict."

Readings

- Cronon 1987, "Revisiting the Vanishing Frontier: The Legacy of Frederick Jackson Turner"
- Opie 1982, "Frederick Jackson Turner, the Old West, and the Formation of a National Mythology"
- Ridge 1991, "The Life of an Idea: the Significance of Frederick Jackson Turner's Frontier Thesis"
- Turner [1893] (1962), "The Significance of the Frontier in American History"

UNIT 2. LEARNING TO READ A FOREST

Nature may offer continuous and infinite interpretive flexibility. One seemingly unambiguous natural phenomenon—a forest—is better understood as several different entities, resources, and phenomena. A forest is actually a complex of meanings belonging to different human groups. This flexibility counters environmental determinism. One starts with the different social groups, such as Europeans or Indians, and looks through their eyes at the forest. Indeed, it is impossible not to look through someone's eyes at the forest; it cannot be examined autonomously. The forest is the same though its reality is unknowable since it is always seen through someone's filter. This could also be called the Rashomon effect, and it is akin to the Heisenberg indeterminacy principal in physical science.

In all these cases, the forest is a "black box" which we only know from different points of view but which we can still learn about from comparisons. What we really learn is that each human community has problems with the forest for which it finds solutions. The forest is gradually constructed (or deconstructed) for use through the different community interactions with it. This contingency, or dependence upon highly individualized human viewpoints, is unnerving because it challenges any sense of fixity or permanence, or "constancy in history." An environmental determinism would give such permanence, but it would remove possibilities for change and circumscribe freedom of choice.

In fact, when a forest is cut down for firewood or to build a fence, or the trees cleared to plant corn, certain cultural choices are made which reduce or eliminate possibilities for change. (But does the forest have its own purpose, and can we discover this purpose?) When Indians burned the forest regularly to create a better habitat for more deer, they also began to limit their own future choices. Thus interpretive flexibility need not mean total relativism. A human community cuts down or burns the forest based on its cultural goals, while the forest is definitely changed when it is cut down or burned. Other human groups might have left it in its primeval state or replaced it with "another" forest.

Reading
• Williams 1989, *Americans and Their Forests*

California's Environmental History: Farewell Promised Land? (a full course)

Course Description and Objectives. An environmental approach brings a fresh look at the history of several American regions. Such courses are usually upper level undergraduate and sometimes graduate courses. The studies by Cronon (1983) and Merchant (1989) reinvented New England's historical environment. Donald Worster's (1979) study of the Dust Bowl compelled another look at human impacts upon the Great Plains of the 1930s. No American region has received more attention as an environmental problem than California. Each of the units listed below is intended for two weeks (six class sessions). Since many of California's environmental problems are connected with national agendas, several of the units can be readily applied to non-California courses.

Long ago C. S. Lewis (1947) observed in *The Abolition of Man* that "what we call Man's power over Nature turns out to be a power exercised by some men over other men with Nature as its instrument." This course explores the meteoric transformation of California's physical geography. As such, it also records the rise to power of certain interests, particularly urban elite in San Francisco and Los Angeles. We can travel to any region in the state and observe the profound role of human beings as environmental agents. For example, over the past 150 years, California's vast interior valley, the Great Central Valley, was transformed from "the Serengeti of North America" into a "vanished landscape." In the valley's southeastern reaches, the Tulare Lake basin, a naturally occurring lake once the size of Rhode Island, no longer exists as such today. Its waters have been siphoned off, at great taxpayer expense, for private agricultural and urban use. Tulare Lake was drained, its wetlands plowed under and replaced by agribusiness. Today the lake bed is only visible as architectonic grids superimposed on a fleetingly lucrative, pliable landscape. While dramatic, the Tulare Lake Basin is only one of thousands of such examples one can cite in the environmental alteration of California.

Additional readings, not included in the course plans, are identified in the section of the Resources list entitled "The Environmental Destruction of California" at the close of this chapter. This course can make creative use of a mix of fictional and nonfictional accounts, articles, still photography, films, museum visitations, on-site field studies, and existing primary historical materials, to document environmental change in California. For those willing to invest the time and energy, it can also serve as a model for constructing a course based on other regions of the country.

UNIT 1. SAN FRANCISCO, HETCH HETCHY VALLEY, AND THE FOUNDING OF THE SIERRA CLUB

In its bid to grab water for further urban expansion, San Francisco's elite triggered a backlash. Hetch Hetchy is the legendary valley that, like its Sierran neighbor, Yosemite Valley, sparked an environmental movement. The Glenn Canyon of its day, Hetch Hetchy was stoppered like a bathtub to make a city bloom. San Francisco's water travels underground some 148 miles from the watery remains of the 1,970 acre valley to Crystal Springs Reservoir. Today the 430-foot O'Shaughnessy Dam is the only structure of its kind within the existing boundaries of a national park. While conservationists like Gifford Pinchot argued that the project was an "improvement upon Nature," the decision to build the dam was principally about political power. Opposition to its construction was led by naturalist John Muir and sparked the founding of the Sierra Club. However it was not an easy contest. San Francisco's argonauts fought a protracted, 12-year, Congressional struggle that culminated in the 1913 signing of the Raker Act and the flooding of a magnificent landscape.

Readings

- Black in press, *California's Last Salmon: The Unnatural Policies of Natural Resource Agencies,* chapter 1
- Hanson 1987, *Beyond San Francisco Water and Power: A History of the Municipal Water Department and Hetch Hetchy System*
- Muir 1988, *The Yosemite*
- Wilkinson 1991, "No Holier Temple: Responses to Hodel's Hetch Hetchy Proposal"

UNIT 2. FREDERICK LAW OLMSTED VERSUS WILLIAM HAMMOND HALL: THE CREATION OF SAN FRANCISCO'S GOLDEN GATE PARK

Landscape architect Frederick Law Olmsted toured California and the arid West between 1863 and 1865. The co-creator of New York's famed Central Park, Olmsted urged San Franciscans to think twice before establishing a water-thirsty, English pastoral park along the city's western edge. After extensive observation, Olmsted concluded that replicating an English, Constable-like landscape with great expanses of luxuriant lawns would be wholly inappropriate to an arid western landscape. He reasoned that California required a unique style of regional landscape, one best suited to a dry Mediterranean climate. In part because of his views, Olmsted was refused the commission to build Golden Gate Park.

In 1871, William Hammond Hall, San Francisco's new park superintendent, undertook the controversial task of forging a park out of what critics then described as a "Sahara Desert." Consisting of 1,017 acres of lawns, gardens, arboretum, lakes, and woodland, the park was built upon shifting Pacific sands. The park used local and imported water and made few concessions to the fundamental climate of the region.

Readings
- Black in press, "Searching for a Genius of Place: The Ambiguous Legacy of Golden Gate Park"
- Clary 1987, *The Making of Golden Gate Park, The Early Years: 1865–1906*
- Beveridge 1990, "Introduction to the Landscape Design Reports: The California Origins of Olmsted's Landscape Design Principles for the Semiarid American West"

Site Visitation. Take a walking tour throughout the park and contrast this landscape with that found just to the north in San Francisco's historic "Presideo." For a truer sense of arid California's landscape, contrast these contrived landscapes with that found on the "barren" Marin headlands, just beyond the Golden Gate Bridge. Why are the two landscape aesthetics irreconcilable?

UNIT 3. THE GREAT WATER GRAB: LOS ANGELES VERSUS
THE OWENS RIVER VALLEY

In California, it is said that "water flows uphill toward money." Los Angeles versus the Owens River Valley dramatically illustrates this proposition, whereby a sleepy, mountainous eastern agricultural community awoke one morning to learn its waters had been corralled by LA's powerful Metropolitan Water District (MWD). LA's power brokers—men like Floyd Dominy and Robert Mullholland—were urban water rustlers of the first order. They cast their water-thirsty shadows regionwide, constructing a massive water retrieval system. Immortalized in the film "Chinatown," Owens Valley ranchers suddenly discovered that their chief water supply sources had been clandestinely bought up by MWD representatives. Owens Valley residents mobilized to challenge the aqueous land-grab, but to no avail. Finally, out of sheer frustration laced with desperation, some valley residents responded by blowing up a portion of LA's Owen's Valley pipeline. Thanks to its imperial water architects, LA was free to grow at its neighbors' expense.

Readings

- Walton 1992, *Western Times and Water Wars: State, Culture, and Repression in California*
- Reisner 1986, *Cadillac Desert: The American West and Its Disappearing Water*, chapter 10, "Chinatown"
- Worster 1985, *Rivers of Empire: Water, Aridity and the Growth of the American West*, chapter 2, "The Flow of Power Through History"
- See also the films: "The Milagro Beanfield War" and "Chinatown"

UNIT 4. EDIBLE ICONS: THE PASSING OF CALIFORNIA'S SALMON

California's Sacramento River is, after the Columbia River, the second largest waterway in the western United States and the 43rd largest worldwide by volume. It remains California's premiere habitat for salmon and steelhead. Yet as Joel Hedgpeth and Nancy Reichard lament, what distinguished Central Valley rivers from the rest is that "probably no river system in the country is under the stress of greater use in proportion to its size than California's Central Valley rivers."

Nowhere is that evidence of adverse pressure more visible than among dwindling salmon stocks. As fish conservationist William Kier observes, among today's Central Valley streams as a whole, "salmon and steelhead are cut off from 95 percent of their traditional spawning grounds." The Sacramento has always accounted for roughly 70 percent of California's anadromous fisheries stocks. Today, the winter and spring Chinook salmon runs on the Sacramento River are nearing extinction. During calendar year 1993, the river's surviving winter run numbered 186 fish; few spawned. In 1994, less than 1,000 spring-run Chinook returned to complete their epochal cycle. Both stocks of fish are now listed under the state's Endangered Species Act. Dams alone wiped out a total of 19 Central Valley populations of spring-run chinook. Other indignities included extreme overfishing, the wholesale destruction of wetlands, extensive water diversion, and the rise of industrial agriculture. Our dwindling salmonids, like canaries in the proverbial mineshaft, remind us that whole chains of California's ecosystems are in a virtual state of collapse.

Readings

- Black in press, *California's Last Salmon: The Unnatural Policies of Natural Resource Agencies*
- Lufkin 1991, *California's Salmon and Steelhead: The Struggle to Restore an Imperiled Resource*, chapters 1, 4, 5, 6, and 9
- McEvoy 1990, *The Fisherman's Problem*, chapters 1–5

UNIT 5. HYDRAULIC MINING, METALLURGY, AND ENVIRONMENTAL
APOCALYPSE

In 1848, the primary means of harvesting California's gold was a sheath
knife or prospector's pan. As the sources for gold diversified, the technology of choice abruptly shifted toward extraordinary reliance upon
water. In March 1853, New Englander Edward E. Matteson invented
hydraulic mining by dropping vast quantities of water some 400 feet or
more onto the site of an ancient river bed. Under immense pressure, 16-
foot, cast iron water cannons called "monitors" or "dictators" redirected
nature's stored energy against mountainsides and river bottoms.
Through 9-inch nozzles, 30,000 gallons a minute poured onto dissolving
hillsides, carrying anything and everything in its wake. "Hydrauliking,"
as it was dubbed, constituted a form of virtual warfare against the earth
itself. Within its first five years of operation, California's hydraulic army
constructed 5,000 miles of ditches and flumes statewide, a figure that
would double by decade's end. It is estimated that within a 30-year
period (circa 1850–1880) some 1.5 billion cubic yards of debris cascaded
out of the mountains and into California's Central Valley. As Alan Lufkin
(1991) notes, that's enough debris to "pave a mile-wide superfreeway one
foot thick from Seattle to San Diego." With staggering environmental
consequences, a displaced glacier of rock and earth worked its way into
the valley below, covering 18,000 acres of farmland and raising the Yuba
River's bed some 60 feet above its previous elevation. It wasn't until January 1884 that Judge Lorenzo Sawyer of the Federal Ninth Circuit Court
in San Francisco ordered an immediate halt to hydraulic mining. However, far from a strike for environmental protection, the "Sawyer Decision" was a victory of one kind of private property over another, of agriculture over gold fever.

Readings
- McPhee 1993, "Annals of the Former World"
- Brechin in press, *Imperial San Francisco,* chapter 2, "Mining as
  Model and Apocalypse"
- Smith 1987, *Mining America: The Industry and the Environment,
  1800–1980*

Fine Arts Photography. A fine collection of selected prints from photog-
rapher Carlton Watkin's early work hangs in the west corridor of the
Hearst Mining Building at the University of California, Berkeley. Repro-
ductions of still photography are from the mid to late 1800s and show the
devastation wrought by the mining of Sierran landscapes.

Site Visitations
- New Almaden State Historic Park, 12 miles south of San Jose, Cali-

fornia, where cinnabar (mercury/quicksilver) was quarried. By 1860 this was the largest single hardrock mine in the West. Since quicksilver was essential to recovering gold ore, "this mine was the master gear that made everything else work" (Brechin in press).

- Malikoff State Historic Park, near the town of North San Juan, California, in Yuba County. The Malikoff diggings were among the most famous examples of hydraulic mining in California. One passes through the remains of many hydraulic mines en route to this state historic park.

Resources

Annotated Background Readings for the Instructor

THE CONCEPT OF ENVIRONMENTAL HISTORY

To enter some of the most recent discussions, see "Environmental History: A Round Table" (1990); White (1985), "American Environmental History: The Development of a New Historical Field"; and Worster's essay, "The Vulnerable Earth: Toward a Planetary History," in Worster (1988). See also essays by Bird (1987), "The Social Construction of Nature: Theoretical Approaches to the History of Environmental Problems," and Merchant (1987), "The Theoretical Structure of Ecological Revolutions." Any review of the meaning of environmental history must include a look at Worster's two books, *The Ends of the Earth* (1988), and *The Wealth of Nature* (1993). See also the contrasting views by Flores (1994), "Place: An Argument for Bioregional History," and compare to Worster (1994), "Nature and the Disorder of History."

A special curriculum issue of *Environmental History Review* (Piasecki 1992) contains 18 detailed syllabi covering environmental history, interdisciplinary studies, natural science, and humanities, including courses by Cronon, Merchant, Dunlap, and Rothenberg. A professional society, The American Society for Environmental History, was established in 1976. It seeks an interdisciplinary understanding of the human experience of the environment by emphasizing the perspectives of history, the liberal arts, technology, and science. ASEH publishes the professional journal, *Environmental History Review,* available from the Center for Technology Studies, New Jersey Institute of Technology, Newark, NJ 07102.

Recent attempts at international environmental histories, with mixed results, are two volumes by Simmons (1989, 1993), *Changing the Face of the Earth* and *Environmental History*, as well as Ponting (1991), *A Green History of the World.* Cronon's (1991) *Nature's Metropolis* is said to be the forerunner of a fresh environment-based interpretation of American history. While the historical geographer D. W. Meinig (1986, 1993) claims not to do environmental history in his massive multivolume survey, *The Shaping of America*, it is a gold mine of resources. Thus far two volumes have been published, taking the story from 1500 to 1867.

Teachers who want to expand on specific areas can find assistance in Thomas (1956), *Man's Role in Changing the Face of the Earth;* Glacken (1967), *Traces on the Rhodian Shore;* Hughes (1972), *Ecology of the Ancient World*; Bilsky (1980), *Historical Ecology*; Bailes (1985), *Environmental History;* and Turner et al. (1992), *The Earth as Transformed by Human Action.* See also *State of the World* reports by the Worldwatch Institute (Brown et al.). Major aspects of global environmental history can also be found in complementary disciplines, particularly historical geography (see Chapter 5, Geography), economic history (Chapter 4, Economics), cultural anthropology (Chapter 2, Anthropology), as well as studies in climate change and other major global environmental issues.

We also recommend screening three computer simulations which can be a valuable adjunct to a number of courses.

(1) *SimCity* allows students to manage urban environmental infrastructures (city budgets, public works projects, roads and airports, electrical and water systems, factories, housing and lifestyle, waste and pollution problems) of seven existing cities around the world, or they can create their own city.

(2) *SimEarth* is based on James Lovelock's Gaia principle that treats the entire earth as a living organism that undergoes constant changes that are both natural and human-induced. Students learn the global implications of large-scale forces like the greenhouse effect, ozone damage, and acid rain, and local or regional impacts of urbanization, desertification, pollution, and toxic wastes.

(3) *SimLife* allows students to build their own ecosystems and give life to existing or new creatures at the genetic level. Students learn about genetics, food webs, mutations, extinctions, natural disasters, and the environmental effects of landforms, climate, fire, and human societies.

Each simulation works its effects through global, geological, and human time. The software is available in Macintosh or MS-DOS versions from most computer stores or from Maxis, 2 Theatre Square, Suite 230, Orinda, CA 94563-3346. Other environmental infrastructure simulations are beginning to appear on the educational, commercial, and consumer markets.

EUROPEAN EXPANSION AND IMPERIALISM

McNeill's (1964) classic undergraduate textbook, *The Rise of the West,* is a particularly lucid description of how Western values and institutions, often unique, parochial, and destructive, arose and spread worldwide. McNeill's themes are elaborated brilliantly by Headrick (1981) in *The Tools of Empire: Technology and European Imperialism in the Nineteenth Century*, and (1988) *The Tentacles of Progress: Technology Transfer in the Age of Imperialism, 1850–1940*, and also by Woodruff's (1966) largely ignored but insightful and comprehensive work, *A Study of Europe's Role in the World Economy, 1750–1960*. While difficult to read, Braudel's (1972, and 1981–84) two classic studies listed below concern the linkages between geography and material culture. Crosby's studies of the global environmental changes wrought by European invasion of the New World are equally essential reading and more accessible: (1972) *The Columbian Exchange* and (1986) *Ecological Imperialism: The Biological Expansion of Europe, 900–1900*. McNeill's (1976) *Plagues and Peoples* should not be missed.

INDUSTRIALIZATION AND GLOBAL ENVIRONMENTAL LIMITS TO ECONOMIC GROWTH

Mumford's (1967, 1970) two volumes, *The Myth of the Machine*, remain the classic critique of technology, industrialization, capitalism, and consumerism as destructive human and environmental forces worldwide. They are nicely complemented by Berman's (1981) *The Reenchantment of the World*, which is a vivid and critical analysis of the rise of secular rationalism in the early modern era. America's love affair with technology, notably railroads, bridges and skyscrapers, factories, electric power, the space program, and even nuclear weapons, is described well in Nye (1994), *American Technological Sublime*. For contrasting views on the debate over the "limits to growth" and sustainable development, compare Meadows et al. (1972), *The Limits to Growth*, and Cole et al. (1973), *Models of Doom: A Critique of the Limits to Growth*. This was followed up by a second edition of the Meadows book in 1974 and Mesarovic and Pestel's (1974) *Mankind at the Turning Point*. The debate was further enlarged by Hirsch's (1978) study, *Social Limits to Growth*. A pointed criticism of the concept of finite limits to earth's resources was presented in 1976 by Herman Kahn of the Hudson Institute in *The Next 200 Years*. See also Kahn's (1978) *World Economic Development: Projections from 1978 to the year 2000*.

The debate over limits to growth and environmental sustainability continued with Tinbergen's (1976) *Rio: Reshaping the International Order*, sponsored by the Club of Rome, as was Laszlo's (1977) *Goals for Mankind*. Aurelio Peccei, President of the Club of Rome, reviews this material in *One Hundred Pages for the Future*. A formidable addition to the debate came with *The Global 2000 Report to the President: Entering the Twenty-First Century*, commissioned by President Jimmy Carter in 1977. This received a rebuttal from many circles, notably in the volume edited by Simon and Kahn (1984), *The Resourceful Earth: A Response to 'Global 2000.'*

The most recent discussion opened in 1987 with the so-called "Bruntland Report" by the World Commission on Environment and Development. The Meadows team (1992) updated and revised their 1972 work in *Beyond the Limits.* To this should be added the major planning document, *Agenda 21,* for the Earth Summit '92, the United Nations Conference on Environment and Development, held in Rio de Janeiro in June 1992 (United Nations 1993). Many studies reported on the impact of the conference, such as Rogers' (1993) book, *The Earth Summit: A Planetary Reckoning.*

ECOSYSTEMS AND BIOLOGICAL TRANSFORMATIONS

Agriculture and food production is receiving fresh attention in environmental terms. See Hobhouse (1986), *Seeds of Change,* which looks at quinine, the potato, sugar cane, cotton, and tea, as well as Heiser (1990), *Seed to Civilization,* and the important specialized studies, Salaman's (1985) classic, *The History and Social Influence of the Potato,* and Fussell's (1992) popular *The Book of Corn.* See also Carter and Dale (1974), *Topsoil and Civilization,* a discussion of the pivotal role played by soils in the maintenance of long-surviving societies, and Crosby's (1986) "Weeds," from *Ecological Imperialism,* a fascinating account that connects damaged earth with the arrival of opportunistic, nonindigenous plant species. Jackson's (1980) *New Roots for Agriculture,* is a speculative venture into an alternative, ecologically adaptive perennial agriculture. An idiosyncratic but provocative overview that combines ecology and human existence is offered by Ehrlich (1986), *The Machinery of Nature.*

LANDSCAPE HISTORY

The best introduction remains the group of provocative essays in Meinig (1978), *The Interpretation of Ordinary Landscapes.* For cognitive mapping, see Gould and White (1974*), Mental Maps,* and Downs and Stea (1977), *Maps in Minds.* See also Evernden's (1992) philosophical analysis, *The Social Creation of Nature.* Especially useful are several studies of nature tourism: Sears (1989), *Sacred Places: American Tourist Attractions in the Nineteenth Century;* Jakle (1985), *The Tourist: Travel in Twentieth-Century North America;* and Stilgoe's (1982) modern classic, *Common Landscape of America: 1580–1845.*

ENVIRONMENTAL HISTORY OF THE AMERICAN WEST

Survey textbooks in American environmental history are still rare. Opie's forthcoming *United States Environmental History* puts the American experience in the context of contemporary global environmental issues. Merchant (1993) has edited an excellent interpretation and compilation of readings in *Major Problems in American Environmental History*, while the first textbook was Petulla's (1977) *American Environmental History*, since revised (1988). The best places to start remain R. Nash (1983), *Wilderness and the American Mind*, and Oelschlaeger (1991), *The Idea of Wilderness*. The connection between modern environmental history and the 1893 Turner Thesis are explored in Cronon (1987), Opie (1982), and Ridge (1991), which all should be compared with Frederick Jackson Turner's famous 1893 paper, "The Significance of the Frontier in American History," available in many versions in separate editions or in anthologies. For the environmental aspects of "the new western history," see the collection of essays edited by Limerick et al. (1991), *Trails*; Limerick's (1987) *The Legacy of Conquest*; and G. D. Nash (1991), *Creating the West*. For several more traditional viewpoints, also see Athearn's (1986) *The Mythic West in Twentieth-Century America*; Goetzmann's (1966) *Exploration and Empire*; Michener's (1960) novel, *Centennial*; and Worster's (1979) *Dust Bowl*. See also Frederick Jackson Turner's (1962) collected essays in *The Frontier in American History*, and the modern Turnerian approach in Billington, *Westward Expansion: A History of the American Frontier*, originally published in 1949 and later revised four times.

EARLY AMERICAN ENVIRONMENTAL HISTORY

There is no place better to start than with Cronon's (1983) pathfinding comparison between native and Puritan uses of the wilderness, *Changes in the Land*. Besides Cronon above see Lemon (1972), *The Best Poor Man's Country: A Geographical Study of Early Southeastern Pennsylvania*; McManis (1975), *Colonial New England*; Merchant (1989), *Ecological Revolutions: Nature, Gender, and Science in New England;* Silver (1990), *A New Face on the Countryside: Indians, Colonists, and Slaves in South Atlantic Forests, 1500–1800;* and Williams (1989), *Americans and Their Forests*.

NATIVE AMERICAN ALTERNATIVES

The best places to begin a modern revisionist review that treats Native Americans with dignity are Brown's (1981) classic, *Bury My Heart at Wounded Knee,* and the journalistic but insightful book by Farb (1968), *Man's Rise to Civilization as Shown by the Indians of North America from Primeval Times to the Coming of the Industrial State*. The misunderstanding and mistreatment of Indians is also trenchantly reported by Jennings (1975), *The Invasion of America: Indians, Colonialism, and the Cant of Conquest*. This can be contrasted with the comprehensive but traditional anthropological study by Driver (1969), *Indians of North America*, and Stewart (1973), *The People of America*. The connections between the natural world and Indian spirituality are effectively described in Martin (1978), *Keepers of the Game*; Albanese (1990), *Nature Religion in America;* and the marvelous portrayal of a single New England tract of land in Mitchell (1984), *Ceremonial Time*. The connection between Indians, whites, and buffalo extermination is examined by Krech (1994) in "Ecology and the American Indian." These and other major issues are also addressed in Vecsey and Venables (1980), *Ecological Issues in Native American History*.

DUST BOWL AND ENVIRONMENTAL FAILURE ON THE HIGH PLAINS

Readers can find no more enjoyable and profitable way of starting to learn more about the High Plains than with Webb's (1931) classic, *The Great Plains,* that opened the subject. This should be followed by a look at Powell's (1878) *Lands of the Arid Region of the United States,* arguably the best government report ever written. Both Webb and Powell are available in paperback reprints. A solid overview of mid-America farming can be found in Fite (1966), *The Farmer's Frontier, 1886–1900,* and more details are in the articles collected by Whittaker (1974) in *Farming in the Midwest, 1840–1900,* and Wessel (1977) in *Agriculture in the Great Plains, 1876–1936*. There are also important and provocative essays on the Plains in *The Great Plains: Environment and Culture,* edited by Blouet and Luebke (1977), and *The Great Plains: Perspectives and Prospects,* edited by Lawson and Baker (1981). *The Great Plains Quarterly,* a journal published in Lincoln, Nebraska, helps to update analysis and interpretation of the Plains. The environmental study of the Plains has also been greatly enriched by several highly suggestive and controversial interpretations. Readers should not miss the writings of the irascible James C. Malin as collected by Swierenga (1984). Several relevant essays by the pathfinding geographer, Carl Ortwin Sauer, are in the collection edited by Leighly (1963), *Land and Life.* Study of Plains environmental history has also been shaped by Sear's (1980) *Deserts on the March,* first published in 1935, and Hollon's (1966) *The Great American Desert.* No reader should leave the subject of the High Plains, however, without a full reading of Worster's (1979) classic, *Dust Bowl: The Southern Plains in the 1930s,* which reshaped the modern study of the High Plains. One hopes that Frank and Deborah Popper will produce a book out of their provocative articles on the future of large parts of the High Plains as a "Buffalo Commons." For a recent analysis, see Opie's (1993) *Ogallala: Water for a Dry Land,* which, despite its title, is a broader environmental and historical analysis of the High Plains.

THE ENVIRONMENTAL DESTRUCTION OF CALIFORNIA

On the relationship between city building and environmental destruction, see Brechin's (in press) *Imperial San Francisco.* Brechin and Dawson's forthcoming *Farewell Promised Land* is intended as a sequel to Dasmann's (1966) *The Destruction of California*. Sweeping regional treatments of the Sacramento River Valley, the Tulare Lake Basin, and the Great Central Valley, respectively, are contained in Kelly's (1989) *Battling the Inland Sea*; Preston's (1981*) Vanishing Landscapes*; and Johnson, Haslam, and Dawson's (1993) *The Great Central Valley: California's Heartland*. McEvoy (1990*), The Fisherman's Problem*, remains the best historiographic overview of the decline of California fisheries. To explore the disappearance of California's Sacramento River salmon, see Black's forthcoming, *California's Last Salmon: The Unnatural Policies of Natural Resource Agencies*.

Literature Cited

Entries are cited either in a course plan or in the section "Annotated Background Readings for the Instructor" above. Page numbers appearing in brackets at the end of each entry indicate where the reference is cited.

Albanese, C. L. 1990. *Nature Religion in America: From the Algonkian Indians to the New Age.* Chicago: University of Chicago Press. [p. 142]

Athearn, R. G. 1986. *The Mythic West in Twentieth-Century America.* Lawrence: University Press of Kansas. [p. 141]

Bailes, K. E., ed. 1985. *Environmental History: Critical Issues in Comparative Perspective.* Lanham, MA: University Press of America. [p. 138]

Barbour, I. et al. 1982. *Energy and American Values.* New York: Praeger. [p. 129]

Berman, M. 1981. *The Reenchantment of the World.* Ithaca: Cornell University Press. [pp. 123, 129]

Beveridge, C. 1990. "Introduction to the Landscape Design Reports: The California Origins of Olmsted's Landscape Design Principles for the Semiarid American West." In *The Collected Papers of Frederick Law Olmsted.* V. Post-Ranney, ed. Vol. 5, *The California Frontier.* Baltimore: Johns Hopkins University Press. [p. 134]

Billington, R. A. 1949.*Westward Expansion: A History of the American Frontier.* New York: Macmillan. [p. 141]

Bilsky, L. J., ed. 1980. *Historical Ecology: Essays on Environment and Social Change.* Port Washington, NY: Kennikat Press. [p. 138]

Bird, E. A. R. 1987. "The Social Construction of Nature: Theoretical Approaches to the History of Environmental Problems." *Environmental Review*, Winter. [p. 137]

Black, M. In press. *California's Last Salmon: The Unnatural Policies of Natural Resource Agencies*. Berkeley: University of California Press. [pp. 133, 135, 143]

Black, M. In press. "Searching for a Genius of Place: The Ambiguous Legacy of Golden Gate Park." *American Quarterly*. [p. 134]

Blouet, B. W. and F. C. Luebke, eds. 1977. *The Great Plains: Environment and Culture*. Lincoln: University of Nebraska Press. [p. 142]

Braudel, F. 1972. *The Mediterranean and the Mediterranean World in the Age of Philip II*. 2 vols. New York: Harper Collins. [p. 139]

Braudel, F. 1981–1984. *Civilization and Capitalism: 15th–18th Century*. 3 vols. Berkeley: University of California Press. [p. 139]

Brechin, G. In press. *Imperial San Francisco*. Berkeley: University of California Press. [pp. 136, 137, 142]

Brechin, G. and R. Dawson. In press. *Farewell Promised Land*. Berkeley: University of California Press. [pp. 142–143]

Brown, D. 1981. *Bury My Heart at Wounded Knee: An Indian History of the American West*. New York: Henry Holt and Company. [p. 141]

Brown, L. et al. Annual. *State of the World: A Worldwatch Institute Report on Progress toward a Sustainable Society*. New York: Norton. [p. 138]

Carter, V. G. and T. Dale. 1974. *Topsoil and Civilization*. Norman: University of Oklahoma Press. [p. 140]

Clary, R. 1980, *The Making of Golden Gate Park, The Early Years: 1865–1906*. San Francisco: California Living Books. [p. 134]

Cole, H. S. D. et al. 1973. *Models of Doom: A Critique of the Limits to Growth*. New York: Universe Books. [p. 139]

Cronon, W. 1983. *Changes in the Land*. New York: Hill and Wang. [pp. 128, 132, 141]

Cronon, W. 1987. "Revisiting the Vanishing Frontier: The Legacy of Frederick Jackson Turner." *The Western Historical Quarterly* 18:157–176. [pp. 131, 141]

Cronon, W. 1991. *Nature's Metropolis: Chicago and the Great West*. New York: Norton. [p. 137]

Crosby, A. W. 1972. *The Columbian Exchange*. Westport, CT: Greenwood Publishers. [pp. 124, 127, 139]

Crosby, A. W. 1986. *Ecological Imperialism: The Biological Expansion of Europe, 900–1900*. New York: Cambridge University Press [pp. 124, 127, 139, 140]

Dasmann, R. 1966. *The Destruction of California*. New York: Collier Books. [p. 143]

Downs, R. M. and D. Stea. 1977. *Maps in Minds: Reflections on Cognitive Mapping.* New York: Harper and Row. [p. 140]

Driver, D. 1969. *Indians of North America,* 2nd ed., rev. Chicago: University of Chicago Press. [p. 141]

Ehrlich, P. R. 1986. *The Machinery of Nature: The Living World Around Us—And How It Works.* New York: S & S Trade. [p. 140]

"Environmental History: A Round Table." 1990. *Journal of American History,* March. [p. 137]

Evernden, N. 1992. *The Social Creation of Nature.* Baltimore: John Hopkins University Press. [p. 140]

Farb, P. 1968. *Man's Rise to Civilization as Shown by the Indians of North America from Primeval Times to the Coming of the Industrial State.* New York: Viking Penguin. [p. 141]

Fite, G. C. 1966. *The Farmer's Frontier, 1886–1900.* New York: Holt, Rinehart, Winston. [p. 142]

Flores, D. 1994. "Place: An Argument for Bioregional History." *Environmental History Review,* Winter. [p. 137]

Fussell, B. 1992. *The Book of Corn.* New York: Knopf. [p. 140]

Glacken, C. 1967. *Traces on the Rhodian Shore: Nature and Culture in Western Thought.* Berkeley: University of California Press. [p. 138]

The Global 2000 Report to the President: Entering the Twenty-First Century. 1980. Washington, DC: Government Printing Office. [p. 139]

Goetzmann, W. H. 1966. *Exploration and Empire: The Explorer and Scientist in the Winning of the West.* Austin: Texas State Historical Association. [p. 141]

Goldfarb, T. D. 1993. *Taking Sides: Clashing Views on Controversial Environmental Issues,* 5th ed. Guilford, CT: Dushkin Publishing Group. [p. 129]

Gould, P. and R. White. 1974. *Mental Maps.* Los Angeles: Rutledge Press. [p. 140]

Hanson, W. D. 1987. *Beyond San Francisco Water and Power: A History of the Municipal Water Department and Hetch Hetchy System.* San Francisco: Department of Water and Power. [p. 133]

Headrick, D. 1981. *The Tools of Empire: Technology and European Imperialism in the Nineteenth Century.* New York: Oxford University Press. [pp. 123, 139]

Headrick, D. 1988. *The Tentacles of Progress: Technology Transfer in the Age of Imperialism, 1850–1940.* New York: Oxford University Press. [p. 139]

Heiser, Jr., C. B. 1990. *Seed to Civilization: The Story of Food,* rev. ed. Cambridge: Harvard University Press. [p. 140]

Hirsch, F. 1978. *Social Limits to Growth*. Cambridge: Harvard University Press. [p. 139]

Hobhouse, H. 1986. *Seeds of Change: Five Plants That Transformed Mankind*. New York: HarperCollins. [p. 140]

Hollon, W. E. 1966. *The Great American Desert, Then and Now*. New York: Oxford University Press. [p. 142]

Hughes, J. D. 1972. *Ecology of the Ancient World*. Albuquerque: University of New Mexico Press. [p. 138]

Jackson, W. 1980. *New Roots for Agriculture*. Lincoln: University of Nebraska Press. [pp. 124, 140]

Jakle, J. A. 1985. *The Tourist: Travel in Twentieth-Century North America*. Ann Arbor, MI: Books Demand. [p. 140]

Jennings, F. 1975. *The Invasion of America: Indians, Colonialism, and the Cant of Conquest*. New York: Norton. [p. 141]

Johnson, S., G. Haslam, and R. Dawson. 1993. *The Great Central Valley: California's Heartland*. Berkeley: University of California Press. [p. 143]

Kahn, H. 1976. *The Next 200 Years: A Scenario for America and the World*. New York: Quill Books. [p. 139]

Kahn, H. 1978. *World Economic Development: Projections from 1978 to the year 2000*. Boulder, CO: Westview Press. [p. 139]

Kelly, R. 1989. *Battling the Inland Sea: American Political Culture, Public Policy, and the Sacramento Valley, 1850–1986*. Berkeley: University of California Press. [p. 143]

Kimbrough, R. ed. 1988. *Joseph Conrad, Heart of Darkness*, 3rd ed. New York: W. W. Norton. [p. 125]

Krech III, S. 1994. "Ecology and the American Indian." *Ideas from the National Humanities Center* 3(1):4–22. [p. 142]

Laszlo, E. 1977. *Goals for Mankind*. New York: New American Library. [p. 139]

Lawson, M. P. and M. E. Baker. 1981. *The Great Plains: Perspectives and Prospects*. Ann Arbor, MI: Books Demand. [p. 142]

Leighly, J. 1963. *Land and Life*. Berkeley: University of California Press. [p. 142]

Lemon, J. T. 1972. *The Best Poor Man's Country: A Geographical Study of Early Southeastern Pennsylvania*. Baltimore: Johns Hopkins University Press. [p. 141]

Lewis, C. S. 1947. *The Abolition of Man*. New York: Collier Books. [p. 132]

Limerick, P. N. 1987. *The Legacy of Conquest: The Unbroken Past of the American West*. Lawrence: University Press of Kansas. [p. 141]

Limerick, P. N., C. A. Milner II, and C. E. Rankin, eds. 1991. *Trails: Toward A New Western History.* Lawrence: University Press of Kansas. [p. 141]

Lufkin, A., ed. 1991. *California's Salmon and Steelhead: The Struggle to Restore an Imperiled Resource.* Berkeley: University of California Press. [pp. 135, 136]

Martin, C. 1978. *Keepers of the Game: Indian–Animal Relations and the Fur Trade.* Berkeley: University of California Press. [p. 142]

McEvoy, A. F. 1990. *The Fisherman's Problem: Ecology and Law in the California Fisheries, 1850–1980.* New York: Cambridge University Press. [pp. 135, 143]

McManis, D. R. 1975. *Colonial New England: A Historical Geography.* New York: Oxford University Press. [p. 141]

McNeill, W. 1964. *The Rise of the West.* Chicago: University of Chicago Press. [pp. 123, 138]

McNeill, W. 1976. *Plagues and Peoples.* New York: Doubleday. [p. 139]

McPhee, J. 1993. "Annals of the Former World." *The New Yorker,* Sept. 14. [p. 136]

Meadows, D. H. et al. 1972. *The Limits to Growth,* 2nd ed. New York: Universe Books. [pp. 125, 139]

Meadows, D. H., D. L. Meadows, and J. Randers. 1992. *Beyond the Limits: Confronting Global Collapse, Envisioning a Sustainable Future.* Post Mills, VT: Chelsea Green Publishing Company. [pp. 126, 140]

Meinig, D. W., ed. 1978. *The Interpretation of Ordinary Landscapes.* New York: Oxford University Press. [pp. 126, 140]

Meinig, D. W. 1986, 1993. *The Shaping of America: A Geographical Perspective on 500 Years of History.* 2 vols. New Haven: Yale University Press. [p. 138]

Merchant, C. 1987. "The Theoretical Structure of Ecological Revolutions." *Environmental Review,* Winter. [p. 137]

Merchant, C. 1989. *Ecological Revolutions: Nature, Gender, and Science in New England.* Chapel Hill: University of North Carolina Press. [pp. 128, 132, 141]

Merchant, C., ed. 1993. *Major Problems in American Environmental History.* Lexington, MA: D. C. Heath. [pp. 129, 141]

Mesarovic, M. and E. Pestel. 1974. *Mankind at the Turning Point: The Second Report to the Club of Rome.* New York: New American Library. [p. 139]

Michener, J. 1960. *Centennial.* New York: Random House. [p. 141]

Mitchell, J. H. 1984. *Ceremonial Time: Fifteen Thousand Years on One Square Mile.* Boston: Houghton-Mifflin. [p. 142]

Muir, J. [1912] 1988. *The Yosemite.* San Francisco: Sierra Club Books. [p. 133]

Mumford, L. 1967. *The Myth of the Machine: Technics & Human Development.* New York: Harcourt Brace Jovanovich. [p. 139]

Mumford, L. 1970. *The Myth of the Machine: The Pentagon of Power.* New York: Harcourt Brace Jovanovich. [pp. 123, 139]

Nash, G. D. 1991. *Creating the West: Historical Interpretations 1890–1990.* Albuquerque: University of New Mexico Press. [p. 141]

Nash, R. 1983. *Wilderness and the American Mind,* 3rd ed. New Haven: Yale University Press. [pp. 129, 140]

Nye, D. E. 1994. *American Technological Sublime.* Cambridge, MA: MIT Press. [p. 139]

Oelschlaeger, M. 1991. *The Idea of Wilderness.* New Haven: Yale University Press. [pp. 129, 140]

Opie, J. 1982. "Frederick Jackson Turner, the Old West, and the Formation of a National Mythology." *Environmental Review* 5(winter):79–90. [pp. 131, 141]

Opie, J. 1993. *Ogallala: Water for a Dry Land.* Lincoln: University of Nebraska Press. [p. 142]

Opie, J. Forthcoming. *United States Environmental History.* New York: Harcourt Brace. [pp. 129, 140]

Peccei, A. 1981. *One Hundred Pages for the Future.* New York: Pergamon Press. [p. 139]

Petulla, J. M. 1988. *American Environmental History,* rev. ed. New York: Macmillan. [pp. 129, 141]

Piasecki, B., ed. 1992. "Special Curriculum Issue." *Environmental History Review* 16(Spring). [p. 137]

Ponting, P. 1991. *A Green History of the World: The Environment and the Collapse of Great Civilizations.* New York: St. Martin's Press. [p. 137]

Popper, F. J. and D. E. Popper. 1987. "The Great Plains from Dust to Dust." *Planning* 53(12):1–18. [p. 142]

Powell, J. W. 1878. *Lands of the Arid Region of the United States.* Washington, DC: Government Printing Office. [p. 142]

Preston, W. L. 1981. *Vanishing Landscape: Land and Life in the Tulare Lake Basin.* Berkeley: University of California Press. [p. 143]

Reisner, M. 1986, *Cadillac Desert: The American West and Its Disappearing Water.* New York: Viking Press. [p. 135]

Ridge, M. 1991. "The Life of an Idea: The Significance of Frederick Jackson Turner's Frontier Thesis. *Montana: the Magazine of Western History* 41(fall):2–13. [p. 131, 141]

Rogers, A. 1993. *The Earth Summit: A Planetary Reckoning*. Hollywood, CA: Global View. [p. 140]

Salaman, R. 1985. *The History and Social Influence of the Potato*, rev. ed. New York: Cambridge University Press. [p. 140]

Sear, P. B. [1935] 1980. *Deserts on the March*. Norman: University of Oklahoma Press. [p. 142]

Sears, J. F. 1989. *Sacred Places: American Tourist Attractions in the Nineteenth Century*. New York: Oxford University Press. [p. 140]

Silver, T. 1990. *A New Face on the Countryside: Indians, Colonists, and Slaves in South Atlantic Forests, 1500–1800*. New York: Cambridge University Press. [p. 141]

Simmons, I. G. 1989. *Changing the Face of the Earth: Culture, Environment, History*. Cambridge, MA: Blackwell Publishers. [p. 137]

Simmons, I. G. 1993. *Environmental History: A Concise Introduction*. Cambridge, MA: Blackwell Publishers. [p. 137]

Simon, J. L. and H. Kahn. 1984. *The Resourceful Earth: A Response to 'Global 2000'*. Cambridge, MA: Blackwell Publishers. [p. 140]

Smith, D. 1987. *Mining America: The Industry and the Environment, 1800–1980*. Lawrence: University Press of Kansas. [p. 136]

Stewart, T. D. 1973. *The People of America*. New York: Charles Scribner's Sons. [p. 141]

Stilgoe, J. R. 1982. *Common Landscape of America: 1580–1845*. New Haven: Yale University Press. [p. 140]

Swierenga, R. P. 1984. *History and Ecology: Studies of the Grasslands*. Lincoln: University of Nebraska Press. [p. 142]

Tallmadge, J. 1987. "Anatomy of a Classic." In *Companion to a Sand County Almanac*. J. B. Callicott, ed. Madison: University of Wisconsin Press. [p. 121]

Thomas, W. L., ed. 1956. *Man's Role in Changing the Face of the Earth*. 2 vols. Chicago: University of Chicago Press. [p. 138]

Tinbergen, J. 1976. *Rio: Reshaping the International Order*. New York: New American Library. [p. 139]

Turner, B. L., III, et al. 1992. *The Earth as Transformed by Human Action*. New York: Cambridge University Press. [p. 138]

Turner, F. J. [1893] 1962. "The Significance of the Frontier in American History." In *The Frontier in American History*. Melbourne, FL: Krieger. [pp. 131, 141]

United Nations. 1993. *Agenda 21: Programme of Action for Sustainable Development*. New York: United Nations Publications. [p. 140]

Vecsey, C. and R. W. Venables, eds. 1980. *Ecological Issues in Native American History*. Ann Arbor, MI: Books Demand. [p. 142]

Walton, J. 1992, *Western Times and Water Wars: State, Culture, and Repression in California*. Berkeley: University of California Press. [p. 135]

Watts, M. T. 1975. *Reading the Landscape of America*, rev. ed. New York: Macmillan. [p. 127]

Webb, W. P. 1931. *The Great Plains*. Boston: Ginn and Company. [p. 142]

Wessel, T. R. 1977. *Agriculture in the Great Plains, 1876–1936*. Washington, DC: Agricultural History Society. [p. 142]

White, R. 1985. "American Environmental History: The Development of a New Historical Field." *Pacific Historical Review*, August. [p. 137]

Whittaker, J. W. 1974. *Farming in the Midwest, 1840–1900*. Washington, DC: Agricultural History Society. [p. 142]

Wilkinson, N. L. 1991. "No Holier Temple: Responses to Hodel's Hetch Hetchy Proposal." *Landscape* 31(1): 1–9. [p. 133]

Williams, M. 1989. *Americans and Their Forests: A Historical Geography*. New York: Cambridge University Press. [pp. 128, 132, 141]

Woodruff, W. 1966. *A Study of Europe's Role in the World Economy, 1750–1960*. New York: St. Martin's Press. [pp. 122, 139]

World Commission on Environment and Development. 1987. *Our Common Future*. New York: Oxford University Press. [p. 126]

Worster, D. 1979. *Dust Bowl: The Southern Plains in the 1930s*. New York: Oxford University Press. [pp. 132, 141, 142]

Worster, D. 1985. *Rivers of Empire: Water, Aridity and the Growth of the American West*. New York: Pantheon. [p. 135]

Worster, D. 1988. *The Ends of the Earth*. New York: Cambridge University Press. [p. 137]

Worster, D. 1993. *The Wealth of Nature: Environmental History and the Ecological Imagination*. New York: Oxford University Press. [p. 137]

Worster, D. 1994. "Nature and the Disorder of History." *Environmental History Review*, Summer. [p. 137]

Chapter 7

Literature

Vernon Owen Grumbling
University of New England

As the enduring record of creative imagination, literature potentially encompasses all subjects of human thought and experience. A central and recurring theme is the relation between humankind and the earth, with all its living creatures, its habitats, and landscapes. Because literature works through value-laden images and offers itself to the interpretation of the reader, its peculiar value is to personalize the moral and aesthetic issues that inevitably arise in exploring conservation of biodiversity and sustainable development. Those teaching in disciplines other than literature can easily "borrow" a particular literary text as a means of stimulating students to respond in personal terms to the environmental consequences of attitudes and behaviors. Conversely, the infusion of environmental awareness into the study of literature often results in unusually lively discussion. Sometimes its students even develop an abiding affection for literature itself.

Physical Description as Evocation

In its descriptive mode, literature is often highly valued for conveying physical appearance. It can record graphically an environmental condition, as well as dramatize change in a system. Crevecoeur's depiction of the immense flocks of passenger pigeons inhabiting America in the mid-18th century, for example, contrasts dramatically with the species' subsequent extinction. A literary description may contain insights about a particular environmental problem, such as the overgathering of specimens by amateur collectors, implied in Sara Orne Jewett's "A White Heron" (1886; in Begiebing and Grumbling 1990). In still other cases, literature may record the perception of an environment by an individual or social group, for example, the "virginal" prairie of American frontier literature (Kolodny 1975).

Literature's graphic depiction provides stimulus for emotional reaction. A lovely landscape, an endangered animal, or a destroyed habitat in literature evokes a sense of value and poses implicit and even explicit moral questions. A character or a narrative voice, in expressing individual experience, directly dramatizes feelings and values. Thus readers have opportunity to consider, in a hypothetical "person," the relation between perception, emotion, ethic, and behavior. In D. H. Lawrence's *Lady Chatterley's Lover* (1928), for example, Clifford's obsessive extraction of coal deposits on his ancestral lands is caused by, and in turn enlarges, his insensitivity to both humanity and nature—as judged by the narrative voice, which consistently assigns value to the integrity of the environment and the individual. Thus literature presents "whole" human models as benchmarks to which individual readers can compare—and evaluate—their own attitudes and behaviors.

Environment as Subtext

Much literature takes place within a setting that represents or implies an environment. Consequently, literary texts from one or another canon, in many different courses, present opportunities for analysis of environmental values. Twain's *Huckleberry Finn* (1884), for example, a novel appropriate to an American survey course, might there be considered primarily in regard to the theme of human freedom. Yet its setting on the Mississippi River calls attention to related choices in human use of the riverine ecosystem, namely, the conflict between impending industrialism and appreciation of the wild beauty of the river.

By considering the environment as a subtext submerged in setting, one can infuse discussions of environmental concerns into most literature courses, even standard surveys required by general education mandates. With *Huck Finn*, for example, one may explore the consequences of the steamboat, not only for Huck's journey, but for the future of other species—and ask how the reader feels about that obviously doomed future. If a text does not admit nonhuman attributes to its environment, that fact is itself significant.

Nature Literature: Canon and Criticism

Courses on many common literary canons, such as British Romanticism, Transcendentalism, American Western Literature, Native American Literature, Canadian Literature, Women's Literature, Men's Literature, and others, typically may explore themes of human relationship with nature. Traditional courses on these topics, then, might be designed to focus on biodiversity by means of texts that

- narrate direct personal experience with animals or plants;
- examine the relationships of humans with particular landscapes (bioregions), including both emotional ties and physical impacts;
- create, imply, or critique myths of genesis, eschatology, cosmogony, and cosmology;
- dramatize competition for and depletion of resources;
- dramatize or critique cultural attitudes toward environmental issues; and
- speculate on the essential nature of humanity as member of the biotic community.

Some instructors may have opportunities to design courses that deal specifically with "environmental literature" or "nature literature," as it is variously defined. From one perspective "modern nature writing" begins with the onslaught of industrialism in England during the 18th century, with its transfer of populations from the farm and rural life to factories and shops in the city (Begiebing and Grumbling 1990). Nature writing, initially poetry, emerged in reaction to discovery of the sense of alienation from rural nature. Another perspective emphasizes the force of the American wilderness experience in generating the "nature essay," which combines natural history description with emotion and considers philosophical or moral questions (Finch and Elder 1990). Some critics find significant nature writing throughout the entire canon of Western European literature, while many are interested in non-Western literatures, particularly the oral traditions of tribal cultures.

Many agree that a tradition of nature writing in Western literature has repeatedly reaffirmed human connectedness with and responsibility for the whole of the earth; in doing so, they argue, the tradition has heroically attempted to subvert the dominant Western industrial paradigm of human domination over the biosphere (Begiebing and Grumbling 1990).

However it may be defined, there has been a renaissance in the teaching of nature writing, beginning roughly with the first Earth Day (1970), a little over a generation ago. An inspiring early anthology, now unfortunately out of print, was David McKain's (1974) *The Whole Earth: Essays in Appreciation, Anger, and Concern.* A watershed of sorts was passed, no doubt, when the Modern Language Association underwrote the publication of *Teaching Environmental Literature* (Waage 1985), a compendium of course descriptions and teaching techniques. Recently, a new journal, *Interdisciplinary Studies in Environmental Literature,* has been instituted. A substantial number of anthologies, assembled according to various perspectives, are now available. (See "Resources," below.) Theoretical approaches based on ecofeminism, culture studies, and deep ecology have emerged. What appears to be a landmark critical study of Wordsworth's ecological awareness, *Romantic Ecology: Wordsworth and the Environmental Tradition* (Bate 1991), may go a long way to rehabilitate canons and critics denatured by the excesses of poststructuralism.

Genres

Anthologists and other critical writers have suggested a wide variety of genres in the canon of nature writing. Most forms of poetry have, no doubt, enclosed themes of nature; natural themes have, conversely, structured a number of poetic forms, such as the animal poem, the landscape poem, and the poem of meditation. The "nature novel," a subgenre, is primarily concerned with the relation between character and the attraction of nature (Alcorn 1977).

The nature essay and the nature journal evolved from natural history description and border on science writing. They may deal with a particular locale, ecosystem, or bioregion, particularly, the wilderness. Science fiction utilizes the relation between technology and nature to project its utopias and disutopias. Environmental polemics, such as Carson's (1962) *Silent Spring,* may depict, analyze, and attempt to rectify particular destructive impacts of human behavior, while essays of ecological inquiry, such as Aldo Leopold's "The Land Ethic," aim systematically to arrive at new conceptions of what "humanity" and "nature" mean. Clearly, much nature writing defies simple classification into genre, and much connects intimately with other disciplines.

Interdisciplinarity

Environmental literature typically evokes the need for interdisciplinarity—the approach that assumes sound understanding demands study of a question from several integrated perspectives. Discussion of almost any text requires detailed information about ecology and related sciences, about ethics, social behavior, language, aesthetics, and philosophy. Most significantly, the imaginative, value-laden substance of literature tends to personalize questions of environmental concern. Students become aware of the importance of the environment to their own lives, whether considering the value of a "special place" or learning about threats to their very survival posed by degradation, such as loss of the ozone screen that prevents damage from ultraviolet rays.

Consequently, motivation for active learning can run high, causing students to cross disciplinary borders looking for the physical sources of environmental degradation, for example, or for the cultural attitudes that have sanctioned destructive behaviors. Such personal engagement can lead, even in introductory courses, to interdisciplinary study at a high cognitive level, including an understanding of the limitations of any one discipline.

References for the Introduction

Alcorn, J. 1977. *The Nature Novel from Hardy to Lawrence.* New York: Columbia University Press.

Bate, J. 1991. *Romantic Ecology: Wordsworth and the Environmental Tradition.* London: Routledge.

Begiebing, R. J. and O. Grumbling, eds. 1990. *The Literature of Nature: The British and American Traditions.* Medford, NJ: Plexus Publishing, Inc.

Finch, R. and J. Elder, eds. 1990. *The Norton Anthology of Nature Writing.* New York: Norton.

Kolodny, A. 1975. *The Lay of the Land: Metaphor as Experience and History in American Life and Letters.* Chapel Hill: University of North Carolina Press.

McKain, D., ed. 1974. *The Whole Earth: Essays in Appreciation, Anger, and Concern.* New York: St. Martin's Press.

Waage, F., ed. 1985. *Teaching Environmental Literature.* New York: Modern Language Association of America.

COURSE PLANS

The materials include a syllabus for a course, "The Nature Writers," as a model for those who wish to design a new introductory (or, with some modification, advanced) literature course; for those without the opportunity to design new courses, the section presents two course units that might fit into standard introductory courses in literature, composition, or, perhaps, other disciplines as well. Also included is a syllabus for "Contemporary Nature Writing," an advanced-level literature course.

Introductory Courses and Units

The Nature Writers (a full course)

Course Description. This course explores literature that depicts the natural world with affection, respect, imagination, and concern, as created by authors such as William and Dorothy Wordsworth, John Fowles, Henry Thoreau, Sarah Orne Jewett, and Edward Abbey. To provide a context for the literature, we will consider how current environmental dilemmas are the consequence of attitudes toward nature, shaped by historical influences such as religion, economics, and philosophy; at the same time we will examine how the tradition of nature literature has expressed values and attitudes critical of the dominant paradigm. As we read the various authors' expressions of their relationships with nature, each of us will discover, articulate, and, perhaps, revise individual beliefs. (In the course description and throughout the syllabus I attempt to reveal the link with environmental issues and to establish that active learning is an expectation.)

Course Objectives. (1) To read texts in the British and American traditions of nature literature, both as artistic creations and as portrayals of value-laden relationships with the natural world. (2) To analyze cultural factors—technology, science, religion—that have shaped the evolution of these traditions, and that have shaped our culture's ideas about nature. (3) To consider environmental themes and values expressed in the literature in the context of our society and in terms of our own lives.

Texts and Films

- Abbey, E. [1968] 1990. *Desert Solitaire.* In addition to the anthologies, I've found it useful to use a novel or a book of essays by a single author.
- Silko, L. M. 1977. *Ceremony.* This is a powerful novel by a Native American woman of the Laguna Pueblo. It shows a definition of human health that is indistinguishable from the health of the land. Undergraduates enjoy this reading.
- Begiebing, R. and O. Grumbling. 1990. *The Literature of Nature: The British and American Traditions.* This anthology includes poetry, essays, journal entries, and short stories and, in its frontmatter, provides extensive historical frames.
- Anderson, L. 1991. *Sisters of the Earth.* This anthology balances the selection of writers offered in *The Literature of Nature.*
- *A White Heron* (film), *Never Cry Wolf* (film), *Dances With Wolves* (film)

Assignments

(1) A Learning Journal, recorded on a weekly schedule, encompassing both assigned writings and independent explorations. The journal is to be

reread regularly and its contents are to be revised and/or commented on. The journal is evaluated in terms of its substance, its preparation related to assigned texts, its independent entries, and its recursive (reconsidered) entries. Use of assigned questions in the journal ensures that students will deal with specific issues in response to questions the instructor assigns, and that the student will construct learning in response to the assignment for independent entries. Also, the journal's recursive aspect encourages students to internalize concepts and reconsider moral questions. (For examples of assigned questions, see Course Units below.)

(2) A Creative Project dealing with environmental perception, interpretation, or concern. It could take the form of a short story, a poem, an essay, a photoessay, a song, a video, a "letter to the editor," an editorial, a sculpture, a game. This assignment allows students to express emotion in "right brain" activity. Creating a gallery atmosphere for viewing their productions builds both self-esteem and a sense of community for the group; both are necessary to promote the trust necessary for grappling with the issues that arise in discussion. Other devices that help accomplish these goals are community dinners (pot luck), hikes, camping trips, ski tours, and ropes courses.

Nature as Source of Personal Regeneration (unit for an introductory course)

Unit Description and Objectives. This unit serves an introductory function in "The Nature Writers" and might be transferred into other courses with little problem. Its goal is to apprehend the possibility that direct experience of the natural world can enrich human life in nonmaterial, nonconsumptive ways, leading to the insight that nature possesses intrinsic value (see Chapter 9, Philosophy, for fuller discussion). A second goal is to question received assumptions about the absolute value of human "productive activity."

The first task is to introduce the text. In order for the students to encounter the poem without preconception, I postpone giving historical background on Wordsworth and the Romantic era. Instead, so that they can begin reading, I clarify the rhetorical context of the poem: William Wordsworth's "To My Sister" (from *Lyrical Ballads* [1798]) is a narrative poem, ostensibly a note written on the first warm day of spring in an English countryside and sent by a young man in his twenties to his sister.

For those readers who are not familiar with the poem, I will attempt a brief synopsis (with heartfelt apologies to those who know the work). The writer begins with the lines "It is the first mild day of March;/Each minute sweeter than before" and goes on to assert that "There is a blessing in the air." He enjoins his sister to quit her tasks and "Come forth and feel the sun." In consequence, "No joyless forms shall regulate/Our living calendar." A key line, repeated in the final stanza, asks the sister to ". . . bring no book: for this one day/We'll give to idleness." Then comes the first of several assertions that he and his sister can anticipate spiritual regeneration:

> One moment now may give us more
> Than fifty years of reason;
> Our minds shall drink at every pore
> The spirit of the season.

The writer asserts that the benefit will be lasting: their hearts will make "silent laws" that they "shall long obey," and their souls "shall be tuned to love."

Preparatory Journal Questions. After hearing about the rhetorical context of the poem (but *not* hearing the synopsis!), the students respond in their journals to a series of questions and tasks:

(1) What might be "joyless forms" (line 17) and "living calendar" (line 18)? The question aims to evoke an understanding of the use of symbolism, namely synechdoche (a part stands for the whole), and in the process to introduce the idea of organic connections.

(2) In the lines "Love, now an universal birth/From heart to heart is stealing," what is the "universal birth"? Why "now"? This question aims to reveal how the writer connects biological regeneration with the human concept of love.

(3) "One moment now may give us more/Than fifty years of reason." More what? And what does "reason" mean? This question points to the poet's suggestion of an apparent dichotomy between feeling and reason.

(4) Do you agree that the speaker and his sister are spending their day in "idleness"? Is it good or bad? Define what you mean by "idleness," and what the term means in the poem. This question sets up potential debate on several levels.

(5) Try to verify the writer's thesis: have you ever experienced "'idleness in nature," in a way you think approximates the poem's theme? If so, describe your experience, taking care to analyze any benefit you find.

(6) (Optional) Go outside and enjoy yourself. Then ask, "Have I received any lasting benefit? Has the 'outside' benefited?"

Class Discussion. Discussion of responses to the prepared questions leads to assertions about the meaning of the poem, and about its correspondence to the experience of individuals. The question about "idleness" may open debate on several levels: initially, about the responsibility to work rather than to exist on welfare, then about the meaning of "work" and "benefit." In facilitating the discussion, the instructor can ask individuals to explain what kind of knowledge validates the assertions, and can attempt to uncover the assumptions of value that underlie students' arguments. The instructor might ask, for example, "Is what one receives from such an experience worthwhile?"; "Why must one justify such an experience?"; "If the characters (or if we) did not give the day to idleness, what else might they (we) do with it?"; "For this alternative action, what are the range of consequences?"; "What might be the consequences to the biosphere of other behaviors associated with 'productivity'?"

Learning Summary and Follow-up Activities. At the end of class the instructor attempts to represent areas of agreement and conflict and asks students to write in their journals in order to reflect upon their initial experiences. The goal is to connect the perceived value of the natural world with the need for sustaining it in the future:

(1) Write notes describing a place in nature which you have found satisfying. Keep writing. Then read your notes and write a couple of paragraphs that explain why the place is important to you.

(2) The poem "To My Sister" suggests that direct experience in nature is valuable to humans in ways other than satisfying our material needs for food and shelter. What is it about nature that needs to be sustained or preserved for you to continue finding such experiences?

(3) If people cannot live only by the kind of experience narrated in "To My Sister," what must you do to satisfy physical needs? Does meeting physical needs ever hinder your direct experience of nature?

(4) Is there any place that you feel should continue to exist even if you will never get to experience it personally again? If no humans ever will experience it directly?

Follow-up Background Information. After discussion of this and other poems of the period, such as Blake's "The Ecchoeing Green," the following concepts might be introduced, and emphasized differently in a general introduction, a survey of British literature, or a composition course:

- symbol, narrative, rhetorical context, poetic form—as related to theme;

- the movement of population from rural areas to urban ones consequent to the rise of industrialism in 18th and 19th century England;

- biographical information: Wordsworth's affection for the Lake District where he was born and raised, and where he returned to live as an adult; his sympathy with the democratic movement in England and France; his disillusionment with politics, and his subsequent attempt to create a philosophy of "natural piety"; and

- the complexity of distinguishing a "natural" place unimpacted by humans: the rural as opposed to the wild.

The Intrinsic Value of Nonhuman Species *(a unit suitable for either an introductory or advanced course)*

Unit Description. This unit examines imaginative renderings of experience with nonhuman animals and plants. Its goal is to develop a felt sense of the integrity of the Other, leading to intuition of intrinsic value as a nonanthropocentric, nonutilitarian reason for preservation of species. (See Chapter 9, Philosophy, for fuller discussion of this kind of intrinsic value.) Of many useful texts, two stand out: D. H. Lawrence's poem "Snake," and Sarah Orne Jewett's short story "A White Heron."

A. "Snake" (In Begiebing and Grumbling, pp. 496–498).

Introduction to the Text. In an introductory course the rhetorical context of the poem should be explained: a man, living in Sicily in sight of Mount Etna, goes one morning to fetch water at a nearby spring, where he encounters a venomous snake. Students should be advised to note how the character behaves, and to speculate about what causes his behavior. (For those unfamiliar with the poem, the narrator eventually succumbs to fear of the snake and acts violently, only to feel acute remorse.)

Preparatory Journal Questions

(1) After reading the poem, make a synopsis of the action. Elaborate on why you think the speaker acts as he does.

(2) Have you ever witnessed or performed (if you feel safe to admit it) an act of wanton cruelty to an animal? Describe the event and try to explain why people acted as they did.

(3) How do you feel about snakes? Do a free writing exercise to discover the source of your feelings.

(4) How does the narrator feel about the snake at the end of the poem? Can you identify with him?

Class Discussion. The task here is to facilitate an honest discussion of emotions and beliefs. Usually students will raise issues about the "sliminess" or "sneakiness" of snakes; typically other students will refute them, and discuss reptile morphology and life history, which may lead to instruction in predator/prey relations and population dynamics. A second useful topic is to explore how negative feelings about snakes arise both from personal experience, received cultural attitudes, and perhaps innate biological endowment. The role of the snake in *Genesis* is apt to emerge as a factor in the individual's concept.

Learning Summary. One concept to be summarized is that attitudes toward species stem from both personal experience and cultural influence. A related concept is the power of testimony to form feelings, whether from this poem or from stories heard from parents or peers. Follow-up questions and activities should attempt to focus on more complex questions regarding the ecological significance of a species and especially the conflict between existence of a species and an apparent material need for human society.

Journal Follow-up Questions

(1) If you were in the scene of the story, when would you feel justified in acting violently toward the snake?

(2) Is there any species that does deserve to be exterminated?

(3) What do you imagine would happen if humans succeeded in exterminating snakes?

Extended Activities. Some or all students might be assigned to choose one of the following:

(1) Research and report to the class on the question "What would happen if humans succeeded in exterminating snakes in a locality?" You could research textbooks, or interview a professor of ecology or biology.

(2) With partners, set up a debate on the public policy question of whether grey wolves, which some perceive as a threat to livestock (creating an unacceptable economic cost to ranchers), should be reintroduced in the northern Rockies, where they ranged prior to the advancement of human settlement.

(3) With partners, establish a public policy on grizzly bears in national parks such as Yellowstone, given that the bears have attacked and killed tourists there. Focus on the question of what rights the bears should have: continued existence only in zoos? a minimal population only in the most remote areas of public lands? the chance to expand their population at the expense of human convenience? at the expense of human safety?

B. "A WHITE HERON" (In Begiebing and Grumbling, pp. 439–446).

Introduction to the Text. In an introductory course the historical and geographical setting of the story should be described: an isolated small homestead in a small inland Maine town at the end of the 19th century; the characters are poor and uneducated. The story is told by a third-person narrator who sometimes comments on the characters' internal feelings. (For those unfamiliar with the story, it is the encounter of a young girl and her grandmother, on an isolated farm, with a hunter from the city who is collecting specimens of birds. He has heard of a rare bird in the locale and offers the girl money to reveal its nesting site. Her decision is complicated by her affection for the young man, who in fact teaches her about natural history and who represents a different world: urbane, educated, traveled, wealthy.)

Preparatory Journal Questions

(1) Consider the "conflict"—a literary term meaning that the protagonist must take action or make a decision, and consequently changes in some way. What is Sylvie's conflict? And how does she resolve it?

(2) How would you have resolved it? Why?

(3) Write questions that might be asked of each character to find out what they value, and why they act the way they do. Then try to imagine you are each of the three main characters, one at a time. Answer the questions that you wrote, and try to express what you (the character) value.

(4) A "symbol" is a physical thing in literature that reminds the reader of something else; often a symbol reminds us of personal associations that we have made with abstract qualities such as courage or freedom or love. Pick out two obviously central physical things—symbols—in the story and *free associate* what they evoke for you.

Follow-up Background Information. In several ways, the text calls for treatment from the perspective of feminist criticism. The characters in the story all offer positive traits, and the resolution of the conflict, according to the narrator, is ambiguous. In other words the story emphasizes relationships more than conflict, in keeping with other works by Jewett. Furthermore, the story sets at odds two ways of understanding nature: the objective, rational method of biological science, versus an intuitive, holistic approach that does not eliminate emotion and that assumes relationship between the knower and the living thing to be known. One can proceed from this point to a lecture on the Newtonian world view and its critique by Merchant (1983). Subsequent units might develop these themes, using, for example, Wordsworth's "The Tables Turned," Blake's "Mock On, Voltaire, Mock On Rousseau," or other works from the wealth of selection available in the anthologies listed in the Resources section below.

On the other hand, follow-up should attempt to understand the motivations of the amateur scientist, including his sincere desire to collect dead specimens, in terms of the evolution of biological science. More simply, it is important to communicate that behavior takes place in a cultural context, that historical characters act in terms of what they know.

One might ask "If ornithologists had never collected specimens, would we be as prepared today to understand the needs of species for their preservation?" From this line, the subsequent unit might be the essay by John James Audubon (namesake of the Audubon Society) about how he captured and killed birds in order to paint them ("My Style of Drawing Birds," in Begiebing and Grumbling 1990, pp. 268–271).

Extended Activity. After an initial discussion of the story, students return to the next class prepared for the following group activities:

(1) Two teams prepare to play the roles of the story's characters: in the second team students play roles of the opposite sex. The rest of the class prepares to interview the characters in order to understand their values and motivations.

(2) A team of students researches causes of extinction of birds in the United States during the 19th century and reports to the class.

(3) A team of students researches critical writing about the life and works of Sarah Orne Jewett, and dramatizes to the class what might be her own interpretation of the story, along with her rationale for writing it.

Follow-up Journal Question. If scientific knowledge, in the case of the snake, is necessary for understanding the creature, are there other kinds of knowledge, beyond science, that are also necessary for understanding?

Upper Division Course

Contemporary Nature Writing

Course Objectives

(1) To read contemporary forms of nature literature both as artistic creations and as portrayals of value-laden relationships with the natural world, and to place these forms in the evolving tradition.

(2) To analyze and compare significant contemporary forms: regional writing, environmental polemic, the literature of ecofeminism and of deep ecology, ecological speculation, wilderness writing, popular music, and journalism.

(3) To consider environmental themes and values of the literature in the context of our society and in terms of our own lives.

(4) To function as a learning community, each member acting as both teacher and learner. Primary concern in the course is for each learner to construct personal meaning from the texts and the problems posed there; then to express that meaning to members of the class; finally, to reflect upon others' constructions of meaning.

Texts and Assignments. In this advanced course I would provide background lectures on the authors and present excerpts of provocative
reviews and other criticism. Each book implies questions about an environmental issue of some depth that call for a subtle examination of values. Brief annotations and some possible questions follow.

- Dillard, A. [1974] 1988. *Pilgrim at Tinker Creek.* Dillard expresses
  horror at the immensity of death and "fecundity" in natural processes
  such as predation and evolution. Her attitude is based on religious
  assumptions. Is this horror similar to or different from the environmentalist's fear of species extinction? *Assignment in the community:*
  Find a forum where you can advocate for zero population growth (letter, church forum, town selectmen), and report to the class on your
  experience.

- McPhee, J. 1991. *Coming into the Country.* The Alaskan settlers
  treated sympathetically by McPhee do not, in their activities, fit
  within new land regulations devised to preserve the bioregion. Yet the
  impact of their activities, given their low population density (*a research assignment*), it can be argued, is negligible. Should opportunity for individuals to sustain themselves in the wilderness be incorporated in policy that attempts to preserve biodiversity?

- Abbey, E. [1968] 1990. *Desert Solitaire.* In the chapter on "The Dead
  Man at Grandview Point" and elsewhere Abbey raises the issue of
  human population expansion as a threat to the integrity of bioregions, speaking sometimes bitterly. Given that U.S. fecundity rates
  remain high and immigration is increasing, how do you appraise the
  values inherent in this conflict, and what policies can you imagine to
  alleviate it? (*a research assignment*).

- Ehrlich, G. 1985. *The Solace of Open Spaces.* Ehrlich finds spiritual
  communion with nature in an economic activity condemned by many
  environmental thinkers as destructive to the integrity of ecosystems,
  and hence to biodiversity. *Policy investigation:* Research current policy on grazing of stock on public lands, take a position, locate a like-
  minded environmental advocacy group, and somehow support their
  effort. Remembering that humans, like all other organisms, impact
  their environment in every activity, how do you evaluate her celebration of this experience in her publication?

- Anderson, L., ed. 1991. *Sisters of the Earth.* See annotation in
  Resources section under "Anthologies."

- Snyder, G. 1990. *Practice of the Wild.* San Francisco: North Point
  Press. Snyder's concern with preservation of "wild"-ness among both
  humans and nonhumans has implications for the design of human
  communities. In terms of your own values, what is an appropriate
  balance of rural land, wilderness, habitation, and commons in your
  region? *Creative assignment:* Map out how your bioregion would be

meeting human needs to ensure sustainability and conservation of other species if it had been planned ideally. Emphasize Snyder's concept of community.

- Berry, W. [1977] 1986. *The Unsettling of America.* Berry praises traditional rural culture and condemns thoughtless use of technological innovation. Because the visions of rural culture and of wilderness preservation have potential for conflict, try to analyze the respective values underlying these visions. *Research assignment:* Find the effects of agricultural development on wetland loss (a major cause of species extinction) and decide whether Berry's ideas might have prevented the problem—or might still remediate it.

- Lopez, B. 1989. *Crossing Open Ground.* Is the vandalism of ancient monuments described by Lopez the consequence of an innate and inevitable human tendency to destroy? From your general education draw knowledge from other disciplines to formulate for yourself the balance between the tendency toward destruction and the countervailing one toward sustenance.

Term Assignments. I've included two term assignments I find useful for eliciting active response from students.

- *Assignment 1.* A Learning Journal, recorded on a weekly schedule, should include for each week (a) informal responses to the featured new text written prior to class, (b) reflections on the text after class discussion, and (c) responses to occasional summary questions posed by the instructor. The journal is evaluated in terms of its substance, its depth, and its consistency of preparation. The student can raise the quality of the Learning Journal by regularly writing additional self-directed entries about the texts, about one's personal reaction to the texts, and/or about environmental concerns related to the texts studied.

- *Assignment 2.* Choose either (a) or (b).

(a) A Creative Project dealing with environmental perception, interpretation, or concern that is clearly related to the literature discussed in the course. It could take the form of a short story, a poem, an essay, a photoessay, a song, a video, a "letter to the editor," an editorial, a sculpture, or a game. It might be an imitation, a response to, or a parody of one of the course's featured writers. The creative project will be evaluated according to the qualities of originality of treatment, difficulty of medium, and vitality of theme.

(b) A three-page (typed) review of an environmentally oriented magazine or journal, or the environmental aspect of a regular department in a general journal. Examples of the former would be magazines like *E, Buzzworm, Garbage, Mother Earth News,* and *Sierra,* and journals like *Environmental History Review, Inquiry,* and *Environmental*

Ethics; examples of the latter would be magazines like *Outside, Mother Jones, Time, and Harpers,* or journals like *College English, MLA,* and *Science.* The review should (1) describe the periodical in general: how often it appears, how long it has been published, how widely it circulates, its advertising profile, its likely market; (2) judge the degree to which it deals with environmental matters and the perspective or bias it generally takes; (3) survey a list of themes or topics it has examined over the course of a recent year; (4) list the genres it has employed (fiction, poetry, science essay, nature essay, journalism, polemic, etc.); and (5) evaluate the journal.

Resources

Course Texts *(annotated above)*

Abbey, E. [1968] 1990. *Desert Solitaire.* New York: Ballantine.

Berry, W. [1977] 1986. *The Unsettling of America,* rev. ed. San Francisco: Sierra.

Dillard, A. [1974] 1988. *Pilgrim at Tinker Creek.* New York: Harper-Collins.

Ehrlich, G. 1985. *The Solace of Open Spaces.* New York: Viking Penguin.

Lopez, B. 1989. *Crossing Open Ground.* New York: Random.

McPhee, J. 1991. *Coming into the Country.* New York: Farrar, Strauss & Giroux.

Merchant, C. 1983. *The Death of Nature: Women, Ecology, and the Scientific Revolution.* New York: Harper and Row.

Silko, L. M. 1977. *Ceremony.* New York: Penguin Books.

Snyder, G. 1990. *Practice of the Wild.* San Francisco: North Point Press.

Anthologies of Literature

Anderson, D. D., ed. 1971. *Sunshine and Smoke: American Writers and the American Environment.* New York: J. B. Lippincott Company.

Inspired directly by Earth Day, this early anthology contains a long list of essays, stories, poems, and excerpts of longer works by a wide range of U.S. authors from colonial times up to its publication date. Though out of print, it is worth examination for the uniqueness of some selections, as well as inclusion of classic pieces. It is organized by thematic "Visions": "Abundance," "Fulfillment," and "Hope and Despair."

Anderson, L., ed. 1991. *Sisters of the Earth: Women's Prose and Poetry about Nature.* New York: Vintage Books.

A consistently fine anthology that can stand alone or complement one of the more traditional anthologies. It tends more toward contemporary writers, though earlier periods are represented. Also useful is its thematic arrangement: "Kinship," "Pleasures," "Rape," and "Healing" serve as section headers. Author biographies are included.

Beebe, W., ed. [1944] 1988. *The Book of the Naturalists*. Princeton, NJ: Princeton University Press.

As the name implies, this anthology focuses upon naturalist writers, from Aristotle up to Rachel Carson. Selections provide the sharp scientific observation of biota that is founded in care; moreover, many selections would as supplements enrich discussion of the ecological issues underlying short stories and poems.

Begiebing, R. J. and O. Grumbling, eds. 1990. *The Literature of Nature: The British and American Traditions*. Medford, NJ: Plexus Publishing, Inc.

This anthology includes poetry, short stories, and essays of 50 classic writers from the 18th century to the date of publication. It includes extensive essays on the evolution of nature writing in Britain and America, along with author headnotes. Unlike many anthologies, it tends to include complete texts; like many of the historical anthologies, however, its selection is short on women writers.

Bergeron, F., ed. 1980. *The Wilderness Reader*. New York: Penguin.

The narrow focus on prose nonfiction descriptions of the American wilderness dating from the 18th century makes this anthology especially useful in structuring a course similarly defined. It offers a fine introduction and well-chosen samples of the genre.

Caduto, M. J. and J. Bruchac. 1988. *Keepers of the Earth: Native American Stories and Environmental Activities for Children*. Golden, CO: Fulcrum, Inc.

Despite the title, stories from this collection should prove most useful in college courses because of the complex assumptions of value implied in the stories. Included is a lengthy section on pedagogical technique, again, much of it adaptable to the college classroom. Sections are organized by themes such as "Earth," "Water," "Sky," and "Plants and Animals." Bruchac has edited several other anthologies of native stories, such as *Keepers of the Animals*.

Diamond, I. and G. F. Orenstein, eds. 1991. *Reweaving the World: The Emergence of Ecofeminism*. San Francisco: Sierra Club Books.

The text presents biographies and bibliographies of ecofeminists with 26 selections from the movement's canon, organized around such thematic categories as "Reconnecting Politics and Ethics," and "Healing Ourselves; Healing Our Planet."

Erdoes, R. and A. Oriz. 1984. *American Myths and Legends*. New York: Pantheon Books.

This huge and in some ways definitive anthology compiles representative stories from a wide range on Native American tribal cultures. Selections are arranged by theme: human creation, world creation, coyote tales, animal stories, and so on. Includes a bibliography.

Finch, R. and J. Elder, eds. 1990. *The Norton Anthology of Nature Writing*. New York: Norton.

This vast collection (over 900 pp. and 94 authors) is informed by the idea that the "nature essay" has its roots in the European encounter with the American continent, the subject of its Introduction. It presents many classic authors and titles but relies exclusively on nonfiction prose, and includes no poetry or fiction. A thoughtful introduction and a selected bibliography accompany the selections.

Halpern, D., ed. 1986. *On Nature: Nature, Landscape, and Natural History*. San Francisco: North Point Press.

Focused, as the title indicates, on nature, this anthology includes excerpts from a wide variety of authors, including women, Native Americans, and scientists. Selections operate at a sophisticated conceptual level, generally with a naturalist orientation. Also included are useful bibliographies and an introduction by John Hay.

Kieran, John. ed. 1957. *John Kieran's Treasury of Great Nature Writing*. Garden City, NY: Hanover House.

The collection presents a long list of excerpts from British and American writers, slightly emphasizing naturalist writing. Some authors are well-known (Isaac Walton, Thoreau, Leopold, even one of William Cobbet's *Rural Rides*); many of the selections by lesser known writers are engaging. Out of print, but worth examining.

Knowles, K., ed. 1992. *Celebrating the Land: Women's Nature Writing, 1850–1991*. Flagstaff, AZ: Northland Publishing.

This anthology includes works by Cooper, Bird, Thaxter, Austin, Rawlings, Kumin, Zwinger, LeGuin, Hubbell, Dillard, Silko, and others.

Lyon, T. J., ed. 1989. *This Incomperable Lande*. New York: Viking Penguin.

Nonfiction prose from 22 American authors makes up this anthology, which is also distinguished by an excellent introductory essay of nearly 100 pages on American nature writing. Older texts are well-represented, with nearly half the book drawn from the 17th through 19th centuries. It includes an extensive bibliography. Like other anthologies set up historically, it offers few selections from women and minority authors.

Mabey, R., ed. 1984. *Second Nature*. London: Jonathan Cape.

An anthology of British contemporaries—both writers and artists—in an attempt to "promote the importance of . . . local distinctiveness." What results is marvelously concrete writing and art, connected to actual locales. A persistent theme, predictable in the British tradition, is the pervasive relation between nature and human culture, in the sense of an ancient tradition, felt rather than theorized. This collection would be most useful in a course dealing with contemporary British literature or environmental policy, or as a supplement to a survey course on British literature.

McKain, D., ed. 1974. *The Whole Earth: Essays in Appreciation, Anger, and Concern*. New York: St. John's Press.

An early anthology, *The Whole Earth,* presents a brief but unique selection of excerpts arranged to support the themes named in the title. The readings come from a wide variety of writers, including some not typically considered nature writers—like Jack Kerouac ("Desolation in Solitude") and the architect Frank Lloyd Wright. Unfortunately it is out of print; check libraries for a copy.

Mills, S., ed. 1990. *In Praise of Nature*. Washington, DC: Island Press.

As a reaction to the 20th anniversary of Earth Day, this text collects and comments on brief selections from major texts, organized by chapters on "Earth," "Air," "Fire," "Water," and "Spirit."

Slovick, S. H. and T. F. Dixon, eds. 1992. *Being in the World: An Environmental Reader for Writers*. New York: Macmillan.

This is a reader for freshman composition courses, with appropriate teaching apparatus, and a table of contents arranged not only in terms of writing modes, but also by geographical region.

Trimble, S., ed. 1988. *Words from the Land*. Layton, UT: Peregrine-Smith Books.

The focus is on naturalist observation drawn in lengthy selections from 15 of the most prestigious contemporary nature writers, supported by lengthy biographies.

Walker, M., ed. 1993. *Reading the Environment*. New York: Norton.

This is a reader for freshman composition classes, with the appropriate teaching apparatus. It is structured thematically, beginning with a section called "Entering the Conversation"—a good strategy for engaging masses of students who may not already have encountered the conversation. Included are many classic pieces, along with excerpts dealing with current environmental questions.

Willers, B., ed. 1991. *Learning to Listen to the Land.* Washington, DC: Island Press.

A powerful collection of generally brief essays that explore the value of biodiversity. These selections provide excellent practical suggestions for changing attitudes in order to accomplish what David Brower calls "the Green Shift" of paradigms. Authors include Lovelock, Wilson, Ehrenfeld, Stegner, Berry, and Abbey, often with startlingly apt pieces not often anthologized elsewhere. *Learning* might be the single most valuable anthology on biodiversity per se. Every selection offers passages worth introducing into a course discussion at some point.

Representative Scholarship Useful for Teaching

This sampling, focused on tools for teaching, is selected from a rapidly burgeoning scholarly canon. The scholarly literature can best be approached through review of several bibliographies, supplemented by the annual ASLE bibliography (first item below) for current work. Note that many of the anthologies listed above contain valuable bibliographies.

Association for the Study of Literature and the Environment. *Annual Annotated Bibliography of Scholarship on Literature and the Environment.* San Marcos, TX: Department of English, Southwest Texas State University.

Gross, M., R. Wilke, and J. Passineau, eds. 1989. *Working Together to Educate about the Environment.* Available from the North American Association for Environmental Education, P.O. Box 400, Troy, OH 45373. Selected Papers from the Joint Conference of the North American Association for Environmental Education and the Conservation Education Association.

This collection includes a number of articles on teaching approaches that use literature and that stress interdisciplinary approaches. In other articles it also provides a useful introduction to principles of environmental education.

Hilbert, B., ed. 1991. "The Literature of Nature." *Critic* 54(Fall). A special issue of The College English Association.

The focus of this collection is on approaches to teaching, and teaching nature writing rather than environmental literature, as the title indicates.

Nonetheless, it presents a wide range of approaches in its selections of "Practicum," actual course descriptions with strategies and activities, including those using ideological approaches. A. Zwinger, author of *Beyond the Aspen Grove,* contributes an essay describing her own work. Scott Slovic's "Annotated Booklet for Teachers of Environmental Literature" is a useful guide.

Piasecki, B., ed. 1992. "Special Curriculum Issue." *Environmental History Review* 16(Spring).

The hallmark of this Curriculum Issue is its rich, practical description of courses in several disciplines, that is, courses that frequently cross disciplinary boundaries. Sections deal with "Environmental History," "Humanities," "Natural Science," and "Integrated Studies." All of the course descriptions in all of the sections have potential to enrich literature courses.

Sherman, P. and R. F. Sayre, eds. 1991. "Nature Writers/Writing." Special Issue of *North Dakota Quarterly* 59(Spring).

Twenty provoking articles by respected contemporaries on prominent American nature writers. Of special interest is Thomas J. Lyon's essay "Nature Writing as Subversive Activity." Includes a half dozen creative works.

Waage, F., ed. 1985. *Teaching Environmental Literature.* New York: Modern Language Association of America.

The MLA funded this early teaching tool, a very useful hands-on guide to structuring college courses. It is divided by sections on environmental literature, nature writing, field-based teaching, and regional approaches. The book contains an extensive "Environmental Bibliography," which includes information centers and a bibliography of periodicals.

Periodicals

The following lists only a few journals of particular relevance. Many literary journals not named here occasionally run articles connected in some way with nature literature or environmental issues in ways that can prove useful to the teacher.

Several journals (all quarterlies) consistently include articles and reviews that deal with literature and, at least tangentially, the theme of biodiversity. Mostly the focus is on criticism, but some have offered special issues on teaching environmental literature (see above, Hilbert 1991; Piasecki 1992). Others, such as *ISLE,* include departments on classroom activities.

The Wordsworth Circle (New York: New York University), devoted to the first generation of British Romantics, frequently deals with nature writing and environmental issues in that context. Political issues revolving around reactions to industrialism also provide contexts for classroom discussions. *Western American Literature* (Logan, UT: Utah State University), probably more than any other academic journal of literature, consistently deals with nature literature, as a consequence of its focus on western American authors. Each issue includes articles, reviews, and essay reviews representing a wide range of perspectives. A recently established journal, *Interdisciplinary Studies in Literature and the Environment (ISLE)* suggests in its editorial stance a preoccupation with theory. Its stated mission includes the goal of creating "a more self-conscious... theoretical foundation. . . ." Published at the Indiana University of Pennsylvania, it includes a section on "Classroom Practice." The scholarly association affiliated with *ISLE*, the Association for Interdisciplinary Studies in Literature and the Environment, provides in its *Newsletter* a valuable means of networking with environmental advocacy groups and journals and magazines representing a wide range of approaches to the subject, and it offers much that is of practical value for teaching college courses. Since 1993 the *Newsletter* has subsumed *The American Nature Writing Newsletter*, which was a fine source for brief articles, notes, and reviews on American nature writing. A delightful newsletter highly useful for networking is *Writing Nature: An Annual of Fine Nature Writing*, published by J. Parker Huber, 35 Western Avenue, Brattleboro, VT 05301. It offers reviews, articles, notes, and personal "catching up" in a pleasantly informal structure.

Useful journals in related fields include *Environmental Ethics: An Interdisciplinary Journal* (Denton, TX: University of North Texas). Many classroom discussions of nature literature lead toward the kinds of questions discussed in its articles; it is useful, therefore, in providing a context when the literature opens questions about the rights of humans, for example, as opposed to other species. (See Chapter 9, below, Philosophy, for several specific references to this journal.) *Environmental History Review* (Newark: New Jersey Institute of Technology), formerly *Environmental Review*, has somewhat more immediate relevance in that many of its articles directly involve a literary text. Its book review section is particularly valuable, examining books from a wide range of disciplines and perspectives, and it has shown a continuing interest in providing materials and perspectives for teachers. (See Chapter 6, above, History, for specific references. Chapter 6 co-author, John Opie, was founding editor of *EHR*.) Another interdisciplinary journal, *Forest & Conservation History*, offers articles and book reviews in which literature figures as part of environmental history. It is published by the Forest History Society, Inc., Durham, North Carolina.

The magazines and journals of major environmental advocacy organizations can be depended upon for discussion of current issues relevant to biodiversity, and they sometimes include approaches that draw upon literature. Of these the venerable *Appalachia* (Boston: Appalachian Mountain Club) and *Sierra* (San Francisco: The Sierra Club) deserve mention for presentation of personal responses to wilderness landscapes. Similar regional publications are too numerous to mention.

Finally, many "environmentally concerned" popular magazines possess elements useful in literature courses; the best and most relevant is *Orion: People and Nature* (New York: Orion Society), which is consistently filled with thoughtful, intelligent articles that often arise out of literary traditions.

Chapter 8

Media and Journalism

Karl Grossman
State University of New York, College at Old Westbury
and
Ann Filemyr
Antioch College

The role of the communications media in helping people gain an understanding of environmental issues has been mixed. The publication in 1962 of Rachel Carson's seminal work, *Silent Spring,* spurred the development of a new branch of journalism: environmental journalism. Conversely, the decades of silence by major media on the environment and the sometimes inadequate media handling of environmental subjects today have been factors in discouraging environmental understanding.

"It has not taken the nation's newspapers very long to demonstrate their effectiveness as crusaders to protect the environment," John Hohenberg, professor emeritus at the Columbia University Graduate School of Journalism, wrote in the 1970s in his *The Professional Journalist,* long a widely used introductory journalism text. "Through their accomplishments, they have gone far toward making up for the long years during which they neglected the issue. It has seemed to make no difference whether a paper is large or small; if it has a public-spirited publisher, a determined editor, and a talented and devoted staff, it can—and does—obtain results" (p. 500).

Because it is a relatively new area of journalistic activity, reporting on environmental issues is a new subject of consideration in lower division college and university courses in media and journalism. Upper division courses devoted to the practice and history, as well as critical analysis, of the new field of environmental journalism have, likewise, not entered journalistic curricula until recently.

Environmental Journalism as Deep Journalism

Today, environmental issues are part of our daily news programming. Students are aware of and concerned about a wide range of these issues before they enter college. Their lives have already been directly affected by environmental degradation. When asked, students often list suburban development projects (shopping malls, parking lots, and housing), loss of wilderness and/or "green space," air and water pollution, and exposure to hazardous waste through incineration and landfills as the most pressing environmental issues with which they have had direct experience. Many of them are also aware of global issues such as the greenhouse effect, ozone depletion, over-population, species extinction, soil erosion and desertification, hunger, and homelessness. Students entering colleges today are seeking answers to these social and ecological problems. They are demanding that their courses prepare them to meet the challenges of the changing world, including the skills to communicate effectively about environmental issues. Despite this urgency, few courses and fewer textbooks address the particular role of the media in furthering public awareness of the requirements for an environmentally sustainable future.

Environmental journalists serve the public's right to know as they report on environmental issues (Carson 1962). Environmental reporting requires substantial preparation not just in understanding fundamental scientific concepts but also in addressing social, political, and philosophical questions concerning how we live in relation to the natural world. For example, an environmental journalist covering a story about a toxic chemical leak must be prepared to report not just about the effects on employees exposed to the chemical, but also about pertinent regulations and legislation governing the chemical in question. Any health effects tied to exposure of the chemical must be included. A well-written story would also include the larger environmental impacts of the chemical on air, water, and soil. It should point out who manufactures and distributes the chemical, what industrial uses it has, and what less toxic materials or processes could be substituted for it. The article could point out who benefits and who suffers by the current use of this chemical. In gathering and reporting on this information, the reporter strives for fair and accurate coverage in order to respond to community concerns regarding past, present, and future exposure to the chemical.

Public access to information is the cornerstone of democracy. Without information, citizens cannot participate meaningfully in public decision-making processes. Providing information to the general public on environmental issues is the job of environmental reporters, so many students of environmental communications are interested in sharpening their skills as writers and researchers. As we enter the next century, the public's need for better information on the environment will continue to increase.

A debate has raged in the practice of environmental journalism over whether it should involve advocacy or the traditional journalistic standard of objectivity. This controversy is central in deciding how to teach the subject. Michael Frome, director of the Environmental Journalism Program at Huxley College at Western Washington University, is convinced of the need to make students advocates for environmental protection. "I don't teach objectivity because I don't believe it exists. I'm very definitely teaching advocacy journalism" (*The Chronicle of Higher Education*, March 20, 1991, A35).

On the other side, Everette E. Dennis, executive director of the Freedom Forum Media Studies Center at Columbia University, declares in *Media and the Environment* (LaMay and Dennis 1991):

> The idea that a reporter would openly expose a point of view on a public issue violates the accepted canons of journalistic practice. . . . The American media's ideological code of objectivity describes both a philosophical commitment to what media people call 'fairness' and a style of news presentation that differs greatly from the textured interpretative essays of European journals. Beyond the separation of fact and opinion (ostensibly distinguishing news stories from editorials, columns, and commentary), traditional journalists in America strive for emotional detachment—an essential element of their professionalism, they say — as well as balance—typically stated as giving 'both sides' on conflicting interests a shot at a level playing field. (pp. 58–59)

But as Teya Ryan, an environmental journalist and senior producer of Turner Broadcasting System's program "Network Earth," says in the same book, "I think the environment may be the one area where you can say advocacy journalism is appropriate, indeed, vital... [because] we're talking about survival in the grandest sense of the word. Moreover the environment may be the one area where the issues are so crucial and so complex that it is imperative reporters offer the public some guidance" (pp. 84–85).

The authors of this chapter believe in practicing—and teaching—what we call Deep Journalism. Environmental reporters should be prepared to ask probing questions, to challenge fundamental assumptions, and to make clear connections. Those who have chosen to work at this kind of reporting have an unusual responsibility as messengers who raise issues which directly affect the health and survival of humankind and the biosphere.

The role of media in value change for sustainable development and planetary survival was the theme of an international gathering of environmental journalists, co-sponsored by UNICEF and the Global Forum on Media and Value Change for Human Survival, in Okayama, Japan, in 1993. Many journalists resist the idea that they are involved in value change, but the undeniable influence of the press is obvious in every nation.

An international perspective is vital in practicing—and teaching—environmental journalism. There are profound differences around the world in how the environment itself is defined, how environmental topics are addressed, and how far journalists are willing to go in questioning the status quo. These differences mark us as being from North or South, the richer nations or the poorer ones. Journalists in developing countries look at environment and development issues as inseparable. Overpopulation, hunger, and homelessness are considered critical environmental issues, as is international debt and the pressure it puts on small domestic economies to use up natural resources at an unprecedented rate. In the United States journalists often fail to make these kinds of connections.

There is also the insightful perspective of the late Varinda Tarzie Vittachi, a well-known international environmental journalist committed to journalism education. He stated,

> In the past five years—not much longer—we have changed our news values considerably to include the *Processes* which are endangering the very survival of all living things and not merely environmentally disastrous *Events* such as Chernobyl, Bhopal, forest devastation in Kalimantan and the Amazon, and the ravaging of the Aral Sea—as a regular and necessary item in our news menu. This is fine as long as we realize that it calls for (1) change in journalism training—educating ourselves in the sciences which touch on ecology; not to become experts but to become expert enough to ask the right questions from experts and understand their response well enough to make it interesting and intelligible to non-experts; (2) change in our time-scales of attention because process-reporting demands more persistence and follow-through than event-reporting; and (3) change in our ways of writing so that we are able to make our product as compelling as our reporting of events. (Letter to journalists participating in the Global Forum on Media and Value Change for Human Survival, March 1993, Okayama, Japan)

In addition, different cultural world views define different aspects of the natural environment as living versus nonliving. Native American Indians and other indigenous peoples hold that certain mountains, rivers and streams, rocks and minerals are living, that is, fully conscious beings. Many news stories show the clash between this world view and the world view that nature is primarily a resource for human use and human consumption. The struggle over Big Mountain in Northern Arizona between the Hopi, Diné, and Peabody Coal is only one example (Gedicks 1993). Another involves nuclear testing and nuclear waste dumping on Shoshone land in Nevada (Churchill 1993). There are many other examples (Bullard 1990; Bryant 1992; Churchill 1993; Gedicks 1993). For many indigenous people, cultural survival and cultural diversity are tied directly to the international debates in conservation and preservation of biodiversity. Environmental reporters need to be sensitive to these cultural differences when reporting on conflicts over natural resources and land use which involve indigenous people.

In short, as Sharon Friedman, Iacocca Professor and Director, Science and Environmental Writing Program, Lehigh University, concludes, environmental journalism reaches very far indeed: "To define environmental reporting just by the issues it includes may be too narrow. A much broader definition states that since the environment involves the active relationship between people and their living and non-living environs there is very little reporting that is not environmental" (*Asian Forum*, p. 28).

We try to encourage our students to make connections between their own identities, their privileges as citizens of the United States, and the social and environmental issues they think are important. We try to enlarge the circle of connection so that students are able to see how the environmental impact of one group or nation is connected to the entire ecosystem. We all live downstream, downwind, upstairs, or next door. How can journalists use their power to communicate, to speak to large numbers of people, to increase knowledge and respect between groups? It seems crucial to us that we must begin to provide education about the interrelationships between power and privilege on the one hand, and powerlessness, poverty, and environmental degradation on the other.

The idea that social systems of privilege need to be challenged has been foreign to most U.S. environmental journalism. There appears to be great reluctance to connect any issues of gender, race, or class to environmental issues. Journalists in the United States have long been silent regarding environmental racism. A good example, difficult to overlook, is the obvious targeting of communities of color, communities with less financial resources, less political influence, and less visibility, for toxic waste facilities and landfills.

We believe that the most effective form of environmental journalism is one that relies on the principles of investigative reporting, building on the foundation laid by Carson in *Silent Spring*.

We also teach our students that "...Environmental Reporting Can Be

Hazardous to Your Career," as *Extra!*, the magazine of the media watchdog group, Fairness and Accuracy in Reporting, headlined an article in its April/May 1992 issue, "After Earth Day: A Survey of Environmental Reporting." This *Extra!* issue is an important "reality check" for students. The article ends by noting that "it isn't only journalists at little papers who have to be careful: Phil Shabecoff, who covered the environment for the *New York Times* for 14 years, left the paper after being switched to the IRS beat. 'I was told my coverage was considered pro-environment, whatever that means,' Shabecoff told the *Washington Post* (May 5, 1991). The only example the *Times* gave him of what he was doing wrong: He used the word 'slaughter' to describe the mass killing of dolphins" (p. 16).

Environmental journalism regularly upsets some of the most powerful vested interests in society. The backlash by industry against environmental monitoring of all kinds, including environmental journalism, has become more and more intense. Students should learn that, practically speaking, there are limits to what environmental reporters can do. Students should be taught to ask difficult questions when investigating and writing environmental stories. It is not acceptable simply to poke a microphone in front of the face of the spokesperson for Exxon and be told that the mess in Prince Edward Sound is not *that bad*, and then write an article which simply juxtaposes the ecological destruction with the corporation's denial. These journalists should be prepared to dig, to seek to determine what really happened, how things really work. That is the necessary direction, the start toward Deep Journalism. And some may be fortunate and work at media locations where they will be fully free to practice Deep Journalism in environmental reporting.

Despite the emerging importance of media coverage of environmental issues, no central textbook exists for college faculty who are preparing to teach environmental journalism. Most journalism texts do not even include a chapter on this topic. However, students in undergraduate and graduate programs have indicated a keen interest in environmental communications, and it is likely that this interest will not abate in the future. Rather, it seems clear that we will need more students trained to take an interdisciplinary and multidisciplinary approach to environmental journalism in order to grasp the wide range of issues and their interrelationships. The demand for students with this expertise continues to grow. As Paul Nowak at the University of Michigan stated recently, "This is a very salable major. These students are in demand."

COURSE PLANS

The Environmental Journalism course, developed by Ann Filemyr, is presented here in two forms of organization, one focusing on topics and reading assignments and the other on journalistic writing assignments. Karl Grossman has added a unit on environmental racism, a relatively new and pressing issue, and one which, as he makes clear, is likely to reach students who might not otherwise show interest in environmental concerns. The emphasis throughout is on developing a cross-cultural and international perspective from which to understand the pressing environmental issues facing us today. Students will be actively involved in reading, discussion, research, and writing on current environmental issues, as well as learning about the recent development of environmental journalism worldwide as a specialization within the field of journalism. Following the course syllabus is a brief discussion of how to structure a major in Environmental Communications that includes work in television/video, radio, film, and photography, in addition to print media.

Environmental Journalism (organized by topic)

WEEK 1: INTRODUCTION TO ENVIRONMENTAL JOURNALISM

Topic: What is environmental journalism? The environmental journalist searches for a voice—voice in the wilderness, voice of opposition, factual voice, impassioned voice, voice of the people, voice of the planet. Introduction to current environmental specialty periodicals: *E Magazine, Earth Island Journal, Z Magazine, The Ecologist,* etc.

Readings

- Asian Forum of Environmental Journalists 1988, "Defining Environmental Reporting," chapter 3
- Carson 1962, "The Obligation To Endure," chapter 2
- Friedman 1991, "Two Decades of the Environmental Beat." In LaMay and Dennis 1991
- Ryan 1991, "Network Earth: Advocacy, Journalism, and the Environment." In LaMay and Dennis 1991
- Detjen 1991, "The Traditionalist's Tools (And a Fistful of New Ones)." In LaMay and Dennis 1991

WEEK 2: INTRODUCTION TO THEORY AND PRACTICE OF ENVIRONMENTAL JOURNALISM

Topic: The environmental journalist as educator. We will discuss the ideas of objectivity, fairness, and accuracy; gaining the reader's trust; media's role in influencing public opinion and shaping public policy; basic newswriting; the Freedom of Information Act (FOIA), and how to conduct a search for information.

Reading

• Asian Forum of Environmental Journalists 1988, "Check-lists for Reporters Working on Environmental Stories," chapter 7

WEEK 3: ENVIRONMENTAL JOURNALISM AND COMMUNITY PARTICIPATION

Topic: The environmental journalist as community member. Advocacy journalism; media as an instrument of social change; media as a mechanism for organizing/mobilizing around an issue; journalist as a public informant; journalism as a public service.

Readings

• Introducing an issue: Moyers 1990, "The Paths of Least Resistance," chapter 1
• Interview: The Cousteau Society 1985, "The Environment, the Press, and the Public"
• Personal experience: Watson 1991, "Raid on Reykjavik"
• Investigative report: O'Callaghan 1992, "Whose Agenda for America"
• Book review: Nash 1992, "The Beef Against..."
• Profile: Williams 1992, "The Spirit of Rachel Carson"
• Editorial: Valdez 1992, "Looking Beyond the Snail Darter"

WEEK 4: ENVIRONMENTAL JOURNALISM: CROSS CULTURAL PERSPECTIVES

Topic: The environmental journalist as cross-cultural communicator. Indigenous versus immigrant people's relationship to the land; concepts of the natural world; scientific methods and cultural perception; cultural survival versus development.

Readings

• Mander 1991, "What Americans Don't Know about Indians," chapter 11, and "Indians Are Different from Americans," chapter 12
• Gwaganad 1990, "Speaking the Haida Way." In Andrus et al. 1990
• Linden 1991, "Lost Tribes, Lost Knowledge"
• Alston, ed. 1990, *We Speak for Ourselves: Social Justice, Race, and Environment*

WEEK 5: MEDIA BIAS: WHAT IS IT?

Topic: The environmental journalist as an employee. Restrictions and realities of working for the "boss"; framing the issue; the media's participation in limiting public discourse.

Readings
- Spencer 1992, "U.S. Environmental Reporting: The Big Fizzle"
- Lee and Solomon (n.d.) *The Media Bias Detector*
- Grossman 1994, "A Nuclear Conflict of Interest? 20/20 Blurs the Lines"
- Fairness and Accuracy in Reporting (n.d.), *The Media Business.* Lists media ownership
- Mander 1991, "Television: Audiovisual Training for the Modern World," chapter 5

WEEK 6: RESEARCH METHODS FOR ENVIRONMENTAL JOURNALISTS

Topic: The environmental journalist as an investigator. EcoNet and computer networks; the Meeman Archive of Environmental Journalism (see Nowak 1987); "State of the World" annual reports and world atlas; accessing government reports and government files; informal video taping, photographic records, and eyewitness accounts; oral history gathering; reaching and questioning the experts; dealing with contradictory information; informing the public.

Reading
- Kessler and McDonald 1987, chapters 6–10

WEEK 7: THE ENVIRONMENTAL JOURNALIST AND ENVIRONMENTAL MOVEMENTS

Topic: Expressing opinion—editorials and commentaries. The relationship between reporters and movements; writers for the movement; challenging the status quo.

Readings
- Grossman 1992, "Every Breath We Take, of Toxic Racism and Environmental Justice"
- King 1993, "Feminism and Ecology"
- Plant 1990, "Revaluing Home: Feminism and Bioregionalism"
- Dodge 1990, "Living by Life and Practice, Some Bioregional Theory"

WEEK 8: ENVIRONMENTAL JOURNALISM AND INTERNATIONAL POLITICS

Topic: The environmental journalist as world citizen. Post-U.N. and NGO conferences on Environment and Development; "Agenda 21"; North/ South divisions and distribution of international decision-making power;

impact of poverty on the environment—environmental degradation caused by the unequal distribution of wealth; environmental impact of the military; the role of the World Bank and other major funding sources; multinational corporations; looking for connections in the BIG picture.

Readings

- Barnaby 1988, "Civilization in Crisis," chapter 5
- United Nations 1992, *Agenda 21: Report of the United Nations Conference on Environment and Development*
- Bliss-Guest 1992, *United States National Report for the United Nations Conference on Environment and Development*

WEEK 9: ENVIRONMENTAL JOURNALISM AND GLOBAL PERSPECTIVES

Topic: The environmental journalist as a change agent. Influence of Gaia hypothesis; beyond national boundaries; planet as home; bioregionalism and remapping the earth; sloganeering and the meaning behind slogans like "Think Globally, Act Locally" and "Earth Day Everyday"; home-based economics in the global marketplace; the role of the media in creating new images and metaphors for defining/shaping our relationship to the environment; sustainable development as the new mission for planetary survival.

Reading

- Brown (annual), *State of the Earth* (see Worldwatch Institute in Resource list, below), chapters selected as relevant from the current edition

WEEKS 10 AND 11: PRESENTATIONS OF INVESTIGATIVE REPORTS

Remember to include visual information—charts, graphs, clips from video, film or radio documentaries, photographs, etc.

Environmental Journalism (organized by writing assignments)

(1) EDITORIAL OR COMMENTARY: ENVIRONMENTAL JOURNALISM AS PERSUASIVE WRITING TO INFLUENCE THE PUBLIC.

This has been an important function of environmental journalism beginning with Rachel Carson and continuing in the present. Most students enter the course with very strong opinions on at least one environmental topic. Some feel passionately about the dangers of acid rain; others feel strongly about animal rights and embrace a vegetarian (or vegan) lifestyle; still others are strongly opposed to biotechnology. Prior to writing an editorial, students critique an environmental op/ed piece from a newspaper or magazine. In addition, the class reads hand-outs with numerous examples of editorials on a range of environmental issues. In class discussion, these editorials are critiqued for their effectiveness. Are they convincing? Why or why not? What information is the most persuasive? What kinds of information are used as the basis for building and sustaining an argument—statistical? moral or ethical? emotional? What are the sources for this information? Is the writer appealing to head or heart or both?

In writing their own editorials, they must address the arguments for or against their chosen topic in an intelligent and lively manner. They must rely on data gathered from valid sources to support their arguments. They must focus on solutions to problems and not just the problems themselves. They bring their written editorials to class to read. Students respond to each other's work. Everyone gets involved immediately in an atmosphere of exchange and debate that is necessary for journalists who want to engage in these topics. I establish ground rules for listening, for offering criticism or praise, and for asking questions in a fair and open manner. I insist that we do not need to agree, but that we learn to hear each other out.

(2) INTRODUCING A GLOBAL ENVIRONMENTAL TOPIC TO A GENERAL AUDIENCE: ENVIRONMENTAL JOURNALISM AS INFORMATIVE WRITING TO EDUCATE THE PUBLIC.

This second assignment is designed to help students consider audience as the key element in writing an article. The idea here is to present a global environmental issue (deforestation, desertification, soil erosion, global warming, population growth, loss of biodiversity, ozone depletion, nuclear energy, militarization, the relationship between poverty and environmental degradation, the relationship between gender and environmental issues, environmental racism, etc.) in a straightforward manner. Students are encouraged to incorporate visual elements, such as graphs, maps, and charts, to help communicate their message. Students are introduced to materials prepared and distributed by the United Nations, particularly Agenda 21 and the agreements reached during the 1992 Conference on Environment and Development. The focus here is on information presented in as clear and concise a manner as possible.

This article should present a broad, general overview of the problem for an average adult reader. This often requires students to create their own metaphors or seek out metaphors to explain problems and to find ways to break down technical language into terms more readily understood. Once a student has chosen a topic, the entire class works together to prepare questions. What exactly is the problem? What are the biological factors and conditions that create the problem? What historical/cultural/political/economic factors contribute to this problem? What are the solutions? I encourage students to begin with secondary sources, research already published on the topic, before seeking out available experts to interview.

These reports are presented to the class as a stimulus for discussion of the issues.

(3) SPECIAL COVERAGE OF A LOCAL ISSUE FOR THE CAMPUS NEWSPAPER: ENVIRONMENTAL JOURNALISM AS COMMUNITY-BASED PUBLIC SERVICE.

This is one of the most important assignments because it encourages students to serve a specific community and focus on local problems and solutions. It provides the opportunity to see how a well-researched story can serve as an instrument of change: values-change, awareness-change, or even action-change.

We brainstorm possible stories and try to prioritize them in order of timeliness or urgency or greatest impact. From this list students select stories to pursue; they often work together. They are responsible to the editors of the campus newspaper to meet the weekly deadline. The articles then appear (one or two in each issue) over the course of the quarter. Some students include photographs. Past student articles have been on a wide range of local issues with a focus on useful information. For example, an article on water quality in the Yellow Springs Creek explained the reasons why swimming is forbidden due to high pesticide and herbicide use by local farmers, resulting in skin and eye irritations. Other stories have focused on energy conservation on campus, cafeteria food sources, the student-run organic garden, asbestos in old buildings, strategies to reduce paper waste on campus, campus recycling, the environmental costs of vandalism, the health effects of inappropriate exposure to darkroom chemicals, cleaning solvents used by housekeeping staff, herbal medicine, students arrested for protesting hazardous waste burning at a local cement kiln, and the local impacts of proposed changes to environmental regulations by the Contract with America.

(4) PROFILE OF SOMEONE INVOLVED IN AN ENVIRONMENTAL ISSUE: ENVIRONMENTAL JOURNALISM AS FEATURE WRITING/HUMAN INTEREST STORIES.

The focus here is on developing student interview skills. We practice interviewing in class, develop questions, and create a list of possible interview subjects that are available in the area. Students are required to conduct these interviews as professionals. They use tape recorders as well as taking notes. We discuss the proper use of quotes, description, etc. by looking at numerous examples of profiles of environmental leaders.

Students enjoy this assignment. They have written profiles of local environmental activists that have been published in the town paper. They may interview science faculty involved in environmental research. They have interviewed environmental educators in local schools and programs. They have interviewed fellow students who have sailed with Greenpeace or marched against the nuclear testing on the Shoshone Reservation in Nevada. In addition, I try to bring in at least two or more speakers on environmental topics. In the past I have had bioregionalist author Stephanie Mills, my colleague and Antioch alumnus Karl Grossman, Eugene Linden of *Time* magazine, speakers from the local Indian Councils, local environmental activists, and representatives from environmental regulatory agencies and businesses. Students may interview guest speakers and write profiles for the school paper.

(5) IN-DEPTH INVESTIGATIVE PIECE: ENVIRONMENTAL JOURNALISM AS ACTIVISM FOR SOCIAL AND ENVIRONMENTAL JUSTICE.

In the spirit of the muckrakers of the early 20th century, investigative environmental journalists are often seeking to inform the public in order to inspire action to right injustices, correct misunderstanding and misinformation, and reveal cover-ups. Students are given approximately two weeks to complete each of the assignments listed above, but this final assignment is given four weeks. From all of the topics addressed and discussed in prior articles, introduced through the reading or by the speakers, students now select a final topic to investigate. They may work in E-Teams (Environmental Reporter Teams) as small groups of not more than four students.

Past investigative reports have been both creative and informative. Some have investigated local topics such as paper use and paper recycling on campus, local water quality, and asbestos in old buildings. Others have looked at larger issues which affect all of us. A few examples of these topics include food irradiation as a form of disposal of low level nuclear waste; the history of agent orange, its development and uses, and current health problems/birth defects attributed to exposure to agent orange by Vietnam vets; international perspectives on population growth and the impact of sterilization campaigns on Third World women; the historical relationship between deforestation and civilization beginning with the Tigris and Euphrates River Valley and ending with the Amazon; Judaism and earth-centered spirituality; consumerism as an extension of corporate culture and the environmental and social implications of the market economy; the philosophy of Deep Ecology Earth First! activists and Redwood Summer; monoculture farming versus permaculture and sustainable agriculture; the long-term consequences of nuclear bomb testing by the U.S. military on Bikini atoll and the health consequences to both the indigenous peoples and military personnel involved in the testing; the environmental and social impact of logging in the Pacific Northwest and the Endangered Species Act; the growing popularity of ecotourism and its potential impact on biodiversity.

Many of these reports are published in the school newspaper and serve to inform the local community of wider social and environmental issues. Each student or E-Team presents the final investigative report in class.

Course Unit: Environmental Racism

An advantage of presenting environmental racism as a component of an introductory journalism or communications course is that, because of its social and political nature, it interests students with concerns about fairness, health, racism, and social equity who otherwise might not be reached by other environmental themes. The components of this unit are: (1) an overview of the nature of environmental racism; (2) a class discussion—and it is highly likely that there will be students in one's class who are victims or who know victims of environmental racism; (3) an overview of the media handling of the matter; and (4) a discussion of that performance.

A good starting point for an overview is the 1987 report, *Toxic Wastes and Race in the United States*, of the Commission for Racial Justice of the United Church of Christ. It is summarized by Grossman (1991, 1992, 1994). An explanation of how the report came about is helpful for students. The Commission for Racial Justice began exploring the link between environmental degradation and race in 1982 after it was asked by residents of Warren County, North Carolina, for help in fighting the siting by the state of North Carolina of a dump for PCBs in predominantly African-American Warren County. A campaign of civil disobedience followed, in which more than 500 people were arrested, among them the commission's then executive director, Benjamin Chavis, Jr. It was during this struggle that Chavis began considering the connection between the Warren County dumping and the siting of toxic facilities in other black areas. These included the U.S. government's Savannah River nuclear facility (a source of radioactive leaks) in a largely black area of South Carolina, and the largest hazardous waste landfill in the nation, located in Emelle, Alabama, a community that is 80 percent African-American.

That led to the Commission correlating what the U.S. Environmental Protection Agency deemed commercial "hazardous waste facilities" and "uncontrolled toxic waste sites" with the ethnic composition of the communities in which they were located. The commission's report found:

- Communities with the greatest number of commercial hazardous waste facilities had the highest composition of ethnic residents.

- Although socio-economic status played an important role in the location of such facilities, race proved still more significant. This represented a consistent national pattern.
- Three out of the five largest commercial hazardous waste landfills in the United States were located in predominantly black or Hispanic communities. These three landfills accounted for 40 percent of the total estimated commercial landfill capacity in the nation.
- Three out of every five black and Hispanic-Americans lived in communities with at least one uncontrolled toxic waste site.
- Blacks were heavily over-represented in the populations of metropolitan areas with the largest number of uncontrolled toxic waste sites.
- Los Angeles had more Hispanics living in communities with uncontrolled toxic waste sites than any other metropolitan area in the United States.
- Approximately half of all Asian/Pacific Islanders and American Indians lived in communities with uncontrolled toxic waste sites. (Grossman 1994, 277–78)

As he prepared to present the report at the National Press Club in Washington, D.C., Chavis coined the term "environmental racism." His definition: "Environmental racism is racial discrimination in environmental policy making, the enforcement of regulations and laws, the deliberate targeting of people of color communities for toxic waste facilities, the official sanctioning of the life-threatening presence of poisons and pollutants in our communities and the history of excluding people of color from the leadership of the environmental movement" (Grossman 1994, 278).

The work of Robert Bullard is critical in teaching about the issue. A professor of sociology at the University of California, Riverside, Bullard began his research into environmental racism in 1979, while assisting his wife, an attorney, in preparing a class-action lawsuit to challenge the planned siting of a municipal landfill in Northwood Manor, a black middle class neighborhood of Houston, Texas. He discovered that since the 1920s, all five of Houston's landfills and six of its eight incinerators had been sited in black neighborhoods (Bullard 1990, 1993).

Bullard's (1990) book, *Dumping in Dixie*, concludes:

Limited housing and residential options combined with discriminatory facility practices have contributed to the imposition of all types of toxins on black communities through the siting of garbage dumps, hazardous waste landfills, incinerators, smelter operations, paper mills, chemical plants and a host of other polluting industries. These industries have generally followed the path of least resistance, which has been in economically powerless black communities. Poor black communities are by no means the only victims of siting disparities, however. Middle-income black communities are confronted with many of the same land-use disputes and environmental threats as their low-income counterparts. (pp. xiv–xv)

Bullard details the fight against environmental racism, how African-Americans in Houston and Dallas; in Alsen, Louisiana; Institute, West Virginia; and Emelle, Alabama, "have taken on corporate giants who would turn their areas into toxic wastelands" (p. xiv). And, he explores the struggle further in *Confronting Environmental Racism: Voices from the Grassroots* (1992) and *Unequal Protection: Environmental Justice and Communities of Color* (1994).

Other valuable teaching resources include the writings of Bunyan Bryant and Paul Mohai, professors at the School of Natural Resources at the University of Michigan, especially their book, *Race and the Incidence of Environmental Hazards* (1992).

It is then appropriate for the class to consider why the press, which in the United States is ideally supposed to be a watchdog, a monitor revealing social injustices and seeking to rectify them, has not been in the forefront of exposing this issue. Why did it take the Commission for Racial Justice and several African-American academics to reveal what the media could—and should—have begun dealing with years ago?

A classroom discussion of these questions can lead to two principal areas of concern: (1) On environmental racism—as on many environmental issues—the media have been slow to respond. Students should be encouraged to explore the overlapping ownership and directorates of the major media and large corporations who are likely to be the targets of investigation. For example, when a corporation like General Electric with a long record of pollution owns a major media outlet such as the National Broadcasting Company, it is a case of the entity that should be monitored owning the would-be monitor. Bagdikian (1992) shows a shrinking number of corporations owning much of the U.S. media, with many of the remaining media connected to corporations they should be watchdogging, through direct control, interlocking boards of directors, and other links. (2) Media in the United States has a history of ignoring institutional racism in general. Students should read the Kerner Commission report of 1968, which stressed how the media is derelict in examining racism in the United States and is itself reflective of a racist society—dominated by white males (still the case). Students might discuss how they think the domination of media by a segment of the population personally untouched by environmental racism might impact on media deciding "what's news."

The American Society of Newspaper Editors found in 1994, more than 25 years after Kerner, that minority daily newspaper staff members made up only 8 percent of newsroom employees and that minorities constitute only 18.2 percent of broadcast journalists, while they compose 25 percent of the population (Young 1994). Nonwhites in newspaper management remained at about 1 percent. In electronic media, subject to post-Kerner government pressure through the Federal Communications Commission, as of 1989 some 8 percent of radio news people and 16 percent of TV news employees—mainly lower-level—were minorities, according to the National Association of Black Journalists (Jones 1989).

An article by Martinez and Head (1992), "Media White-Out of Environmental Racism," is helpful in discussions of media performance on environmental racism. The article begins:

> The young Anglo environmental reporter at the *Albuquerque Journal* stared blankly when SouthWest Organizing Project co-director Jeanne Gauna spoke about environmental racism. Still, to help him read up on the subject, she offered him a copy of *Toxic Wastes and Race in the United States.* . . . About a week later, he returned the study. Regarding its findings, he said, "This may be true in other places, but it's not the case in Albuquerque." (p. 29)

Martinez and Head conclude that there are "three major reasons" for the media failure to highlight environmental racism:

(1) Corporate interests are at stake, and the mass media hesitate to thoroughly scrutinize them;

(2) societal racism encourages the media to be uninterested in people of color unless there's a sensational (usually negative) story; and

(3) government agencies, especially the U.S. Environmental Protection Agency, have actively pursued strategies to divert public attention from the issue of environmental racism. (p. 29)

The Liberal Arts Major in Environmental Communications

The major in Environmental Communications at Antioch College could be replicated on other campuses where sufficient courses exist in various departments to allow a comprehensive, integrated program of study. This self-designed major incorporates courses in Environmental Science, Ecological Economics, Environmental Policy and Law, Environmental Ethics, Gender, Race, and Class in Environmental Movements, Women and Nature, Nature Writing, and other related courses. This interdisciplinary approach prepares students who are also developing their skills in production techniques in a nonprint medium (film, video, radio, photography). Their upper level coursework must reflect a synthesis of these concerns as they produce work in documentary film, video, and/or photography concerning environmental issues. Senior projects in Environmental Communications have included a video documentary on local environmental issues; a photo essay on ecologically based intentional communities; a photo essay on the impact of tourism on a rural community; outdoor public signage for an environmental education center; a video documentary on the conflict over land at Big Mountain, Arizona, from the perspective of the Diné (Navajo) People; a photo essay and investigative report on women and water in Palestine; investigative report and photo essay on water and international aid in Cape Verde, West Africa.

Students in environmental communications have also been encouraged to participate in cooperative education experiences or internships with environmental organizations working in public relations and related areas in order to polish their skills in communicating with large, general audiences about environmental issues. Many students continue to work with organizations and educational programs to make documentary materials on environmental issues, and some students continue their studies in Environmental Communications at a graduate level.

Resources

Page numbers appearing in brackets at the end of some entries indicate where the reference is cited in a course plan.

Books Specifically for Environmental Journalists

The Asian Forum of Environmental Journalists. 1988. *Reporting on the Environment: A Handbook for Journalists*. Bangkok: The U.N. Economic and Social Commission for Asia and the Pacific. [pp. 180, 181]

This is an excellent practical guide for reporting on the environment. Chapters on the importance of environmental issues; their complexity; specific strategies for researching stories; suggestions for how to write stories that will both educate and inform the public, etc. Includes an excellent glossary with concise explanations of scientific terms. Available from United Nations Economic and Social Commission for Asia and the Pacific, the United Nations Building, Rajadamnern Avenue, Bangkok, 10200, Thailand.

Bliss-Guest, Patricia, ed. 1992. *United States of America National Report for the United Nations Conference on Environment and Development*. One volume, 420 pages, available from the Executive Office

of the President, Council on Environmental Quality, Washington, DC
20503. [p. 183]

Each participating nation was required to prepare a national report before
the conference.

Carson, R. 1962. *Silent Spring.* Boston: Houghton Mifflin Company.
[p. 180]

As a scientist who began to write for a general audience, Rachel Carson is
the first who could be called an environmental reporter in the United States.
Her research and reporting on pesticide use caused an enormous stir and
changed the way many North Americans thought about the use of chemicals
in daily life. Certainly the struggle is not over. Though her work resulted in
the banning of DDT in the United States, it is still manufactured and distributed worldwide. She has been the inspiration of many who have followed
her. This should be required reading for all serious students of environmental journalism and science writing.

Davis, J., ed. 1991. *The Earth First! Reader: Ten Years of Radical Environmental Journalism.* Salt Lake City: Peregrine Smith Books.

This book is a collection of articles published over a 10-year period
(1980–1990) in the *Earth First! Journal,* the publication of the Earth First!
environmental movement. These articles will spark much discussion as they
chronicle the viewpoints and strategies of activists directly involved in grassroots action from road blockades in old growth forests to the sinking of whal-
ing ships. Some have accused Earth First! of ecoterrorism; others considered
it the brave leading edge of citizen action to protect and preserve nature.
Excellent for a discussion of ethical issues and imperatives of human and
natural survival.

Kessler, L. and D. McDonald. 1987. *Uncovering the News: A Journalist's
Search for Information.* Belmont, CA: Wadsworth Publishing Co. [p.
182]

This book provides an overview for journalism students in how to research
information for stories as well as in ethical and legal issues. An excellent
primer.

LaMay, C. L. and E. E. Dennis, eds. 1991. *Media and the Environment.*
Washington, DC: Island Press. [p. 180]

Collection of articles by journalists and environmental writers on controversial issues: Should the media serve as environmental advocates? Is the environment a new kind of story requiring a new kind of reporting? Are there
contradictions between the media's role in advertising and their role in environmental reporting? Can the media respond to the need to place environ-

mental reporting into larger contexts, such as philosophy, politics, economics, and culture? Features writing by Teya Ryan, producer of Turner Broadcasting's *Network Earth;* Emily Smith, science and technology writer for *Business Week;* Jim Detjen, reporter for the *Philadelphia Enquirer* and president of the Society for Environmental Journalists; Herman E. Daly, senior economist at the World Bank and author of *Steady-State Economics;* Donella H. Meadows, syndicated columnist and professor of environmental studies at Dartmouth College, as well as author of *The Global Citizen.* Based on *Gannett Center Journal,* Summer 1990 issue, "Covering the Environment."

Moyers, B. and Center for Investigative Reporting. 1990. *Global Dumping Ground: The International Traffic in Hazardous Waste.* Washington, DC: Seven Locks Press. [p. 181]

Documents a number of case studies of illegal and legal dumping of toxic hazardous waste from the United States and Europe into African, Caribbean, and South American nations. Includes interviews with both senders and receivers; documents deaths and other serious health problems resulting from exposure to toxic waste; points out the moral issues of richer nations dumping in poorer nations where people are unaware of the danger they are in as a result of toxic chemicals dumped in their neighborhoods; discusses the United Nations Accord in Montreal to halt the exporting of toxic waste, as well as the persistent problem in industrialized nations to alter production practices so as not to continue creating this unwanted garbage.

Nowak, P. F., ed. 1987. *Environmental Journalism: The Best from the Meeman Archive.* Scripps Howard Foundation. School of Natural Resources, University of Michigan, Ann Arbor, MI 48109. [p. 182]

The Meeman Archive was established by the Scripps Howard Foundation at the University of Michigan to preserve and make accessible to the public outstanding journalism in the areas of conservation, environment, and natural resources. It is housed in the School of Natural Resources in Ann Arbor. This unique collection reprints the award-winning series on hazardous waste dumping in Alabama. In addition, the Meeman Archive will conduct on-line searches for articles on any environmental topic from their electronic data bank. Contact Paul F. Nowak or Jonathan Friendly (313) 763-0445 for more information.

Prato, L. 1991. *Covering the Environmental Beat: An Overview for Radio and TV Journalists.* Washington, DC: Environmental Reporting Forum.

Useful and practical tips for any professional working this beat. Great resource for advanced students.

United Nations. *Report of the United Nations Conference on Environment and Development*. Rio de Janeiro, June 3–14, 1992. Five Volumes available from the United Nations, New York, NY. [p. 183]

A compendium of all the treaties and agreements and accompanying documentation from the Earth Summit.

Books and Articles on Environmental Racism

Alston, D., ed. 1990. *We Speak for Ourselves: Social Justice, Race, and Environment*. Washington, DC: The Panos Institute, 1717 Massachusetts Avenue NW, Suite 301, Washington, DC 20036. (202) 483-0044. [p. 181]

Boulard, G. 1993. "Combating Environmental Racism." *The Christian Science Monitor*, March 17:8.

Brough, H. September/October 1990. "Minorities Define 'Environmentalism'." *World Watch* 3(5):5–7.

Bryant, B. and P. Mohai. 1992. *Race and the Incidence of Environmental Hazards*. Boulder, CO: Westview Press. [p. 189]

Bullard, R. D. 1983. "Solid Waste Sites and the Black Houston Community." *Sociological Inquiry* 53:273–88.

Bullard, R. D. 1990. *Dumping in Dixie: Race, Class, and Environmental Quality*. Boulder, CO: Westview Press. [p. 188]

Bullard, R. D., ed. 1992. *Confronting Environmental Racism: Voices from the Grassroots*. Cambridge, MA: South End Press. [p. 189]

Bullard, R. D. 1993. *Confronting Environmental Racism: Voices from the Grassroots*. Boston: South End Press. [p. 188]

Bullard, R. D., ed. 1994. *Unequal Protection: Environmental Justice and Communities of Color*. San Francisco: Sierra Club Books. [p. 189]

Bullard, R. D., and B. H. Wright. 1987. "Politics of Equity: Emergent Trends in the Black Community." *Mid-American Review of Sociology* 12(2):21–38.

Bullard, R. D. and B. H. Wright. 1990. "Mobilizing the Black Community for Environmental Justice." *The Journal of Intergroup Relations* 17(1):34–43.

Churchill, W. 1993. *Struggle for the Land: Indigenous Resistance to Genocide, Ecocide, and Expropriation*. Monroe, ME: Common Courage Press.

Commission for Racial Justice. 1987. *Toxic Wastes and Race in the United States: A National Report on the Racial and Socio-Economic Characteristics of Communities with Hazardous Waste Sites*. New York: Commission for Racial Justice, United Church of Christ. 475 Riverside Drive, New York, NY 10115. (212) 870-2077. [p. 187]

Faupel, C. E., C. Bailey, and G. Griffin. 1991. "Local Media Roles in Defining Hazardous Waste as a Social Problem: The Case of Sumter County, Alabama." *Sociological Spectrum* 11:293–319.

Frampton, G. T., Jr. 1991. "Bringing Racial Diversity to the Environmental Movement." *Reconstruction* 1(3):41–45.

Gedicks, A. 1993. *The New Resource Wars: Native and Environmental Struggles Against Multinational Corporations*. Boston: South End Press.

Grossman, K. 1991. "Environmental Racism." *The Crisis*, April, 14–32. [p. 187]

Grossman, K. 1992. "Every Breath We Take, of Toxic Racism and Environmental Justice." *E, The Environmental Magazine*, May/June, 30–35. [pp. 182, 187]

Grossman, K. 1994. "The People of Color Environmental Summit." In *Unequal Protection*. R. D. Bullard, ed. San Francisco: Sierra Club Books. [pp. 187, 188]

Gwaganad. 1990, "Speaking the Haida Way." In Andrus et al. 1990. [p. 181]

Jaimes, M. A., ed. 1992. *The State of Native America: Genocide, Colonization, and Resistance*. Boston: South End Press.

Jones, A. S. 1989. "Black Journalists Seeking New Gains in the Newsroom." *The New York Times*, Aug. 17.

Kerner Commission. [1968] 1988. *The Kerner Report: The 1968 Report of the National Advisory Commission on Civil Disorders*. New York: Pantheon Books.

King, Y. 1993. "Feminism and Ecology." In *Toxic Struggles: The Theory and Practice of Environmental Justice*, R. Hofrichter, ed. Philadelphia: New Society Publishers. [p. 182]

Linden, E. 1991. "Lost Tribes, Lost Knowledge." *Time*, Sept. 23: 46–55. [p. 181]

Mander, J. 1991. *In the Absence of the Sacred: The Failure of Technology and the Survival of the Indian Nations*. San Francisco: Sierra Club Books. [pp. 181, 182]

Martinez, E. and L. Head. 1992. "Media White-Out of Environmental Racism." *Extra!* Special issue, "Focus on Racism in the Media," July/August, 29-31. [p. 190]

Matthiesson, P. 1984. *Indian Country*. New York: Penguin.

Schwab, J. 1994. *Deeper Shades of Green: The Rise of Blue-Collar and Minority Environmentalism in America*. San Francisco: Sierra Club Books.

Young, M. R. 1994. "Black Journalists Snub Daily News." *Newsday*, July 28: A15. [p. 190]

A highly effective video for students examining environmental justice is "Documentary Highlights of The First National People of Color Environmental Leadership Summit," available from the United Church of Christ, Cleveland, OH. (800) 325-7061.

Additional Texts

Andrus, V., C. Plant, J. Plant, and E. Wright, eds. 1990. *HOME! A Bioregional Reader*. Philadelphia: New Society Publishers.

Bagdikian, B. H. 1992.. *The Media Monopoly*, 4th ed. Boston: Beacon Press. [p. 189]

Barnaby, F., ed. 1988. *The Gaia Peace Atlas: Survival into the Third Millennium*. New York: Doubleday. [p. 183]

Danziger, G. 1992. *The Solid Waste Mess: What Should We Do With the Garbage?* Troy, OH: NAAEE Publishers (see below under "Organizations").

Dodge, J. 1990. "Living by Life and Practice: Some Bioregional Theory." In Andrus et al. 1990. [p. 182]

The Environmental Health Center/National Safety Council. *Covering the Coasts: A Reporters Guide to Coastal and Marine Resources* (n.d.), *Reporting on Municipal Solid Waste: A Local Issue* (1993), and *Reporting on Climate Change: Understanding the Science*. Booklets available, 1019 19th Street, NW #401, Washington, DC 20036. (202) 293-2270.

Fairness and Accuracy in Reporting (n.d.) *The Media Business*. Booklet published by FAIR (see below under "Organizations"). [p. 182]

Fellowship for Intentional Communities. 1990. *Intentional Communities 1990–91 Directory: A Guide to Cooperative Living*. Stelle, IL: Communities Publications Cooperative. 105 Sun St. 60919. (815) 256-2252.

Goldman, B. A. 1991. *The Truth About Where You Live: An Atlas on Toxins and Mortality*. New York: Random House.

Grossman, K. 1980. *Cover Up: What You Are Not Supposed to Know about Nuclear Power*. Sag Harbor, NY: Permanent Press.

Grossman, K. 1983 *The Poison Conspiracy*. Sag Harbor, NY: Permanent Press.

Grossman, K. 1986. *Power Crazy*. New York: Grove Press.

Grossman, K. 1994. "A Nuclear Conflict of Interest? 20/20 Blurs the Lines." *EXTRA!* 7(1):12–18. [p. 182]

Hilz, C. 1992. *The International Toxic Waste Trade*. New York: Van Nostrand Reinhold.

Hofrichter, R., ed. 1993. *Toxic Struggles: The Theory and Practice of Environmental Justice*. Philadelphia: New Society Publishers.

Kessler, L. and D. McDonald. 1987. *Uncovering the News: A Journalist's Search for Information*. Belmont, CA: Wadsworth.

Lee, M. and N. Solomon (n.d.). *The Media Bias Detector*. Booklet published by FAIR: Fairness and Accuracy in Reporting (see below under "Organizations"). [p. 182]

McKibben, B. 1992. *The Age of Missing Information*. New York: Random House.

Miller, C. and K. Swift. 1988. *The Handbook for Non-Sexist Writing: For Writers, Editors, and Speakers*. New York: Harper and Row.

Nash, J. M. 1992. "The Beef Against. . . ." Review of J. Rifkin, *Beyond Beef: The Rise and Fall of the Cattle Culture. Time*, April 20: 76–77. [p. 181]

O'Callaghan, K. 1992. "Whose Agenda for America?" *Audubon* 94(5):80–91. [p. 181]

Plant, J. ed. 1988. *Healing the Wounds: The Promise of Ecofeminism*. Philadelphia: New Society Publishers.

Plant, J. 1990. "Revaluing Home: Feminism and Bioregionalism." In Andrus et al. 1990. [p. 182]

Sandman, P. M, D. B. Sachsman, and M. R. Gochfield. 1987. *Environmental Risk and the Press*. New Brunswick, NJ: Transaction Publishers.

Seager, J., ed. 1990. *The State of the Earth Atlas*. New York: Simon and Schuster.

Spencer, M. 1992. "U.S. Environmental Reporting: The Big Fizzle." *Extra!* A publication of FAIR: Fairness and Accuracy in Reporting, April/May, 12-22. [p. 182]

Valdez, L. 1992. "Looking Beyond the Snail Darter." *Quill*, April, 45-47. [p. 181]

Walter, M. L., ed. 1994. *Reporting on RISK: A Journalist's Handbook*. Michigan Sea Grant Communications, University of Michigan, 2200 Bonisteel Boulevard, Ann Arbor, MI 48109. (313) 764-1138.

Watson, P. 1991. "Raid on Reykjavik." In *The Earth First! Reader*. J. Davis, ed. Salt Lake City: Peregrine Smith Books. [p. 181]

Williams, T. T. 1992. "The Spirit of Rachel Carson." *Audubon* 94(4):104-107. [p. 181]

World Resources Institute. 1994. *World Resources 1994–95: A Guide to the Global Environment*. New York: Oxford University Press.

Audio Cassettes/Radio

"Common Ground." This professional world affairs radio series has covered environmental issues since 1980. The Stanley Foundation. Call (800) 767-1929 to order a catalog of cassettes. Excellent resource.

"Earth on the Air," produced by the Earth on the Air Radio Cooperative, a nonprofit organization with the mission of empowering the public by involving it in radio. Students can make programs to submit for broadcast. Broadly defined the show is about "How we treat our planet and how we treat each other." Includes commentary, satire, poetry, music, interviews, etc. The show is hosted by Peter Malof and Janice Kayne. Contact Pacifica Program Service: (800) 735-0230.

"GoodKind of Sound." Has audio cassettes available from all of the sessions of the annual Society for Environmental Journalists' meetings as well as speeches from UNCED and the Global Forum in Rio. An excellent resource. Particularly recommended are these two from the 2nd National Conference of the SEJ, November 6–8, 1992: J. Edelson, E. Linden, W. Minis, S. Curwood, and R. Manning, "Is the Environmental Beat Endangered?"; and J. Detjen, E. Hayes, and J. Alexander, "Environmental Reporting 101: A Basic Introduction." Route 3, Box 365AA, Sylva, NC 28779. (800) 476-4785.

Television, Films, and Videos

Bullfrog Films, Inc. P.O. Box 149, Oley, PA 19547. (800) 543-3764.

Rents films and videos with environmental themes. Write to request a free catalog.

CNN. Barbara Pyle, producer for CNN environmental stories, and Teya Ryan, producer for Turner Broadcasting System's "Network Earth." One CNN Center, Box 105366, Atlanta, GA 30348. (404) 827-1500.

Corporation for Public Broadcasting. PBS Adult Learning Satellite Service. 1320 Braddock Place, Alexandria, VA 22314. (800) 257-2578.

Produced a 1990 Year of the Environment/Environmental Resource Compendium. Also produced two programs on Nuclear Power: "Nuclear Waste in the West" and "Nuclear Power: Re-Emerging in the 1990s." Other programs available. Contact them for more information.

EnviroVideo. Box 311, Ft. Tilden, NY 11695. (800) ECO-TV-46.

Produced and distributes "Nukes in Space: The Nuclearization and Weaponization of the Heavens," a 60-minute documentary on how the U.S. government is pushing ahead with the deployment of nuclear technology in space, and "Three Mile Island Revisited," a 30-minute documentary that shows that despite the claims of government and industry officials, people did die and that the illness continues as a result of the nuclear accident near Harrisburg, Pennsylvania, in March 1979. The catalog also lists some 100 of Enviro Video's other environmental videos.

Facets. 1517 W. Fuller Avenue, Chicago, IL 60614. (800) 311-6197.

Video distribution center that carries hard-to-find environmental education videos. Write or call for a free catalog.

Media Network. 121 Fulton, 5th floor, New York, NY 10038. (212) 619-3455.

Environmental education films and videos; distributes "Greenjems," a guide listing available and new films and videos on environmental subjects.

National Film Board (NFB) of Canada. "Green Video Guide," P.O. Box 6100, Station A, Montreal, Quebec H3C 3H5.

NFB has a long track record of generating public awareness of the present global environmental crisis. Get their catalog. They also have regional 800 numbers to call for purchase and rental arrangements.

One World 92. One World Group of Broadcasters. Ritchie Cogan, BBC One World Unit, E219 BBC Television Centre, Wood Lane, London, Great Britain W12 7RJ. Phone: (44-81) 576 7987; fax: (44-81) 576 7250.

International linkage of television broadcasters from Eastern and Western Africa, Portuguese-speaking Africa, Brazil, and Japan who planned a programming season from January–June 1992 in preparation for the Earth Summit in Rio. Programs included "documentaries, drama, children's programs and light entertainment to show that problems of environment and Third World development are two sides of the same coin."

Television Trust for the Environment (TVE). Bruno Sorrentino, Programme Executive, 46 Charlotte Street, London W1P 1LX United Kingdom. Phone: (44-71) 637 4602; fax: (44-71) 580 7780.

Produces and distributes film documentaries on environmental issues in developing nations for educational purposes and public information.

The Video Project: Films and Videos for a Safe and Sustainable World. 5332 College Avenue, Suite 101, Oakland, CA 94618. (800) 4-PLANET

Produces an annual catalog of over 190 independently produced video documentaries on environmental problems and solutions distributed by this nonprofit organization.

Worldlink. 8755 W. Colgate Avenue, Los Angeles, CA 90048. (213) 273-2636.

Produced a video series, "Spaceship Earth: Our Global Environment," to present segments on environmental problems and solutions. Hosted entirely by young people. Includes teacher guide.

English Language Periodicals Whose Primary Focus Is Environmental News

Alternatives: Perspectives on Society, Technology and Environment. c/o Faculty Environmental Studies, University of Waterloo, Waterloo, Ontario, Canada N2L 3O1.

Common Sense on Energy and Our Environment. P.O. Box 215, Morrisville, PA. 19067-0215.

E Magazine. P.O. Box 5098, Westport, CT 06881. [p. 180]

Earth First! P.O. Box 1415, Department NN, Eugene, OR 97440.

Earth Island Journal. Gar Smith, Editor. Published by Earth Island Institute, 300 Broadway, Suite 28, San Francisco, CA 94133. (415) 283-3200. [p. 180]

Earthwatch. 680 Mt. Auburn Street, P. O. Box 403, Watertown, MA 02272.

The Ecologist. Editorial Office, Corner House, Station Road, Sturminster, Newton, Dorset, DT101BB UK. Phone: 44-258-73476; fax: 44-258-73748; E-mail GN: Ecologist. [p. 180]

Ecology Center Newsletter. 2530 San Pablo Ave., Berkeley, CA 94702. (415) 548-2220.

Environmental Action. Environmental Action, Inc. 1525 New Hampshire Ave. NW, Washington, DC 20036. (202) 745-4870.

Environment Writer and *Journ E.* Resources for environmental journalism educators published by the Environmental Health Center, a division of the National Safety Council, 1019 19th St. NW, Suite 401, Washington, DC 20036.

Green Magazine. Windsor House, London Road, Norbury, London SW164DH, England. Phone: (44-81) 679-1899; fax: (44-81) 679-1899.

Greenpeace: Greenpeace U.S.A., 1436 U Street NW, Washington, DC 20009.

The New Catalyst. P.O. Box 97, Lillooet, British Columbia, Canada, V0K 1V0.

Our Planet: The United Nations Environment Programme Magazine for Sustainable Development. P.O. Box 30552, Nairobi, Kenya. Phone: (2542) 621 234; fax 226 831; telex 22068 UNEP KE.

Rachel's Environment and Health Weekly: Providing News and Resources for Environmental Justice. Environmental Research Foundation, P.O. Box 5036, Annapolis, MD 21403.

Rocky Mountain Institute Newsletter. Rocky Mountain Institute, 1739 Snowmass Creek Road, Snowmass, CO 81654-9199.

Searching for Success. Renew America, 1400 16th St. NW, Suite 710, Washington, DC 20036. (202) 232-2252.

SEJournal. Quarterly publication of the Society for Environmental Journalism. 9425 Stenton Avenue, Suite 209, Philadelphia, PA 19118.

The Trumpeter: Voices from the Canadian Ecophilosophy Network. Light Star, 1138 Richardson Street, Victoria, British Columbia, Canada V8V 3C8.

UnderCurrents. c/o Faculty of Environmental Studies, York University, 4700 Keele St., North York, Ontario, Canada M3J 1P3.

Whole Earth. 27 Gate Five Road, Sausalito, CA 94965. (415) 332-1716.

Wild Earth. Cenozoic Society, Inc. P.O. Box 455, Richmond, VT 05477.

World Climate: A Quarterly Review of Issues Concerning Global Climate Change. Department of Environmental Sciences, Clark Hill, University of Virginia, Charlottesville, VA 22903.

World Ecology Report. World Information Transfer. 866 Third Ave., New York, NY 10022. Phone: (212) 702-3750; fax: (212) 888-4960.

World Watch. Worldwatch Institute, 1776 Massachusetts Ave., NW, Washington, DC 20036.

Selected International Publications

Folhado Meio Ambiente. Published by Forest Cultura Viva e Promocoes, Ltda. SCS, Q, 08, Ed. Venancio 2000, Bloco B-60, sala 228, Brasilia, Brasil 70333.

The only Portuguese language news magazine devoted exclusively to environmental news in Brazil, includes English summaries of articles.

Japan Environment Monitor. Published monthly by an independent group of writers. Editors: Rick Davis at 400 Yamanashi-ken, Kofu-shi, Saiwai-cho 18-11, Kofu, Japan. Phone/fax: 0552-28-5386; and Maggie Suzuki at 769-29 Kagawa-ken, Okawa-gun, Hiketa-cho,Kureha 279-1, Japan. Phone/fax: 0879-33-6763.

This volunteer effort is aimed at grassroots organizers both inside and out of Japan. It is an English language publication.

Jornal "A Semana." Jorge Soares, Director, Avenue Cidade Lisboa, Caixa Postal 36-C, Praia, Cabo Verde, West Africa.

A private Portuguese language newspaper owned by a collective of 50 Caboverdeans covering local environmental issues as well as other news. The only non–government controlled media outlet (including radio and television) in Cabo Verde.

Electronic Bulletin Boards

EcoNet. An electronic network for environmental information. Institute for Global Communication, 3228 Sacramento Street, San Francisco, CA 94115. (415) 923-0900

Organizations and Organizational Resources

Arena Press: Specialists in Environmental Printing. 207 Main Street, Point Arena, CA 95468. (800) 882-2833.

Excellent resource if your campus is ready to make the switch to recycled paper and soybean-oil based inks in their newspaper and publications. As educators, we can take the leadership not simply to teach the issues but to make the necessary lifestyle and production changes when and where we can in our homes and communities.

Center for Foreign Journalists. 11690A Sunrise Valley Drive, Reston, VA 22091. (703) 620-5984.

Co-sponsors international gatherings of environmental journalists and provides education and networking for journalists with an interest in this beat.

Consortium for International Earth Science Information Network. CIESIN, 2250 Pierce Road, University Center, Saginaw, MI 48710. (517) 797-2700; E-mail: CIESIN. Info@ciesin.org.

A nonprofit corporation founded to facilitate access to, use, and understanding of global change information worldwide. CIESIN has been commissioned by NASA to extend the benefits of NASA's Earth Observing System (EOS) to a broad array of international research and nonresearch users, including policy makers, federal agencies, educators, resource managers, and the general public.

Earth Council/Consejo de la TierraConseil de la Terre. P.O. Box 2323-1002, San José, Costa Rica. (506) 255-2197; E-mail: ecouncil@igc.apc. org.

An international trilingual organization following up on the agreements at the United Nations Conference on Environment and Development, June 1992. Dedicated to ongoing international dialog on sustainable development.

FAIR: Fairness and Accuracy in Reporting. 130 West 25th Street, New York, NY 10001. (212) 633-6700.

Members receive *Extra!,* a monthly magazine of media criticism including critical analysis of mainstream media coverage of the environment. The July/August 1992 issue of *Extra!* was devoted to an analysis of environmental journalism, "After Earth Day: A Survey of Environmental Reporting." Watchdog organization for media bias in reporting.

International Women's Tribune Center. 777 United Nations Plaza, New York, NY 10017.

Provides books and other resources, participates in international efforts on women's development with an analysis of environment and gender.

North American Association for Environmental Education (NAAEE). Suite 400, 1255 23rd Street NW, Washington, DC 20037. (202) 467-8753. Publications and Member Services Office, P.O. Box 400, Troy, OH 45373. (513) 339-6835.

This is an excellent resource for communications educators on environmental issues, topics, and teaching methods. Books in the "Environmental Issues Forum" series are designed to help local organizations and schools conduct public meetings and study circles addressing difficult environmental issues. Excellent resource for role-playing exercises on community decision-making processes that can be used in the classroom.

Nuclear Information & Resource Service. 1424 16th Street NW, Suite 601, Washington, DC 20036. Phone: (202) 328-0002; fax: (202) 462-2183; E-mail: nirsnet@igc.apc.org.

Superb source of information on nuclear technology especially commercial nuclear power, nuclear waste, and radiation. Publishes *The Nuclear Monitor Bi-weekly.* Sends out alerts on legislative and regulatory actions via fax and internet.

Safe Energy Communication Council. 1717 Massachusetts Ave. NW, Suite 805, Washington, DC 20036. Phone: (202) 483-8491; fax: (202) 234-9194.

A coalition of national energy, environmental, and public-interest media groups working to increase awareness about energy efficiency and renewable-energy technologies. Issues reports, provides camera-ready art, and offers training to grassroots citizen-organizations on interacting more effectively with media.

The Scientists' Institute for Public Information (SIPI). Media Resource Service (MRS), 355 Lexington Avenue, New York, NY 10017. (800) 223-1730.

In 1980 SIPI began the MRS, a free referral service for journalists who need information sources in science, technology, medicine, and the environment. SIPI staff provide journalists with names, affiliations, and phone/fax numbers to make direct contact with qualified experts. They have also provided assistance to student journalists. Send them a fax with a description of the story and your needs. For more information contact Roshi Pelaseyed, Director, Global Change Program.

Society for Environmental Journalists. Box 27506, Philadelphia, PA 19118. (215) 247-9710; E-mail: SEJOffice@aol.com.

Members receive a quarterly publication with pertinent news and coverage of issues. Sponsors an annual meeting. Membership includes both professionals and academics in environmental media.

Union of Concerned Scientists. 2 Brattle Square, Cambridge, MA 02238. Phone (617) 547-5552; fax: (617) 864-9405; E-mail: ucsatucsusa.org.

Dedicated to advancing responsible public policies in areas where technology plays a critical role. Publishes books, brochures, briefing papers, and the quarterly newsletter, *Nucleus.*

WEDO: Women's Environment and Development Organization. 845 Third Avenue, 15th Floor, New York, NY 10022. (212) 759-7982; E-mail: wedo@igc.org.

Provides an analysis of environment and development issues from a gender perspective. Newsletter available. Organizes conferences and supports grassroots organizing efforts.

World Information Service on Energy. P.O. Box 18185, 10001 ZB Amsterdam, The Netherlands. Phone: 31-20-6392681; fax: 31-20-6391379; E-mail: wiseamster@gn.apc.org.

Publishes *WISE News Communique* bi-weekly, which contains information on energy, mainly nuclear power, and effects of radiation, seldom seen in mainstream media.

Worldwatch Institute. 1776 Massachusetts Ave, NW, Washington, DC 20036. (202) 452-1999. [p. 183]

Produces the annual *State of the World Report on Progress Toward a Sustainable Society,* L. R. Brown et al. New York: W.W. Norton.

Conferences
(a sample of conference activity, listed chronologically)

Ann Filemyr has attended these conferences and has materials available if anyone is interested.

"Early Warnings Conference on Media and the Environment." Sponsored by *Utne Reader*, Minneapolis, Minnesota, May 1990.

"Imprensa Verde 92." International Green Press Conference. Co-sponsored by International Journalists Organization (OIJ); Brazilian National Federation of Journalists (FENAJO); and the Professional Journalist Union in Brazilian State of Minas Gerais (SJPMG). Belo Horizonte, Minas Gerais, Brazil, May 20–24, 1992.

Society for Environmental Journalists: Second National Annual Conference. Ann Arbor, Michigan, November 6–8, 1992.

"Value Change for Global Survival: The Role of the News Media." Co-sponsored by the Center for Foreign Journalists and UNICEF, Okayama, Japan, April 17–20, 1993.

"Communication and Our Environment." Third Biennial Conference, Chattanooga, Tennessee. Sponsored by the West Chair of Excellence in Communication and Public Affairs, University of Tennessee at Chattanooga. Chattanooga, March 30–April 2, 1995.

Chapter 9

Philosophy

Holmes Rolston III
Colorado State University

Teaching Environmental Ethics

Few discussions of environmental conservation continue long without
reaching the question "Why?", and the answers are seldom elaborated
for long without reaching the question of values. What we wish to conserve depends on what we value. What we ought to conserve depends on
what we ought to value. Environmental ethics is entwined with values
carried by nature. What is of value there? How are values to be discovered and judged? That is a philosophical question.

What we must do to achieve conservation is importantly a biological
question. How much habitat do these endangered species require? What
is their minimum breeding population? After that, what we must do is,
secondly, a social and political question. How can we protect this amount
of habitat from the social forces that encroach upon it? What laws or
environmental policy, strategy, or incentives will be effective? Conservation is an economic question. Who will pay and can we afford it? But the
biological, political, social, and economic questions presuppose that
philosophical questions have been or can be answered. Why ought we to
care for these endangered species? What are they good for? Why save

them? Is this a matter of prudence or principle? What is the character of our duties to, or concerning, nonhuman creatures? Do they count morally? How do we count their value?

Fortunately, persons may often agree on a course of action without entirely agreeing on their reasons why. Values are often nonrival, and though people use different premises with which to obtain the consensus, they may converge on a single course of action. That is, in fact, regularly the case in a democracy, where legislation is often supported by a coalition of interests. Within individuals themselves, as well as within groups acting in concert, reasons may add up and reinforce each other. Unfortunately, often they do not, as the controversy over cutting old growth forests in the Pacific Northwest illustrates. Almost every piece of environmental legislation passed in the last half century has been fought over.

Cut two ways, environmental ethics is of two broad kinds:

(1) An anthropic ethic concerns the environment instrumentally but is concerned about humans intrinsically. That is the ethics most readily reached from the humanistic philosophical tradition, which takes traditional ethics (whether utilitarian, rights-based, pragmatic, or whatever) and applies it to the environment. Ethical concern for humans is primary; ethical concern about the environment is secondary, tributary to the primary ethic.

(2) A naturalistic ethic (without denying that humans are a major concern of ethics) is also concerned directly about some nonhuman creatures—perhaps animals who suffer or species that become extinct. Such an ethics is more radical, theoretically as well as practically, since it challenges the prevailing humanism and ascribes values to nonhuman nature. It takes nature as sometimes ethically primary. There are duties to nonhumans, not just duties concerning them.

The two-way cut is only introductory, and early in the debate it became clear that environmental ethics could be cut three ways: (1) an anthropic ethic, as before. But now the naturalistic domain is divided into (2) an animal ethics, concerned with the welfare of sentient creatures, and (3) a land ethics, concerned with nature as a whole, with ecosystems. In the memorable injunction of Aldo Leopold, "A thing is right when it tends to preserve the integrity, stability, and beauty of the biotic community. It is wrong when it tends otherwise." Fortunately again, integrity in the biotic community is entwined with the welfare of sentient creatures. Unfortunately again, this is not always so. We might need to cull or hunt excess elk, for instance, if they are overpopulating and range is being degraded.

Even the three-way cut proves inadequate, and, with further analysis, there are at least five levels of concern. The principles of moral concern differ at each level.

(1) An anthropic ethic, interhuman ethics. Environmental ethics nowhere denies that humans are a primary focus of ethical concern; typically what's good for the environment is good for people, and vice versa.

(2) An animal ethic, since animal welfare counts morally. Humans, though they may sometimes override animal welfare, ought at least to consider it.

(3) A respect for all life, plant as well as animal, if it is true that plants embody values. For there does seem to be some sense in which plants defend their own vitality, even though they do not suffer pains and pleasures. They can be helped or harmed, in better or worse condition.

(4) A concern for endangered species, respect for life at the species level, since we are much more concerned with the death of a dozen whooping cranes than with the death of a dozen Canada geese, although approximately equal avian well-being and suffering is involved in each case. We may prefer endangered plants over feral animals or permit the hunting of common animals but forbid the hunting of endangered ones.

(5) A concern for biotic community, for the web of life that incorporates animals, and plant species with which human culture is entwined. This is often called a land ethics.

Perhaps these multiple levels of concern drive us into a pluralism. Those who conclude so have recently taken a pluralist turn, maintaining that there are and ought to be several different kinds of environmental ethics. Is there a unifying theory, one that can guide us in practice when the different kinds of ethics seem to conflict? These axiological problems lie at the center of environmental ethics as the discipline has developed over the last two decades.

There are other ways of approaching the same territory and these can also prove seminal. These approaches may be better suited to the interests of some instructors or with some classes. An appropriate respect for life is a religious challenge; instructors should consult Chapter 11, Religion. Still others think that the value problems can best be solved with Asian worldviews. Whether the Asian assistance succeeds or fails, it throws into relief our Western axioms about valuing nature. Deep ecology is a philosophical worldview so life-orienting as to become in many respects a religion. Biocentrism, a life-centered account, tends to focus more on the organismic individual, less on wholes. Feminists have been active in environmentalism; ecofeminists may claim that a large part of the inappropriate conduct that characterizes the environmental crisis lies in male dominance. Suggestions for proceeding with each of these approaches are presented in the following section.

Global concerns increasingly loom large. These are sometimes physical ones, such as climate change or the loss of the ozone layer. They are sometimes social issues such as the seemingly inequitable distribution of wealth between developed nations and developing ones. Nations of "the North," so-called, with one-fifth of the world's population, produce and consume about fourth-fifths of the worlds goods. Nations of "the South," with four-fifths of the world's population, produce and consume about one-fifth. Overconsumption, overpopulation, and maldistribution all seem to be sources of the environmental crisis.

Environmental ethics is sometimes greeted with a smile—romantics concerned about the chipmunks and daisies—or with disdain—tree-huggers who ignore the problems of war, justice, human suffering, and digress to marginal frivolities. Environmental ethics is in fact urgent and relevant, as shown by the recent Earth Summit in Rio de Janeiro. The four most critical issues that humans currently encounter are peace, environment, development, and population. All are interrelated, and no solution for one can be found without solutions for the others. Human desires for maximum development drive population increases, escalate exploitation of the environment, and fuel the forces of war. Those without moral principles will exploit humans as readily as nature. Those at peace with nature will seldom need to be urged to seek peace with their neighbors. Nor can anyone be at peace with neighbors or nature until he or she has a concept of nature and of community, a philosophy of residence in the world.

Ethics until recently was almost exclusively concerned with other humans. Ethics can exclusively be practiced by humans, who are the only moral agents on Earth, the only ones concerned. But are humans the only objects of moral concern? There seems something amiss about an ethic that regards the welfare of only one of the several million species on Earth as an object of duty. Ought not *Homo sapiens*, the sole moral species, seeking to be the wise species, seeking to be a philosopher (who *loves wisdom*), appropriately respect life at all its panoramic levels? Socrates said that the unexamined life is not worth living, and we can add that life in an unexamined world is not worthy living either. Any comprehensive education requires examination of what kind of place we live in, the worth of the world. There is something morally naive about living in a reference frame where one species takes itself as absolute and values everything else relative to its utility. There is something incomplete about an education without an environmental ethics.

Ethics is at once the most challenging and the most ready philosophy to teach. Some say teaching ethics is impossible, or even wrong. Since one cannot make somebody else do right, they must discover the right for themselves, and one ought not to impose one's values on others. According to this viewpoint, one can only coach ethics. Yet students are ready to talk ethics; environmental issues are front page news; good cases abound to launch discussions. Students have other majors, in many of which environmental issues will arise. For example, see Chapter 4, Economics, where Smith argues that ethical assumptions about what constitutes a fulfilled life lie at the root of economic theories and that students must be challenged to examine these. What anthropologists have learned about humans relating to their environment in other societies may also inform the discussion (Chapter 2, Anthropology). Orr (Chapter 1, Reinventing Higher Education) presents a uniquely educational perspective on these same issues. Students will disagree with each other, or be puzzled about what they think, but they are ready to become intellectually involved. The instructor may lecture, but philosophy since its origins has been dialogue (the Socratic method).

There is much good audio-visual material, often best used as short excerpts to introduce issues. Lots of projects, from abstract theory to on-the-ground practice, are possible, either singly or in groups. (See Chapter 1, Reinventing Higher Education, for examples of practical, locally based projects.) Teaching ethics, especially environmental ethics, can be quite an adventure. You will learn something about teaching methods, as well as about ethics and the environment.

COURSE PLANS

Introductory Course Units

Unit Description and Objectives. Suggestions for introductory units follow, with readings listed that will raise the central questions in environmental ethics. For complete references, see the Resources. See also Vitek (1992), "Teaching Environmental Ethics" and, earlier, Sagoff (1980a), "On Teaching Environmental Ethics." These units will be suitable for students who are in their first philosophy course, which will perhaps also be the only philosophy class that they ever take.

Readings (To construct a unit, choose three from among the following suggestions.)

- Rolston (1981), "Values in Nature"; Rolston (1994b), "Value in Nature and the Nature of Value"; Rolston (1988b), "Human Values and Natural Systems"; and Rolston (1988d), "Values Deep in the Woods." Any of these four will introduce the values questions by itemizing values with which the reader can identify. The reader will be drawn further than first expected into wondering whether the values that humans find to be carried by nature are not, in part at least, objectively there. Readers will feel clearer about what sorts of values nature has, but confused about whether these values are humanist or natural. Part of the difficulty will be working within and, at the same time, beginning to break out of a human-centered concept of value.

- Rolston (1994a), *Conserving Natural Value.* Any of the chapters entitled, "Natural and Cultural Values," "Anthropocentric Values," "Intrinsic Natural Values," or "The Home Planet," will introduce the nature–culture question and lead into questions similar to those above. Here, all the articles are in one place, written for freshmen and sophomores, with nonphilosophy majors in mind.

- Callicott (1986), "The Search for an Environmental Ethic." A good summary of the field that will reduce somewhat the sense of confusion above, beginning to introduce order into the different theoretical approaches. Callicott advocates a land ethic, but nevertheless hopes to use a humanist value theory to value nature intrinsically.

- Naess (1973), "The Shallow and the Deep, Long-Range Ecology Movement: A Summary." This uses a short, pioneering article in the field to set out sharp contrasts: a humanist, resource-oriented ethic now lamented as "shallow" versus a "deep" ethic that relates humans to a community of natural value.

- Callicott (1980), "Animal Liberation: A Triangular Affair." Although it seemed, reading Naess, that there were two sides in the debate, Callicott here returns to convince us that there are at least three. Even if one is convinced that there are duties to and values in the natural world, there is still homework to do. A classic article that no one can read without becoming worried that there may be irreconcilable differences among those who love animals and those who are environmentalists (Humane Society types versus Sierra Club types).

- Leopold (1949), "The Land Ethic." Probably the most famous article in the field, simply written, elusive, and subtly persuasive in its mix of argument and appeal to experience.

- Rolston (1994c), "Winning and Losing in Environmental Ethics." Useful for its focus on the question whether humans will or ought to lose when they do the right thing in environmental ethics, always an issue to which students soon come. Does appropriate respect for nature combine with human interests in a sustainable biosphere so that solutions are always win–win?

Complete Upper Division Courses

A Systematic Environmental Ethics Course

Course Description and Objectives. The author has taught environmental ethics at Colorado State University for many years, and the syllabus presented below has evolved with the developing literature. The book *Environmental Ethics* (Rolston 1988a), which grew out of essays collected in *Philosophy Gone Wild* (Rolston 1986), digests that teaching experience and reflects a mixture of theory and practice. The class is junior/senior level, attended by majors from throughout the university, many in the sciences and natural resource fields, with perhaps one-fifth of the class being philosophy majors.

The course begins with the 19th century, with a backward look at the philosophical roots of current concepts of nature in the strong contrast between Emerson's ([1844] 1926, 1961) romanticism and Mill's ([1874] 1969) scientific empiricism. It notes the sources of conservation both in romanticism and in the resource use tradition, two perspectives later embodied in Muir and Pinchot at the turn of the 20th century. Emerson gives a 19th century portrait of life in harmony with nature. Mill gives a hard-nosed, critical, scientific approach. Nature is amoral or immoral, an odious scene of violence, to be conquered by human ingenuity; following nature is irrelevant to morality.

The course is thereafter contemporary. There is first a taxonomy of values carried by nature (Rolston 1988a, *Environmental Ethics*, chapter 1), then a progression through levels of concern: animal welfare (Rolston 1988a, chapter 2, and Callicott 1980, "Animal Liberation"); respect for organismic life (Rolston 1988a, chapter 3, and Taylor 1981, "The Ethics of Respect for Nature," which takes a biocentric approach); endangered species (Rolston 1988a, chapter 4); and ecosystems (Rolston 1988a, chapter 5, and Leopold's [1949] land ethic). Subsequent topics include faking nature (Elliot 1982—faked nature has less value than pristine nature), then an introduction to religion and environment. I use White (1967), "The Historical Roots of Our Ecological Crisis," which needs to be adequately criticized. Then there is an Eastern turn. Smith (1972), "Tao Now," persuasively idealizes Taoism and Buddhism. Earhart (1970), "The Ideal of Nature in Japanese Religions and its Possible Significance for Ecological Concerns," is appreciative but has more critical skepticism and many doubts. Afterward, students are stimulated and divided by attitudes toward the American Indian in Callicott's (1982) "Traditional American Indian and Western European Attitudes toward Nature." This is a perceptive, well-written account that romanticizes the American Indian and criticizes European attitudes sufficiently to stimulate considerable discussion. Redford (1990), "The Ecologically Noble Savage," challenges Callicott's idealization: Indigenous peoples did and continue to do whatever they need to to survive, which sometimes shows ecological insight but more often does not. (See Chapter 2, Anthropology, for a parallel treatment.)

The course then focuses on value theory in systematic form (Rolston 1988a, chapter 6), which is theoretical, controversial, and relatively difficult for students. It then drops from theoretical to practical levels: environmental ethics applied with common sense maxims to environmental policy, to an ethic of the commons (Rolston 1988a, chapter 7), to environmental business (Rolston 1988a, chapter 8), and finally to an embodied ethic, one that is lived with a sense of residence in natural place as culture is superposed on nature (Rolston 1988a, chapter 9. See also Chapter 6, History, "Cognitive mapping: Learning to read your personal history in your neighborhood environment.")

There is frequent use of discussion cases, often introduced by videotapes. Only extracts may be used to start discussion. *Fence at Red Rim* pits animal welfare against a rancher's rights. The extract on rescuing the drowning bison, against park policy, from *Yellowstone in Winter* raises the issue of compassion for animals suffering in the wild. Trophy hunting is at issue in *Black Bear Hunting Secrets,* and *The Ancient Forests* asks whether the abuse of land is not because we regard land as a commodity rather than a community.

A Course Emphasizing Theoretical Issues

Course Description and Objectives. Choose three of the following principal systematic treatments and work through them, comparing and contrasting each with the others. There is a wealth of literature now available, and the principal treatments are listed below, alphabetically. All are serious reading. Students will find Wenz (1988) and Attfield (1992) the hardest. Naess (1989) is expensive. Des Jardins (1993) is the easiest but is not a primary source. See further notes in Resource section.

Readings

- Attfield (1992), *Ethics of Environmental Concern.* The most historically oriented of these works, good not only for its careful analysis of Western philosophical and religious traditions, but excellent as an education in the history of ideas. Reading this book is an example of classical liberal arts, here applied to a survey of the concept of nature in the primary Western sources.
- Brennan (1988), *Thinking About Nature.* The most ecologically informed of these works, a well-argued attempt to think through which philosophical positions do have strong empirical, scientific support and which ones do not. Brennan advocates an ecological humanism.
- Callicott (1995), *Earth's Insights: A Survey of Ecological Ethics from the Mediterranean Basin to the Australian Outback.* The only globally comparative environmental ethics, with the sustained intent to see what everybody else outside the Western world thinks about the relation between humans and nature and to set this beside the Western traditions. A Herculean effort, ending in the conclusion that many

indigenous peoples, and, fortunately, Leopold's land ethic as well, already were almost postmodern.

- Des Jardins (1993), *Environmental Ethics: An Introduction to Environmental Philosophy.* Unlike the others in this section, this book is not written as a primary contribution to the field but rather attempts to describe at the freshman and sophomore levels what the main writers in the field have been arguing. In that sense it is the first "secondary" text in environmental ethics. But Des Jardins does critically assess the primary writers and leads students to see where the principal issues lie.

- Hargrove (1989), *Foundations of Environmental Ethics.* Hargrove pays more attention than others to the 19th century roots of 20th century environmentalism in the United States. He advocates an appreciation of aesthetic creativity in nature as the foundation of an environmental ethic. This book will have to be coupled with others to examine the full range of issues currently being discussed in environmental ethics.

- Johnson (1991), *A Morally Deep World: An Essay on Moral Significance and Environmental Ethics.* We morally ought to consider whatever has interests, and this includes not only humans but also animals, plants, species, and ecosystems. Johnson is surprised to find that the latter three have interests but argues that such logic is inescapable. Such interests are much like traditional concepts of goods or welfare.

- McLaughlin (1993), *Regarding Nature: Industrialism and Deep Ecology.* Deep ecology explained by drawing out areas of continuity and discontinuity between deep ecology and progressive political thought. Examined are the fundamental assumptions of the ideologies within which we find ourselves caught—capitalism, socialism, anthropocentrism, and egocentrism. McLaughlin does social more than scientific ecology.

- Marietta (1995), *For People and the Planet: Holism and Humanism in Environmental Ethics.* An effort to place humans in a holistic, planetary perspective, with an emphasis on the ways in which humans constitute their worlds (a phenomenological approach), with more or less adequacy in their environmental relationships. Perhaps the most sustained inquiry into environmental holism and individual humans and their place in nature.

- Naess (1989), *Ecology, Community, and Lifestyle.* The most systematic deep ecology approach. Arguing that shallow approaches are not going to resolve the current crisis, the Norwegian philosopher and environmental activist Arne Naess advocates deep ecology, a nonanthropocentric movement calling for the overthrow of the current social, political, and value systems in favor of biospheric egalitarianism.

- Rolston (1988a), *Environmental Ethics*. A systematic account, with chapters devoted to the ways humans value nature, to duties to animals, plants, species, ecosystems, an account of natural value theory, and concluding with chapters on environmental policy, business and the environment, and an ethics of personal residence. This book features many cases that can be used in class discussions.
- Sagoff (1988), *The Economy of the Earth*. More oriented to law and environmental policy than are the other introductions here. Useful if your students come more from political science or business, or if they come from the sciences but need this perspective.
- Stone (1987), *Earth and Other Ethics*. Stone is easy to read, literate in both philosophy and law, with a pragmatic outlook that concludes in a working pluralism. He despairs of finding any comprehensive theory for environmental ethics, then concludes that this really is not necessary, and that an operational ethics, mixing different principles appropriately for relevant occasions, will suffice for environmental conservation.
- Sylvan and Bennett (1994), *The Greening of Ethics*. Environmental ethics from "down under" (Australia) showing how topsy turvy the uppermost Western, first world view really is, and analyzing Australia's unique contribution to the greening of ethics. Forceful, critical, subversive, even satirical, and, ultimately quite constructive. Australia is a bellwether territory, though if conservation fails there, little hope remains of convincing the rest of the world of its importance. This one is not to be overlooked because it is from afar, a good complement to the other treatments.
- Taylor (1986), *Respect for Nature*. Taylor locates value in organisms that are teleological centers of life, entities having a good of their own that can be furthered or damaged by moral agents. Normatively, no species is superior. Challenging for most undergraduates, but it gives them good exposure to sustained and careful argument, leading them to conclusions that seem right given the premises, but which they also may not want to accept. A vigorous biocentrism, denying anthropocentrism.
- Wenz (1988), *Environmental Justice*. Wenz views environmental ethics as the just distribution of resources, ending with a pluralist, concentric circle theory, where humans have differing kinds of obligations to persons and to domestic and wild animals, plants, species, and ecosystems. Somewhat demanding reading for undergraduates, but this is also exposure to serious and sustained philosophical argument. Wenz is more sympathetic to the animal rights perspective than are the others.
- Westra (1994), *An Environmental Proposal for Ethics: The Principle of Integrity*. Extended analysis of the philosophical meaning and the

operational value of the concept of integrity in natural and social systems in environmental ethics.

Courses Based on Anthologies

Course Description and Objectives. Topically oriented courses will use selected readings from any of numerous anthologies, almost an embarrassment of riches in the last few years, with virtually every major publisher offering an anthology. These anthologies are already arranged topically. Examples include defining an environmental ethic; environmental ethics and moral theory; animal rights; preservation of rare species; wilderness; economics, ecology, and ethics; pollution; energy; global justice; ecojustice; ecofeminism; environmental racism; future generations; agriculture; cost–benefit analysis; and individual versus collective choice. Such a course can be open-ended, and you can decide where to go next even when midway through. There are notes on each anthology in the Resources section at the end of the chapter.

Readings

- Armstrong and Botzler (1993), *Environmental Ethics: Divergence and Convergence*
- Attfield and Belsey (1994), *Philosophy and the Natural Environment*
- Bormann and Kellert (1991), *Ecology, Economics, Ethics: The Broken Circle*
- Cooper and Palmer (1992), *The Environment in Question*
- Elliot (1995), *Environmental Ethics*
- Engel and Engel (1990), *Ethics of Environment and Development: Global Challenge and International Response*
- Ferré and Hartel (1994), *Ethics and Environmental Policy: Theory Meets Practice*
- Gruen and Jamieson (1994), *Reflecting on Nature: Readings in Environmental Philosophy*
- List (1993), *Radical Environmentalism: Philosophy and Tactics*
- Newton and Dillingham (1993), *Watersheds: Classic Cases in Environmental Ethics*
- Pierce and VanDeVeer (1995), *People, Penguins, and Plastic Trees*
- Pojman (1994), *Environmental Ethics: Readings in Theory and Application*
- Scherer (1990), *Upstream/Downstream: Issues in Environmental Ethics*
- Scherer and Attig (1983), *Ethics and the Environment*
- Sterba (1995), *Earth Ethics: Environmental Ethics, Animal Rights, and Practical Applications*

- VanDeVeer and Pierce (1994), *The Environmental Ethics and Policy Book: Philosophy, Ecology, Economics*
- Westphal and Westphal (1994), *Planet in Peril: Essays in Environmental Ethics*
- Zimmerman et al. (1993), *Environmental Philosophy: From Animal Rights to Radical Ecology*

A Course Based on Professional Articles

Course Description and Objectives. The preceding section has introduced upper division courses based primarily on systematic texts and anthologies. Further possibilities drawing more on professional articles than on systematic treatises are given below. These articles pursue the questions of value, anthropocentric and naturalistic, and pose questions about what sorts of things count morally. This material is more challenging than in the preceding syllabuses but is central to the theoretical issues in the field. The student will probably be taking two or three other philosophy classes but is not necessarily a philosophy major.

Readings (Choose from the following selections.)
- Rolston (1975), "Is There an Ecological Ethic?" This article begins with an analytic style and will give the student the feeling that he or she is doing serious philosophy, perhaps coupled with some frustration about having to read it twice to understand it. The article then passes to a more discursive style, invoking experience and ethical intuitions, and the author passes from being an analyst to being an advocate. The reader may conclude with the author that an environmental ethic, though as yet unsettled and still on the horizon, has at least his vote to be so if it can be.
- Rolston (1982), "Are Values in Nature Subjective or Objective?" or chapter 6 in *Environmental Ethics*. Serious value theory again, this time focusing on the much debated "subjective or objective" distinction, with the reader being led from the primary–secondary qualities distinction familiar in modern philosophy (trees aren't really green; they only seem so in the eye of the beholder), to its application in environmental ethics. This time, besides the analysis, there are some sketches and diagrams to launch and stimulate discussion. Again, the student is drawn deeper than was expected into a concept of intrinsic natural value, perhaps left uncomfortable both with merely anthropocentric value and with the proposed naturalistic alternative.
- Callicott (1984), "Non-Anthropocentric Value Theory and Environmental Ethics." In an article from a professional philosophical journal, Callicott both summarizes value theory in environmental ethics and makes his own proposal, a theory that combines a humanist value theory with assigning intrinsic value to natural things, especially to ecosystems.

- Attfield (1981), "The Good of Trees." A British philosopher maintains, in the leading journal of value theory, that trees can have a good of their own. If so, the question is not always what are trees good for (their uses), but what is the good of trees (their intrinsic value). Here is an analysis of what it means to have interests, whether trees can have interests, welfare, a good of their own, even though they have no felt experiences, and whether this kind of good can count morally.
- Partridge (1986), "Values in Nature: Is Anybody There?" An enticing title, and the student will soon bog down in the technicalities of argument about objective and subjective value, need some rescuing from the feeling that philosophy becomes too academic or scholastic, but, if rescued, come away with the feeling that here are serious philosophical issues, being seriously debated.
- Taylor (1981), "The Ethics of Respect for Nature." Careful, step-by-step biocentric argument, leading the student where he or she may by now want to go, into the conviction that all and each living thing deserves respect as a teleological center of life. The student may then realize with some dismay that to plunge into biocentrism also takes one to places he or she is unwilling to go. It threatens to paralyze judgment, since every organism seems to have equal inherent worth, and worse, threatens to make one misanthropic. One does not want to be arrogantly anthropocentric, but still there seem to be relevant ethical differences between humans and mosquitoes!
- Frankena (1979), "Ethics and the Environment." The dean of American ethicists, whom the student may also have read in other ethics classes, turns his attention to environmental ethics, sympathetically but conservatively, unwilling to take the plunge into this deeper ethic, puzzled by what it could mean for there to be value in nonsentient creatures. Frankena analyzes a number of different types of environmental ethics, arguing for respect for sentient life.
- Callicott (1992), *The Intrinsic Value of Nature,* theme issue of *The Monist.* Seven articles by leading figures in the field, all addressed to the question of intrinsic value in nature. Copies of the single back issue are available. Professional philosophical material, suitable for a senior seminar: varieties of intrinsic value, of anthropocentric value, subjectivism and objectivism and beyond, pragmatism and value in nature, disvalues in nature.

Upper Division Course Units

Environmental Ethics with an Animal Welfare Emphasis

Unit Description and Objectives. The animal rights movement has surprised almost everyone with its increasing strength in recent years. It has many concerns kindred to those in environmental ethics, making it an effective way to approach environmental ethics by making use of comparisons and contrasts in the two movements. Ecosystem degradation, the loss of tropical forests and endangered species, global warming, or the good of trees may seem remote to students, but everyone, especially those with pets, can wonder whether animals can suffer. It is important here not just to raise the issue of eating meat, significant in itself, but to use this as a route into a concept of nature, of whether what is the case in nature (meat eating by carnivores and omnivores) ought to be the case in human life, and of the valuation of ecosystems and natural processes.

Readings

- Callicott (1980), "Animal Liberation: A Triangular Affair." See notes on p. 16. The student who has somewhat casually thought that all environmentalists and nature lovers are pretty much alike has a sudden awakening.

- Singer (1986), "Animals and the Value of Life" or Singer (1979), "Not for Humans Only: The Place of Nonhumans in Environmental Issues." Higher, sentient animals, count morally, but lower ones and plants do not. Consideration stops somewhere between a shrimp and an oyster.

- Regan (1975), "The Moral Basis of Vegetarianism." In a typical philosophy class most of the students will take vegetarianism as being oddball; but a few (more than the instructor may think) will be vegetarians by conviction. Most who eat meat will find it hard to believe that they are doing wrong but will be unsure about their justifications. This article and the preceding one will confront students with professional philosophers arguing that one ought not to eat meat.

- Ferré (1986), "Moderation, Morals, and Meat." Next come two philosophers on the meat eating side. Both argue from nature. After all, animals eat each other; humans evolved as hunter-gatherers; thus, should we deny the nutrient cycles of our ecology? An organicist ethic realizes that all life other than the primary producers has to feed on other life, and respect for nature as readily enjoins meat eating as denies it.

- Rolston (1988a), "Higher Animals: Duties to Sentient Life," chapter 2 in *Environmental Ethics*. There are duties to animals, though animals do not have rights, but duties to animals need not be extrapolated from duties to humans. The moral rules in culture and in amoral wild nature are different.

- Hargrove (1992), *The Animal Rights/Environmental Ethics Debate*. This anthology contains the principal 11 papers of the debate, of which the Callicott paper, "Animal Liberation: A Triangular Affair" is an example.

Five further approaches to environmental ethics are listed below, as significant as those above, but they can only be suggested here.

Environmental Ethics with a Western Religious Emphasis

See Chapter 11, Religion, for ideas and references.

Environmental Ethics with an Eastern Turn

Readings (There is a much larger literature available, but start with the selections below.)
- Smith (1972), "Tao Now: An Ecological Testament"
- Callicott and Ames (1989), *Nature in Asian Traditions of Thought*, selections
- Rolston (1987a), "Can the East Help the West to Value Nature?"

See also Chapter 11, Religion, for additional references.

Environmental Ethics: Confrontational Style

Unit Description and Objectives. Arrange the class pro and con, but be careful not to generate more heat than light. This is a good way to wake up sleepy students, but the danger is that there will be only argument and no growth toward resolution. There is also a danger that students will think there is only argument and not considerable consensus in ethics about practical matters of right and wrong. Adversarial in debate is only one route to insight.

Readings
- Goldfarb (1993), *Taking Sides: Clashing Views on Controversial Environmental Issues*. Drawn largely from the popular press and designed for confrontation and debate. There is a new edition frequently, so the issues will be quite contemporary.

Environmental Ethics with an Economic/Business Emphasis

The economics of natural resources intersects with philosophical assessments of value. Begin here and consult Chapter 4, Economics.

Readings
- Sagoff (1981), "At the Shrine of Our Lady of Fatima or Why Political Questions Are Not All Economic"
- Rolston (1984), "Just Environmental Business" from *Just Business*

Environmental Ethics as Deep Ecology

Unit Description. Deep ecology orients the whole of life with a respect for nature; the self-realization of humans is inseparably entwined with the autonomy and integrity of the larger biotic community.

Readings
Start here and see also the Naess book and comments above and below.
- Devall and Sessions (1985), *Deep Ecology,* selections
- Naess (1973), "The Shallow and the Deep, Long-Range Ecology Movement: A Summary"
- Mathews (1991), *The Ecological Self*
- McLaughlin (1993), *Regarding Nature: Industrialism and Deep Ecology*

Resources

Page numbers appearing in brackets at the end of some entries indicate where the reference is cited in a course plan.

Bibliographies

Four introductory bibliographies are:

Katz, E. 1989. "Environmental Ethics: A Select Annotated Bibliography, 1983–1987." *Research in Philosophy and Technology* 9:251–285.

Katz, E. 1992. "Environmental Ethics: A Select Annotated Bibliography II, 1987–1990." *Research in Philosophy and Technology* 12:287–334.

Nash, R. F., 1989. "Selected Bibliography." In R. F. Nash, *The Rights of Nature.* See listing below.

Simmons, D. A., 1988. "Environmental Ethics: A Selected Bibliography for the Environmental Professional." Council of Planning Librarians, CLP Bibliography 213, March.

A *Master Bibliography in Environmental Ethics* is maintained by the International Society for Environmental Ethics (see below) on computer disk. This annotated bibliography contains all the bibliographic entries from the *Newsletter* of the society, volumes 1–5 (1990-1994), all the articles and abstracts from the journal *Environmental Ethics,* volumes 1–16 (1979–1994), all the articles and abstracts from the journal *Environmental Values,* volumes 1–3 (1992–1994), and the two Katz bibliographies, above. The format is either WordPerfect DOS or Macintosh, which can be easily translated into other word processing programs. The bibliography can be searched on computer, or printed out in two volumes, about 300 pages each, and spiral bound for both faculty and student use. It is inexpensive and not copyrighted. Contact the Secretary of the International Society for Environmental Ethics for details. See entry below.

This bibliography can also be reached on World Wide Web, through an international society for environmental ethics site at the University of North Texas. The address is: <http://www.cep.unt.edu/ISEE.html>. There is a search engine with which you can search for particular key words.

Anthologies and Systematic Books

See also the earlier comments on these various works.

Armstrong, S. J., and R. G. Botzler, eds. 1993. *Environmental Ethics: Divergence and Convergence*. New York: McGraw Hill. [p. 216]

An excellent anthology all around.

Attfield, R. 1992. *The Ethics of Environmental Concern*, 2nd ed. Athens: University of Georgia Press. [p. 213]

Attfield, R. 1994. *Environmental Philosophy: Principles and Prospects*. Aldershot, Hampshire, UK: Avebury.

Sixteen essays.

Attfield, R. and A. Belsey, eds. 1994. *Philosophy and the Natural Environment*. Cambridge, UK: Cambridge University Press. [p. 216]

A series of careful philosophical analyses: intrinsic values in nature, environmental restoration, persons in natural history, anthropocentrism, the moral considerability of nonhumans, the idea of environment, natural capital, environmental disobedience, and global environmental justice.

Blackstone, W. T., ed. 1974. *Philosophy and Environmental Crisis*. Athens: University of Georgia Press.

Eight important early articles that, though now dated, emphasize the basic problems and options.

Bormann, F. and S. Kellert, eds. 1991. *Ecology, Economics, Ethics: The Broken Circle*. New Haven: Yale University Press. [p. 216]

A collection that has enjoyed especially widespread attention for its mix of the three areas, more interdisciplinary than most of the anthologies.

Brennan, A. 1988. *Thinking About Nature: An Investigation of Nature, Value and Ecology*. London: Routledge, and Athens: University of Georgia Press. [p. 213]

Cahn, R. 1978. *Footprints on the Planet*. New York: Universe Books.
An easy to read, nonacademic approach.

Callicott, J. B. 1989. *In Defense of the Land Ethic*. Albany: State University of New York Press.
A collection of essays by the principal philosophical interpreter of Aldo Leopold's land ethic.

Callicott, J. B., ed. 1992. *The Intrinsic Value of Nature*. Theme issue of *The Monist*, 75(2). [p. 218]

Callicott, J. B. 1995. *Earth's Insights: A Survey of Ecological Ethics from the Mediterranean Basin to the Australian Outback*. Berkeley: University of California Press. [p. 213]

Callicott, J. B. and R. T. Ames. 1989. *Nature in Asian Traditions of Thought: Essays in Environmental Philosophy*. Albany: State University of New York Press. [p. 220]

Cooper, D. E. and J. A. Palmer, eds. 1992. *The Environment in Question*. London: Routledge. [p. 216]
British anthology with an international emphasis. Contributions from the United States, India, and Australia. Environmental ethics, nuclear wastes, rainforests, obligations to future generations, and the nature of technological risk.

Des Jardins, J. R., 1993. *Environmental Ethics: An Introduction to Environmental Philosophy*. Belmont, CA: Wadsworth. [pp. 213, 214]

Devall, W. and G. Sessions. 1985. *Deep Ecology*. Salt Lake City, UT: Peregrine Smith Books. [p. 221]
Easy reading and a handbook of the movement.

Drengson, A. R., 1989. *Beyond Environmental Crisis: From Technocrat to Planetary Person*. New York: Peter Lang.
Another deep ecology approach.

Elliot, R., ed. 1995. *Environmental Ethics*. New York: Oxford University Press. [p. 216]

About a dozen articles selected to feature the principal issues. Manageable size.

Elliot, R. and A. Gare, eds. 1983. *Environmental Philosophy.* State College, PA: Pennsylvania State University Press.

An Australian-produced collection for upper level undergraduates.

Encyclopedia of Bioethics. 1995. Rev. ed. New York: Macmillan Library Reference, Simon and Schuster.

Contains useful articles on a variety of topics pertinent to environmental ethics, such as animal rights in a variety of contexts, deep ecology, ecofeminism, and conservation management.

Engel J. R. and J. G. Engel, eds. 1990. *Ethics of Environment and Development: Global Challenge and International Response.* Tucson: University of Arizona Press. [p. 216]

Twenty authors address the challenge of an environmental crisis resulting from industrialization in developed countries, simultaneously with increased poverty and escalating populations in developing countries. They ask whether and how environmental conservation, a sustainable biosphere, and sustainable human development can be achieved, with equity and justice.

Ferré, F. and P. Hartel, eds. 1994. *Ethics and Environmental Policy: Theory Meets Practice.* Athens: University of Georgia Press. [p. 216]

A general collection with an emphasis on putting theory into practice, also on international and global issues.

Fritsch, A. S. with The Science Action Coalition. 1980. *Environmental Ethics: Choices for Concerned Citizens.* New York: Doubleday.

An easy to read, nonacademic approach.

Goldfarb, T. D. 1993. *Taking Sides: Clashing Views on Controversial Environmental Issues,* 5th ed. Guilford, CT: Dushkin Publishing Group. [p. 220]

Gruen, L. and D. Jamieson, eds. 1994. *Reflecting on Nature: Readings in Environmental Philosophy.* New York: Oxford University Press. [p. 216]

Excellent. Organized around sections on images of nature, ethics and the environment, alternative perspectives, sustainable development and international justice, and contemporary issues (wilderness, animals, population and consumption, and biodiversity).

Gunn, A. S. and P. A. Vesilind, eds. 1986. *Environmental Ethics for Engineers*. Chelsea, MI: Lewis Publishers.

Hargrove, E. C., 1989. *Foundations of Environmental Ethics*. Englewood Cliffs, NJ: Prentice-Hall. [p. 214]

Johnson, L. E. 1991. *A Morally Deep World: An Essay on Moral Significance and Environmental Ethics*. Cambridge: Cambridge University Press. [p. 214]

List, P. C., ed. 1993. *Radical Environmentalism: Philosophy and Tactics*. Belmont, CA: Wadsworth Publishing Co. [p. 216]
Sections on deep ecology, on ecofeminism, on social ecology and bioregionalism, on radical ecoactivism and ecotactics. Features the "radical" environmentalists, but intends to help "moderates" sharpen their resolve to find and act on a theoretically coherent and practically feasible environmental ethics.

McLaughlin, A. 1993. *Regarding Nature: Industrialism and Deep Ecology*. Albany, NY: State University of New York Press. [pp. 214, 221]
Deep ecology compared with progressive political thought. The fundamental assumptions of the leading ideologies—capitalism, socialism, anthropocentrism, egocentrism.

Marietta, D. E., Jr. 1995. *For People and the Planet: Holism and Humanism in Environmental Ethics*. Philadelphia: Temple University Press. [p. 214]

Mathews, F. 1991. *The Ecological Self*. Savage, MD: Barnes and Noble. [p. 221]
A sophisticated metaphysics for deep ecology.

Naess, A. 1989. *Ecology, Community, and Lifestyle: Outline of a Ecosophy*. New York: Cambridge University Press. First published in Norwegian in 1976. [pp. 213, 214]

Nash, R. F. 1982. *Wilderness and the American Mind*, 3rd ed. New Haven: Yale University Press.
A historical approach that has been a bestseller for decades.

Nash, R. F. 1989. *The Rights of Nature: A History of Environmental Ethics*. Madison: University of Wisconsin Press.
Continues Nash's earlier history of wilderness with expanding ethical concern through contemporary events.

Newton, L. H. and C. K. Dillingham. 1993. *Watersheds: Classic Cases in Environmental Ethics*. Belmont, CA: Wadsworth. [p. 216]

Nine pivotal cases in environmental ethics: Love Canal, the ozone layer and its depletion, UNCED at Rio, the *Exxon Valdez*, the Northwest forests and the spotted owl, Chernobyl, Chico Mendez and the tropical rainforests, the global greenhouse and our changing climate, Bhopal. Impressive detail and documentation of the cases combined with insightful ethical analysis.

Norton, B. G., ed. 1986. *Preservation of Species*. Princeton, NJ: Princeton University Press.

The best philosophically oriented collection on the preservation of species.

Norton, B. G. 1987. *Why Preserve Natural Variety?* Princeton, NJ: Princeton University Press.

Norton, B. G. 1991. *Toward Unity Among Environmentalists*. New York: Oxford University Press.

Environmentalists can find convergent interests, agreeing what they ought to do, even if they operate with differing philosophical positions.

Passmore, J. 1974. *Man's Responsibility for Nature*. New York: Scribner's.

An influential early treatment, easy reading. Passmore takes an anthropocentric and resource (utilitarian) approach.

Pierce, C, and D. VanDeVeer, eds. 1995. *People, Penguins, and Plastic Trees: Basic Issues in Environmental Ethics*, Rev. ed. Belmont, CA: Wadsworth. [p. 216]

A popular anthology, containing several of the articles already mentioned, often thought to be the easiest anthology, now in an enlarged second edition.

Pojman, L. P., ed. 1994. *Environmental Ethics: Readings in Theory and Application*. Boston: Jones and Bartlett. [p. 216]

A big reader arranged in a pro and con dialogue, 72 readings on 20 topics, in 18 sections, emphasizing a mix of theory and practice. Historical roots, animal rights, biocentrism, a land ethic, deep ecology, intrinsic natural value, ecofeminism, the Gaia hypothesis, biodiversity, obligations to future generations, Asian concepts of nature, world population, hunger, pollution, wastes, energy policy, nuclear power, climate change, sustainable development, economics, ethics, and environmental policy.

Regan, T., 1982. *All That Dwell Therein: Essays on Animal Rights and Environmental Ethics*. Berkeley: University of California Press.

Regan, T., ed. 1990. *Earthbound: New Introductory Essays in Environmental Ethics*. Prospect Heights, IL: Waveland Press.

The 10 articles in this anthology were written for beginning students. The book was published by Random House in 1984 and has been reissued by Waveland Press. Articles in it are still useful because they are specifically written for beginners.

Rolston, H., III. 1986. *Philosophy Gone Wild*. Buffalo: Prometheus Books. [p. 212]

The 15 essays can be read individually or in topically related groups. Nature has nonanthropocentric intrinsic and systemic value, as well as instrumental value. Some values are natural in the sense that they objectively emerge out of ecosystems and natural processes.

Rolston, H., III. 1988a. *Environmental Ethics*. Philadelphia: Temple University Press. [pp. 212, 213, 215, 219]

Rolston, H., III. 1994a. *Conserving Natural Value*. New York: Columbia University Press. [p. 211]

Written not only for philosophy students but also for natural resource and conservation biology students, this book can be used outside philosophy departments, and in combination with books and articles from other disciplines in environmental studies. Freshman and sophomore level.

Sagoff, M. 1988. *The Economy of the Earth: Philosophy, Law, and the Environment*. New York: Cambridge University Press. [p. 215]

Scherer, D., ed. 1990. *Upstream/Downstream: Issues in Environmental Ethics*. Philadelphia: Temple University Press. [p. 216]

Eight articles that explore the main issues: norms and environments, future generations, public policy and scientific uncertainty, international and transboundary environmental problems, takings, just compensation, pollution, and cost–benefit analysis.

Scherer, D., and T. Attig, eds. 1983. *Ethics and the Environment*. Englewood Cliffs, NJ: Prentice-Hall. [p. 216]

A solid introductory anthology, though now a decade old.

Shrader-Frechette, K. 1984. *Environmental Ethics*. Pacific Grove, CA: Boxwood Press.

Sterba, J. P., ed. 1995. *Earth Ethics: Environmental Ethics, Animal Rights, and Practical Applications*. Englewood Cliffs, NJ: Prentice-Hall. [p. 216]

Three dozen authors, a major anthology in the field, arranged in a theoretical and a practical section.

Stone, C. F. 1987. *Earth and Other Ethics*. New York: Harper and Row. [p. 215]

Sylvan, R., and D. Bennett. 1994. *The Greening of Ethics*. Cambridge, UK: White Horse Press; Tucson, AZ: University of Arizona Press. [p. 215]

Taylor, P. 1986. *Respect for Nature*. Princeton, NJ: Princeton University Press. [p. 215]

VanDeVeer, D., and C. Pierce, eds. 1994. *The Environmental Ethics and Policy Book: Philosophy, Ecology, Economics*. Belmont, CA: Wadsworth. [p. 216]
Features interdisciplinary crossovers between philosophy, politics, and economics. Ethical theory; western religions and environmental attitudes; animals; constructing an environmental ethic; deep ecology, social ecology, ecofeminism; cost–benefit analysis; ecological sustainability; population; biodiversity; forests and wilderness; degrading the planet. A wide-ranging and well-conceived text.

Wenz, P. S., 1988. *Environmental Justice*. Albany: State University of New York Press. [pp. 213, 215]

Westphal, D. and F. Westphal, eds. 1994. *Planet in Peril: Essays in Environmental Ethics*. Fort Worth, TX: Harcourt Brace College Publishers. [p. 216]
A reasonably slim anthology, one that uses fewer, but complete articles. Biocentric ethics, wilderness, inherent value in nature, pollution, animals. More selective than comprehensive, modest and manageable in size and price, and contrasts with the much bigger collections.

Westra, L. 1994. *An Environmental Proposal for Ethics: The Principle of Integrity*. Lanham, MD: Rowman and Littlefield Publishers, Inc. [p. 215]

Zimmerman, M. E., J. B. Callicott, G. Sessions, K. J. Warren, and J. Clark, eds. 1993. *Environmental Philosophy: From Animal Rights to Radical Ecology*. Englewood Cliffs, NJ: Prentice-Hall. [p. 216]
Excellent, with main sections on environmental ethics, deep ecology, ecofeminism, and social ecology.

Books on Animal Rights

Clark, S. R. L. 1977. *The Moral Status of Animals*. Oxford: Oxford University Press.

An Aristotelian approach to animals; animals ought to have lives according to their kind. Vegetarianism is endorsed. Readable but wordy.

Hargrove, E. C., ed. 1992. *The Animal Rights/Environmental Ethics Debate*. Albany: State University of New York Press. [p. 219]

Linzey, A. 1987. *Christianity and the Rights of Animals*. New York: Crossroad.

Linzey, an Anglican priest, is the principal theological defender of animal rights. Sensitive and caring, though quite nonecological, he regards wild nature as fallen, under a curse, and in need of redemption.

Midgley, Mary. 1983. *Animals and Why They Matter*. Athens, GA: University of Georgia Press.

Regan, T. 1983. *The Case for Animal Rights*. Berkeley: University of California Press.

Massive and detailed arguments for animal (mammal) rights by their principal philosophical defender. Readable, although some parts will be difficult for undergraduates.

Regan, T. and P. Singer, eds. 1989. *Animal Rights and Human Obligations*, 2nd ed. Englewood Cliffs, NJ: Prentice-Hall.

Singer, P. 1975a. *Animal Liberation*. New York: New York Review Books.

Classical (hedonistic) utilitarianism extended to animals. Singer exposes the abuses of factory agriculture and concludes that vegetarianism is morally obligatory. He also criticizes medical and scientific uses of animals. Quite readable.

Books on Ecofeminism

The following are places to start in an actively growing field.

Griffin, S. 1978. *Women and Nature*. New York: Harper and Row.

Merchant, C. 1983. *The Death of Nature: Women, Ecology, and the Scientific Revolution*. New York: Harper and Row.

Warven, K., ed. 1994. *Ecological Feminism*. New York: Routledge.

Articles and Chapters in Books

The chief sources of academic articles are the journals *Environmental Ethics* and *Environmental Values*. See also the bibliographies listed above.

Attfield, R. 1981. "The Good of Trees." *Journal of Value Inquiry* 15:35–54. [p. 218]

Callicott, J. B. 1980. "Animal Liberation: A Triangular Affair." *Environmental Ethics* 2:311–338. [pp. 211, 212, 219]

Callicott, J. B. 1982. "Traditional American Indian and Western European Attitudes toward Nature." *Environmental Ethics* 4:293–318. [p. 212]

Callicott, J. B. 1984. "Non-Anthropocentric Value Theory and Environmental Ethics." *American Philosophical Quarterly* 21:299–309. [p. 217]

Callicott, J. B. 1986. "The Search for an Environmental Ethic." In *Matters of Life and Death*, 2nd ed. T. Regan, ed. New York: Random House. [p. 211]

Callicott, J. B. 1991. "The Wilderness Idea Revisited: The Sustainable Development Alternative." *Environmental Professional* 13:235–247. Reprinted in Gruen and Jamieson 1994; see anthology listing.

Argues that the wilderness idea is flawed, incoherent, and anthropocentric. Rolston's (1991b) reply (see listing below) defends the wilderness idea. The two articles form an exchange that will stimulate students about the idea of the natural, nature versus culture, and the human relation to the wild.

Earhart, H. B. 1970. "The Ideal of Nature in Japanese Religion and its Possible Significance for Environmental Concerns." *Contemporary Religions in Japan* 11:1–26. [p. 212]

Elliot, R. 1982. "Faking Nature." *Inquiry* 25:81–93. [p. 212]

Emerson, R. W. [1844] 1926, 1961. "Nature." In *Emerson's Essays*. 1st and 2nd series. New York: Thomas Crowell. [p. 212]

Ferré, F. 1986. "Moderation, Morals, and Meat," *Inquiry* 29:391–406. [p. 219]

Frankena, W. K. 1979. "Ethics and the Environment." In *Ethics and*

Problems of the 21st Century. K. E. Goodpaster and K. M. Sayre, eds. Notre Dame, IN: University of Notre Dame Press. [p. 218]

Gunn, A. S. 1990. "Preserving Rare Species." In *Earthbound*. T. Regan, ed. (See anthology listing.)

Leopold, A. 1949. "The Land Ethic." In *A Sand County Almanac*. A. Leopold. Oxford: Oxford University Press. [pp. 211, 212]

Mill, J. S. [1874] 1969. "Nature." One of *Three Essays on Religion*, in *Collected Works*, vol. 10. Toronto: University of Toronto Press. [p. 212]

Naess, A. 1973. "The Shallow and the Deep, Long-Range Ecology Movement: A Summary." *Inquiry* 16:95–100. [pp. 211, 221]

Partridge, E. 1986. "Values in Nature: Is Anybody There?" *Philosophical Inquiry* 8:96–110. [p. 218]

Redford, K. H. 1990. "The Ecologically Noble Savage." *Orion Nature Quarterly* 9(3):25–29. [p. 212]

Regan, T. 1975. "The Moral Basis of Vegetarianism." *Canadian Journal of Philosophy* 5:181–214. Reprinted in Regan 1982. (See anthology listing.) [p. 219]

Rolston, H., III. 1975. "Is There an Ecological Ethic?" *Ethics* 85:93-1–9. Reprinted in Scherer and Attig, eds. 1983. (See anthology listing). [p. 217]

Rolston, H., III. 1981. "Values in Nature." *Environmental Ethics* 3: 113–128. Reprinted in Rolston 1986. (See anthology listing.) [p. 210]

Rolston, H., III. 1982. "Are Values in Nature Subjective or Objective?" *Environmental Ethics* 4:125–151. Reprinted in Rolston 1986; also in Elliot and Gare 1983. (See anthology listing.) [p. 217]

Rolston, H., III. 1984. "Just Environmental Business." In *Just Business: New Introductory Essays in Business Ethics*. T. Regan, ed. New York: Random House. Reprinted in Rolston 1986; also in Westphal and Westphal 1994. (See anthology listings.) [p. 220]

Rolston, H., III. 1985. "Duties to Endangered Species," *BioScience* 35:718–726. Reprinted in Rolston 1986; also in Sterba 1995; also in VanDeVeer and Peters 1994. (See anthology listings.) Also in Regan and Singer 1989. (See animal rights listing.)

Rolston, H., III. 1987a. "Can the East Help the West to Value Nature?" *Philosophy East and West* 37:172–190. [p. 220]

Rolston, H., III. 1987b. "On Behalf of Bioexuberance." *Garden* 11(4):2–4, 31–32.

Rolston, H., III. 1988b. "Human Values and Natural Systems." *Society and Natural Resources* 1:271–283. [p. 210]

Rolston, H., III. 1988c. "In Defense of Ecosystems." *Garden* 12(4):2–5, 32.

Rolston, H., III. 1988d. "Values Deep in the Woods," *American Forests* 94(5 and 6):66–69. [p. 210]

Rolston, H., III. 1991a. "Environmental Ethics: Values in and Duties to the Natural World." In Bormann and Kellert 1991. Reprinted in Gruen and Jamieson 1994; also in VanDeVeer and Pierce 1994. (See anthology listings.)
A convenient summary of Rolston's book *Environmental Ethics*.

Rolston, H., III. 1991b. "The Wilderness Idea Reaffirmed." *Environmental Professional* 13:370–377. Reprinted in Gruen and Jamieson 1994. (See anthology listing.)
Replies to Callicott 1991, "The Wilderness Idea Revisited." See above.

Rolston, H., III. 1992a. "Ethical Responsibilities toward Wildlife." *Journal of the American Veterinary Medical Association* 200:618–622.
Based on case studies that raise tough questions; short, easy to read.

Rolston, H., III. 1992b. "Wildlife and Wildlands: A Christian Perspective." In *After Nature's Revolt: Eco-justice and Theology*. D. T. Hessel, ed. Minneapolis, MN: Fortress Press.

Rolston, H., III. 1994b. "Value in Nature and the Nature of Value." In Attfield and Belsey 1994. (See anthology listing.) [p. 210]

Rolston, H., III. 1994c. "Winning and Losing in Environmental Ethics." In Ferré and Hartel 1994. (See anthology listing.) [p. 211]

Sagoff, M. 1980a. "On Teaching Environmental Ethics." *Metaphilosophy* 11:307–325. [p. 210]
Useful for teaching introductory students.

Sagoff, M. 1980b. "On the Preservation of Species." *Columbia Journal of Environmental Law* 7:33–67.

Sagoff, M. 1981. "At the Shrine of Our Lady of Fatima *or* Why Political Questions Are Not All Economic." *Arizona Law Review* 23:1283–1298. [p. 220]

Saleh, A. K. 1984. "Deeper than Deep Ecology: The Eco-Feminist Connection." *Environmental Ethics* 3:339–345.

Singer, P. 1986. "Animals and the Value of Life" In *Matters of Life and Death*, 2nd ed. T. Regan, ed. New York: Random House. [p. 219]

Singer, P. 1975b. "Down on the Factory Farm." In Singer 1975a. Reprinted in Regan and Singer 1989. (See animal rights listings.)

Singer, P. 1979. "Not for Humans Only: The Place of Nonhumans in Environmental Issues." In *Ethics and Problems of the 21st Century*. K. E. Goodpaster and K. M. Sayre, eds. Notre Dame, IN: University of Notre Dame Press. [p. 219]

Smith, H. 1972. "Tao Now: An Ecological Testament." In *Earth Might Be Fair*. I. G. Barbour, ed. Englewood Cliffs, NJ: Prentice-Hall. [pp. 212, 220]

Taylor, P. 1981. "The Ethics of Respect for Nature." *Environmental Ethics* 3:197–218. [pp. 212, 218]
A biocentric approach, enlarged upon in Taylor 1986, *Respect for Nature*.

Vitek, W. 1992. "Teaching Environmental Ethics." *Teaching Philosophy* 15:151–173. [p. 210]
Good suggestions for class and student projects.

Warren, K. J., 1990. "The Power and Promise of Ecological Feminism." *Environmental Ethics* 12:125–146.
Includes a recent bibliography.

White, L., Jr., 1967. "The Historical Roots of Our Ecological Crisis." *Science* 155:1203–1207. [p. 212]

Videotapes, Films, and Other Sources

Many audio-visual resources are available. The following are only illustrations. Probably the best single source of environmental films is Bullfrog Films, Oley, PA 19547, with a catalog of over 300 titles on environmental and related social and development issues. *Switching on to the Environment*, a book by Television Trust for the Environment, 46 Charlotte Street, London W1P 1LX, in cooperation with the United Nations Environment Programme, describes and evaluates 100 films.

Fence at Red Rim. Does a rancher have a right to build a fence that destroys an antelope herd, enclosing public land though built on private land, protecting his cattle and preventing a designation of critical habitat that might prevent strip mining? Focus Productions, distributed by University of California Extension Media Center, Berkeley, California. [p. 213]

Wetlands in Crisis. United States Fish and Wildlife Service videotape urging "no net loss" of wildlands. Distributed by their Audio Visual Office, Washington, D.C., and regional centers.

The Ancient Forests. Clearcutting in the Pacific Northwest, devastating forests there. Project Lighthawk, Santa Fe, New Mexico. [p. 213]

Yellowstone in Winter. The harsh and beautiful Yellowstone winter, including a provocative extract of an attempted and failed rescue of a drowning bison, against park policy, raising the issue of compassion toward wildlife. Wolfgang Bayer Productions, Jackson Hole, Wyoming. [p. 213]

Black Bear Hunting Secrets. Produced to extol hunting, but the hunting scenes (shooting a sow in spring, the bow and arrow shooting of a treed bear) raise the larger questions of whether merely recreational trophy hunting is moral. 3M Sportsmen's Video Collection, Bloomington, Minnesota, on sale at sporting goods stores and video outlets. [p. 213]

From Sea to Shining Sea. CIBA GEIGY, a multi-national corporation, discharges toxic wastes into the Atlantic Ocean off the coast of New Jersey, of disputed content and with disputed permit. Greenpeace divers partially plug the pipes and are arrested, though supported by a citizens' rally. Illustrates corporate power, government ineffectiveness, civil disobedience, pollution, and toxic threats. Available through Bullfrog Films (see address above).

The International Society for Environmental Ethics (ISEE), a membership organization, is devoted to advancing environmental ethics and its teaching. There is a quarterly newsletter noting resource materials. Back issues of these newsletters are available both in print and on the internet through gopher at Morehead State University, Morehead, Kentucky. At your internet system prompt, send the telnet message: <gopher infoserv.morehead-st.edu>, and follow the prompts searching the MSU Gopher Server using Jughead with the search words: International Society for Environmental Ethics to get to the *ISEE NeIwsletter*. The Society maintains a master bibliography in environmental ethics (see above). Contact Professor Laura Westra, Secretary, Department of Philosophy, University of Windsor, Windsor, Ontario N9B 3P4, Canada.

Chapter 10

Political Science

Michael E. Kraft
University of Wisconsin at Green Bay

Environmental issues are of increasing interest to political scientists and other students of public affairs, both in their research and in teaching. Concern for environmental degradation and public policies designed to deal with it finds its way into courses in the discipline itself and in the related fields of public administration and public policy. Topics include the long-established natural resources and environmental protection issues, such as creation and maintenance of national parks and wilderness areas, protection of endangered species, and air and water pollution control. Increasingly they extend to the newer global threats of stratospheric ozone depletion, climate change, loss of biological diversity, and the implications of rapid economic growth in a world where a population of 5.7 billion in 1995 is expected to balloon to between 8 and 10 billion people over the next 50 years.

In some areas of the discipline these subjects, particularly environmental protection policies, have become so familiar and accepted that they are now on a par with such widely acknowledged subfields as economic and foreign policy. For example, many introductory public policy texts have one or more chapters on environmental and energy policies. International relations texts in recent years often have included a discussion of global natural resources and environmental threats and their political implications. The massive media coverage of the June 1992 U.N. Conference on Environment and Development (the Earth Summit) and the September 1994 U.N. Conference on Population and Development in Cairo, Egypt, can only accelerate the trend.

Similarly, for almost a decade, many American government texts have included at least some reference to environmental policies, if not in a separate chapter then as examples of challenges facing executive agencies, the courts, or legislatures. Some of the newest texts include supplementary material (videos, audio tapes, and short monographs) that focus on environmental policy (e.g., Kraft 1994). These developments are one sign of the salience of these issues.

In some subfields of the discipline, however, environmental or conservation issues continue to be viewed as peripheral at best. That seems to be the case in comparative government and politics as well as political theory, although in the past several years political theorists have taken more interest in the normative issues of politics and resource scarcity and the political implications of a sustainable society (Ophuls and Boyan 1992; Eckersley 1992; Paehlke 1989; Kraft 1992). Similarly, the field of comparative environmental politics and policy is attracting much more interest (Kamieniecki 1993).

Scholarly research on environmental issues has also become more common within the discipline of political science and the affiliated areas of public policy and public administration. Evidence can be found in the published literature, professional society membership directories, annual program panels and papers, doctoral dissertations and articles appearing in the disciplinary journals (Lester 1995; Vig and Kraft 1994; Ingram and Godwin 1985; Kamieniecki, O'Brien, and Clarke 1986). As one example of this increased interest and the quality of current scholarship, for over ten years the State University of New York Press has had one or more series focusing on environmental politics and policy.

Some professional associations (for example, the American Society for Public Administration) have formal sections on natural resources and the environment. Other associations subsume these topics under related subfields. For instance, the public policy section of the American Political Science Association (APSA) includes a strong representation of political scientists interested in environmental politics and policy, as does the section on science, technology, and environmental politics. Each section has its own newsletter. The APSA itself now records environmental policy as one of the standard specializations for its members, making possible the preparation of mailing lists of individuals within the subfield.

Despite these developments, several significant obstacles face political scientists who emphasize environmental issues in their scholarship, and sometimes even in their teaching. The discipline exhibits a strong preference for conventional social science approaches, particularly the use of rigorous analytic frameworks and quantitative data in hypothesis testing and theory building. The behavioral revolution of the 1950s and 1960s continues to exert a powerful influence on graduate instruction in political science and on the expectations for publication in the leading journals. Regrettably, most of the major graduate schools have shown little interest in the study of environmental politics and policy, and very few offer advanced training in this subfield at the Ph.D. level. That doesn't close the door entirely, but it does mean that determined students need to seek the assistance of willing graduate faculty and will likely have to pursue environmental studies within one of the standard political science subfields, such as public policy, American government, public administration, or international politics.

A further obstacle is the continuing skepticism on most campuses toward interdisciplinary study, which is often criticized for making little contribution to the discipline or for having a perceived lack of rigor. In a tight academic job market, and with budgetary constraints sharply limiting support for new programs, scholars who favor interdisciplinary and applied environmental research may find themselves at a significant disadvantage. These conditions are not cause for despair. Yet they do indicate the need for creative efforts to push the discipline toward the study of environmental politics and policy, both at the level of the professional societies and journals and on individual college and university campuses where interdisciplinary environmental studies programs and courses are not yet well accepted.

Fortunately, there is noticeable growth in demand for such courses and training, particularly at the master's level, and often in combination with schools of public administration and public policy. Natural scientists also recognize the value of understanding governmental policy making, especially the relationship between science and policy, and they often welcome courses on environmental policy. Several universities (including Duke, Yale, and the University of California campuses at Santa Barbara and Berkeley) have recently begun graduate programs in environmental science, policy, and management that reflect these trends, and they report sharp increases in applications for admission.

Similarly, since the late 1980s, there has been a rising demand from undergraduates for coursework in environmental politics, policy, and law. This has resulted in new environmental studies programs at leading colleges and universities in the East. Eventually these forces may have more impact on graduate education in political science and on undergraduate programs across the nation.

To help spur these developments, I have selected the material presented below as a sample of what might be done to introduce environmental concerns in introductory and advanced courses in political science and related fields. As its practitioners know well, the discipline includes a wide range of subject matter and may overlap with the study of history, philosophy, law, economics, international relations, and public policy. Yet at its core, political science deals with the characteristics of political institutions and decision making, political rights and authority, political power, political attitudes and behavior, leadership, political parties and elections, interest group activities and influence, and public policies and their implementation. I focus here on courses in American government and public policy, although some of what is suggested below may also be used in introduction to political science courses or introduction to international relations or world politics. I present an outline for one full upper-level course in environmental politics and policy and for several components that may fit into other courses.

The selection of readings, assignments, and projects is designed to further several teaching goals:

(1) to build student understanding of environmental conditions and trends and their political implications;

(2) to describe through case studies and analytic articles why public officials and governments respond to environmental challenges the way they do, and how individuals might influence them to act more responsibly;

(3) to build student capacity for independent analysis of environmental problems and policies and for effective participation in decision making.

Much of the material described below can be used by instructors in a range of courses where there is some emphasis on government, politics, and public policy, including those in environmental science, conservation biology, science and technology studies, and environmental sociology, history, and economics.

References for the Introduction

Eckersley, R. 1992. *Environmentalism and Political Theory: Toward an Ecocentric Approach*. Albany: State University of New York Press.

Ingram, H. M., and R. K. Godwin, eds. 1985. *Public Policy and the Natural Environment*. Greenwich, CT: JAI Press.

Kamieniecki, S., ed. 1993. *Environmental Politics in the International Arena: Movements, Parties, Organizations, and Policy*. Albany: State University of New York Press.

Kamieniecki, S., R. O'Brien, and M. Clarke, eds. 1986. *Controversies in Environmental Policy*. Albany: State University of New York Press.

Kraft, M. E. 1992. "Ecology and Political Theory: Broadening the Scope of Environmental Politics." *Policy Studies Journal* 20(4):712-718.

Kraft, M. E. 1994. *Environmental Policy and Politics in the 1990s*. New York: HarperCollins Political Pamphleteer Series.

Lester, J., ed. 1995. *Environmental Politics and Policy: Theories and Evidence*. 2nd ed. Durham, NC: Duke University Press.

Ophuls, W., and A. S. Boyan, Jr. 1992. *Ecology and the Politics of Scarcity Revisited*. New York: W. H. Freeman.

Paehlke, R. 1989. *Environmentalism and the Future of Progressive Politics*. New Haven: Yale University Press.

Vig, N. J., and M. E. Kraft. 1994. *Environmental Policy in the 1990s: Toward a New Agenda*. 2nd ed. Washington, DC: Congressional Quarterly Press.

COURSE PLANS

Units for Introductory Courses

Global Environmental Conditions and Politics

Instructors might consider a lecture (or series of lectures) that reviews global environmental threats, from climate change to population growth and risks to biological diversity, and asks about the political implications. This topic could fit easily within courses in world politics, international relations, introduction to political science, American government, or broad introductions to contemporary government and politics. The data are easily available in texts such as Ophuls and Boyan (1992); L. Brown's annual edited volume, *State of the World*; the World Commission's (known as the Brundtland Commission) (1987) *Our Common Future*; MacNeill, Winsemius, and Yakushiji's (1991) *Beyond Interdependence*; the National Commission on the Environment's (1993) *Choosing a Sustainable Future*; or the World Resource Institute's biennial reference work, *World Resources*.

Chapters 2 and 3 of Ophuls and Boyan offer a detailed survey of global environmental conditions and trends, as do the introductory chapters to the Brundtland Commission report and MacNeill et al.'s volume. Students will likely find Ophuls and Boyan provocative, inasmuch as they challenge conventional ideas about the possibility of continued growth. The case for sustainable development is made succinctly in an introductory summary statement in the National Commission's report and in its chapter 1. Any of these analyses and position statements would serve well to introduce students to the facts, issues, and controversies over global environmental problems and sustainable development. All chapters are suitable for lower-division students.

Dissenting views are equally available and might help to put the consensus arguments for environmental protection efforts into a useful context to encourage critical thinking. Such views can be found in collections such as Goldfarb's (1993) *Taking Sides: Clashing Views on Controversial Environmental Issues*; Bernards's (1991) *The Environmental Crisis: Opposing Viewpoints*; and Dwyer and Leeming's (1995) compilation of *Washington Post* articles from the last five years, *Earth's Eleventh Hour*. Solid scientific appraisals can be found in collections such as Scientific American's (1990) *Managing Planet Earth*.

Students need to learn how to deal with conflicting scientific arguments and scientific uncertainty over long-term trends such as climate change and population growth, and references like these should help. When is governmental action justifiable? When is it best to defer action to await improvements in scientific knowledge? Special attention might be given to the dilemma of political leadership in response to problems where the benefits of public policy are long-term and uncertain and the costs short-term and highly visible.

There is no shortage of good sources for international environmental policy. Many articles and books leading up to the 1992 Earth Summit or following it (MacNeill et al. 1991; Mathews 1991; Meadows, Meadows, and Randers 1992; Grubb et al. 1993; Haas, Levy, and Parson 1992; Parson, Haas, and Levy 1992; United Nations 1993a and 1993b) offer useful information. So too do the various texts on international environmental policy (e.g., Caldwell 1990; Porter and Brown 1991). A recent comprehensive collection on population issues related to the 1994 Cairo population conference is Mazur (1994). They would be easily readable by lower-division students.

Instructors may want to highlight population variables, for which current data and useful sources are included in Kraft (1994b) or the annual Population Reference Bureau's (PRB) (1994) *World Population Data Sheet*. Organizations such as Zero Population Growth and PRB have extensive libraries of films and slide presentations that can assist. Other topics that can be emphasized include global climate change, deforestation, and loss of biological diversity.

In all cases, the emphasis in political science, government, or public policy classes can be on how political systems have responded to these challenges to date. If action has been insufficient (which is generally the case), why is that? What are the major reasons governments have been unwilling or unable to do more? What might be done to improve governmental capabilities to understand and respond to such problems? What role do environmental and other organizations play in shaping such governmental decisions? What about public opinion? The Gallup Health of the Planet survey offers a wealth of intriguing data on public attitudes toward the environment in 24 nations, both developed and developing countries (Dunlap, Gallup, and Gallup 1993a and 1993b).

At a different level, students might be encouraged to think about their own preferences for governmental intervention. What do students believe is the proper role for government on environmental and resource issues, both domestically and internationally? Do they agree with conservative critics who argue for limited governmental involvement and reliance on free markets? Do they think governments should be more actively engaged with these issues? How do students feel personally about government and politics? Are they themselves playing an active role, and why or why not?

U.S. Government and Environmental Policy

Focusing on the U.S. government, instructors might offer a summary and analysis of environmental policy since 1970. This topic could work well in courses in American government and politics and introductions to public policy. Review the enactment of the major environmental policies, and the political conditions that facilitated such action, such as high levels of public concern for environmental degradation. What have these policies achieved? How successful have they been? If they have not been very successful, why is that? What conclusions are warranted on the responsiveness of the U.S. government to public concern about the environment. What are the implications for the future of environmental policy? Attention could be focused on one or more cases, such as the Endangered Species Act of 1973 or the Clean Air Act of 1970 and their later amendments.

Another approach that should appeal to students is to review and analyze the major criticisms directed at U.S. environmental policy from conservative think tanks (such as the Cato Institute and Heritage Foundation) and from the new Republican majority in the U.S. Congress. Much of the emphasis in 1995 on mandatory cost–benefit analysis and risk assessment for new regulations, protection of established property rights, and an end or limit to "unfunded mandates" for state and local governments have been promoted intensively over the past several years by the so-called Wise Use and property rights movements and by their ideological allies in think tanks (e.g., Anderson and Leal 1991; Greve and Smith 1992). The critiques and their origins could be examined and their likely effects assessed. Should environmental policy be radically altered in this manner? Would doing so be consistent with public opinion on environmental issues? How is it that such conservative critiques have become so widespread and so politically prominent in light of the strong bipartisan history of environmental policy and consistent public support for it?

There is plenty of text material that provides such an overview and assessment (including Rosenbaum 1995; Vig and Kraft 1994; Kraft 1995b; Switzer 1994; Portney 1992). Those seeking a single chapter to cover these issues might consider the introductory chapter in Vig and Kraft, which offers a review of 25 years of U.S. environmental policy and politics as well as a modest appraisal of environmental achievements and costs. At least one publisher (HarperCollins) offers a monograph series that accompanies one of its leading American government texts, with one of the volumes covering U.S. environmental policy and politics (Kraft 1994c). That can be a starting point for instructors who are not very familiar with the subject. So too can the brief treatments of opposing viewpoints offered in Goldfarb (1993), which may be especially appropriate in light of increasing criticism of environmental policy.

Upper Division Course

Environmental Politics and Policy

This course is designed to provide a survey of environmental politics and policy, both in the United States and globally. It examines the nature of environmental problems; contrasting views of global environmental futures; the philosophies, strategies, and tactics of environmental groups; ideological, political, and institutional forces shaping governmental policy making and implementation; and selected issues and problems in environmental policy. Students work on three individual projects and papers drawn from extensive lists of possible topics handed out at equal intervals in the course. Many variations are possible, including group research projects.

UNIT 1. ENVIRONMENTAL PROBLEMS AND POLITICS

Lectures can review the character of global environmental problems and their political implications. Several perspectives may be offered, including scientific, historical, ethical, economic, and political. Because the course focuses on political institutions and the policy-making process, it is helpful to begin with other perspectives. Several weeks might be spent reviewing the way different disciplines approach environmental problems and their solutions, from natural scientists and engineers to economists and philosophers.

Students are encouraged to think of the contribution each perspective makes to understanding the causes and implications of environmental problems. Why do natural scientists place so much faith in the contribution of scientific research? Why do economists favor market-based solutions? Why are some philosophers convinced that only development of an environmental ethic will provide sufficient public support for progressive environmental change? What does a study of the history of environmental problems and society's responses to them tell us about the prospects for action today? What is unique about a political perspective on environmental problems?

Given the emphasis of the course on government and politics, and widespread cynicism toward both in the 1990s, instructors might think of creative ways to underscore the imperative of public policy intervention to protect the "public good" of environmental quality, and the implications for citizen involvement.

Such an exercise should speak to the question of the strengths and limitations of traditional disciplines. Thus it contributes to an appreciation of the need for an interdisciplinary orientation and may suggest how colleges and universities can build such an orientation into their curricula. Readings and lectures may be drawn from Worster's (1988) collection on environmental history, particularly his own introductory chapter; Lacey's (1989) edited volume on historical aspects of U.S. environmental policy; Freeman's chapter in Vig and Kraft on the approach taken by economists (1994); Paehlke's excellent book (1989) and his chapter in Vig and Kraft (1994) on environmental values; Rosenbaum's (1995) text, particularly chapters 1 and 10; and other contributions to Vig and Kraft (1994) on the role of political science and policy analysis. The reader is urged to make use of the resources provided in other chapters of this book, particularly those on history, economics, philosophy, and "Reinventing the Classroom," in developing these ideas.

Among the papers and projects suitable for this section of the course are the relationship between environmental science and public policy. Why is there so much dispute over scientific facts regarding, for example, global climate change or protection of biological diversity? What constitutes "scientific consensus"? At what point is such consensus sufficient to promote public policy solutions to environmental problems?

Other possible topics for papers and projects concern the nature of an environmental ethic. What does it mean? What are its component parts? How much agreement is there among environmentalists and among environmental writers? To what extent would belief in such an ethic contribute to changes in human behavior?

Similarly, to what extent does an economic perspective on environmental problems and solutions offer important insights and guidance for public policy? What are the advantages of an economic view of the environment? The disadvantages? How do conventional economic treatments of environmental problems compare to those found in the emerging "ecological economics" literature (Daly and Cobb 1994; Costanza 1991). What are the implications for public policy? For the "greening of industry" trend? For "green consuming" on the part of the public? (See Chapter 4, Economics, for further discussion.)

UNIT 2. ENVIRONMENTAL CONDITIONS AND TRENDS

The purpose of this section of the course is to review selected scientific data and analyses on the severity of contemporary environmental conditions and projections for the future. The exercise provides a good opportunity to discuss the scientific basis for environmentalist policy, and to understand the need to ground arguments for environmental change in valid scientific assessment.

Readings can be diverse, using text material (e.g., Rosenbaum 1995; MacNeill et al. 1991) and excerpts from *Scientific American* (1990). Students can be alerted to the extensive sources of information on the subject, including governmental studies and compilations (e.g., Council on Environmental Quality and Environmental Protection Agency reports) and volumes from environmental research institutes (e.g., the World Resources Institute's *World Resources* series; and the Worldwatch Institute's *State of the World* series, see Brown et al. in Resources Section).

With such material, students might investigate the extent of environmental threats using primary-source data and reach their own conclusions regarding the severity of problems and appropriate governmental response. Governmental reports on trends in air and water quality, release of toxic chemicals, energy use, and population growth are readily available in depository libraries. Among topics that might be encouraged are disagreements between environmentalists and their critics over environmental and public health risks posed by climate change, threats to biodiversity, deterioration of the stratospheric ozone layer, urban air quality, drinking water quality, pesticides, toxic chemicals, hazardous wastes, nuclear wastes, and so forth. What do the data show? How well are the risks understood? On what points are there conflicting judgments, and what is the source of this disagreement? To what extent might conflicts be resolved through scientific research? What are the implications for public policy?

Such projects might work best if the object of concern is a local or state environmental problem on which students might gather data first-hand and interview the parties in dispute about the actual risks to public health or to the environment and the data on which such judgments are based. Local air quality or water quality issues might work well, or public exposure to toxic chemicals, where Toxics Release Inventory data are available from the federal and state governments on industrial emissions to the air, water, and land. Students might also examine the concerns of local environmental groups and the responses by industry or governmental bodies to these concerns.

UNIT 3. POLITICAL AND ECONOMIC IMPLICATIONS OF ENVIRONMENTAL TRENDS

What are the implications for political and economic systems of global environmental trends? Can we cope with environmental challenges through democratic systems of government? What are the strengths and weaknesses of democratic politics in this context? Are free-market economic systems compatible with resource scarcity and environmental protection? What are their advantages or disadvantages?

Readings and class discussions might emphasize sharply contrasting views, including Ophuls and Boyan (1992) and Paehlke (1989) on the prospects for democratic politics. A class debate on the capacity and limitations of democratic politics could be arranged. Among the possible questions to examine: Can democratic governments move swiftly enough to respond effectively to environmental threats? How far will the public be willing to go in its support of environmental policies? If democracy falls short, what are the alternatives? Do we need, as Ophuls and Boyan say, some form of ecological mandarins, an environmentally informed elite, to make policy decisions? Can the public become sufficiently informed to make democratic environmental politics a reality? Through what kinds of political discourse and interaction can the public play a significant role in environmental policy decisions?

UNIT 4. ENVIRONMENTALISM AND POLITICAL BEHAVIOR

This section of the course reviews public opinion on the environment and assesses the diverse environmental movement. Using readings and lectures from Dunlap and Mertig (1992), Dunlap (1991); Mitchell (1990), and Bosso (1994), among others, explore the degree of public support for environmental activities of government. What kinds of environmental issues most concern the public? How much support exists for environmental policies?

Instructors might encourage discussion of the strategies used by environmental groups. Are mainstream groups more effective than grassroots organizations or the more radical "green" groups? Which do students prefer, based on what assumptions about government and politics or the effectiveness of certain kinds of actions? Films might be used to portray environmental protest (e.g., by Earth First!) or more conventional political activities such as lobbying of policymakers and public education. Exercises here might involve designing a strategy for a local environmental group, drafting letters to local industry or government officials, examining voting records of members of Congress or state and local officials by using one of the scorecards compiled by environmental groups.

The addresses and phone numbers of environmental groups are available in several of the sources listed in the reference works and almanacs noted below. The *Conservation Directory* (National Wildlife Federation 1993) is particularly useful for this purpose, as is the volume prepared for the 1990 Earth Day, the *Global Ecology Handbook* (Global Tomorrow Coalition 1990).

One topic that may appeal to students is exploration of grassroots environmentalism. Several variants merit consideration, including those groups involved in the environmental justice movement (reflecting concerns over how environmental problems and policies affect poor and minority communities), other citizen groups concerned about toxic chemicals and hazardous wastes, and the recently mobilized grassroots groups loosely affiliated with the western Wise Use and property rights movements. Who joins these groups, what are their political philosophies, what do they do, and how effective are they? Does the rise of grassroots groups pose a fundamental challenge to the mainstream established groups such as the Sierra Club, Wilderness Society, Natural Resources Defense Council, and Audubon Society? Can the Washington-based groups coexist easily with the grassroots groups?

At another level, students could be encouraged to examine the role of environmental issues in election campaigns. How do Democrats and Republicans differ on environmental issues? What do party platforms tell us? What about documents such as the Republicans' Contract with America? How do voting records of each of the major parties compare, using the League of Conservation Voters (LCV) analyses of congressional voting? LCV scores are available for congressional voting over the past two decades, and new scores are compiled and made available annually. Students also might be encouraged to ask about the extent to which environmental issues have been prominent in recent presidential election campaigns. What role have environmental groups played in election campaigns and how well have they done? How successful have "green parties" been in the United States? What is their promise for the future?

UNIT 5. THE POLICY-MAKING PROCESS

Text material (Rosenbaum 1995; Vig and Kraft 1994) covers most of the essentials, such as the characteristics of governmental institutions and policy processes. Students should be led to ask about the organization and operation of institutions such as Congress, the presidency, the bureaucracy, the courts, and state and local governments. What are the chief characteristics of each of the major institutions, and how well have they performed on environmental issues? Students also need to learn how policy making occurs, what forces affect decision making in government, and how policy making changes over time and under different administrations. Class discussion might focus on what students and others can do to affect the making of environmental policy, whether at the national or state and local level.

Many good case studies or assessments of U.S. environmental policy making are available for this purpose to supplement core texts and edited books. These include Bosso (1987) on pesticide policy, Tobin (1990) on endangered species and biodiversity, Kraft (1994b) and Mazur (1994) on population policy, and Cohen (1995) and Bryner (1993) on the Clean Air Act of 1990. At the state and local level, DeWitt John's (1994) *Civic Environmentalism* contains insightful analyses of environmental policy innovation. For a review of work in political science that focuses on Congress, the bureaucracy, the courts, interest groups, federalism, and the like, see Lester (1995).

Class lectures and discussions might deal with recent controversies such as the Clean Air Act Amendments of 1990, proposed changes in the Clean Water Act, the Safe Drinking Water Act, the Superfund, and federal pesticides policy, among other major federal acts. Other suitable topics include protection of biological diversity in old growth forests, governmental response to global climate change, and action on world population growth. In each case, attention could focus on the nature of the disputes over the accomplishments of present policies and needed reforms. Which side is most persuasive? Given the different perspectives on such policies, how does the political system build public consensus for policy action?

Alternatively, attention can be given to the major policy actions taken by various presidential administrations (Nixon to Clinton) and their success or failure. Ronald Reagan's presidency merits special consideration. Why did Reagan adopt such a hostile posture on environmental policy, and to what extent did his administration realize its radical reform agenda? What was the long-term legacy? Did George Bush's efforts merit the label he gave himself, the environmental president? How well have Bill Clinton and Al Gore measured up? What does the record for these presidents say about the institution of the American presidency and its potential to provide national leadership on the environment?

In a similar vein, lectures or student papers or projects might focus on decision making within major federal or state bureaucracies such as EPA, the Department of Energy, the Interior Department, or state environmental protection agencies. How are they organized, and how well funded and staffed are they? How well are they doing at implementing environmental policies? What influences their decision making? How can the agencies and their decision making be made more effective or more responsive to environmental needs?

One of the most promising developments has been environmental policy innovation at the state and local level. Lectures or class papers and topics might focus on some of these actions, such as clean air and toxic chemical policies in California; energy conservation efforts in Colorado, California, and other states; restoration of the Everglades in Florida; control of agricultural chemicals in Iowa; or use of ecosystem management approaches for restoration of the Great Lakes basin and other areas (see John 1994; Ringquist 1993; Lowry 1992).

UNIT 6. ENVIRONMENTAL POLICY ANALYSIS

Instructors could review and discuss the various approaches to analyzing environmental policy, whether global, national, or local, including economic analysis, risk assessment, political analysis, and ethical analysis.

Is economic cost–benefit analysis helpful or not? Does it merit the enormous attention given to it in recent years? Can it be used in the manner that critics of environmental policy have in mind? Is it possible to compare costs and benefits of environmental policy fairly when so many benefits are intangible or difficult to measure precisely in relation to the costs of public policies? What role should cost–benefit analysis play in policy making? To what extent is it compatible with the inevitable political judgments about the desirability of policy action?

What about risk assessment? What do current methods of health risk assessments allow us to determine about the effects of environmental pollution on human health, and with what degree of certainty? How about the emerging practice of ecological risk assessment for estimating damage to natural systems? How well do both approaches help to clarify threats to human and ecological health? Are these methods reliable enough to play the role in policy choices favored by many critics of environmental policy in the 1990s? Examination of leading cases such as EPA's studies of environmental tobacco smoke (ETS), radon, dioxin, and lead—or studies by the Intergovernmental Panel on Climate Change and the National Academy of Sciences on climate change—might be useful ways to bring the abstraction of risk assessment down to a practical level.

What does political analysis contribute to our ability to measure environmental policy success and failure? How well can we assess policy implementation? What are the most appropriate standards for judging policy success and failure? Based on appropriate criteria, how well are governmental institutions such as the Congress, the presidency, the courts, and the bureaucracy doing in responding to environmental problems?

In this context, some attention needs to be given to ethical analysis. How might it supplement the common emphasis on economics in environmental policy decisions?

For all of these topics, readings might be drawn from chapters by Freeman, Andrews, and Paehlke in Vig and Kraft (1994); Ophuls and Boyan (1992); Bartlett (1986 and 1994); Milbrath (1989); or Daly and Cobb (1994). Class projects might include an effort to examine a local or state environmental issue and the full range of costs and benefits. For example, should local wetlands be preserved or developed? Should utilities build more power plants or encourage energy conservation? Should city and state governments encourage (and subsidize) use of public transit or continue to rely heavily on private automobiles? Some campus policies might be investigated in a similar manner, particularly those related to energy use and materials recycling. (See Chapter 1, Reinventing Higher Education, and Chapter 8, Media and Journalism, for further examples.)

UNIT 7. GLOBAL ENVIRONMENTAL POLITICS AND POLICY

Although this course focuses on U.S. environmental policy, there is no sharp line between domestic and international policy. Domestic policy has global implications, and actions taken outside of the United States have implications for domestic policy. A host of issues might be addressed at this point in the course.

What are the prospects for international environmental politics and policy, particularly in light of the 1992 Earth Summit? Review the key issues of the Earth Summit, using, for example, excerpts from Parson, Haas, and Levy (1992) or original documents from the United Nations (1993a and 1993b), and debate the U.S. role at the meeting. Discuss the prospects for North–South cooperation on funding for environmental programs and technology transfer (Jordan 1994a and 1994b). Instructors could use cases of international trade and the environment, climate change treaties, protection of biodiversity, or population growth, among others, to explore international tensions and ways to achieve environmental goals.

One volume listed in the references, *Environmental Profiles*, contains examples of environmental and conservation activities in some 115 countries (Katz, Orrick, and Honig 1992). The Worldwatch Institute's papers and annual volumes have many examples as well. The most notable cases of international trade and the environment recently have been the North American Free Trade Agreement (NAFTA) and the General Agreement on Tariffs and Trade (GATT). A number of articles and book-length treatments are available on NAFTA. Many of these kinds of conflicts are best examined using case studies of particular nations and local disputes. Class projects might involve selection of several such cases from the sources noted, investigation of the pertinent issues, and class discussion of the implications for public policy, national and international.

Among the key issues meriting attention in this segment of the course are the way in which national security is being redefined to include environmental and resource concerns (including the massive cleanup effort directed at the legacy of the Cold War), conflicts over the relationship of international trade and environmental protection, the development of environmental policy in the new European Community, the struggle to improve environmental conditions in the former Soviet Union, the implementation of international environmental agreements approved over the past 25 years, the capacity of international institutions such as the United Nations and the World Bank to foster sustainable development, and the relationship between developed and developing nations in funding and otherwise influencing the direction of economic development in the 21st century. Excellent treatments of most of these topics are available and are listed in the resource list at the end of the chapter.

UNIT 8. SELECTED ISSUES IN ENVIRONMENTAL POLICY

Using texts or case study material, instructors can select several major policy areas for more intensive review to illustrate some of the themes addressed earlier in the course. At the national level, abundant material is available in core texts (e.g., P. Portney 1990; K. Portney 1992; Ringquist 1993; Rosenbaum 1995; Kraft 1995b) to afford thorough coverage of topics such as pollution control, energy, and natural resource policies. An international dimension can be added with selections from the Worldwatch Paper series or the annual *State of the World* volume. Excellent books are available for even more in-depth coverage of selected public policies such as the Clean Air Act (Cohen 1995; Bryner 1993) and the Endangered Species Act (Yaffee 1994).

One useful way to proceed is to assess how well various national policies are working. What policies do we have, what are their goals and objectives, how well have they been implemented, and what have they achieved to date? On the whole, are they successful at resolving the problems to which they are directed? Why are they working or not working, and what are the implications for either redesigning the policies or improving implementation of them? What does the record suggest about the capacity of the U.S. political system to formulate and carry out appropriate environmental policies?

Students might also be asked to investigate the particulars of one or more of the leading federal policies. Sources such as *Congressional Quarterly Weekly Report* and its annual *Almanacs* provide fairly extensive descriptions of the policies, the leading actors in Congress, the major interest groups involved, and the key issues. Congressional hearings, executive branch documents, and court records provide elaborate information on issues, participants, and decisions.

Student projects might also involve examination of state and local environmental conditions (e.g., air and water quality or protection of biological diversity) and policy actions. Information about environmental conditions should be available from local or regional offices of the state environmental protection or natural resources agencies, and from local environmental groups. Debates could be organized around the costs of environmental programs and whether the benefits justify the costs, broadly defined.

Students also could explore cases of particularly innovative or successful programs at the local, state, or national level. Alternatively, cases of environmental gridlock over hazardous or nuclear waste sites could be explored to understand the political forces at work. What causes the NIMBY ("Not in My Back Yard") phenomenon and how can communities and states deal with it? What are the plans of local utilities for construction of additional power plants or promotion of energy conservation, and on what are they based? Many other lines of inquiry are possible.

UNIT 9. THE FUTURE OF ENVIRONMENTAL POLITICS

As the 21st century approaches, inquiries about long-term environmental challenges and the efficacy of government and politics become even more pertinent than usual. Instructors might focus on the major issues on the environmental agenda for the rest of the 1990s and the early 21st century. What are they? Various authors have their own lists (e.g., Vig and Kraft 1994; Kraft 1995b; National Commission 1993). Nearly everyone would agree that further improvements are needed in environmental protection policies, and in energy, population, and natural resource policies, both domestically and internationally. Topics such as sustainable development, promotion of environmental technologies, the greening of business, trade and the environment, environmental justice, the urban environment (transportation, housing, infrastructure), computers and the environment, public education, and environmental restoration, among others, are also suggested. Class discussions could focus on creative suggestions for societal change, the obstacles to achieving such changes, and appropriate action strategies.

More philosophically, class lectures and discussions might focus on how well equipped governments are to deal with the challenges that lie ahead. What new approaches (such as integrated decision making, pollution prevention, full cost accounting, improved environmental research, and greater use of cost–benefit analysis and risk assessment) are needed to develop and implement effective environmental policies?

For these and other questions, class debate could be organized around a book such as Al Gore's (1992) *Earth in the Balance*, or chapters in the annual *State of the World*. For more advanced courses, some of the most provocative books (or chapters from them) could be used to stimulate discussion. These include Ophuls and Boyan's (1992) *Ecology and the Politics of Scarcity*, particularly chapter 8, and Martin Lewis's (1994) *Green Delusions*. Lewis's introductory chapter would serve as a suitable counter to Ophuls and Boyan and other "radical" or deep ecology positions.

Upper Division Course Modules in Environmental Politics and Policy

Environmental Policy Analysis

Central to debates over environmental politics and public policy in the 1990s are issues of costs, benefits, and risks, and the value of market incentives as a supplement to regulation. Instructors in several kinds of course could develop a module for a week or two of emphasis on these topics. Readings might include chapters by Freeman and Andrews in Vig and Kraft (1994), the report by Stavins (1991) on market-based environmental strategies, selections from P. Portney's (1990) collection of economic analyses of environmental protection and natural resource policies, EPA's widely cited study of comparative risk assessment, *Reducing Risk* (1990), among others.

Lectures might review the logic of such policy analysis as a purportedly rational way to make difficult policy choices; summarize studies of environmental program costs and benefits; indicate how cost–benefit analysis is done, its strengths, and its weaknesses; review methods and concepts of risk assessment and report on the comparative risks of different environmental problems.

Students might debate the value of such methods and whether their use is acceptable or not. Case studies of particular issues might be used to review how assessment of costs, benefits, and risks might clarify the factual issues in disputes, whether over environmental health or ecological preservation. Can local disputes be resolved in this way? What about major national conflicts over protection of biological diversity or prevention of climate change? Should we have stringent but very costly regulations on exposure to hazardous wastes or toxic chemicals? Should all of the many former Department of Defense and Department of Energy sites be cleaned up to the same degree and within the same time frame, even though the cost may run to hundreds of billions of dollars and the risks may vary significantly across the universe of sites? Current data on such facilities and the policy dilemmas the nation faces may be found in Funke (1994) and Kraft (1994a).

Public Opinion and Environmental Politics

The public's understanding of environmental issues is crucial to its support for governmental action. Instructors might draw from research on public opinion and political behavior to create a module on public attitudes toward the environment. There is a great deal of survey data available for review and discussion, as well as assessments of environmental groups and their efforts to mobilize the public (e.g., Dunlap 1991; Dunlap and Mertig 1992; Mitchell 1990; Bosso 1994). As noted above, comparable data is available for other nations through the Gallup Health of the Planet survey (Dunlap, Gallup, and Gallup 1993a, 1993b). Lectures on this subject could emphasize the degree of public concern and support for public policy, and how it has changed over time. The public seems to be especially concerned about threats to its health (e.g., from toxic chemicals or radioactive waste), but much less so with ecosystem risks such as loss of biological diversity or even with common problems of indoor air pollution. Why is this? What kinds of information might make a difference in the public's appraisal of environmental conditions and risks?

Projects might involve student review of the poll data and preparation of a profile of public concerns. Or students might want to conduct a survey of the student body or the community. They might want to ask about environmental education in the public schools and whether such programs are likely to alter public perceptions and attitudes over time.

Political Theory and the Environment

Beyond the specific issues of environmental ills and public policy, there are looming normative questions around which course modules might be constructed. What is the role of individual freedom and governmental authority under conditions of what Ophuls and Boyan (1992) call ecological scarcity? Are conventional assumptions about individual rights (including property rights) still as defensible as they used to be given the constraints imposed by growing environmental threats? Are democracy and environmental values compatible? How does an environmental ethic compare to other bases for political choice?

There are excellent sources from which instructors might draw to address these questions. Several recent books are discussed in a review essay (Kraft 1992). Ophuls and Boyan (1992) offers many provocative assertions, with counterarguments available from Paehlke (1989 and 1990), Dryzek (1987), Eckersley (1992), among others. At a more concrete level, volumes such as Milbrath (1989) and Daly and Cobb (1994) offer discussions of what a sustainable society might look like and the ethical dilemmas facing environmentalists.

Projects for students in this module might involve writing critical essays on these authors' works and debating questions of how individual rights and ecological needs may conflict, the issues related to equity between rich and poor nations (or among segments of the U.S. population), and the extent to which individuals can be persuaded to alter their behavior ("sacrifice" in some way) to protect future generations. Much useful material on such basic ethical issues can be found in the journal *Environmental Ethics.*

Resources

Page numbers appearing in brackets at the end of some entries indicate where the reference is cited in a course plan.

General Works on Environmental Politics and Policy

Anderson, T. L., and D. R. Leal. 1991. *Free Market Environmentalism*. Boulder, CO: Westview Press. [p. 241]

The authors are sharply critical of mainstream environmental policy and argue for a free market alternative. Helps in understanding the philosophical and economic basis for conservative and property rights critiques of environmental policy.

Andrews, R. N. L., 1994. "Risk-Based Decisionmaking." In Vig and Kraft (2nd ed.). [p. 248]

A critique of environmental policy focusing on dilemmas associated with the conduct and use of risk assessment and comparative risk analysis.

Bartlett, R. V. 1994. "Evaluating Environmental Policy Success and Failure." In Vig and Kraft (2nd ed.). [p. 248]

Sets out multiple criteria for evaluating how well environmental programs are working. An original and challenging analysis for upper-level undergraduates and graduate students.

Bernards, N., ed. 1991. *The Environmental Crisis: Opposing Viewpoints*. San Diego: Greenhaven Press. [p. 240]

As the title indicates, the text offers clashing points of view on environmental problems and public policies, with an emphasis on pollution control.

Bosso, C. J. 1987. *Pesticides and Politics: The Life Cycle of a Public Issue*. Pittsburgh: University of Pittsburgh Press. [p. 246]

A thorough and excellent case study of congressional action on pesticide issues. Nicely illustrates the policy process in the U.S. Congress for environmental issues. Suitable for upper-level undergraduate students.

Brown, L., et al. Annual. *State of the World: A Worldwatch Institute Report on Progress toward a Sustainable Society*. New York: W. W. Norton. [pp. 239, 244, 250, 251]

A widely used annual collection of well-written and well-documented assessments of environmental problems. Suitable for all levels, and available at a very modest price if ordered directly from Worldwatch.

Bryner, G. C. 1993. *Blue Skies, Green Politics: The Clean Air Act of 1990*. Washington, DC: Congressional Quarterly Press. [pp. 247, 250]

A thorough, scholarly assessment of the enactment of the Clean Air Act of 1990. Best for upper-level courses in environmental policy. Second edition available by late 1995.

Cohen, R. E. 1995. *Washington at Work: Back Rooms and Clean Air.* 2nd ed. New York: Macmillan. [pp. 247, 250]

A journalistic case study of how Congress dealt with the Clean Air Act of 1990. Can be read at all levels.

Costanza, R., ed. 1991. *Ecological Economics: The Science and Management of Sustainability.* New York: Columbia University Press. [p. 243]

A collection that advances the concept of ecological economics as a counter to conventional economic thinking.

Dryzek, J. S. 1987. *Rational Ecology: Environment and Political Economy.* New York: Basil Blackwell. [p. 253]

An insightful but rather densely argued book on the adequacy of social choice mechanisms in light of ecological needs. Best for graduate courses.

Dwyer, W. O., and F. C. Leeming, eds. 1995. *Earth's Eleventh Hour: Environmental Readings from The Washington Post.* [p. 240]

An extensive and balanced compilation of articles from the Post on environmental issues, from population growth and air pollution to pesticides and federal land use. Although the articles are quite brief, they should alert students to political controversies over environmental policy and stimulate them to seek more detailed accounts.

Freeman, A. M., III. 1994. "Economics, Incentives, and Environmental Regulation." In Vig and Kraft (2nd ed.).

An assessment of the potential for making greater use of economics in environmental policy. Includes a discussion of cost–benefit analysis and the use of market incentives for achieving environmental quality goals.

Goldfarb, T. D. 1993. *Taking Sides: Clashing Views on Controversial Environmental Issues,* 5th ed. Guilford, CT: Dushkin Publishing Group. [pp. 240, 242]

A well-tested and highly readable collection that presents opposing arguments on major environmental issues. Regularly updated.

Greve, M. S., and F. L. Smith, Jr., eds. 1992. *Environmental Politics: Public Costs, Private Rewards.* New York: Praeger. [p. 241]

Ten authors, reflecting diverse ideological positions, offer critiques of environmental policy, arguing that environmental regulation is used for many political and economic objectives that have little to do with environmental protection.

256 Michael E. Kraft

Henning, D. H., and W. R. Mangun. 1989. *Managing the Environmental Crisis: Incorporating Competing Values in Natural Resource Administration*. Durham, NC: Duke University Press.

A text focusing on natural resource issues, with much useful historical data.

Ingram, H. M., and R. K. Godwin, eds. 1985. *Public Policy and the Natural Environment*. Greenwich, CT: JAI Press.

Collection of original studies illustrating work by political scientists.

Ingram, H. M., and D. E. Mann. 1983. "Environmental Protection Policy." In *Encyclopedia of Policy Studies*. S. S. Nagel, ed. New York: Marcel Dekker.

An overview of environmental policy issues suitable for graduate students.

John, D. 1994. *Civic Environmentalism: Alternatives to Regulation in States and Communities*. Washington, DC: Congressional Quarterly Press. [p. 247]

An illuminating exploration of innovation in environmental policy at the state and local level, with emphasis on alternatives to conventional regulation. Includes many excellent case studies of state and local environmental policy.

Jordan, A. 1994a. "Financing the UNCED Agenda: The Controversy over Additionality." *Environment* 36 (April):16–20, 26–34. [p. 249]

Along with the companion piece just below, it provides a thorough review of the costs of implementing Agenda 21.

Jordan, A. 1994b. "Paying the Incremental Costs of Global Environmental Protection: The Evolving Role of GEF." *Environment* 36 (July–August):12–20, 31–36. [p. 249]

Kamieniecki, S., R. O'Brien, and M. Clarke, eds. 1986. *Controversies in Environmental Policy*. Albany: State University of New York Press.

A diverse collection focusing on major controversies in environmental policy, including cost–benefit analysis, regulation and its alternatives, market-based incentives, privatization, evaluation of environmental agencies and policies, and the viability of democratic politics. A new edition is in progress.

Kraft, M. E. 1992. "Ecology and Political Theory: Broadening the Scope of Environmental Politics." *Policy Studies Journal* 20(4):712–718. [p. 253]

Reviews and critiques four books dealing with environmentalism and political theory and suggests new areas for political science research.

Kraft, M. E. 1994a. "Searching for Policy Success: Reinventing the Politics of Site Remediation." *The Environmental Professional* 16 (September):245–253. [p. 252]

An examination of issues involved in siting hazardous and nuclear waste facilities and remediating contaminated sites, such as former military installations. Emphasizes the importance of democratic participation.

Kraft, M. E. 1994b. "Population Policy." In *Encyclopedia of Policy Studies*, 2nd ed. S. Nagel, ed. New York: Marcel Dekker. [pp. 240, 246]

Current data on population rates, policy controversies, and scholarly work in the field as of late 1992. Emphasizes the history of U.S. population policy.

Kraft, M. E. 1994c. *Environmental Politics and Public Policy in the 1990s.* New York: HarperCollins. [p. 242]

Prepared as a monograph to supplement American government textbooks. Contains basic survey of U.S. environmental policy and politics, with emphasis on the Reagan and Bush years and Clinton administration initiatives.

Kraft, M. E. 1995a. "Congress and Environmental Policy." In *Environmental Politics and Policy.* J. P. Lester, ed. Durham, NC: Duke University Press.

A review of the scholarly literature on Congress and the environment and suggestions for new research. Intended for graduate students.

Kraft, M. E. 1995b. *Environmental Policy and Politics: Toward the 21st Century.* New York: HarperCollins. [pp. 241, 250, 251]

A moderate-length text on U.S. environmental policy and the political process, with attention given to both pollution control and natural resource policies. Emphasizes the application of policy analysis to environmental problems and offers an historical and evaluative treatment of U.S environmental policies and politics.

Lester, J. P., ed. 1995. *Environmental Politics and Policy: Theories and Evidence.* Durham, NC: Duke University Press. [p. 247]

A collection geared to political scientists and graduate students. Useful as a review of political institutions and scholarly studies of environmental politics.

Lewis, M. W. 1994. *Green Delusions: An Enviromentalist Critique of Radical Environmentalism.* Durham, NC: Duke University Press. [p. 251]

A provocative critique of deep ecology and other radical environmentalist theories.

Lowry, W. R. 1992. *The Dimensions of Federalism: State Governments and Pollution Control Policies.* Durham: Duke University Press. [p. 247]

An informative analysis of state environmental policies, with case studies drawn from four states. Lowry focuses on the conditions for innovative state leadership in environmental policy.

Mazur, L. A., ed. 1994. *Beyond the Numbers: A Reader on Population, Consumption, and the Environment.* Washington, DC: Island Press.

A well-balanced collection on contemporary population trends and issues in population policy. [pp. 240, 246]

National Commission on the Environment. 1993. *Choosing a Sustainable Future.* Washington, DC: Island Press. [pp. 239, 251]

Reflections of mainstream corporate and governmental perspectives on sustainability that is surprisingly strong on the need for social and political change.

Ophuls, W., and A. S. Boyan, Jr. 1992. *Ecology and the Politics of Scarcity Revisited.* New York: W. H. Freeman. [pp. 239, 245, 248, 251, 253]

A revision of a classic work in environmental politics from the mid-1970s, providing a thorough review of global environmental conditions and a strong critique of political responses to date.

Paehlke, R. C. 1989. *Environmentalism and the Future of Progressive Politics.* New Haven: Yale University Press. [pp. 243, 245, 253]

An original argument about the capacity of environmentalism to serve as the center for progressive political coalitions.

Portney, K. E. 1992. *Controversial Issues in Environmental Policy.* Newbury Park, CA: Sage. [pp. 241, 250]

A recent brief text on environmental policy.

Portney, P., ed. 1990. *Public Policies for Environmental Protection.* Washington, DC: Resources for the Future. [pp. 250, 252]

An excellent collection of original assessments of the economics of environmental policy.

Ringquist, E. J. 1993. *Environmental Protection at the State Level: Politics and Progress in Controlling Pollution.* Armonk, NY: M.E. Sharpe. [pp. 247, 250]

A rigorous and original examination of state-level pollution control policies and their effects on environmental quality in the states.

Rosenbaum, W. A. 1995. *Environmental Politics and Policy*, 3rd ed. Washington, DC: Congressional Quarterly Press. [pp. 241, 243, 244, 246, 250]

The leading text, in various titles and editions since the early 1970s.

Stavins, R. N. 1991. *Project 88—Round II, Incentives for Action: Designing Market-Based Environmental Strategies*. Washington, DC: Offices of Senators Tim Wirth and John Heinz. [p. 252]

One of the best compilations of ways in which market incentives can be used to further conservation and environmental protection.

Switzer, J. V. 1994. *Environmental Politics: Domestic and Global Dimensions*. New York: St. Martin's. [p. 241]

A survey of environmental problems and public policies, with descriptive coverage of some issues (such as indoor air quality, oceans, tropical forests, the arctic environment, and population) not addressed in much detail in other texts on environmental politics.

Tobin, R. 1990. *The Expendable Future: U.S. Politics and the Protection of Biological Diversity*. Durham, NC: Duke University Press. [p. 246]

One of the best treatments of biodiversity politics in the United States, offering a thorough assessment of bureaucratic decision making.

Vig, N. J., and M. E. Kraft, eds. 1994. *Environmental Policy in the 1990s*, 2nd ed. Washington, DC: Congressional Quarterly Press (1st ed. 1990). [pp. 241, 243, 246, 248, 251, 252]

The latest collection of original work by political scientists and other policy scholars, with new material on international environmental issues. Covers major governmental institutions and policy processes as well as selected policy dilemmas. A third edition will be available by fall 1996.

Yaffee, S. L. 1994. *The Wisdom of the Spotted Owl: Policy Lessons for a New Century*. Washington, DC: Island Press. [p. 250]

A careful and original examination of the case of the spotted owl and preservation of old growth forests in the Pacific Northwest, focusing on the decision-making process.

International Environmental Issues

Axelrod, R. S. 1994. "Environmental Policy and Management in the European Community." In Vig and Kraft (2nd ed.).

An overview of the development of the European Community and an appraisal of its environmental policy actions.

Benedick, R. E. 1991. *Ozone Diplomacy: New Directions in Safeguarding the Planet.* Cambridge: Harvard University Press.

A fine case study of diplomatic negotiations leading to the Montreal Protocol on protection of the ozone layer, written by the U.S. official who played the leading role. Lessons here for other international treaties, including those associated with the Earth Summit of 1992.

Caldwell, L. K. 1990. *International Environmental Policy: Emergence and Dimensions,* 2nd ed. Durham, NC: Duke University Press. [p. 240]

The newest edition of a classic work on the history of international environmental agreements.

Funke, O. 1994. "National Security and the Environment." In Vig and Kraft (2nd ed.). [p. 252]

An extended analysis of new perspectives on national security based on environmental threats. Includes a discussion of the challenge of environmental cleanup at military installations.

Gore, A. 1992. *Earth in the Balance: Ecology and the Human Spirit.* New York: Plume Books. [p. 251]

Bestseller by Vice President Al Gore, offering a broad and often personal assessment of global environmental issues.

Grubb, M., et al. 1993. *The Earth Summit Agreements: A Guide and Assessment.* London: Royal Institute of International Affairs, Energy and Environmental Programme. [p. 240]

Describes the "road to Rio," the outcomes of the UNCED meeting, and themes and lessons. Also contains a summary and analysis of the five main UNCED agreements.

Haas, P. M., M. A. Levy, and E. A. Parson. 1992. "Appraising the Earth Summit: How Should We Judge UNCED's Success?" *Environment* 34 (October):6–11, 26–32. [p. 240]

One of the best summary assessments of the Earth Summit.

Kamieniecki, S., ed. 1993. *Environmental Politics in the International Arena:* Movements, Parties, Organizations, and Policy. Albany: State University of New York Press.

A unique collection of political analyses focusing on environmental movements and parties in both developing and developed nations. Authors relate political cultures to politics and environmental policy in Latin America, Asia, and Eastern and Western Europe.

MacNeill, J., P. Winsemius, and T. Yakushiji. 1991. *Beyond Interdependence: The Meshing of the World's Economy and the Earth's Ecology*. New York: Oxford University Press. [pp. 239, 240, 243]

Offers a good overview of global environmental problems and the imperative of continued economic growth in the years ahead. Follow-up to *Our Common Future* (see below).

Mathews, J. T., ed. 1991. *Preserving the Global Environment: The Challenge of Shared Leadership*. New York: W. W. Norton. [p. 240]

Diverse collection on global environmental problems, though a little short in treatment of politics and government.

Meadows, D. H., D. L. Meadows, and J. Randers. 1992. *Beyond the Limits: Confronting Global Collapse, Envisioning a Sustainable Future*. Post Mills, VT: Chelsea Green Publishing Company. [p. 240]

In this sequel to the classic *The Limits to Growth* (1972), the authors argue that present trends, without significant changes in human behavior, are likely to lead to a global economic collapse in the next century. The book outlines the conditions for global environmental sustainability.

Parson, E. A., P. M. Haas, and M. A. Levy. 1992. "A Summary of the Major Documents Signed at the Earth Summit and the Global Forum." *Environment* 34 (October):12–15, 34–36. [pp. 240, 249]

Summary of the key documents approved at the Earth Summit.

Porter, G., and J. W. Brown. 1991. *Global Environmental Politics*. Boulder, CO: Westview Press. [p. 240]

Short text on international environmental politics.

Scientific American. 1990. *Managing Planet Earth*. New York: W. H. Freeman. [pp. 240, 242]

A solid collection of scientific appraisals of environmental problems covering the changing atmosphere, climate shifts, water, biodiversity, population growth, energy use, agriculture, and strategies for sustainable development. Clearly written and succinct treatments of the issues.

Starke, L. 1990. *Signs of Hope: Working Towards Our Common Future*. New York: Oxford University Press.

Overview of treaties and other agreements enacted after the 1987 *Our Common Future* (see below).

United Nations. 1993a. *The Global Partnership for Environment and Development: A Guide to Agenda 21, Post-Rio Edition.* [pp. 240, 249]

Summarizes the programs and themes of the Earth Summit for a general audience.

United Nations. 1993b. *Agenda 21: Programme of Action for Sustainable Development.* [pp. 240, 249]

Contains the final text of agreements negotiated by governments at the Earth Summit. Agenda 21 (the full action plan) is included, as is the Rio Declaration on Environment and Development and the Statement of Forest Principles.

World Commission on Environment and Development. 1987. *Our Common Future.* New York: Oxford University Press. [p. 239]

A classic on the global environmental predicament and the need for institutional and policy reforms. First major report to stress the concept of sustainable development. Known as the Brundtland Commission report because of its chair, Prime Minister Gro Brundtland of Norway.

Environmental History and Ethics

Bartlett, R. V. 1986. "Ecological Rationality: Reason and Environmental Policy." *Environmental Ethics* 8:221–239. [p. 248]

An examination of different kinds of rationality, with a proposal for "ecological rationality" as a new concept.

Daly, H. E., and J. B. Cobb, Jr. 1994. *For the Common Good: Redirecting the Economy Toward Community, the Environment, and a Sustainable Future,* 2nd ed. Boston: Beacon Press. [pp. 243, 248, 253]

Original and provocative examination of ethics, economics, and creation of a sustainable future.

Eckersley, R. 1992. *Environmentalism and Political Theory: Toward an Ecocentric Approach.* Albany: State University of New York Press. [p. 253]

An examination of the impact of environmental ideas on contemporary political theory.

Hays, S. P. 1987. *Beauty, Health, and Permanence: Environmental Politics in the United States, 1955–1985.* New York: Cambridge University Press.

Useful history of environmental politics, though by an historian, not a political scientist.

Lacey, M. J., ed. 1989. *Government and Environmental Politics: Essays on Historical Developments Since World War II.* Baltimore: Johns Hopkins University Press. [p. 243]

A first-rate collection that reviews the history of U.S. environmental policies and the actions of organized groups.

Orr, D. W. 1992. *Ecological Literacy: Education and the Transition to a Postmodern World.* Albany: State University of New York Press.

A provocative set of essays drawing from normative theory that makes a strong case for promoting interdisciplinary environmental education in light of needs for sustainable development. Contains a useful "syllabus for ecological literacy." (See Chapter 1, Reinventing Higher Education.)

Paehlke, R. C. 1990. "Environmental Values and Democracy: The Challenge of the Next Century." In Vig and Kraft (1st ed.). [p. 253]

A rejoinder to critics such as Ophuls and R. Heilbroner, arguing that democracy and environmentalism are indeed compatible.

Paehlke, R. C. 1994. "Environmental Values and Public Policy." In Vig and Kraft (2nd ed.).

A highly readable survey of the values of contemporary environmentalism and their relationship to public policy.

Wandesforde-Smith, G. 1990. "Moral Outrage and the Progress of Environmental Policy: What Do We Tell the Next Generation about how to Care for the Earth?" In Vig and Kraft (1st ed.).

An historical treatment arguing that public outrage has been a determining factor in U.S. environmental policy development.

Worster, D., ed., 1988. *The Ends of the Earth.* New York: Oxford University Press. [p. 243]

Collection on environmental history.

Public Opinion and the Environmental Movement

Bosso, C. J. 1994. "After the Movement: Environmental Activism in the 1990s." In Vig and Kraft (2nd ed.). [p. 245, 252]

Overview and assessment of contemporary environmental groups and their strategies.

Dunlap, R. E. 1991. "Public Opinion in the 1980s: Clear Consensus, Ambiguous Commitment." *Environment* 33 (October):9–37. [pp. 245, 252]

Discusses a range of public opinion surveys to clarify the extent of public commitment to environmental protection.

Dunlap, R. E., and A. G. Mertig, eds. 1992. *American Environmentalism: The U.S. Environmental Movement 1970–1990.* Philadelphia: Taylor and Francis. [pp. 245, 252]

Excellent collection on history of environmental movement and public attitudes toward environmental issues.

Dunlap, R. E., G. H. Gallup, Jr., and A. M. Gallup. 1993a. "Of Global Concern: Results of the Health of the Planet Survey." *Environment* 35 (November):7–15, 33–40. [pp. 240, 252]

A summary of the 1992 study listed below.

Dunlap, R. E., G. H. Gallup, Jr., and A. M. Gallup. 1993b. *Health of the Planet Survey.* Princeton, NJ: George H. Gallup International Institute. [pp. 240, 252]

Report of a major survey of international opinion on environmental issues conducted in 1992. Results from 24 nations.

Dunlap, R. E. 1995. "Public Opinion and Environmental Policy." In *Environmental Politics and Policy: Theories and Evidence*, 2nd ed. J. P. Lester, ed. Durham, NC: Duke University Press.

An extensive review and assessment of public opinion data and the relationship of public opinion to environmental policy making.

Global Tomorrow Coalition, 1990. *The Global Ecology Handbook: What You Can Do About the Environmental Crisis.* Boston: Beacon Press. [p. 245]

One of the best collections prepared for the 1990 Earth Week activities. Particularly useful for information about environmental organizations and concrete proposals for citizen action arranged by substantive problem area. A good source for class projects.

Kraft, M. E., and D. L. Wuertz. 1996. "Environmental Advocacy in the Corridors of Government." In *Environmental Discourse: Perspectives on Communication and Advocacy.* J. G. Cantrill and C. Oravec, eds. Lexington, KY: University Press of Kentucky, in press.

Reviews the major approaches used by environmental groups to lobby government, with emphasis on political communication strategies and their impact on environmental policy.

McCormick, J. 1989. *Reclaiming Paradise: The Global Environmental Movement.* Bloomington: Indiana University Press.

Analysis of environmental movement worldwide.

Milbrath, L. W. 1989. *Envisioning a Sustainable Society: Learning Our Way Out.* Albany: State University of New York Press. [pp. 248, 253]

Suggestive of personal and social changes needed to achieve a sustainable future.

Mitchell, R. C. 1990. "Public Opinion and the Green Lobby: Poised for the 1990s?" In Vig and Kraft (1st ed.). [pp. 245, 252]

Short overview of public opinion on the environment and conflicts within environmental movement.

Reference Works and Almanacs

Bureau of National Affairs, Inc. *Environment Reporter.*

One of the leading reference sources for current developments in environmental policy and for coverage of environmental statutes and regulations. In 1994, it became available in a CD-ROM format that provides easy access to the full text of all federal environmental statutes, regulations, and executive orders. Comparable disks are available for each of the 50 states. Will soon contain all court decisions as well.

Council on Environmental Quality. Annual. *Environmental Quality.* Washington, DC: Council on Environmental Quality. [p. 244]

Published more or less annually since 1970.

Environmental Protection Agency, Science Advisory Board. 1990. *Reducing Risk: Setting Priorities and Strategies for Environmental Protection.* Washington, DC: Environmental Protection Agency. [p. 252]

Report on comparative risk by the Science Advisory Board of the EPA. Summary volume and technical reports.

Hall, B., and M. L. Kerr. 1991. *1991–1992 Green Index: A State-by-State Guide to the Nation's Environmental Health.* Washington, DC: Island Press.

An extensive compilation of environmental conditions and policies in the 50 states.

Island Press. Annual. *Island Press Environmental Sourcebook*. Washington, DC: Island Press.

An extensive and very useful catalog of books on biological diversity and a wide range of other environmental topics. Includes books by other publishers as well.

Katz, L. S., S. Orrick, and R. Honig. 1992. *Environmental Profiles: A Global Guide to Projects and People*. Hamden, CT: Garland Publishing. [p. 249]

Includes detailed descriptions of thousands of environmental projects, programs, and campaigns in 115 countries. Coverage of successful campaigns helps to illustrate how environmental problems have been addressed in particular settings around the world.

League of Conservation Voters. 1994. *National Environmental Scorecard*. Washington, DC: League of Conservation Voters.

An annual report on environmental voting records of members of Congress.

National Wildlife Federation. 1993. *1993 Conservation Directory*, 38th ed. Washington, DC: National Wildlife Federation. [p. 245]

A comprehensive list of organizations, agencies, and officials involved with natural resource use and management. Includes names, addresses, and phone numbers for international, national, regional, and state bodies. Extensively indexed for easy use.

Population Reference Bureau. 1994. *1994 World Population Data Sheet*. Washington, DC: Population Reference Bureau. [p. 240]

The best single source of population data, issued annually. Compiled from United Nations and Census Bureau data.

U.S. Environmental Directories, Inc. 1992. *Directory of National Environmental Organizations*. 4th ed. St. Paul, MN: U.S. Environmental Directories, Inc.

Includes over 600 nongovernmental environmental and conservation groups in alphabetical order, with addresses, phone numbers, contact persons, founding dates, current membership, and description of the groups' goals and activities. Also includes 50 federal agencies involved in environmental and natural resources policy. Indexed by subject and state.

World Resources Institute. 1993. *The 1993 Information Please Environmental Almanac*. Boston: Houghton Mifflin.

A series (presumably annual) that pulls together an array of useful environmental data on national and global environmental problems and issues. Includes profiles of nations of the world and the 50 American states.

World Resources Institute. 1994. *World Resources 1994–95: A Guide to the Global Environment*. New York: Oxford University Press. [pp. 239, 244]

Extensive biennial guide to world resource conditions prepared in cooperation with the United Nations Environment Programme and the United Nations Development Programme. Contains elaborate tables of data, many of which are also available in computer files for separate purchase.

Zero Population Growth, Inc. *The ZPG Reporter* (bimonthly), a newsletter devoted to population issues.

ZPG also produces a variety of population–environment fact sheets showing the relationship of human population growth to environmental problems, and it has available a variety of teaching materials related to population growth and its effects as well as to environmental concerns generally. See the organization's "Selected Resources on Population," a seven-page list of books on population and the environment, periodicals that cover these subjects, handbooks and wall charts, films and videos, software, and teaching materials. The collection includes references to books, videos, and curriculum guides geared to pre-collegiate audiences, including children. The list is available from Zero Population Growth, 1400 Sixteenth Street, N.W., Suite 320, Washington, DC 20036 (202) 332-2200. Other materials on population and environment are available from the Population Reference Bureau, the Population Institute, the National Audubon Society, and the Sierra Club's population program. Among the best films are the Audubon Society's *What is the Limit?* (1987). ZPG has a six-minute video, *World Population* (1990), that dramatically simulates world population growth from A.D. 1 to the present and projects it to the year 2020.

Chapter 11

Religion

Steven C. Rockefeller
Middlebury College

In his well-known essay on "The Land Ethic," published in 1949, the forester and ecologist Aldo Leopold called for an "extension of the social conscience from people to land." He further noted that this would not occur without the support of philosophy and religion, neither of which had yet awakened to the problem. Today Leopold's insights are widely regarded as prophetic, and he was in general correct about the state of affairs in philosophy and religion when he wrote. However, over the past 25 years the situation has changed dramatically in the field of religion, as well as in philosophy. For example, a 1991 meeting on Capitol Hill in Washington, D.C., of the Joint Appeal by Religion and Science for the Environment involved an historic coalition of outstanding scientists and leading Jewish, Protestant, and Roman Catholic clergy and North American Indian spiritual leaders. In spite of their many differences, these scientists and religious leaders were united by a shared moral concern over environmental deterioration, ecological literacy, and government action. A rapidly growing number of American religious thinkers and educators are now listening to the voices of ecologists like Leopold, and many scientists and social thinkers recognize that religion and a sense of moral responsibility have a critical role to play in helping society get on the path of sustainable development and environmental protection.

This turn of events is linked with a rapidly expanding body of new scholarship in the field of religion and the environment. The rich resources in this emerging field of study create a wide range of possibilities for academic courses. Such courses are of interest today not only to religion majors but also to students working in the larger field of environmental studies, which in many colleges is being developed as an interdisciplinary program involving the humanities as well as the sciences.

The major religious traditions are expressions of the worldviews and values that have emerged as different peoples throughout the world have struggled to respond creatively to the challenge of their unique environments and histories in the light of their awareness of the sacred. The study of religion and the environment provides, then, an excellent opportunity to explore past and present ideas, attitudes, and values pertaining to nonhuman species, the land, and the universe. This involves a very promising new field of inquiry that had been given only limited attention by scholars of religion prior to the rise of public concern about the environment.

Research, writing, and teaching in the field of religion and the environment tend to focus on a variety of environmentally significant topics and issues that include:

- Visions of the divine (the sacred), nature, and human nature and their interrelationships, and the influence of these visions on attitudes toward nature
- The elements of an ecological spirituality that nurtures wonder, fosters reverence for life, and integrates the sacred and secular, spiritual life and everyday life
- An ethics of respect and care for the whole community of life, including future generations
- The new science (biology, cosmology, ecology, physics, etc.) and its implications for a knowledge of reality, an ecological spirituality, and an ethics of respect for nature and sustainable living
- Analysis of the links between institutional religion, social and economic oppression, and environmental degradation; feminism, ecology, the sacred, and eco-social liberation; the poor, minorities, and environmental justice
- The religions, world community, and a shared global ethic that recognizes the indivisibility of peace, human rights, economic opportunity, and environmental restoration and protection

Themes and topics such as these can be used to organize courses, reading assignments, lectures, class discussions, and examination questions.

Exploration of these themes and issues may be undertaken in and through historical studies, comparative studies, and the study of new visions in theology, philosophy, and ethics, involving fresh approaches to spiritual practice and new forms of activism. Historical studies in religion and the environment may focus on a particular religious tradition such as Buddhism, Christianity, Hinduism, Islam, Judaism, Taoism, or other traditions, including, for example, African religions, Goddess worship, Jainism, American Indian religions, Shintoism, and spiritual democracy. A comparative religions approach is useful as a method for bringing out the unique contributions and problems associated with particular traditions and for identifying commonalities as well as differences.

Historical research pertaining to religion and the environment is commonly motivated by one of two primary objectives. On the one hand, the goal is often to determine to what extent sacred texts and religious worldviews have fostered ideas and attitudes that have led humans to abuse the natural environment. Environment has joined race, class, and gender as a focus for critical reappraisals of past religious traditions. On the other hand, inquiry may be engaged in a retrieval of traditions, some of which may have been suppressed or forgotten, that could help with an ecological reorientation of contemporary societies. Such undertakings include, for example, efforts to identify elements of a land ethic in the Torah, new appreciation for the teachings of St. Francis of Assisi, fresh attention to ancient Goddess traditions, and an increased interest in American Indian spiritual values. Some environmentalists find aspects of a number of Asian traditions like Buddhism, Hinduism, and Taoism of special interest in this regard.

In many instances efforts at retrieval of valuable ancient ideas and practices are undertaken in the context of reconstructing a tradition or of developing a compelling new religious worldview that is consistent with contemporary ecology and supportive of sustainable living. It is in this area of reconstructing worldviews and visions of the way that the most creative and exciting work is being done by religious thinkers with environmental concerns. Recognizing that there are connections between the exploitation of nature and the oppression of women, minorities, and the poor, much of the new constructive thinking in the field of religion and the environment draws on various forms of social, political, and economic analysis and is concerned with broad visions that seek to integrate the values of peace, community development, social justice, and environmental protection.

The simplest way to integrate environmental concerns into a religion department's curriculum is to give attention to ideas and attitudes regarding nature in the worldviews of the various religious traditions when teaching courses on the history of religions. One or two essays on this subject can be assigned. Many departments offer a course in myth, symbol, and ritual as an introduction to the study of religion. Environmental themes and issues may be addressed in such a course by giving special attention, for example, to creation myths and related rituals, or to symbols and rituals associated with the Goddess and other deities closely identified with the earth's cycles of birth, death, and regeneration.

Two upper level courses and a first-year seminar are outlined in what follows. In addition, several four- to six-week course units are proposed. The units in the full-length courses and these additional units can be arranged in many different ways to form a variety of diverse courses. Other courses or units can be designed by employing the selected annotated bibliography with which the chapter concludes. The reading assignments have been selected with the idea that they would require an average undergraduate roughly six to seven hours of study per week.

Two of the recommended courses involve a comparative study of a variety of traditions, and one focuses exclusively on a single tradition, Christianity. One could, of course, offer an entire course on ecology and other single traditions. Christianity was chosen because of the major influence of the Judeo-Christian tradition on Western culture and the fact that significantly more work has been done on contemporary environmental issues and Christianity than is the case with any other tradition. This work is contributing to some exceptionally creative new thinking in Christian theology and ethics.

Some of the issues explored in courses on religion and the environment can be made more concrete by looking at the way specific religious organizations are trying to integrate environmental materials into educational programs and spiritual practice and to support environmental activism, including political action. Some students may find it instructive and rewarding to design and conduct their own ecologically oriented religious ritual or service. The ethical values and issues under study can often be brought to life by involving students in the exercise of researching and wrestling with the ethical dimensions of current environmental problems facing a university or the local, regional, or global community.

COURSE PLANS

An Introductory, Upper Division Course

Ecology, Ethics, and Religion

Course Description and Objectives. This course has been designed for students with some basic introductory knowledge of religion who wish to explore the religious and ethical dimensions of the environmental crisis from a variety of different Western and Eastern perspectives. It is an intensive introductory study of religion, ecology, and the ethics of respect for nature and sustainable living for upper level students. A course of this nature is one alternative for a religion department that is able to offer only one course with a primary focus on the environment. It can also be simplified and adjusted so that it may be taught as a 12-week seminar for first-year students. (See lower division seminar immediately following.)

The course begins with Roderick Nash's (1989) history of environmental ethics, which puts the current discussion of ecology, ethics, and religion in historical perspective with special reference to the American context. The book emphasizes the interconnections between the evolution of democratic social values, ecology, and environmental ethics, and it discusses the relation of these ideas and values to religious thought. Recognizing the global nature of the environmental crisis, the course next introduces students to the international debate over sustainable development and the cross-cultural dialogue between the religions over the roots of our environmental problems and alternative ways of addressing these concerns. The remainder of the course focuses special attention on selected traditions and especially important books. The assigned texts will expose students to many perspectives, including that of Buddhism, Christianity, Confucianism, ecofeminism, Goddess religion, Hinduism, Islam, Judaism, North American Indian religions, spiritual democracy, and Taoism.

The readings explore the problems that religions (and related philosophies) have created as well as the positive contributions that have been made and can be made. The social forces that influence religious ideas and values are discussed. In most of the readings the emphasis is on worldviews that are consistent with ecology, on modes of spiritual practice that support environmental awareness, and on the ethics of respect for nature, including discussion of a new world ethic. The course concludes with two books that present new attempts at a broad integrated vision with religious depth. One focuses on the creation story emerging out of contemporary science, which a number of thinkers find of great religious significance for the emerging global community and for the development of a global ecological conscience. The other concluding volume, which is deeply influenced by ecofeminism, demonstrates how a person might develop a profoundly meaningful contemporary worldview, drawing on much of the scientific, social, ethical, and religious material under consideration in the course.

This course can best be taught as a seminar, but it may be offered as a lecture course, even though this may require some adjustments in library reserve reading. Lectures could introduce students to the relevant important ideas in the religions under consideration; discuss the historical background of particular works, issues, and debates; and keep attention focused on major themes and objectives.

Recommended Requirements: A mid-term; a journal; and a final examination or a 10- to 15-page term paper on a theme directly related to the course readings and involving some independent research. If a seminar is being taught, it is often useful to require of each student one oral presentation (7–10 minutes) before the class, involving a critical review of the day's reading assignment or some other relevant subject, followed by questions from the class. Students should write in their journals each week (250–750 words), noting their critical observations about readings and class discussions, identifying especially significant issues and ideas, and formulating questions. Journals may be submitted to the instructor for comment and evaluation midway through the semester (or earlier) and at the end of classes.

Some of the recommended library reserve readings could be eliminated, but these readings are valuable resources for the instructor and for lectures. Books recommended for purchase by students, as distinguished from reserve reading, are noted with an asterisk (*) when first cited.

UNIT: HISTORICAL PERSPECTIVES AND THE AMERICAN CONTEXT

Week 1

• Genesis 1–3 (Creation, Eden, Fall).
• Nash 1989, *The Rights of Nature: A History of Environmental Ethics,** pp. 1–54.
• Film: *The Wilderness Idea: John Muir, Gifford Pinchot and the First Great Battle for Wilderness,* 58 min.

Week 2

• Nash 1989, pp. 55–121.

SUPPLEMENTAL READING

• St. Francis of Assisi, "The Canticle of Brother Sun." Translation available in Linzey and Regan 1989, pp. 15–16.
• Schweitzer 1949, *Out of My Life and Thought,* chapter XIII.
• Leopold, "Thinking Like a Mountain" and "The Land Ethic." In Leopold 1949, *A Sand County Almanac.**

Week 3

• Nash 1989, pp. 121–213.

(1) How does Genesis 1–3, which is an especially influential text in the Western tradition, view the relation of God and the world, God and human beings, human beings and nature, man and woman? What is the nature of the harmony that exists in the Garden of Eden before the

Fall? What causes the Fall? What is the significance of the Fall for the religious quest?

(2) What is the definition and task of ecology?

(3) How have religious traditions hindered and/or supported respect for nature and the development of environmental ethics?

(4) What is the ecological significance of St. Francis's theological vision of nature?

(5) In what ways did John Muir and Gifford Pinchot agree and disagree in their understanding of respect for and protection of nature?

(6) What is Schweitzer's argument in defense of reverence for life? What is Leopold's defense of the Land Ethic? In what ways do Schweitzer and Leopold represent two different approaches to respect for nature and environmental ethics?

(7) What is the relation between the evolution of Western natural rights theory and the ethics of democracy on the one hand and environmental ethics on the other?

(8) What are the basic arguments used to defend the idea of environmental ethics?

(9) What is meant by "the greening of religion?"

UNIT: INTERFAITH DIALOGUE AND A GLOBAL ETHIC

Week 4

- Rockefeller and Elder 1992, *Spirit and Nature,* * Introduction, Appendix (UN World Charter for Nature), chapters 1–3, 5.
- Dwivedi, "Satyagraha for Conservation: Awakening the Spirit of Hinduism." In Engel and Engel 1990, *Ethics of Environment and Development,* pp. 201–12.

Week 5

- Rockefeller and Elder 1992, chapters 4, 7–9, Epilogue.
- World Conservation Union (IUCN) 1991, *Caring for the Earth,* pp. 1–17.
- Film: *Moyers/Spirit and Nature,* 88 min.

SUPPLEMENTAL READING:

- Tu Weiming, "Toward the Possibility of A Global Community." In Hamilton 1993, *Ethics, Religion and Biodiversity,* pp. 65–74.

- "An Open Letter to the Religious Community from the Scientific Community," 1990. In Beversluis 1995, *A Sourcebook for the Community of Religions,* pp. 279–280.
- Mission to Washington Statement of A Joint Appeal by Religion and Science for the Environment, May 12, 1992. The National Religious Partnership for the Environment, 1047 Amsterdam Avenue, New York, NY 10025.

(1) What constitutes the global environmental crisis?

(2) What widely shared ideas, attitudes, and values have contributed to the environmental crisis?

(3) In what ways does the UN World Charter for Nature represent a biocentric point of view that transcends a strictly anthropocentric perspective?

(4) What is the definition of sustainable development? What are the principles of sustainable development? What is the role of ethics in achieving sustainable development?

(5) Is it possible and desirable to develop a world ethic? What role should democratic values and the ethics of sustainable living play in a global ethic?

(6) Compare how different representative religious thinkers argue in defense of respect for nature? What role does the idea of God play in these arguments? What role do scripture, revelation, tradition, science, reason, and religious experience play in their arguments? What spiritual attitudes and values regarding nature do they emphasize?

(7) How have global environmental problems brought scientists and religious leaders into dialogue on issues of ethical responsibility and social policy?

(8) What do the religions have to contribute to a world ethic? Can they agree on a world ethic?

UNIT: JEWISH MYSTICAL THEOLOGY AND ENVIRONMENTALISM

Week 6

- Green 1992, *Seek My Face, Speak My Name: A Contemporary Jewish Theology.**

(1) How does Green understand the origins and nature of the religious quest? What is his view of the role of tradition and the language of the sacred?

(2) How does Green describe the reality and nature of God? What is the relation of God and the universe? What is meant by the Shekhinah?

(3) What is the significance of Green's mystical theology and spiritual practice for an ethics of respect for nature and sustainable living? Is it possible to adopt Green's religious vision of the way as a form of ecological spirituality?

UNIT: CHRISTIAN ECOTHEOLOGY AND ECOFEMINISM

Week 7
- W. Berry, "The Gift of Good Land." In W. Berry 1981, *The Gift of Good Land,* pp. 267–281.
- Moore, "A New Christian Reformation." In Engel and Engel 1990, pp. 104–113.
- Ruether 1983, *Sexism and God-Talk,** pp. 1–71.

Week 8
- Ruether 1983, pp. 72–266.

(1) How does Wendell Berry find a basis for respect for nature and an environmental ethic in the Bible?

(2) What problems do Moore and Ruether identify in traditional Christian thought regarding God and nature? What is their approach to overcoming these problems?

(3) What are the main elements of Ruether's ecofeminist critique of patriarchy and the Christian tradition? What are the guiding ethical values in her ecofeminist Christian vision of social reconstruction? How does Ruether conceive the task of theology? What is her vision of God? Where should a person look for Christ? What role can religion play in social reconstruction and healing the earth?

UNIT: EASTERN RELIGIONS AND ECOLOGY; TAOISM AND CONFUCIANISM

Week 9
- Callicott and Ames 1989, *Nature in Asian Traditions of Thought.* Read the Foreword, Introduction, and essays by Callicott, "The Metaphysical Implications of Ecology," and Tu Wei-Ming, "The Continuity of Being: Chinese Visions of Nature."
- Smith, "Transcendence in Traditional China," and "Tao Now: An Ecological Testament." In Smith 1992, pp. 57–92.
- Tucker, "Ecological Themes in Taoism and Confucianism." In Tucker and Grim 1993, *Worldviews and Ecology.*

(1) Can Eastern religions and philosophies help Western societies in developing ideas and attitudes that support care for the earth?

(2) How are Eastern religions and philosophies related to the findings of the new physics and ecology and their metaphysical implications?

(3) What is the Chinese understanding of "the great transformation?" What is meant by ch'i?

(4) In what sense does Taoism involve a religious ecological worldview? What is the Tao? What is the relation of the Tao and the world? What are the practical implications of Taoism regarding how one should live in relation to nature? What are the distinctive characteristics of Confucian ethics regarding nature?

(5) What views of the self and its relationship to the world are suggested by Chinese philosophy?

UNIT: BUDDHISM AND ECOLOGY

Week 10
- Mettasutta (The Sutta of Loving Kindness).
- Sponsel and Natadecha-Sponsel, "The Potential Contribution of Buddhism." In Hamilton 1993, *Ethics, Religion and Biodiversity,* pp. 75–91.
- Cooke, "The Jewel Net of Indra." In Callicott and Ames 1989, pp. 213–230.
- Dalai Lama, "A Tibetan Buddhist Perspective on Spirit in Nature." In Rockefeller and Elder 1992, chapter 6.
- Piburn 1990, *The Dalai Lama: A Policy of Kindness,* chapters 1, 5, 9, 11, 12.
- Macy, "The Greening of the Self." In Badiner 1990, pp. 53–63 (Reprinted in Macy 1991, *World as Lover, World as Self*).

Week 11
- Snyder, "Buddhism and the Possibilities of a Planetary Culture." In Eppsteiner 1988, pp. 82–85.
- Aitken (1984), *The Mind of Clover: Essays in Zen Buddhist Ethics,* chapters 1–21.

(1) What is the general nature and the scope of the ethical concern expressed in the Mettasutta? For what is the Jewel Net of Indra a metaphor?

(2) What, according to Sponsel, are the fundamental principles forming a Buddhist ecological ethic?

(3) What is the Dalai Lama's understanding of human nature and of the nature of reality? How does he explain "emptiness"? What does he mean by "a sense of universal responsibility?"

(4) What is meant by the ecological self?

(5) What according to Snyder is "the mercy of the East" and "the mercy of the West"?

(6) What is the purpose of the Buddhist precepts? What is the first precept? What is "the mind of clover"? How can animals, trees, and stones "advance and affirm the self"? In what sense does Buddhism support deep ecology?

UNIT: COSMOGENESIS, ECOLOGY, AND FAITH

Week 12
• Swimme and Berry 1992, *The Universe Story,** pp. 1–140, or T. Berry 1988, *The Dream of the Earth,* Introduction, chapters 1–8.

Week 13
• Swimme and Berry 1992, pp. 140–278, or T. Berry 1988, chapters 9–16.

What are the basic principles governing the process of cosmogenesis? In what sense is the story of each person and culture the story of the universe? How have Swimme and Berry tried to integrate science and a sense of the sacred? Are they successful? What is the significance of this story for human civilization in a time of environmental crisis and social turmoil?

Week 14
• Spretnak 1991, *States of Grace,** pp. 1–155.
• Film: *Gorillas in the Mist,* 129 min.

Week 15
• Spretnak 1991, pp. 156–232.

(1) What does Spretnak view as the distinctive contributions of Buddhism, Native American religions, Goddess spirituality, and the Judeo-Christian tradition? In her endeavor to develop a fresh holistic worldview by drawing on insights from these different wisdom traditions, has Spretnak succeeded in expressing the spirit of a promising new outlook? What are the strengths and weaknesses of her approach and vision?

(2) Does Spretnak's worldview harmonize well with "the universe story"?

(3) In the light of your readings in *The Rights of Nature, Caring for the Earth,* and the texts by various religiously oriented authors, what are the conflicts in ethical values raised by Diane Fossey's work as presented in *Gorillas in the Mist?* Does she offer an example of I–thou relationships with animals?

(4) In reflecting on the course readings, how are the concepts of democracy, human rights, ecology, environmental ethics, sustainable development, cosmogenesis, a sense of the sacred, and religious faith interrelated? What is the significance of these ideas for social liberation, individual growth, and healing for the biosphere in the 21st century?

Lower Division, Introductory Seminar

Religion, Ethics, and Environment

Course Description and Objectives. This course may also serve as an introductory religion course that uses the ecological theme to expose students to a variety of world religious traditions and their relevance to contemporary issues. If this first-year seminar is offered by a religion department, the department could also offer an advanced level course like the preceding one, "Ecology, Ethics, and Religion," making adjustments in the syllabus so as to avoid repetition in the readings. The best approach would be to construct a new advanced course that builds on the first-year seminar, continues the exploration of a variety of traditions, and combines units (or parts of units) from several course possibilities suggested in this guide, including the preceding upper division course.

Books recommended for purchase by students are noted with an asterisk (*) when first cited.

UNIT: CIVILIZATION AND NATURE

Week 1

- "World Scientists' Warning to Humanity,"* four-page statement signed by 1,575 scientists from 69 countries and issued November 18, 1992 by the Union of Concerned Scientists, 1616 P Street, NW, Washington, DC 20036, (202) 332-0900. Reprinted in Beversluis 1995, p. 278.
- Leopold, "Thinking Like a Mountain" and "The Land Ethic." In Leopold 1949.*
- L. White 1967, "The Historical Roots of Our Ecologic Crisis."

These opening readings (1) provide a brief scientific definition of the global environmental crisis, (2) describe the science of ecology and the challenge of environmental ethics, and (3) introduce students to the debate over the role of religion in shaping human attitudes toward nature.

UNIT: JEWISH AND CHRISTIAN TRADITIONS

Week 2

- Linzey and Regan 1989, *Love the Animals.**
- Schweitzer 1949, chapter XIII.

Weeks 3–4

- Buber. See Judaism and Ecology (below), Weeks 2–3.

Weeks 5–6

- McFague 1987, *Models of God.**
- Eisler, "The Gaia Tradition and the Partnership Future: An Ecofeminist Manifesto." In Diamond and Orenstein 1990, *Reweaving the World,* pp. 23–34.

UNIT: INTERFAITH DIALOGUE AND A GLOBAL ETHIC

Weeks 7–9

- Rockefeller and Elder 1992. See reading assignments in the section on Interfaith Dialogue in preceding course, Ecology, Ethics, and Religion.

UNIT: HINDU AND BUDDHIST TRADITIONS

Week 10

- Prime 1992, *Hinduism and Ecology: Seeds of Truth.**
- The Mettasutta (Sutta of Loving Kindness).

Week 11

- Macy, "The Greening of the Self." In Badiner 1990, pp. 53–63.
- Nhat Hanh 1991, *Peace Is Every Step.**

UNIT: PROCESS THEOLOGY AND AN ETHICS OF REVERENCE FOR LIFE

Week 12

- McDaniel 1989, *Of God and Pelicans.**
- Film: *Gorillas in the Mist,* 129 min.

A Complete Upper Division Course

Christianity and Ecology

Course Description and Objectives. This course will provide upper level students with (1) an overview of the history of Christian ideas and attitudes regarding nonhuman species, the land, and nature at large, and (2) an understanding of the way a number of representative contemporary Christian thinkers, in response to the environmental crisis and related cultural problems, are endeavoring to reconstruct the idea of God and to redefine what it means to be a Christian. The readings are designed to acquaint students both with environmental and social problems associated with historical Christianity and with the promise of the Christian tradition as a creative source of moral and spiritual wisdom in a democratic, ecological age.

Using a study prepared by scholars associated with the Calvin Center for Christian Scholarship, the first two weeks of the course describe the state of the planet, explore the historical roots of the environmental crisis, and present an outline of a biblically based ethic of stewardship and recommendations for action. In the third and fourth weeks, excerpts from the Bible and a wide variety of Christian thinkers and a study of biblical faith offer a further overview of historical Christian attitudes toward creation with a special focus on animals and the land.

The remainder of the course is devoted to the reading of a number of books and essays by Roman Catholic and Protestant authors whose writings provide additional good examples of the various new directions being taken by contemporary ecotheology and programs of ecojustice (the concept of ecojustice extends the idea of justice to the earth as well as to people). These authors explore the idea of God, the relation between God and the earth, the implications of Whitehead's process philosophy, the meaning of an ecological spirituality, the challenge of ecofeminism, the nature of environmental ethics, questions of animal rights, and issues of public policy and ecojustice.

Regarding recommended requirements, see preceding course, Ecology, Ethics, and Religion. The nine books recommended for purchase by students, as distinguished from reserve reading, are noted with an asterisk (*) when first cited.

UNIT: THE STATE OF THE PLANET AND CHRISTIAN RESPONSIBILITY

Week 1

- L. White 1967, "The Historical Roots of Our Ecologic Crisis."
- Wilkinson 1991, *Earthkeeping in the '90s,** pp. 1–161.

Week 2

• Wilkinson 1991, pp. 162–371.

• Engel, "Introduction: the Ethics of Sustainable Development." In Engel and Engel 1990, *Ethics of Environment and Development,* pp. 1–23.

UNIT: ANIMAL RIGHTS AND A LAND ETHIC

Week 3

• Linzey and Regan 1988, *Animals and Christianity,** Introduction, Parts I–V.

Week 4

• Brueggemann 1991, *The Land.**

• Robb 1991, "Introduction"; and Charles S. McCoy 1991, "Creation and Covenant: A Comprehensive Vision for Environmental Ethics." In Robb and Casebolt 1991, *Covenant for a New Creation,* pp. 1–23, 212–225.

UNIT: AMERICAN PROCESS THEOLOGY AND THE ENVIRONMENT

Week 5

• Cobb and Birch 1981. *The Liberation of Life,** chapters 5–6.

• Daly and Cobb 1989, *For the Common Good,* chapters 1 and 20.

UNIT: CREATION-CENTERED SPIRITUALITY

Weeks 6–7

• Fox 1983, *Original Blessing,** pp. 9–305, or Fox 1988, *The Coming of the Cosmic Christ,* pp. 1–251.

UNIT: ECOFEMINISM AND THEOLOGY

Weeks 8–9

• Ruether 1992, *Gaia and God,** pp. 1–274.

• Williams, "Sin, Nature, and Black Women's Bodies." In Adams 1993, *Ecofeminism and the Sacred,* pp. 24–29.

• Johnson, "New Moon over Roxbury: Reflections on Urban Life and the Land." In Adams 1993, pp. 251–260.

UNIT: ECOLOGICAL SPIRITUALITY

Week 10
• McDaniel 1990, *Earth, Sky, Gods, & Mortals,** pp. 1–194.

UNIT: METAPHORICAL ECOTHEOLOGY

Weeks 11–12
• McFague 1993, *The Body of God,** Introduction, pp. 1–212.

UNIT: ECOLOGICAL ETHICS AND VOICES FROM THE SOUTH

Week 13
• J. Nash 1991, *Loving Nature,** pp. 11–138.

Week 14
• J. Nash 1991, pp. 139–222.
• Bratton 1992, *Six Billion and More,* chapters 3, 5, and 9.

Week 15
• Hallman 1994, *Ecotheology** (selected essays with an emphasis on the South).

Upper Division Course Units

Judaism and Ecology (5 weeks)
Unit Description and Objectives. The reading assignments are designed to introduce students to: (1) the resources within Judaism for developing an ethic of care for creation; (2) the contemporary debate within Judaism pertaining to religion and ecology; and (3) environmental programs being developed within the Jewish community in the United States, Israel, and elsewhere.

The essays selected for the first week discuss the contributions of the Hebrew Bible, Talmud, and early collections of *midrash* and of other Jewish traditions such as Kabbalah and Hasidism. The essays address basic questions: What is the relation of God to creation? What is the purpose of creation? Is God wholly transcendent or is God also immanent, and if so, in what sense? Is Judaism's view of humanity's relation to nature anthropocentric or theocentric or is there another alternative? What are some of the limitations of rabbinic Judaism with regard to attitudes toward nature from Kabbalistic, Hasidic, and feminist perspectives?

Among the issues explored are the role of *halachah* (laws and regulations), the role of ritual and holy days like the Sabbath, the idea of a covenantal relationship between humanity and nature, compassion for animals, vegetarianism, and conservation of resources.

The second and third weeks are devoted to a study of Martin Buber's highly influential book *I and Thou*, which has deep roots in the Hebrew Bible and Hasidic traditions and which provides an example of a Jewish view of reality and the way that involves a theological understanding and spiritual practice supportive of a respect for the intrinsic value of nature and nonhuman species.The fourth week involves the work of a contemporary theologian. The fifth week of readings provides further examples of the way contemporary Jewish theology and ethical thinking are responding to the environmental crisis.

Week 1

- Gendler 1971, "On the Judaism of Nature." This and the following six essays have been reprinted in Swetlitz 1989, *Judaism and Ecology.**
- Shapiro 1975, "God, Man, and Creation."
- Harris 1976, "Ecology: A Covenantal Approach."
- Schwarzschild 1984, "The Unnatural Jew."
- Helfand 1986, "The Earth is the Lord's: Judaism and Environmental Ethics."
- Gordis 1986, "Ecology and the Jewish Tradition."
- Ehrenfeld and Bentley 1985, "Judaism and the Practice of Stewardship."
- David E. Stein 1991, *A Garden of Choice Fruit.*

Weeks 2–3

- Buber, "Hasidism and Modern Man" and "The Way of Man According to the Teachings of Hasidism." In Buber 1958, *Hasidism and Modern Man,** Books I and IV.
- Buber 1970, *I and Thou.**

Week 4

- Green 1992, *Seek My Face, Speak My Name.**

Week 5

- Schorsch, "Learning to Live with Less: A Jewish Perspective." In Rockefeller and Elder 1992, pp. 25–38.
- Plaskow, "Feminist Judaism and Repair of the World." In Adams 1993, pp. 70–84.

• Rose 1992, *Judaism and Ecology*, chapters 6–14.

• "Judaism and Ecology—Our Earth and Our Tradition," Part I in *The Melton Journal* 24, Spring 1991.

• "Towards a Jewish Ecological Paradigm: Essays and Explorations," Part II in *The Melton Journal* 25, Summer 1992.

Of special significance in *The Melton Journal* are the essays in Part I by Eric Katz, "Toward an Ecological Ethic for our Home Planet"; Michael Wyschogrod, "Judaism and the Sanctification of Nature"; Micha Odenheimer, "Environmental Organizations in Israel"; and Robin Aronson, "Animal Life in Light of Jewish and Christian Traditions"; and in Part II by Ismar Schorsch, "Trees for Life"; Lawrence Kushner, "The Self of the Universe"; Nina B. Natelson, "The Treatment of Animals in Israel"; and Eduardo Rauch, "Redeeming the Wilderness from a Dangerous Exile." The essays by Green are excerpts from his book.

American Indian Religious Traditions and Ecology (6 weeks)

Unit Description and Objectives. Indigenous peoples have inhabited the North American continent for thousands of years prior to the arrival of Europeans, and in the face of the environmental crisis there has developed a new appreciation of the significance of their attitudes toward the land and nonhuman species. The readings in this unit, which include the voices of North American Indians as well as other ethnographers and philosophers of religion and ethics, are designed to introduce students to the major features of Native American religious traditions. Emphasis is placed on ideas of the sacred, the role of visions and dreams, the role of myth and ritual, attitudes toward and relations to the natural world, and environmental ethics.

Two brief overviews of North American Indian traditions by Hultkrantz and Brown have been included. Special attention is given to the Shoshoni, Zuni, Lakota Sioux, and Koyukon Athapaskans, whose ways of life provide representative examples of the diversity in Indian traditions. The course unit concludes with two essays on American Indian ecology and the philosophy of environmental ethics and a number of short essays on the environmental and spiritual significance of the Indian legacy and on the contemporary religious situation of the Indian.

MODULE: THE WIND RIVER SHOSHONI AND NEW MEXICO ZUNI, AN OVERVIEW

Week 1

• Momaday, "Native American Attitudes to the Environment." In Capps 1976, *Seeing With a Native Eye,* pp. 79–85.

- Hultkrantz 1979, *Native Religions of North America,** pp. 1–132.

(1) How does Momaday understand the integration of physical and imaginative ways of seeing in Indian traditions?

(2) In what ways are North American Indian religious traditions diverse, and in what sense do they share a common worldview? How do the Shoshoni and Zuni illustrate two basic contrasting religious orientations? What are the ethical implications of their religious worldviews?

MODULE: THE SACRED, NATURE, AND VISIONS OF A LAKOTA SIOUX

Week 2

- Brown 1988, *The Spiritual Legacy of the American Indian,** pp. ix–xiii, chapters 1–5 and 7.
- Neihardt 1988, *Black Elk Speaks,** pp. xi–xix, chapters 1–8.

Week 3

- Neihardt 1988, chapters 9–25, Postscript.
- Reed 1986, "A Native American Environmental Ethic: A Homily on Black Elk." In Hargrove 1986, *Religion and Environmental Crisis,* pp. 25–37.
- Brown 1990, chapters 6 and 8–10.

(1) What are some universal traits of North American Indian religious traditions according to Brown?

(2) What are the major elements in Black Elk's pipe prayer and great vision? What role do animals, trees, and natural forces play in his relation to the sacred powers of the universe? In what sense do his visions involve a holistic and ecological outlook?

(3) What is the purpose and meaning of a vision quest, the sacred pipe, and the Sun Dance? What is the sacred hoop? What is the nature of *Wakan Tanka* and its relation to the natural world, including plants, animals, and people?

MODULE: KOYUKON LIFE IN RELATION TO THE NORTH WOODS

Week 4

- Nelson 1983, *Make Prayers to the Raven,** Introduction, chapters 1–8.

Week 5

- Nelson 1983, chapters 9–13, Epilogue.

How do the Koyukon understand the surrounding natural world in which they live? How is this understanding expressed in their culture and customs? What are the ecological, religious, and ethical dimensions of Koyukon thinking and practice?

MODULE: ENVIRONMENTAL ETHICS AND INDIAN TRADITIONS

Week 6

• Callicott 1989, "American Indian Environmental Ethics." In Callicott 1989, In *Defense of the Land Ethic,* pp. 177–219.

• T. Berry 1988, "Returning to our Native Place," and "The Historical Role of the American Indian." In Berry 1988, *The Dream of the Earth,* chapters 1 and 14.

• Snyder 1969, "Energy is Eternal Delight," and "The Wilderness." In Snyder 1969, *Turtle Island,* pp. 103–110.

• Shenandoah 1992, "A Tradition of Thanksgiving." In Rockefeller and Elder 1992, pp. 15–23.

• Dooling and Jordan-Smith 1989, *I Become Part of It.* Read: Iroquois, "The Roots of Peace"; Amiotte, "The Road to the Center"; Cheyenne, "Sweet Medicine's Prophecy"; Deloria, "Out of Chaos"; and Lyons, "Our Mother Earth."

(1) According to Callicott, how does the Indian worldview differ from the dominant worldview in Western European civilization? In what ways does the Indian outlook support an environmental ethic? Is the idea of a North American Indian land wisdom a romantic exaggeration of the reality?

(2) In the concluding readings, what insights are presented regarding: the relation of the head and the heart, intimacy with the earth, the significance of rituals and ceremonies, the rights of nature, expanding the democratic community, the importance of thanksgiving, the symbol of the Great Tree of Peace, living in harmony with the Sacred Center, and the spiritual crisis facing contemporary North American Indians?

Eco-Feminism and the Goddess (4 weeks)

Unit Description and Objectives. This unit explores the contemporary revival of interest in Goddess spirituality under the leadership of women with strong ties to the larger movement of eco-feminism. From the environmental perspective, the literature and art associated with this movement are especially significant with regard to the way ecological concerns are intimately interrelated with feminist and religious issues.

Scholarship in the field of eco-feminism and Goddess religion has a two-fold focus. First, much work has been done with the aid of archaeological, anthropological, and historical research to rediscover the many forms assumed by Goddess religion in earlier civilizations and to show that some of the ancient civilizations in which the Goddess was worshipped involved matrifocal social structures very different from the patriarchal models that have been the dominant pattern in most societies over the past 5,000 years. Some of the scholarship in this area is speculative and controversial, but it raises critical questions for anyone concerned about religion, ethics, and the environment, as well as the place and role of women in society.

Second, the eco-feminists interested in Goddess religion view it as offering contemporary women and men a spiritual path full of creative possibilities for healing the psychological, social, and environmental ills that afflict life on earth today. The voice of the Goddess is for a significant group of religious thinkers one with the voice of Gaia, the Earth, and it is a voice that a growing number of people find profoundly liberating. Some will find the concern of much Goddess spirituality with the body and sexuality unsettling, but this concern raises important issues for religion in an ecological age seeking a holistic vision of the way.

Week 1
- Gadon 1989, *The Once and Future Goddess,** Introduction, Part I ("In the Beginning: The Sacred Way of the Goddess"), pp. 1–107.
- Gimbutas 1989, *The Language of the Goddess,* Introduction and Conclusion.

Week 2
- Gadon 1989, Part II ("The Patriarchal Takeover: The Taming of the Goddess"), pp. 108–223.
- Preston 1987, "Goddess Worship: An Overview," and "Theoretical Perspectives." In Eliade 1987, volume 6.

Week 3
- Gadon 1989, Part III ("The Reemergence of the Goddess: A Symbol for Our Time"), pp. 225–307.
- Christ 1987, "Journey to the Goddess," "Why Women Need the Goddess," and "Laughter of Aphrodite." In Christ 1987, *Laughter of Aphrodite,* pp. 105–132, 183–205.

Week 4
- Gadon 1989, Part III, pp. 309–377.
- Diamond and Orenstein 1990, *Reweaving the World.* Read: Spretnak, "Eco-feminism: Our Roots and Flowering"; Christ, "Rethinking The-

ology and Nature"; Allen, "The Woman I Love Is a Planet; The Planet I Love Is a Tree"; Starhawk, "Power, Authority, and Mystery: Ecofeminism and Earth-Based Spirituality"; and Jacobs, "Goddess in the Metropolis: Reflections on the Sacred in an Urban Setting."

• See also essays by R. R. Ruether, E.C. Rose, and C. Spretnak in Adams 1993.

Resources

Page numbers appearing in brackets at the end of some entries indicate where the reference is cited in a course plan.

General

Adams, C., ed. 1993. *Ecofeminism and the Sacred*. New York: Continuum Publishing Company. [pp. 282, 284, 289]

In this collection of 20 essays, Buddhist, Christian, Hindu, and Jewish perspectives, among others, are included. Bibliography.

Albanese, C. 1990. *Nature Religion in America*. Chicago: University of Chicago Press.

An introduction to various expressions of "the religion of nature" in the American context, including discussions of Indian religion, 18th century natural religion, and transcendentalism. Annotated bibliography.

Berry, T. 1988. *The Dream of the Earth*. San Francisco: Sierra Club Books. [pp. 278, 287]

An influential cultural historian and religious thinker presents an illuminating critique of Western industrial civilization and calls for a new spiritual awakening to the sacredness of the earth, emphasizing the scientific account of cosmogenesis as the new creation story.

Beversluis, J. D., ed. 1995. *A SourceBook for Earth's Community of Religions*. Grand Rapids, MI: CoNexus Press/SourceBook Project and New York: Global Education Associates. [pp. 275, 279]

A very useful collection that includes many declarations and statements from the world's religions on the environment and global ethics.

Callicott, J. B. and R. T. Ames, eds. 1989. *Nature in Asian Traditions of Thought: Essays in Environmental Philosophy*. Albany: State University of New York Press. [pp. 276, 277]

The best collection of philosophical essays comparing Eastern and Western approaches to the development of an ecological worldview. Much attention is given to the ecological aspects of traditions like Buddhism and Taoism. In *Earth's Insights* (Berkeley: University of California Press, 1994), Callicott offers a pathbreaking "multicultural survey of ecological ethics from the Mediterranean Basin to the Australian Outback."

Carroll, J. E., P. Brockelman, and M. Westfall. 1995. *God, the Environment and the Good Life*. Hanover, NH: University Press of New England.

Fourteen authors writing from a variety of perspectives, including American Indian, Buddhist, Christian, and Jewish, explore the religious and ethical dimensions of environmental and social problems confronting society.

Clebsch, W. A. 1973. *American Religious Thought: A History*. Chicago: University of Chicago Press.

A summary of a distinctive line of religious thought from Jonathan Edwards to Ralph Waldo Emerson to William James, John Dewey, and H. Richard Niebuhr, emphasizing its underlying affirmation that human beings were created to be at home in a "majestically hospitable universe."

Diamond, I. and G. F. Orenstein, eds. 1990. *Reweaving the World: The Emergence of Ecofeminism*. San Francisco: Sierra Club Books. [pp. 280, 288]

A collection of essays by 26 ecofeminists that include essays on the Goddess, religious life, social ethics, eschatology, and healing the earth. Bibliography.

Eliade, M., ed. 1987. *The Encyclopedia of Religion*, 16 volumes. New York: Macmillan. [p. 288]

The best comprehensive reference work available to college students. Articles include annotated bibliographies. Eliade's three-volume *A History of Religious Ideas* (Chicago: University of Chicago Press, 1978-1985) is also a valuable resource.

Engel, J. R., and J. G. Engel, eds. 1990. *Ethics of Environment and Development: Global Challenge and International Response*. Tucson: University of Arizona Press. [pp. 274, 276, 282]

An international group of 22 authors explore the ethics of sustainable development from a variety of religious and secular perspectives that include African, Buddhist, Chinese, feminist, Hindu, Islamic, and Israeli outlooks, as well as diverse Western points of view.

Glacken, C. J. 1973. *Traces on the Rhodian Shore: Nature and Culture in Western Thought from Ancient Times to the End of the Eighteenth*

Century. Berkeley: University of California Press. [Reprint of 1967 edition.]
A monumental history of ideas of nature in the West from ancient to modern times.

Graber, L. H. 1976. *Wilderness as Sacred Space.* Washington, DC: Association of American Geographers.
Utilizing the methodology of the history of religions, Graber argues that many environmentalists are motivated by a religious experience of wilderness.

Hamilton, L. S., ed. 1993. *Ethics, Religion and Biodiversity: Relations Between Conservation and Cultural Values.* Cambridge, UK: White Horse Press. [pp. 274, 277]
Ten essays on environmental and global ethics from a variety of religious and secular perspectives, including studies of conservation practices in Australia, the Pacific Islands, and Southwest China and a very good essay on Buddhist ethics. Bibliography.

Hargrove, E. C., ed. 1986. *Religion and Environmental Crisis.* Athens: University of Georgia Press. [p. 286]
Essays exploring ancient Greek, Jewish, Christian, Taoist, Islamic, and Native American outlooks.

Leopold, A. 1949. *A Sand County Almanac.* Oxford: Oxford University Press. [pp. 273, 279]
This American environmental classic includes Leopold's essay on "The Land Ethic," which is the most influential source of contemporary biocentric or holistic ethics.

Nash, R. F. 1989. *The Rights of Nature: A History of Environmental Ethics.* Madison: University of Wisconsin Press. [pp. 272, 273]
This illuminating study examines the development of Western environmental ethics in the context of natural rights theory and the evolution of the ethics of democracy. There are useful overviews of the greening of religion and philosophy. Annotated bibliography.

Roberts, E., and E. Amidon, eds. 1991. *Earth Prayers from Around the World: 365 Prayers, Poems and Invocations for Honoring the Earth.* San Francisco: HarperSanFrancisco.

Rockefeller, S. C. and J. C. Elder, eds. 1992. *Spirit and Nature: Why the Environment is a Religious Issue.* Boston: Beacon Press. [pp. 274, 277, 280, 284, 287]

Contributors include the Dalai Lama, J. Ronald Engel, Sallie McFague, Seyyed H. Nasr, Ismar Schorsch, Audrey Shenandoah, and others. The volume includes discussion of global ethics, and it contains the UN World Charter for Nature. Bibliography.

Smith, H. 1992. *Essays on World Religion.* New York: Paragon House. [p. 276]

A valuable collection of essays including two instructive studies of Taoism and ecology. An excellent one-volume introduction to the basic beliefs and practices of the major religions is found in H. Smith 1991, *The World's Religions,* San Francisco: HarperSanFrancisco.

Spretnak, C. 1991. *States of Grace: The Recovery of Meaning in the Postmodern Age.* San Francisco: HarperSanFrancisco. [p. 278]

Drawing on the wisdom traditions found in Buddhism, Native American religions, Goddess spirituality, Judaism, and Christianity, Spretnak presents a vision of ideas and values that promise healing for the planet, liberation for the individual, and the creation of community. Bibliography.

Swimme, B. and T. Berry. 1992. *The Universe Story: From the Primordial Flaring Forth to the Ecozoic Era.* San Francisco: HarperCollins. [p. 278]

A mathematical cosmologist and a cultural historian describe the 15 billion year process of cosmogenesis that has generated the earth and life. Their account integrates science with poetic vision and a sense of the sacred. Bibliography.

Tucker, M. E. and J. H. Grim. 1993. *Worldviews and Ecology.* Lewisburg, PA: Bucknell University Press. [p. 277]

Essays exploring American Indian, Bahai, Buddhist, Christian, Confucian, deep ecology, Hindu, Jain, Jewish, Taoist, and Whiteheadian perspectives.

World Conservation Union (IUCN), United Nations Environment Programme (UNEP), and World Wide Fund for Nature (WWF). 1991. *Caring for the Earth: A Strategy for Sustainable Living.* Gland, Switzerland. Available through Island Press, Box 7, Covelo, CA 95428. [p. 274]

A second version of the World Conservation Strategy that puts special emphasis on the ethics of living sustainably.

Buddhism

Aitken, R. 1984. *The Mind of Clover: Essays in Zen Buddhist Ethics.* San Francisco: North Point Press. [p. 277]

Lucid essays on Zen training, the Buddhist precepts, self-realization, ethics, social action, and deep ecology that explore the active interrelation of self and world in the process of enlightenment.

Badiner, A. H., ed. 1990. *Dharma Gaia: A Harvest of Essays in Buddhism and Ecology*. Berkeley, CA: Parallax Press. [pp. 277, 280]

Over 30 essays and meditations on the origins and meaning of Green Buddhism by Buddhist teachers, scholars, and activists.

Cooke, F. H. 1977. *Hua-yen Buddhism: The Jewel Net of Indra*. University Park: Pennsylvania State University Press.

An exposition of a highly influential school of Chinese Buddhist philosophy that stresses the concept of cosmic interdependence and that has a certain affinity with Whitehead's process philosophy.

Eppsteiner, F., ed. 1988. *The Path of Compassion: Writings on Socially Engaged Buddhism*. Berkeley, CA: Parallax Press. [p. 277]

Twenty-five essays by Buddhist teachers, scholars, and activists on spiritual practice and engaged Buddhism. The environment is one focus of concern.

Ives, C. 1992. *Zen Awakening and Society*. Honolulu: University of Hawaii Press.

In this study of the implications of Zen Buddhism for social ethics, Ives includes discussion of emptiness and the intrinsic value of all beings, ecological cosmocentrism and being-in-nature, the rights of nonhuman nature, and the relation between awakening and sustainable development.

Kapleau, P. 1982. *To Cherish All Life: A Buddhist Case for Becoming Vegetarian*. San Francisco: Harper & Row.

A concise presentation by an American Zen teacher and the author of *The Three Pillars of Zen*.

Macy, J. 1991. *World as Lover, World as Self*. Berkeley, CA: Parallax Press. [p. 277]

An exposition of the meaning of the Buddhist concept of dependent co-arising and its implications for contemporary personal liberation, social transformation, and planetary healing.

Nhat Hanh, Thich. 1991. *Peace Is Every Step: The Path of Mindfulness in Everyday Life*. New York: Bantam. [p. 280]

An influential Buddhist teacher explains in this lucid, simply written book the fundamentals of Buddhist philosophy and practice and their relevance to current human and planetary problems.

Piburn, S., ed. 1990. *The Dalai Lama: A Policy of Kindness.* Ithaca, NY: Snow Lion. [p. 277]

An anthology of talks by and conversations with the Dalai Lama that set forth his views on human nature, ethics, compassion, universal responsibility, human rights, democracy, and the environment.

Snyder, G. 1969. *Turtle Island.* New York: New Directions Books. [p. 287]

Poems and short essays that reflect the author's blend of Zen Buddhism, American Indian teachings, and deep ecology. In another book by Snyder, *The Practice of the Wild* (San Francisco: North Point Press, 1990), he explores the meaning and interrelation of freedom, nature, the wild, the good, and the sacred.

SEE ALSO under General the essays on Buddhism in Adams 1993; Callicott and Ames 1989; Hamilton 1993 [note Bibliography]; Rockefeller and Elder 1992; and Tucker and Grim 1993.

Christianity

Austin, R. C. 1988. *Hope for the Land: Nature in the Bible.* Atlanta: John Knox Press.

This is the third volume in a series on environmental theology by a Presbyterian minister and Virginia farmer. He persuasively argues that a variety of biblical traditions provide a basis for a Christian theology that honors the earth and supports environmental ethics.

Berry, W. 1981. "The Gift of Good Land." In *The Gift of Good Land: Further Essays Cultural and Agricultural.* W. Berry, ed. San Francisco: North Point Press. [p. 276]

An influential essay that presents "a biblical argument for ecological and agricultural responsibility" and contributes to formation of a Christian land ethic based on the concept of stewardship.

Birch, C., W. Eakin, and J. B. McDaniel, eds. 1990. *Liberating Life: Contemporary Approaches to Ecological Theology.* Maryknoll, NY: Orbis Books.

These 16 essays provide an overview of currents of Christian thought that are leading contemporary theology to embrace a new concern for animals, endangered species, and the larger earth. The authors include African, American, Asian, and Latin American writers.

Boff, L. 1995. *Ecology & Liberation: A New Paradigm.* Maryknoll, NY: Orbis Books.

Employing ecology as the key to a new theological paradigm and drawing on the mystical tradition, a leading liberation theologian develops a vision of a new ecological–social democracy that addresses the needs of the poor and embraces every part of nature.

Bratton, S. 1992. *Six Billion and More: Human Population Regulation and Christian Ethics*. Louisville, KY: Westminster/John Knox Press. [p. 283]

Bratton reviews the history of population growth and attitudes toward fertility from biblical times to the present. She applies a Christian understanding of social justice, individual rights, and care for the nonhuman creation to contemporary population issues. [p. 282]

Brueggemann, W. 1977. *The Land: Place as Gift, Promise, and Challenge in Biblical Faith*. Philadelphia: Fortress Press. [p. 282]

Brueggemann's work on covenantal traditions and the land in the Bible constitutes a major resource for contemporary Christian theologians who are endeavoring to rethink the place of nature in their tradition.

Cobb, J. B., Jr., and C. Birch. 1981. *The Liberation of Life: From the Cell to the Community*. Cambridge, UK: Cambridge University Press. [p. 282]

Influenced by process metaphysics and ecology, the authors call for rejection of the mechanistic model of the living organism and evolution and argue for a "religion of life" that recognizes the intrinsic value of all beings. They develop the ethical implications of their thinking.

Daly, H. E. and J. B. Cobb, Jr. 1989. *For the Common Good: Redirecting the Economy toward Community, the Environment, and a Sustainable Future*. Boston: Beacon Press.

In this groundbreaking work, Cobb, a theologian, and Daly, an economist, argue for a major transformation of economics. In chapter 20, "The Religious Vision," the authors explain how their own Christian theistic commitments inform their economic proposals and ecological worldview.

DeWitt, C. G., ed. 1991. *The Environment & the Christian: What Can We Learn from the New Testament?* Grand Rapids, MI: Baker Book House.

DeWitt is director of the Ausable Institute of Environmental Studies in Michigan, which is an education center with ties to 80 evangelical colleges and universities. The authors of the six essays in this collection relate major themes in New Testament theology to problems of environmental degradation and ecological sustainability.

Dowd, M. 1991. *Earthspirit*. Mystic, CT: Twenty-Third Publications.

A lucid, short exposition by a pastor in the United Church of Christ that shows how Christians today can embrace the new cosmology and employ it to deepen their understanding of sin, salvation, and Jesus Christ, leading to an ecologically responsible Christianity and a respectful appreciation of other religions. Annotated bibliography.

Engel, J. R., P. W. Bakken, and J. G. Engel. 1995. *Ecology, Justice and Christian Faith: A Critical Guide to the Literature*. Westport, CT: Greenwood Publishing.

Fox, M. 1983. *Original Blessing: A Primer in Creation Spirituality*. Santa Fe, NM: Bear & Company. [p. 282]

In this passionate work, a Dominican theologian offers a critique of the traditional theistic fall/redemption paradigm and recommends that it be rejected in favor of a creation-centered spirituality that is consistent with the teachings of Christian mystics, the new cosmology, ecology, and feminism.

Fox, M. 1988. *The Coming of the Cosmic Christ: The Healing of Mother Earth and the Birth of a Global Renaissance*. San Francisco: Harper & Row. [p. 282]

The author develops a Christology consistent with his panentheistic creation-centered spirituality and presents a vision of the Second Coming as a process of ecological restoration and social transformation.

Granberg-Michaelson, W. 1992. *Redeeming the Creation: The Rio Earth Summit: Challenges for the Churches*. Geneva: WCC Publications.

A member of the World Council of Churches' Unit on Justice, Peace, and Creation explores the connections between Christian theology and ethics and the ideal of sustainable development. Contains the Rio Declaration on Environment and Development.

Gregorios, P. 1978. *The Human Presence: An Orthodox View of Nature*. Geneva: World Council of Churches.

Gregorios presents the classical view of Eastern Christianity that God entered the fallen universe through Jesus Christ to restore the harmony of the whole universe by restoring authentic human nature.

Hallman, D. G., ed. 1994. *Ecotheology: Voices from South and North*. Maryknoll, NY: Orbis Books. [p. 283]

Twenty-six essays by theologians, ecofeminists, indigenous people, and others from around the world.

Kaufman, G. 1993. *In the Face of Mystery: A Constructive Theology.* Cambridge: Harvard University Press.

In this major work, Kaufman fully develops his idea of theology as an imaginative construction of a symbol system for ordering life. "The symbol 'God'," he contends, "refers us not to a particular existent being within or beyond the world, but rather to that trajectory of cosmic and historical forces which, having emerged out of the ultimate mystery of things, is moving us toward a more truly humane and ecologically responsible mode of existence."

Kohak, E. V. 1984. *The Embers and the Stars: A Philosophical Inquiry into the Moral Sense of Nature.* Chicago: University of Chicago Press.

Employing a poetic style, Kohak develops themes from Eastern Orthodox Christian theology, presenting a sacramental view of creation and describing humanity as the "priest of creation."

Küng, H. 1991. *Global Responsibility: In Search of a New World Ethic.* New York: Crossroad Publishing.

A clear, carefully constructed argument in defense of the urgent need for a new world ethic and for peace and cooperation among the religions by an influential theologian.

LaChance, A. J. and J. E. Carroll, eds. 1994. *Embracing Earth: Catholic Approaches to Ecology.* Maryknoll, NY: Orbis Books.

Twenty authors explore "the task of Catholicism in ecology and ecology in Catholicism."

Linzey, A., and T. Regan, eds. 1988. *Animals and Christianity: A Book of Readings.* New York: Crossroad Publishing. [p. 282]

An anthology of selections from the Bible and leading Christian thinkers on the conditions and rights of animals.

Linzey, A. and T. Regan, eds. 1989. *Love the Animals: Meditations and Prayers.* New York: Crossroad Publishing. [pp. 273, 281]

A collection of biblical passages and short readings on the themes of compassion, redemption, and animal rights. Bibliography including films and videos.

Macquarrie, J. 1984. *In Search of Deity: An Essay in Dialectical Theism.* London: SCM Press.

These Gifford Lectures in natural theology offer a critique of classical Christian theism and trace the history of panentheism in the West from Plotinus to Whitehead and Heidegger. In the last chapters Macquarrie presents his own panentheistic vision.

McDaniel, J. B. 1989. *Of God and Pelicans: A Theology of Reverence for Life*. Louisville, KY: Westminster/John Knox Press. [p. 280]

Writing as a Christian and drawing insights from Buddhism, process thought, and feminism, McDaniel integrates a panentheistic view of God, a land ethic, respect for animal rights, a Christian ecological spirituality, and a design for a post-patriarchal mode of community. Bibliography.

McDaniel, J. B. 1990. *Earth, Sky, Gods & Mortals: Developing an Ecological Spirituality*. Mystic, CT: Twenty-Third Publications. [p. 283]

With roots in the tradition of process theology, the author develops a vision of a new ecological Christianity that emphasizes panentheism, the intrinsic value of all life, the interdependence of human and nonhuman life, sustainable living, openness to other religions, and communion with the inner archetypal world of the psyche.

McFague, S. 1987. *Models of God: Theology for an Ecological, Nuclear Age*. Philadelphia: Fortress Press. [p. 280]

Drawing upon an ecological, evolutionary view of reality and conceiving theology as a process of constructing illuminating metaphors and models, the author proposes that we imagine the God–world relationship by thinking of the world as God's body and God as mother, lover, and friend.

McFague, S. 1993. *The Body of God: An Ecological Theology*. Philadelphia: Fortress Press. [p. 283]

McFague reconstructs the classic Christian organic model of reality in the light of "the common creation story" emerging from science, and goes on to explore the theological implications of viewing the universe as God's body, discussing creation, sin, Christology, and eschatology.

Moltmann, J. 1985. *God in Creation: An Ecological Theology*. London: SCM Press.

These 1984 Gifford Lectures by a leading German theologian offer a profound reflection on the doctrine of creation, including an exploration of Trinitarian and Christological issues.

Murphy, C. 1989. *At Home on Earth: Foundations for a Catholic Ethic of the Environment*. New York: Crossroad Publishing.

Considers how recent developments in Catholic theology, especially the encyclicals of Pope John Paul II, support environmentally sound moral virtues and attitudes.

Nash, J. A. 1991. *Loving Nature: Ecological Integrity and Christian Responsibility*. Nashville: Abingdon Press and the Churches' Center for Theology and Public Policy, Washington, DC. [p. 283]

Nash offers the best available systematic study from a Christian theological perspective of the ethics of caring for the earth, including discussion of human environmental rights and the rights of nonhuman creatures.

Oelschlaeger, M. 1994. *Caring for Creation: An Ecumenical Approach to the Environmental Crisis.* New Haven and London: Yale University Press.

An overview of the current state of the debate and of the resources in the Christian tradition for a theology and ethics of sustainable living. Bibliography.

Pinches, C. and J. B. McDaniel. 1993. *Good News For Animals? Christian Approaches to Animal Well-being.* Maryknoll, NY: Orbis Books.

Fifteen theologians and philosophers put the issue in historical perspective and explore the contemporary ethical issues. Bibliography.

Robb, Carol S. and Carl J. Casebolt, eds. 1991. *Covenant for a New Creation: Ethics, Religion, and Public Policy.* Maryknoll, NY: Orbis Books. [p. 282]

These 15 essays call for the formation of "a new covenant in order to heal and sustain a new creation," focusing on "new forms of ownership, new relationships with the rest of creation, and new theories of justice to hold together a society that is sustainable."

Ruether, R. R. 1983. *Sexism and God-Talk: Toward a Feminist Theology.* Boston: Beacon Press. [p. 276]

If one were to read one book on Christian theology, feminism, ecology, and social transformation, this pathbreaking work should be it. Ruether further develops her evaluation of Western Christian culture and related traditions in *Gaia & God: An Ecofeminist Theology of Earth Healing* (San Francisco: HarperSanFrancisco, 1992). [p. 282]

Santmire, H. P. 1985. *The Travail of Nature: The Ambiguous Ecological Promise of Christian Theology.* Philadelphia: Fortress Press.

This substantial study provides a systematic analysis of the theology of nature from Irenaeus to Teilhard de Chardin in an effort to clarify the weaknesses and strengths of the Christian tradition from an ecological point of view.

Schweitzer, A. 1949. *Out of My Life and Thought.* New York: Holt. [pp. 273, 280]

In this autobiographical account, Schweitzer tells the story of the spiritual quest and philosophical argument that led him to his ethic of reverence for life. Schweitzer's philosophy is more fully set forth in *The Philosophy of Civilization* (New York: Prometheus Books, 1987).

Spencer, D. T. 1994. "Pedagogical Issues and Teaching Models for Eco-Justice." State of the Art Paper for the Conference "Theology for Earth Community." Union Theological Seminary, New York. Phone: (515) 271-2885; fax: (515) 271-3977.

Includes sample syllabi. Bibliography.

White, L., Jr. 1967. "The Historical Roots of Our Ecologic Crisis." *Science* 155:1203-7. Reprinted in *Western Man and Environmental Ethics*. I. G. Barbour, ed. Reading, MA: Addison-Wesley, 1973. [pp. 279, 281]

This is White's influential and widely debated essay attacking the biblical tradition and Christianity for encouraging attitudes of domination and exploitation toward nature in Western civilization.

Wilkinson, L., ed. 1991. *Earthkeeping in the '90s: Stewardship of Creation*. Grand Rapids, MI: Wm. B. Eerdmans Publishing Company. [pp. 281, 282]

This substantial work, generated by interdisciplinary research at The Calvin College Center for Christian Scholarship, describes the state of the planet, puts the environmental crisis in historical perspective, wrestles with the economic and technological issues, formulates a biblically based ethic of environmental stewardship, and issues a call to action. It also offers a theological response to ecofeminism, Goddess religion, and other contemporary religious movements. Annotated bibliography.

Goddess Religion

Cashford, J., and A. Baring. 1991. *The Myth of the Goddess: The Evolution of an Image*. London: Penguin Books.

The objective of the authors is to reawaken an appreciation of ancient myths of the Goddess and in this way to assist contemporary civilization in recovering a sacramental view of nature and a full integration of the feminine.

Christ, C. 1987. *Laughter of Aphrodite: Reflections on a Journey to the Goddess*. San Francisco: Harper & Row. [p. 288]

A leader in the Women's Spirituality Movement explains why she became a feminist and ecologist, left the Christian church, and devoted herself to worship of the Goddess. Her writing is pervaded by a deep sense of the holiness of the Earth and the life force within all living things. Bibliography.

Gadon, E. W. 1989. *The Once and Future Goddess: A Symbol for Our Time*. San Francisco: Harper & Row. [p. 288]

This ecofeminist study provides an historical overview of the nature and significance of Goddess worship from prehistoric times (drawing heavily on the research of Marija Gimbutas) to the present. It is beautifully illustrated, including many stunning images by contemporary women artists.

Gimbutas, M. 1989. *The Language of the Goddess: Unearthing the Hidden Symbols of Western Civilization*. San Francisco: Harper & Row. [p. 288]

Drawing upon archaeology, comparative mythology, and folklore, Gimbutas argues in this elaborately illustrated volume that the cultures of Neolithic Europe were characterized by an earth-based spirituality and Goddess worship and were matrifocal and matrilineal. Bibliography. See also Gimbutas, *The Civilization of the Goddess: The World of Old Europe* (San Francisco: HarperSanFrancisco, 1991).

Olson, C., ed. 1983. *The Book of the Goddess, Past and Present: An Introduction to Her Religion*. New York: Crossroad Publishing.

A varied collection of studies of Goddess worship by historians of religion and feminists.

Preston, J. J., ed. 1982. *Mother Worship: Theme and Variations*. Chapel Hill: University of North Carolina Press.

A comprehensive presentation of the data pertaining to Goddess worship from the field of anthropology.

Starhawk. 1979. *The Spiral Dance: A Rebirth of the Ancient Religion of the Great Goddess*. San Francisco: Harper & Row.

An influential feminist account of the significance of Goddess worship designed to revitalize the tradition today.

Whitmont, E. C. 1982. *Return of the Goddess*. New York: Crossroad Publishing.

Employing a Jungian frame of reference, Whitmont endeavors to explain the renewed interest in the myth of the Goddess as a reemergence out of the unconscious of an ancient archetypal ideal, which, if acknowledged, may guide our spiritually impoverished psyches and civilization toward transformation and healing.

Hinduism

Naganathan, G. 1989. *Animal Welfare and Nature: Hindu Scriptural Perspectives*. Washington, DC: Center for Respect of Life and Environment.

A brief but instructive essay on Hindu scriptural teachings regarding respect for nature and compassion for nonhuman creatures.

Nasr, S. H. 1993. *Religion and the Environmental Crisis: The Views of Hinduism and Islam.* New Delhi: Indira Ghandi National Centre for the Arts.

This essay is a brief summary of Nasr's critique of Western secular humanism and science as the major cause of contemporary environmental degradation and an overview of the contributions Hinduism and Islam can make to a spiritual reawakening.

Prime, R. 1992. *Hinduism and Ecology: Seeds of Truth.* London: Cassell Publishers Limited. [p. 280]

A very instructive study on Hindu religious traditions, ecology, and the environmental crisis commissioned by the World Wide Fund for Nature and based in part on interviews with Hindu environmentalists.

SEE ALSO under General the essays on Hinduism in Adams 1993; Engel and Engel 1990; and Tucker and Grim 1993.

Islam

Ba Kader, A. B. A., A. L. T. E. S. Al Sabbagh, M. A. S. Al Glenid, and M. Y. S. Izzidien. 1983. *Islamic Principles for the Conservation of the Natural Environment.* Gland, Switzerland: A Joint Publication of IUCN and MEPA (Meteorological and Environmental Protection Administration), Kingdom of Saudi Arabia.

This instructive booklet was prepared by MEPA and IUCN in connection with the establishment of a central administration for the protection of the environment in Saudi Arabia.

Chittick, W. 1986. "God Surrounds All Things: An Islamic Perspective on the Environment." *The World and Islam Review* 1(6):671–678.

A study of the implications of Islamic theology for attitudes toward nature.

Khalid, F. with J. O'Brien, eds. 1992. *Islam and Ecology.* New York: Cassell.

In a series of short clear essays, seven scholars provide an introductory overview of Islamic teachings regarding the relation of God and nature, the responsibilities of humanity, science, conservation, and environmental ethics. A volume in the World Wide Fund for Nature's series on World Religions and Ecology.

Nasr, S. H. 1968. *Man and Nature: The Spiritual Crisis of Modern Man.* Kuala Lumpur: Foundation for Traditional Studies. New edition— New York: HarperCollins, 1991.

In this pathbreaking book, Nasr, who is a leading authority on Islam, analyzes with exceptional insight the spiritual problems underlying the environmental crisis and urges the world religions to take up the challenge of reawakening humanity to a sacramental view of the cosmos. Nasr's essay "Islam and the Environmental Crisis," in Rockefeller and Elder 1992, is the best introduction to the subject.

SEE ALSO under General the essays on Islam in Engel and Engel 1990 and Tucker and Grim 1993.

Judaism

Bernstein, E. and D. Fink. 1992. *Let The Earth Teach You Torah.* Philadelphia: Shomrei Adamah. Available through Shomrei Adamah, 50 W. 17th St., New York, NY 10011.

An instructive guide to teaching a Jewish understanding of the relation between humanity and nature. It has been designed for high school and adult education use.

Buber, M. 1970. *I and Thou.* Walter Kaufmann, trans. New York: Scribner's. [p. 284]

Buber's I–thou philosophy has profound implications for a theology of divine immanence, a sacramental view of creation, an ethics of respect and care for nature, and an understanding of community. A helpful introduction to his thought may be found in Buber, *Hasidism and Modern Man* (New York: Harper, 1958). [p. 284]

Ehrenfeld, D., and P. J. Bentley. 1985. "Judaism and the Practice of Stewardship." *Judaism* 34:301–311. [p. 284]

The authors defend Judaism as "one of the first great environmental religions" and identify the biblical sources for a Jewish ethic of stewardship.

Gendler, E. 1971. "On the Judaism of Nature." In *The New Jews.* J. A. Sleeper and A. L. Mintz, eds. New York: Random House. [p. 284]

The essay explores "the natural and feminine components of religion" that appear in Kabbalah, Hasidism, and traditions of Jewish poetry.

Gordis, R. 1986. "Ecology and the Jewish Tradition." In *Judaic Ethics for a Lawless World.* R. Gordis, ed. New York: Jewish Theological Seminary. [p. 284]

An insightful analysis of Genesis 1:28, the rabbinic principle regarding "the pain of living creatures," the principle of *bal tashit*, the concept of a sabbatical year for the land, the inherent rights of animals, and God's speeches out of the whirlwind in Job.

Green, A. 1992. *Seek My Face, Speak My Name: A Contemporary Jewish Theology*. New York: Jason Aronson. [pp. 275, 284]

Drawing insights from the Kabbalah, Hasidic masters, and the scientific creation story, Green constructs a panentheistic vision of God and creation that emphasizes both the oneness of God and the intimate relationship of God, the world, and humanity. Rabbinic Judaism, he argues, lost a sense of the divine presence in nature, and Judaism needs a new theology of the world if it is to respond to the environmental crisis and possess a balanced theological vision.

Harris, M. 1976. "Ecology: A Covenantal Approach." *CCAR Journal* 23:101–108. [p. 284]

Harris embraces Buber's I–thou philosophy and a covenantal relationship with nature.

Helfand, J. I. 1986. "The Earth is the Lord's: Judaism and Environmental Ethics." In *Religion and Environmental Crisis*. E. C. Hargrove, ed. Athens: University of Georgia Press. [p. 284]

This introductory essay draws upon halachah, aggadah, and tefillah to establish the foundations for a Jewish environmental ethics.

Heschel, A. J. 1955. *God In Search of Man: A Philosophy of Judaism*. New York: The Jewish Publication Society of America.

A classic in 20th century Jewish philosophy that includes an illuminating discussion of the fundamental religious significance of a sense of the sublime, wonder, awe, and mystery in relation to nature and history.

The Melton Journal: Issues and Themes in Jewish Education. 1991. "Judaism and Ecology—Our Earth and Our Tradition." Part I, 24, Spring. Available through The Melton Research Center, The Jewish Theological Seminary of America, 3080 Broadway, New York, NY 10027. [p. 285]

A collection of short, thoughtful essays from a variety of perspectives that explore the relation of Judaism to nature, ecology, and the environmental crisis. A sequel is found in *The Melton Journal* (1992), "Towards a Jewish Ecological Paradigm: Essays and Explorations." Part II, 25, Summer. [p. 285]

Plaskow, J. 1990. *Standing Again at Sinai: Judaism from a Feminist Perspective*. San Francisco: HarperSanFrancisco.

In this feminist reevaluation of the role of women in Judaism and reconstruction of the conception of God, Plaskow emphasizes "the presence of God in empowered, egalitarian community." She calls for a reassessment of traditional Jewish attitudes toward the earth and "affirmation . . . that all parts of creation have intrinsic value."

Rose, A., ed. 1992. *Judaism and Ecology.* New York: Cassell. [p. 285]

An introductory text for the general reader commissioned by the World Wide Fund for Nature and written by 11 authors who explore resources in Jewish traditions, environmental programs in Israel, animal welfare issues, vegetarianism, tree conservation, and strategies for action.

Schochet, E. J. 1984. *Animal Life in Jewish Tradition: Attitudes and Relationships.* New York: Ktav.

An historical study of the understanding and treatment of animals in Jewish culture from the biblical period to the modern era.

Schwarzschild, S. S. 1984. "The Unnatural Jew." *Environmental Ethics* 6:47–62. [p. 284]

In this polemical essay, the author argues that mainstream Judaism is unabashedly anthropocentric in its attitude toward nature, and he is critical of Kabbalistic and Hasidic perspectives.

Shapiro, D. S. 1975. "God, Man, and Creation." *Tradition* 15:25–47. [p. 284]

Shapiro draws on biblical tradition and a Kabbalistic view of reality to develop a Jewish ethic of respect for nature and to argue that humanity is the key to preservation of the unity of the creation.

Stein, D. E., ed. 1991. *A Garden of Choice Fruit: 200 Classic Jewish Quotes on Human Beings and the Environment.* Wyncote, PA: Shomrei Adamah. Copies are available through Shomrei Adamah, 50 W. 17th St., New York, NY 10011. [p. 284]

Swetlitz, M., ed. 1989. *Judaism and Ecology, 1970–1986: A Sourcebook of Readings.* Unpublished manuscript, originally distributed by Shomrei Adamah. [p. 284]

A collection of essays that includes the essays listed above by Ehrenfeld, Gendler, Harris, Helfand, Schwarzschild, and Shapiro.

SEE ALSO under General the essays on Judaism in Rockefeller and Elder 1992 and Tucker and Grim 1993.

North American Indian Spirituality

Brown, J. E. 1953. *The Sacred Pipe*. Norman: University of Oklahoma Press.

Following publication of Neihardt's book of Black Elk's teachings, Brown lived with Black Elk for over a year and recorded a second set of the teachings of this influential Lakota Sioux holy man.

Brown, J. E. 1990. *The Spiritual Legacy of the American Indian*. New York: Crossroad Publishing. [p. 286]

Essays with an emphasis on the Plains Indians by one of the most skilled and sensitive interpreters of American Indian traditions. The opening essay offers a very useful overview of North American Indian religions.

Callicott, J. B. 1989. *In Defense of the Land Ethic: Essays in Environmental Philosophy*. Albany: State University of New York Press. [p. 287]

Contains two excellent essays (pp. 177–219) on American Indian environmental ethics and their significance by a leading environmental philosopher.

Capps, W. H., ed. 1976. *Seeing with a Native Eye: Essays on Native American Religion*. New York: Harper Forum Books. [p. 285]

Essays on American Indian religious experience, belief, and practice by leading scholars and writers in the field.

Dooling, D.M., and P. Jordan-Smith, eds. 1989. *I Become Part of It: Sacred Dimensions in Native American Life*. New York: Parabola Books. [p. 287]

Thirty stories and short essays on a wide range of themes, representing a variety of Indian traditions, by Native American writers.

Gill, S. D. 1982. *Native American Traditions: Sources and Interpretations*. Belmont, CA: Wadsworth Publishing Company.

An overview of major features of the religious life of North American Indians, involving essays and other contributions by "Native"and "non-Native Americans."

Hughes, J. D. 1983. *American Indian Ecology*. El Paso, TX: Texas Western Press.

Reflecting on Indian sources, the author seeks to identify Indian attitudes toward the natural environment and the practices that flow from these attitudes.

Hultkrantz, Å. 1987. *Native Religions of North America: The Power of Visions and Fertility*. San Francisco: HarperSanFrancisco.

A short introduction with an overview that includes discussion of differences and shared views. Special attention is given to the Shoshoni and Zuni as examples of two basic contrasting types of religious orientation, the hunting pattern and the horticultural pattern. A very useful introduction and survey may be found in Hultkrantz, *The Religions of the American Indians* (Berkeley: University of California Press, 1979). [p. 286]

Neihardt, J. G. 1988. *Black Elk Speaks: Being the Life Story of a Holy Man of the Oglala Sioux.* Lincoln: University of Nebraska Press. [p. 286]

Originally published in 1932, this recording of the visions, prayers, and historical reflections of Black Elk is a classic expression of Plains Indian spirituality that reveals how the Indians experienced an intimate connection between the realm of the sacred and the natural world. Among contemporary North American Indians, it is probably the most influential Indian religious text.

Nelson, R. K. 1983. *Make Prayers to the Raven.* Chicago: University of Chicago Press. [p. 286]

Combining ethnography and natural history, Nelson carefully describes the way that Koyukon Athapaskan Indians, who inhabit the subarctic boreal forests of northwest Alaska, understand and interact with the natural world. The spiritual beliefs, relations with animals and plants, ecological practices, and environmental ethics of the Koyukon are carefully described. Bibliography.

White, R. 1984. "Native Americans and the Environment." In *Scholars and the Indian Experience: Critical Reviews of Recent Writing in the Social Sciences.* W.R. Swagerty, ed. Bloomington: Indiana University Press.

White presents a very instructive critical review of the scholarly literature on Indians and the environment by enthnohistorians and cultural ecologists between 1960 and 1982. The essay seeks to put the popular idea of the Indian as conservationist in critical perspective. Bibliography.

Films

Gorillas in the Mist. 1988. 129 min. Directed by Michael Apted. Available through Facets Multimedia, 1517 West Fullerton Avenue, Chicago, IL 60614. (800) 331-6197. [pp. 278, 280]

This beautiful and moving film is based on the story of Diane Fossey's extraordinary work with gorillas in Central Africa. Fossey's story raises important ethical questions about animal rights versus human rights.

Moyers/Spirit and Nature. 1991. 88 min. Copies may be ordered by writing to: Spirit and Nature, Box 2284, South Burlington, VT 05407. (800) 336-1917. [p. 274]

This beautifully crafted film weaves together art images, music, ritual, scenes from nature, lectures, and religious dialogue from the 1990 Middlebury College Symposium on Spirit and Nature. The lectures from this symposium are published in Rockefeller and Elder 1992, Spirit and Nature.

Shinto: Nature, Gods and Man in Japan, 1977, 48 min. Copies may be ordered by writing Robert Lazzaro, The Japan Society, 333 East 47th Street, New York, NY 10017. (212) 715-1216.

An exceptional film on Japan's native religious tradition.

The Wilderness Idea: John Muir, Gifford Pinchot and the First Great Battle for Wilderness. A film by Lawrence Hott and Diane Garey. 1989. 58 min. Copies may be ordered from Direct Cinema Limited, P.O. Box 10003, Santa Monica, CA 90410. (303) 396-4774. [p. 273]

A superb documentary. The views of Muir and Pinchot represent two divergent approaches to the environment that continue to be of fundamental significance in the debate over how human beings should view and treat nature.

Acknowledgments

In the process of preparing the various parts of this chapter, I have been kindly assisted by a number of colleagues, but I take full responsibility for the bibliographical selections, course materials recommended, and commentary. I am especially grateful to Claire Wilson for assisting me with research and for carefully preparing the computer copy of the manuscript. J. Ronald Engel and Peter Bakken read portions of the manuscript and made helpful contributions regarding the course on Christianity and Ecology and the bibliography. John Grim provided helpful advice pertaining to the North American Indian course unit and bibliography. A number of college, university, and seminary teachers shared with me their course syllabi and helped me with the bibliography, including Richard Clugston, John Elder, Dieter Hessel, Stephanie Kaza, Seyyed Hossein Nasr, Ismar Schorsch, and Donald Swearer. Daniel T. Spencer shared with me his instructive paper on "Pedagogical Issues and Teaching Models for Eco-justice" (1994). Janet Winkler assisted with typing of the manuscript. I wish to express my deep thanks to all of these persons for their contributions to this project.

Chapter 12

Reinventing the Classroom: Connected Teaching

Jonathan Collett
State University of New York, College at Old Westbury

It may be an apocryphal story, but its message still weighs heavily: When asked how they select good teachers at Harvard, the Dean replied, "It's quite simple. We choose the best scholar in the field and he is by definition the best teacher." It should be quickly added that Harvard, of all the Ivies, takes quality teaching seriously, working at it through its Derek Bok Teaching Center. But the majority of faculty across the country, while very concerned with content or subject matter, spend little if any time on the process or pedagogy of their teaching. Faculty have made the correct assessment that they will be judged and rewarded far more for their scholarly output than for their effective teaching. And they have probably never been given any instruction in pedagogy in graduate school, taking the cold plunge on their first teaching job, where with any luck they might be mentored by a wise and caring elder.

As the chapters throughout this book demonstrate, introducing environmental issues into liberal arts courses should help revitalize teaching—and learning—at the same time that it develops more citizen awareness. Because many students in the 1990s find these issues to be a major concern in their lives, they are unlikely to accept a passive role in their classroom study of them. Instead, they will respond to teaching that makes connections—between course content and their lives as local and world citizens, and between content and a learning process that gives them the skills they need to be responsible and effective advocates. They are more likely to learn disciplinary concepts and approaches if these can be shown to help in understanding what it takes to make the future ecologically secure. They may also be less discipline-bound than their instructors, more open to seeing connections across disciplines. Such a process encourages faculty and students alike to think anew about core concepts in their disciplines and how these can be used to elucidate difficult questions about the biosphere and sustainable development. It also leads naturally to links between academic study and action, from the local to the international level.

The student movement for an environmentally sustainable future is large, growing, and well organized. Many faculty may be surprised to learn that there is an active student organization on their own campus, eager to support their efforts to infuse environmental topics into liberal arts courses. In 1994 student delegates from all 50 states, 22 countries, and 6 continents joined faculty and staff at a Campus Earth Summit at Yale University. They drafted a set of recommendations, *Blueprint for a Green Campus*, for institutions of higher education around the world. First among their ten recommendations is to "integrate environmental knowledge into all relevant disciplines." Follow-up to the Campus Earth Summit has included a major gathering of some 1800 students at the University of Pennsylvania in February, 1995. Several national organizations, including the Campus Ecology Program, Campus Green Vote, and the Student Environmental Action Coalition, help coordinate hundreds of student environmental groups and see that the *Blueprint*'s recommendations are enacted (see Resources, below, "Student Activism," for specifics).

Much of the momentum for student and faculty concern on these issues has come from the United Nations Conference on Environment and Development (the Rio Earth Summit) in 1992. "Agenda 21," the program of action agreed to by the world's governments at the conference, calls for nongovernmental organizations and grass-roots groups to become active in environmental policy making within their countries. For higher education, "Agenda 21" offers a timely opportunity to connect the study of environmental subjects with the kind of action that will determine a new direction of sustainable development for the world's societies (see Resources for "Citizens Network" and "Earth Negotiations Bulletin"). Since environmental issues are being addressed on a worldwide as well as local level, there are also many possibilities for building in subjects as well as teaching approaches that appeal to the increasing diversity of students in today's classes: diversity in age, race, country of origin, gender, and social and economic class. A sign of the growing concern about the environment across racial boundaries can be found in an

EcoNet listing of the "People of Color Environmental Groups Directory," which gives over 200 groups, organized in geographic areas throughout the country. (See Chapter 8, Media and Journalism, for a discussion of environmental racism.)

But more than the subject matter will have to change in the classroom if faculty are to successfully engage a more diverse, nontraditional student body. We know, for example, from numerous recent studies that the kind of academic experience that worked for most faculty when they were students (90 percent of all full-time faculty are white and 72 percent are male!) goes against the learning styles of an increasing number of students today (Cross 1976; Anderson and Adams 1992; Collett and Serrano 1992). The competitive, analytic, disciplined, orderly approach that most faculty learned to master is at direct odds with a more participatory, spontaneous, holistic approach characteristic of African-American, Latino, and Native American cultures, and indeed of working-class white students as well. Infusing environmental issues into the liberal arts curriculum provides an ideal opportunity for engaging *all* students in study, debate, and action that spans different learning styles while it crosses over disciplines.

Primary and secondary school teachers traditionally pay close attention to process, preparing an "instructional aim" and a "lesson sequence" for each class: "What is the one point I most want students to understand today and how can I best get it across?" Marjorie Nicolson, Milton scholar and beloved mentor to several generations of graduate students at Columbia University, used to say that she wished all college teachers could spend some time teaching in high school or even primary school. Then they would be forced to think consciously about the elemental points of a subject, how the material could best be broken down for student consumption.

A wealth of good teaching ideas about the environment is available for elementary and high school level teachers. The major environmental organizations usually have an educational program that prepares materials aimed primarily at these teachers. An example is The Wilderness Society, whose booklet, "The Wild, Wild World of Old-Growth Forests," has background information on ecosystems, trees, and wildlife, and a range of imaginative activities to motivate students (900 17th St. NW, Washington, DC 20006). The North American Association for Environmental Education's monthly magazine, *Environmental Communicator*, has an impressive list of new "resources" in each issue: a recent example is an announcement of a new environmental magazine for teachers, *Environmental Connections*, which provides articles and "classroom guides and curricula" (see below for NAAEE. For *Environmental Connections*: Earth Information Center, P.O. Box 387, Springfield, IL 62705). Of course, much of the initiative for the study of environmental concerns in grades K through 12 comes from state and local mandates. In contrast, very few institutions of higher learning have an environmental literacy requirement, although one may well follow in the wake of campus debates on a multicultural curriculum and student concern about the environment. (See Ehrenfeld's Foreword to this book.)

The chapter authors in this book are all known as good teachers as well as respected scholars in their fields. In preparing their chapters, several of them have described how challenging it is to approach environmental issues in their disciplines not in the typical discourse they customarily use in academic journals and books, but instead from a perspective meant for their peers *as teachers*. This different slant has required them to think carefully about how students learn and about what in their own classroom experience has worked and what has not. Much of what they could previously have assumed as the way to talk to students about their disciplines must now be reformulated as discussion spills across disciplinary boundaries and key concepts need redefining. So, for example, William Balée suggests that anthropologists offer a course in ecological anthropology that presents students with rival perspectives in the field: a more traditional focus from cultural anthropology that emphasizes the determining influence of the environment on human culture and a rival approach, coming from historical ecology, that considers how humans impact their surroundings and create human landscapes (see Chapter 2). And Gerald Alonzo Smith finds that the introduction of concern for the biosphere in the study of economics fundamentally changes the way some basic concepts, like the meaning of the terms "value" and "efficiency," have been taught (see Chapter 4).

The teaching strategies described in the course plans in various chapters are not gimmicks, but rather grow organically out of the content point to be conveyed. In their chapter on history, John Opie and Michael Black give students a sense of the importance of geographical place in their personal history by having them draw maps of their neighborhoods as they remember them at age 11 (see Chapter 6). In an upper division course unit on land degradation, Lisa Naughton-Treves and Emily Young would form teams of students playing roles of various local constituencies presenting their interest in an environmental issue like smog or watershed deterioration at a public hearing (see Chapter 5). After assigning D. H. Lawrence's poem, "Snake," Vernon Owen Grumbling suggests as a follow-up activity having students determine what the effect would be of exterminating all snakes in a particular locality (see Chapter 7). A final and most compelling example is David Orr's interdisciplinary chapter, where he creates the content of learning out of its form and context, turning student attention to the ecological soundness of academic buildings: "The design, construction, and operation of academic buildings can be a liberal education in a microcosm that includes virtually every discipline in the catalog" (see Chapter 1).

The resource list that follows begins with some references on teaching in general. The introduction of new material on environmental issues and the likelihood of keen student interest might encourage an instructor using this book to take some risks and try out a variety of classroom activities. Chapter authors provide stimulating ideas about projects, journals, discussions, simulations, and other forms of teaching. Described here are some guides to these and other teaching strategies, regardless of content. How do you lead a genuine discussion, rather than what all too often poses for discussion, a game of "guess what's on my mind," with students addressing the instructor instead of each other? How can the traditional lecture method be enlivened and what students learn from it be reinforced? How do you meet the needs of the diverse student body most of us now teach, where interest levels, previous training, learning styles, and other differences often seem irreconcilable? Specific resources in environmental studies then follow, from books and films to computer games and databases, from activist student organizations to professional and commercial organizations that provide programs and products to help teachers.

Resources

General Teaching Resources

Brookfield, Stephen D. 1990. *The Skillful Teacher*. San Francisco: Jossey-Bass.

Brookfield's specialty at Columbia's Teachers College is teaching and adult learning, but this book also incorporates much of his personal experience of 20 years as a teacher. He assumes the "chaotic unpredictability" of teaching. He treats learners as adults with "rhythms of learning" that the effective teacher will attend to. Good chapters on lecture and discussion, and an excellent final chapter giving 17 "truths" about teaching, summarizing earlier chapters.

Christensen, C. R. 1992. *Education for Judgment: The Artistry of Discussion Leadership*. Cambridge: Harvard Business School.

Coming out of a faculty seminar on discussion leadership that Christensen has offered at Harvard for almost 20 years, this book analyzes discussion sessions and offers skills for making them more effective. Which students should be called on, when should the instructor intervene to summarize or change the direction of the conversation, what if anything should be written on the board? Christensen is also famous for his work on the case-study method now used widely in business education.

Davis, B. G. 1993. *Tools of Teaching*. San Francisco: Jossey-Bass.

An invaluable guide to all aspects of teaching, based on solid research and experience. Best used as a reference for topics of concern, rather than as a book to be read sequentially.

Elbow, P. 1986. *Embracing Contraries: Explorations in Learning and Teaching*. New York: Oxford University Press.

Elbow contends, as he did in his notable books on the writing process (*Writing with Power* and *Writing without Teachers*), that all complex processes, surely teaching and learning, have built-in conflicts that make them messy and difficult. In his section on the teaching process, Elbow describes the eternal struggle that faculty face in their conflicting roles as both student allies and guardians of standards. In this context, Elbow offers helpful advice on evaluation of students and teachers and encourages the teaching of knowledge that embraces both belief and dissent.

Gullette, M. M., ed. 1984. *The Art and Craft of Teaching*. Cambridge: Harvard University Press.

This is a product of the Christensen seminar on teaching at Harvard (see Christensen, above), with practical chapters on lecturing, leading discussions, grading, and understanding the importance of the first class and the potential of pacing in a semester, among other topics.

McKeachie, W. J. 1994. *Teaching Tips: Strategies, Research, and Theories for College and University Teachers*, 9th ed. Lexington, MA: D.C. Heath.

The early editions were aimed at beginning teachers, but McKeachie has added something for everyone. If one were to pick a single book on improving college teaching, this would probably be it. At $18.75 for 444 pages (paperback), buy it!

Jossey-Bass Publishers in San Francisco has two education series that should be watched for the relatively new, mostly high-quality pedagogical "scholarship" now being produced by faculty and teaching center professionals around the country. An early volume in the Higher Education Series was K. P. Cross's (1976) *Accent on Learning*. Cross explains that both faculty and students have "cognitive styles," but that they often conflict. Community college teachers tend to be more "evocative," bringing more structure and warmth to the classroom, while university and especially graduate school faculty are more "didactic," emphasizing individual rather than group achievement among students. The New Directions for Teaching and Learning series, edited paperbacks on specific topics ("Teaching Large Classes Well," "Learning in Groups," etc.), provides useful techniques for improving teaching. A recent volume, L. L. B. Border and N. V. N. Chism, eds. (1992), *Teaching for Diversity*, offers discussion and instructional tips for classes increasingly heterogeneous in gender, race, and ethnicity. Two chapters, cited above, with useful suggestions for dealing with racially and culturally diverse classrooms, are J. A. Anderson and Maurianne Adams, "Acknowledging the Learning Styles of Diverse Student Populations: Implications for Instructional Design," and J. Collett and B. Serrano, "Stirring It Up: The Inclusive Classroom."

Environmental Teaching Resources

A word of caution: Environmental education is a relatively new and fast expanding field. Many of the best resources for teaching are to be found outside the customary books and journals in the disciplines that faculty are accustomed to. Perhaps characteristic of any new field, materials quickly go out of print, or are succeeded by a new, enlarged edition under a different title. An example is Donella Meadows's (1989) *Harvesting One Hundredfold* (New York: UN Environment Programme) which David Orr has called "one of the best short guides to environmental education that I've seen," but which, unfortunately, is now out of print. More important than the specific titles of books, films, computer software, and so on listed below are the directories, sourcebooks, and names of organizations, both nonprofit and commercial, that can serve as guides to the best and most updated resources available. The cheapest, fastest, and most diverse global information about any environmental topic is to be found on the Internet, or more specifically on the environmental networks: EcoNet, EE-Link, and EnviroLink (see below for particulars).

WORKBOOKS, RESOURCE GUIDES, AND CURRICULUM GUIDES

Many of the chapters above include annotated listings of more general references for teaching in addition to those relevant to the discipline. Note particularly in the Resource section of Chapter 10, Political Science, the items under "Reference Works and Almanacs." Another example is Chapter 8, Media and Journalism, which contains a good listing of periodicals, film sources, and organizational resources that are of general use. Several additional resources need to be highlighted:

(1) *Environmental Communicator* magazine has a "Resources" section that covers software, books, and so on in each issue. Although most of these materials are designed for secondary education, many are appropriate

for introductory college courses. North American Association for Environmental Education, P.O Box 400, Troy, OH 45373.

(2) *Island Press Environmental Sourcebook* (since 1987). An annotated listing of books, both Island Press's own and those from other presses, "representing a unique, multidisciplinary approach to environmental problem-solving." Center for Resource Economics/Island Press, 1718 Connecticut Avenue, NW, Suite 300, Washington, DC 20009. Orders: Box 7, Covelo, CA 95428. Phone: 800-828-1302.

(3) The Panos Institute. "From Information to Education." A series of curriculum modules on development issues, including a 16-page module on the effects of underdevelopment and the development process on the environment. The Panos Institute works closely with researchers, journalists, and nongovernmental organization leaders from "the global South" and presents their perspective for educational groups in the North in these curriculum guides. 1717 Massachusetts Avenue, NW, Suite 301, Washington, DC 20036. Phone: 202-483-0044; fax: 202-483-3059.

(4) Piasecki, B. 1992. *Environmental History Review*. Eighteen detailed syllabi in history and other related disciplines. See further description in Resource section under "Annotated Background Readings for the Instructor" in Chapter 6, History.

(5) Savitt, W., ed. 1993. *Teaching Global Development: A Curriculum Guide*. Notre Dame, IN: University of Notre Dame Press. As the Earth Summit made clear, for much of the world environmental issues must be considered in the context of development. This book provides essays on teaching development with a global, interdisciplinary approach; a section of detailed syllabi for seven courses; and a particularly useful annotated bibliography, which includes a section on environment.

(6) Scarisbrick-Hauser, A. M. and W. J. Hauser, eds. 1991. *Environmental Sociology: A Collection of Course Syllabi*. Washington, DC: American Sociological Association Teaching Resources Center. Thirty syllabi for courses on the environment, social impact assessment, technology, and socioeconomic and resource management. Additional resources listed. 248 pages. Through its active Teaching Resources Center, the ASA has led the way among disciplinary organizations in making available syllabi, bibliographies, classroom techniques, and other resources in a wide variety of subject areas. ASA Teaching Resources Center, 1722 N Street NW, Washington, DC 20036. Phone: 202-833-3410.

(7) *World Resources: A Guide to the Global Environment*. New York: Oxford University Press. Biennial reports (about 400 pages) from the World Resources Institute, giving current conditions and trends in the world's natural resource base and in the global environment. Accompanying Teacher's Guide also available. A database diskette contains up-to-date

information on global statistics: 483 variables for 176 countries and 13 regional and economic groupings. World Resources Institute Publications, P.O. Box 4852, Hampden Station, Baltimore, MD 21211. Phone: 800-822-0504.

ELECTRONIC COMMUNICATION, DATABASES

(1) It is a good bet that when the revised version of this Curriculum Guide is "published" in two or three years, it will be in electronic as well as print form. Anyone seriously interested in any aspect of the environment and sustainable development should be taking advantage of the wealth of resources available on an office or home computer screen with a modem and a few clicks of the mouse or strokes of the keyboard.

• "EcoNet" is an electronic network and bulletin board specializing in environmental topics and providing a multitude of resources from the United Nations, the United States government, various university services, and other organizations. Since 1990 it has been on the Internet, a vast worldwide network originally of academic and research institutions, and now including millions of individuals and, increasingly, commercial interests (through the "World Wide Web," a system for organizing and displaying Internet information). EcoNet can be accessed through Internet in most institutions or at home through a local Internet "server" (Prodigy, America Online, Pipeline, etc.). To participate in EcoNet's conferences, which are forums on particular issues, you must join EcoNet itself, which, in turn is a way into the Internet, although a more expensive one. There is a long, constantly growing list of conferences on, for example, biodiversity, the 4th World Conference of Women, animal rights, desertification, and so on, with individuals and organizations contributing ideas and useful resources. Subscriptions can be registered online or by contacting the Institute for Global Communications, 18 De Boom St., San Francisco, CA 94107. Phone: 415-442-0220; fax: 415-546-1794; Internet: <gopher.igc.apc.org:70/1>

• "EE-Link," an environmental education service of the National Consortium for Environmental Education and Training, gives lists of organizations, projects, conferences, and courses. Among its offerings for "Environmental Resources on the Internet" (<gopher.nceet.snre. umich.edu>) are two guides produced at the University of Michigan Library School: (1) C.Briggs-Erickson and T. Murphy (Oct. 1994), "A Guide to Environmental Resources on the Internet." Arranged alphabetically by subject, it then gives Internet tools to locate items. (2) D. K. Kovacs (1995), "Ecology and Environmental Studies." Organized by "discussion name," such as Biodiversity, Ecofem, etc., then gives network resources, forums, addresses, and subscription information.

• "EnviroLink" network claims to be the "largest online environmental information service on the planet." Started by a student at Carnegie

Mellon University, it now has a clearinghouse of information, a directory of products produced by environmentally and socially responsible companies, and an environmental education network serving as a clearinghouse for teaching materials. The Student Environmental Action Coalition, for example, uses EnviroLink, and copies of the Blueprint for a Green Campus (see below, under Student Activism) can be downloaded from EnviroLink.

(2) "Current Contents: Agriculture, Biology, and Environmental Sciences." Multidisciplinary guide to current literature on environmental subjects. Reprints title pages from over 14,000 international science and social science publications as soon as they appear. Contains very complete key word index for article titles and gives addresses for reprint requests. Weekly issues (annual subscription) in print, diskette, or CD-ROM (for PC) form. Abstracts, document delivery available. Expensive for individuals but not for a library that is providing resources for faculty in different areas. If faculty do not have access to a library with an extensive journal collection, then this is the way to see the title pages of hundreds of journals and be able to order reprint articles of interest. Not useful for back issues. Institute for Scientific Information, 3501 Market St., Philadelphia, PA 19104. Phone: 800-336-4474, ext. 1528.

(3) "Earth Negotiations Bulletin" gives daily updates in every area of intergovernmental environment and development negotiations. Electronic versions are accessed through EcoNet or the Internet gopher at <gopher.igc.apc.org>. Hard copies are also available through the International Institute for Sustainable Development (phone: 204-958-7700; fax: 204-958-7710; E-mail: enb@igc.apc.org).

(4) "Earthquest" and "Earthquest Explores Ecology." For Mac users, a large database (about 3 megabytes of hard disk space) of ecological facts, sounds, and illustrations. One part, EcoSimulator, has options that make conditions change for six subsystems. Includes Hypercard 2.1 that allows for customizing the program. Davidson and Associates, Torrance CA. Phone: 800-545-7677.

VIDEO SERVICES, FILMS, VIDEODISKS

(1) Bullfrog Films has a large inventory of environmental films and videos for rent and sale. Holmes Rolston III calls it "probably the best single source of environmental films" (see Resources in Chapter 9). The catalog is available on the Internet through "EcoNet's Guide to Internet Resources on the Environment." P.O. Box 149, Oley, PA 19547. Phone: 800-543-3764; fax: 610-370-1978.

(2) The Canadian Film Distribution Center at SUNY/College at Plattsburgh provides top quality environmental films and videos made in

Canada to educators and cultural groups throughout the United States. Feinberg Library, Room 128, Plattsburgh, NY 12901. Phone: 800-388-6784.

(3) "Environment and Development Kit: The Global Perspective." Thirty-eight high-quality overhead transparencies on topics like "The Living Sea," "Destruction of the Rainforests," and "The Debt Problem." Also a 38-page resource guide that includes specific teaching activities, a listing of major environmental advocacy organizations, and major international agreements. Aimed at high school and college students. Visuell Inform, 1991. c/o AL and LS, 8th Floor, 545 W. 45th St., New York, NY 10036.

(4) Environmental Awareness Series, Films for Educators, Inc./Films for Television. A distributor for the Environmental Protection Agency and other video producers. 420 E. 55th St., Suite 6U, New York, NY 10022. Phone: 212-486-6577; fax: 212-980-9826.

(5) Environmental Media Corporation offers curriculum-based media to support environmental education at all levels. Popular for college students are "The Beaches Are Moving" and the "Green Means" series. P.O. Box 1016, Chapel Hill, NC 27514. Phone: 800-ENV-EDUC or 919-993-3003; fax: 919-942-8785.

(6) EnviroVideo produces interviews, news shows, and documentary specials for television, but also has direct sales. Interviews with Helen Caldicott, Michelle Perreault, and others, and a three-part teleconference on the Earth Summit with a wide range of participants. P.O. Box 29000, El Dorado Hills, CA 95762. Phone: 800-227-8955; fax: 800-852-8000.

(7) "Our Environment Videodisc." 11,000 color photos, maps, graphs, charts, 16 minutes of motion picture, all on a videodisc. A project funded by the U.S. Department of Education at the University of Wisconsin–Stevens Point. Comes with User Index. Teacher Manual and Student Manual also available, as well as HyperCard Stacks for interactive use with a Macintosh. Optilearn, Inc., P.O. Box 997, Stevens Point, WI 54481. Phone: 715-344-6060; fax: 715-344-1066.

(8) "Safe Planet: The Guide to Environmental Film and Video." Annotated guide to over 80 new films and videos. Includes a list of resources and tips on how to use media. Media Network, Alternative Media Information Center, 121 Fulton St., 5th Floor, New York, NY 10038. Phone: 212-929-2663.

(9) The Seventh Generation Environmental Video Collection has 39 of "the best environmental videos" at low prices in a project funded by the Rockefeller Foundation. Colchester, VT 05446. Phone: 800-456-1177; fax: 800-456-1139.

(10) The nonprofit Video Project has produced about 200 programs, many of them festival award winners, for all ages. They also distribute videos of other producers, for sale or rental. 5332 College Avenue, Suite 101, Oakland, CA 94618. Phone: 800-4-PLANET or 510-655-9050; fax: 510-655-9115.

COMPUTER PROGRAMS, SIMULATIONS

Since this is a relatively new and fast-developing resource, what is available is cast for as wide a market as possible. As the market grows, there will be more programs tailored specifically for college students. In the meantime, if some of the materials you scan seem simplistic, don't be discouraged. And remember that eight-year-olds can often run circles around us when it comes to playing computer games and learning from them.

(1) "Eco-Adventures in the Rainforest" and "Eco-Adventures in the Oceans." For Mac and Windows users, imaginative assignments in the rainforest and ocean, requiring that the player get to know basic facts about ecology and conservation issues. One assignment, for example, is to photograph the leaf-tailed gecko within a certain time, while dealing with various human and other complications. A press conference after the assignment is over tests the knowledge students have gained. Chariot Software, 3659 India St., San Diego, CA. 92103. Phone: 800-242-7468; fax: 800-242-7468.

(2) "GAIA/Environmental Resources." A CD-ROM for Mac users, containing over 400 photos and scenes. Also a database of environmental organizations and publications. TigerSoftware, P.O. Box 143376, Coral Gables, FL 33114. Phone: 800-666-2562; fax: 305-529-2990.

(3) "Knowledge Tree on Global Climate Change." A Mac hypercard stack providing material for the study of changes in climate, wind patterns, ocean currents, and weather conditions. For nonmajors in introductory earth sciences courses. Climate Protection Institute, 5833 Balmoral Drive, Oakland, CA 94619. Phone: 510-531-0100.

(4) "SimCity 2000." Highly popular computer game where players start with empty land and build a city, having to make constant decisions about growth, traffic, taxes, and occasional natural disasters. "SimEarth" and "SimLife" are sequels, expanding from the city to the planet and to the ecosystem. See the resources section in Chapter 6 for further description and use in teaching history. All three are products of Maxis Software, available in computer stores or from Broderbund Software, Inc., 17 Paul Drive, San Rafael, CA 94903. Phone: 800-521-6263.

PERIODICALS

Well covered in the Resource sections of various chapters. Two additional ones should be mentioned.

(1) *Environmental Education Research* is a new international journal focusing on the analysis and theory of environmental education. It also reports on conferences, policy issues, and national or regional activities around the world. Carfax Publishing Co., P.O. Box 2025, Dunnellon, FL 34430. Fax: 904-489-6996.

(2) *Hunger Teachnet*, a quarterly publication of the Interfaith Hunger Appeal Office on Education, contains resources helpful for college-level teaching, such as annotated syllabi and reviews from curriculum development institutes sponsored by the IHA. Recent issues covered "Gender, Justice and Development" and "Environment, Development and Peace: Exploring Connections in Undergraduate Education." Institute presentations by John Cobb, Denis Goulet, Elise Boulding, June Nash, among others, are summarized. Interfaith Hunger Appeal, 475 Riverside Drive, Suite 1630, New York, NY 10015. Phone: 212-870-2035.

Organizations, Networks, Conferences

Most environmental organizations have understood the importance of education and have developed educational programs and resources at various levels. See Chapter 10, Political Science, for annotations on directories of organizations, particularly the *Conservation Directory* and the *Directory of National Environmental Organizations*. Listed here are groups that have activities relevant for college-level instruction.

(1) Networking in response to the Earth Summit. There are many entry points to involvement in the organizations and activities growing out of the Earth Summit, depending on location of campus and topic of interest. The best place to start is the Citizens Network for Sustainable Development, formed in 1992 as the network of individuals and organizations in the United States working on issues that follow up the Rio conference. They have an annual conference, online EcoNet conferences, a newsletter, and a directory of their membership. Membership: Sharyle Patton, CitNet, P.O. Box 316, Bolinas, CA 94924. Phone: 415-868-9720. E-mail: mlerner@igc.apc.org. A working group on education, taking as its text the Treaty on Environmental Education signed by the world's leaders in Rio, is headed by Tom Keehn at the American Forum for Global Education (45 John Street, #908, New York, NY 10038. Phone: 212-742-8232).

(2) New England Environmental Conference. Begun in 1979, this annual conference is now presented by Tufts University's Center for Environmental Management. The 1995 conference had Bruce Babbitt, Secretary of the Interior, as a keynote speaker, and featured some 100 workshops, 250 speakers, and 100 exhibits. Workshop subjects run from ecological economics to the university's role in sustainable development to using environmental resources on the Internet. New England Environmental Conference, Tufts University, CEM, 177 College Avenue, Medford, MA 02155. Phone: 617-627-3486; fax: 617-627-3099; E-mail: cemtufts@igc.apc.org.

(3) North American Association for Environmental Education. This organization has an annual conference, publishes *Environmental Communicator* (see above, under "Workbooks, Resource Guides, and Curriculum Guides"), and has projects like Environmental Issues Forums for community discussion of issues. Though strongest at primary and secondary levels, NAAEE has an Environmental Studies section that includes a committee on university-level studies. P.O. Box 400, Troy, OH 45373. Phone/fax: 513-676-2514.

(4) Second Nature, a nonprofit organization dedicated to an environmentally literate citizenry through education, was begun in 1993 with a generous grant from the Heinz Family Foundation. Early projects include partnerships with a consortium of Historically Black Colleges and Universities/Minority Institutions and a consortium of universities in Brazil to train faculty members. Another consortium project involves environmental education in medicine. Second Nature has an ambitious plan for training faculty worldwide and for providing an electronic database on innovative curricula and educational materials. 17 Msgr. O'Brien Highway, P.O. Box 410350, East Cambridge, MA 02141. Phone: 617-227-8888; fax: 617-227-0104.

Student Activism

The *Blueprint for a Green Campus*, the product of the 1994 Campus Earth Summit, gives a clear rationale and specific suggested actions for top administrators, staff, faculty, and students for each of its ten recommendations. It also includes a list of national organizations and a select bibliography of relevant books. It can be ordered through Campus Green Vote (see below).

STUDENT ORGANIZATIONS

(1) Campus Ecology Program. Under the National Wildlife Federation, this program is well organized, with a national staff and regional organizers ready to help any campus group. 1400 16th St., NW, Washington, DC 20036. Phone: 202-797-6858. E-mail for national director: nkeller@nwf.org.

(2) Campus Green Vote. A program of the Center for Environmental Citizenship and a clearinghouse for *Blueprint* distribution and Campus Earth Summit follow-up. Its specialty is keeping campus groups informed of pending and needed legislation from the local to national levels. Updates and distributes "The Campus Green Pages," a directory of individual students, staff, and faculty on campuses in all 50 states working on environmental issues. 1400 16th St., NW, Box 24, Washington, DC 20036. 202-939-3338; fax: 202-797-6646; E-mail: shadow@ igc.apc.org.

(3) The Student Environmental Action Coalition (SEAC). National office for a network of hundreds of campus organizations. Has national staff, three regional offices, and more than 50 volunteer-staffed offices. P.O. Box 1168, Chapel Hill, NC 27514. Phone: 800-700-SEAC; fax: 919-967-4648; E-mail: seac@igc.apc.org.

BOOKS FOR CAMPUS ACTION

(1) Campus Ecology Program. Annual. *Campuses Working for a Sustainable Future*. Available from CEP (see above in student organizations). A directory of campus environmental groups and projects.

(2) Environmental Careers Organization. 1993. *The New Complete Guide to Environmental Careers*, rev. ed. Washington, DC: Island Press. Information on jobs in planning, parks, wildlife management, pollution control, and other environmental career opportunities. Included are educational paths, internships, volunteer possibilities, and strategies for job-hunting in general.

(3) Green Seal. 1994. *Campus Green Buying Guide*. Washington, DC: Green Seal and the University of Maryland Center for Global Change. To help with environmentally responsible purchasing policies on campus, this guide lists appropriate companies. Available from Green Seal, 1730 Rhode Island Ave., NW, Suite 1050, Washington, DC 20036. Phone: 202-331-7337.

(4) Keniry, J. (forthcoming). *Ecodemia: Campus Environmental Stewardship at the Turn of the 21st Century*. Washington, DC: Campus Ecology Program (see above in student organizations). Profiles of leaders among staff and students, chapters on environmentally responsible purchasing policies, and other ways to implement the campus *Blueprint* recommendations.

(5) Smith, A. and the Student Environmental Action Coalition. 1993. *Campus Ecology: A Guide to Assessing Environmental Quality and Creating Strategies for Change*. Washington, DC: Living Planet Press. Students involved in campus ecological design have created this workbook as an action resource. Also included are descriptions of campus projects fea-

turing environmental research and practice. Available from SEAC (see above in student organizations).

(6) Student Environmental Action Coalition. 1991. *Student Environmental Action Guide.* Berkeley, CA Earth Works Press. Examples of dramatic actions, like waste reductions, taken at various campuses and recommendations for other steps in creating an environmentally sound campus. Available from SEAC (see above in student organizations).

Funding

You and your colleagues have great ideas for a project and much student enthusiasm—now to pay for it.

- Make sure that your grants office has *The Environmental Grantmaking Foundations Directory*, which lists major funders who support environmental concerns. The directory gives funding emphases by topic. Published yearly by the Environmental Data Research Institute, 1655 Elmwood Ave., Suite 255, Rochester, NY 14620-3426.

- A directory of "Environmental Education Funders" is available on EcoNet from the Alliance for Environmental Education. At the prompt, give a string of words indicating your funding interests and these will be matched with potential funders.

Contributors

WILLIAM BALÉE is Associate Professor, Department of Anthropology, Tulane University, New Orleans, LA 70118. Author of numerous articles and book chapters on the human ecology of Amazonian Indians and their habitats, he has also published *Footprints of the Forest: Ka'apor Ethnobotany—The Historical Ecology of Plant Utilization by an Amazonian People* (1994), and edited, with D.A. Posey, *Resource Management in Amazonia: Indigenous and Folk Strategies* (1989). At present he is preparing an edited volume on advances in historical ecology.

MICHAEL BLACK is a San Francisco–based policy analyst and environmental historian who writes about issues confronting the arid western United States, the social impact of science and technology, economic planning and development, and the environment. His articles appear in journals and anthologies and cover diverse topics, including land use planning, endangered species, Western water policy, industrial policy, the demilitarization of science and technology policy, and global political economy. He serves on the governing board of the California Studies Association and is past-chair of the subsection on Science and Public Policy of the New York Academy of Sciences. Black is coeditor of *Greening Environmental Policy: The Politics of a Sustainable Future*, published in 1995.

DAVID G. CAMPBELL is Henry R. Luce Professor in Nations and the Global Environment at Grinnell College, Grinnell, IA 50112. He has made 19 research expeditions to the Amazon. He is former Executive Director of the Bahamas National Trust, a member of the research staff of the New York Botanical Garden, and a recipient of a Guggenheim Fellowship. His latest book, *The Crystal Desert: Summers in Antarctica,* published in 1992, won the Burroughs medal.

JONATHAN COLLETT is Professor of Comparative Humanities, State University of New York (SUNY), College at Old Westbury, Old Westbury, NY 11568. He has taught at Columbia and Wesleyan, and was a member of the planning staff that developed the new SUNY campus at Old Westbury where he has served as Acting Academic Vice President. As founder and faculty coordinator of the Teaching for Learning Center at Old Westbury, he has been active in developing innovative teaching methods for use in multicultural and multiethnic settings.

VERN DURKEE is Professor Emeritus of Biology at Grinnell College, Grinnell, IA 50112. He is a plant taxonomist by research and training, has taught courses in zoology, biodiversity, and environmental studies, and has published a number of articles on the taxonomy of tropical flora. For many years he was the advisor for the Associated Colleges of the Midwest programs in Costa Rica.

ANN FILEMYR is Associate Professor of Journalism/Communications and Chair of Interdisciplinary Studies and Director of Communications and the Media Arts Program at Antioch College, Yellow Springs, OH 45387. A member of the Society of Environmental Journalists, she has covered the United Nations Conference on Environment and Development and follow-up conferences in Japan, Brazil, Canada, and the United States.

KARL GROSSMAN is Professor of Journalism at the State University of New York, College at Old Westbury, Old Westbury, NY 11568. He has for more than 25 years specialized in investigative reporting on environmental and energy issues in print and electronic journalism. He is the author of *Power Crazy*, *The Poison Conspiracy*, and *Cover Up: What You Are Not Supposed To Know About Nuclear Power*. Articles by Grossman on environmental and energy issues have appeared in publications including *The New York Times*; *Newsday*; *The Nation*; *Mother Jones*; *The Village Voice*; *The Globe and Mail*; *The Philadelphia Inquirer*; *Environmental Action*; *The San Francisco Bay Guardian*; and *E, The Environmental Magazine*. He hosts, writes and narrates television programs for EnviroVideo.

VERNON OWEN GRUMBLING is Professor of Literature and Environmental Studies at the University of New England, Biddeford, ME 04005, where he has been an active environmental advocate. Among his writings about nature literature are an anthology, *The Literature of Nature: The British and American Traditions*, and a contribution to the Modern Language Association's *Teaching Environmental Literature*. He has also written about land conservation and about interdisciplinary science education.

STEPHEN KARAKASHIAN is Coordinator for Higher Education at the Rainforest Alliance, 65 Bleeker Street, New York, NY 10012. He is a biologist by training, has taught at Reed College and Rice University, and was a Research Associate in Animal Behavior at The Rockefeller University. As a member of the planning staff of the State University of New York, College at Old Westbury, he was instrumental in developing an interdisciplinary program in Health Sciences that was tailored to meet the needs of older and nontraditional students. Dr. Karakashian is also a certified psychotherapist and does antiracism and diversity training.

MICHAEL E. KRAFT is Professor of Political Science and Public and Environmental Affairs at the University of Wisconsin, Green Bay, WI 54311. Among other works, he is coeditor and contributing author of *Environmental Policy in the 1990s: Toward a New Agenda* and *Public Reactions to Nuclear Waste: Citizens's Views of Repository Siting*. His latest book, *Environmental Policy and Politics: Toward the 21st Century*, was published by HarperCollins.

LISA NAUGHTON-TREVES is currently a doctoral candidate in the Wildlife Ecology and Conservation program at the University of Florida, Gainesville, FL 32601. She holds a M.Sc. in geography from the University of Wisconsin–Madison. Ms. Naughton-Treves was formerly a conservation officer for the Wildlife Conservation Society, where she designed field research projects in conservation and consulted with international development agencies regarding local community participation in biological resource management. She has taught field methods in agroecology in Costa Rica and conducted research in South and Central America on land use conflicts around national parks. Her dissertation research is on human agricultural strategies in response to wildlife foraging in farms around Kibale Forest, Uganda.

JOHN OPIE is Distinguished Professor and Director of the Graduate Program in Environmental Policy Studies at New Jersey Institute of Technology, Newark, NJ 07102. In 1976 Opie was the founding editor of the international quarterly, *Environmental Review*, later retitled, *Environmental History Review*. His latest book, published in 1993, is *Ogallala: Water for a Dry Land*, which is a policy history about the consumption of groundwater under the Great Plains for intensive farming and deals particularly with matters of agricultural sustainability under the pressures of human need and climate change. *Ogallala* was co-winner of the George Perkins Marsh book prize in 1995. Opie is currently writing an environmental history text tentatively titled, *Environmental America: A History*, scheduled for publication in 1996. Opie has also written on national water policy, Frederick Jackson Turner's "frontier thesis," what environmental history means, and landscape aesthetics.

DAVID ORR is Professor and Chair of the Environmental Studies Program at Oberlin College, Oberlin, OH 44070. He is author of *Ecological Literacy* (SUNY, 1992) and *Earth in Mind* (Island Press, 1994).

STEVEN C. ROCKEFELLER is Professor of Religion at Middlebury College, Middlebury, VT 05753, where he formerly served as Dean of the College. He is the author of *John Dewey: Religious Faith and Democratic Humanism* and the coeditor of *The Christ and the Bodhisattva*, and *Spirit and Nature: Why the Environment is a Religious Issue*. He recently served as a member of the National Commission on the Environment, which proposed a comprehensive U.S. strategy for long-term economic and environmental well-being in *Choosing a Sustainable Future* (Island Press, 1993).

HOLMES ROLSTON III is University Distinguished Professor of Philosophy, at Colorado State University, Fort Collins, CO 80523. He has taught environmental ethics for two decades. He has written five books, most recently, *Environmental Ethics, Philosophy Gone Wild, Conserving Natural Value*, and *Science and Religion: A Critical Survey*. He is past-President of the International Society for Environmental Ethics and has long been an editor of the journal *Environmental Ethics*.

GERALD ALONZO SMITH is Professor of Economics at Mankato State University, Mankato, MN 56002. His background includes a Licentiate in sacred theology and master's degree in medieval history from St. Louis University, master's degrees in resource economics and in tropical agronomy from the University of Florida, and a doctorate in economics from Louisiana State University, where he studied under Herman Daly's supervision. He has taught environmental economics since 1979.

EMILY YOUNG is currently an Assistant Professor at the University of Arizona, Tucson, AZ 85721. Ms. Young received her Ph.D. in geography from the University of Texas at Austin and her M.Sc. in the same field from the University of Wisconsin–Madison. She is now working to help coordinate binational efforts toward wetland habitat and wildlife conservation in Baja California Sur, Mexico. She has conducted research in Latin America on local conflicts between environmental conservation and economic development activities as well as problems of rural–urban migration and the growth of shanty-towns. Ms. Young is currently engaged in research linking local needs to nature protection through ecotourism and biosphere reserves in coastal and marine areas of Baja California Sur.